Johannes Knoetze (Editor)

Mission
the "labour room"
of theology

CHRISTIAN LITERATURE FUND PUBLISHERS
CHRISTELIKE LEKTUURFONDS UITGEWERS

Mission the "labour room" of theology
© Johannes Knoetze
CLF Publishers
19 Oude Pont Street
Wellington Business Park
Wellington
www.clf.co.za

All rights reserved. No part of this publication may be reproduced, stored in a retrieval system, or transmitted, in any form or by any means, electronic, mechanical, photocopying, recording or otherwise, without any prior written permission of the publisher.

Design and layout by: Anna-Marie Brink
Cover design by: Anna-Marie Brink

ISBN 978-1-86804-525-9

This publication was made possible through sponsorships by NetAct and Christian Literature Fund

Table of Contents

List of Abbreviations 5
List of Contributors 8
Foreword 21
Introduction 23

SECTION A: UNDERSTANDINGS/THEOLOGIES OF MISSION IN AFRICA

Chapter 1: Protestant Mission in Africa –
A Historical Perspective on Translating the Gospel
Gideon van der Watt 26

Chapter 2: Catholic Mission:
A Theological and Historical Survey
Martin Badenhorst 46

Chapter 3: Together Towards Life and Mission:
African Pentecostals' Participation in the Missio Dei
Peter White 62

Chapter 4: African Independent Churches:
Izandla Ziyagezana – Hands Wash Each Other
Johannes Knoetze 76

Chapter 5: Decolonisation of Christian Mission in Africa:
Towards a Missiology of Reconstruction
Buhle Mpofu 88

SECTION B: WHAT IS MISSION?

Chapter 6: Whose Mission? The Mission of God
Piet Meiring 108

Chapter 7: Mission – Where?
Dons Kritzinger 129

Chapter 8: The Place of Missiology as a Theological Discipline in Africa
J.N.J. Kritzinger and H. Kwiyani 149

SECTION C: THE HOW OF MISSION: MISSION AS/IN THE CONTEXT OF...

Chapter 9:	Mission in an Urbanised Context. Cities: 'Wild Spaces Within a New Frontier' *Marinda van Niekerk*	176
Chapter 10:	Not the Future Leaders of Tomorrow! Youth, Missio Dei and the Missiological Research Agenda in (South) Africa *Jacques W. Beukes*	193
Chapter 11:	Collaboration and Networking in Missions in Africa *Nico Mostert*	209
Chapter 12:	A Mission-Centred African Public Theology *Sunday Bobai Agang*	220
Chapter 13:	Dialogue With Other Faiths in Africa *Maniraj Sukdaven*	235
Chapter 14:	Evangelism and Mission *Johannes Knoetze*	248
Chapter 15:	Missional Church and Mission in Africa *Nelus Niemandt*	261
Chapter 16:	Missional Ethical Issues in Africa Through the Lens of 2 Corinthians 2:12-17 *Annette Potgieter*	277
Chapter 17:	Missional Diaconate: A Focused Holistic Ministry *Johannes Knoetze*	292
Chapter 18:	Church and Development in Africa: Looking Back, Moving Forward *Nadine Bowers du Toit*	301
Chapter 19:	Mission as Theological Education (Curriculum) in Africa *Johannes Knoetze and Jones Hamburu Mawerenga*	315
Chapter 20:	Normal(ised) Christianity/Religiosity in the Public Arena – A Mission of the Mind *Christo Lombaard*	330
Chapter 21:	Mission 'and' Ecology in Africa *Ernst Conradie*	344

Conclusion 357

Index 359

List of Abbreviations

AACC	All Africa Conference of Churches
ACC	Anglican Consultative Council
ACNS	Anglican Communion News Service
ACSA	Anglican Church of Southern Africa
AG	Ad Gentes
AGST	Assemblies of God School of Theology
AIC	African Independent/Indigenous/Initiated/Instituted Churches
AIDS	Acquired Immunodeficiency Virus
AM	Africae Munus
ATOR	African Theology of Reconstruction
ATR	African Traditional Religions
AVCSA	Association of Vineyard Churches South Africa
BTh	Bachelor of Theology
BU	Baptist Union
CEO	Chief Executive Officer
CEP	Congregation for the Evangelization of Peoples
CMS	Church Missionary Society
COVID-19	Coronavirus
CWME	Commission on World Mission and Evangelism
DD	Doctoral Divinitatis
DH	Dignitatis Humanæ
DI	Dominus Iesus
DMin	Doctor of Ministry
DRC	Dutch Reformed Church
DRCSA	Dutch Reformed Church of Southern Africa
DSD	Department of Social Development
DTh	Doctoral in Theology
ECD	Early Childhood Development
EHI	The Eleventh Hour Institute

FBO	Faith-Based Organisation
FESA	Fresh Expressions Southern Africa
GBV	Gender-Based Violence
GS	Gaudium et Spes
HIV	Human Immunodeficiency Virus
IDP	Internally Displaced People
IMER	Institute for Missiological and Ecumenical Research
IMF	International Monetary Fund
IPC	Integrated Food Security Phase Classification
IT	Information Technology
JPIC	Justice, Peace and the Integrity of Creation
LG	Lumen Gentium
LGBTQI+	Lesbian, Gay, Bisexual, Transgender, Queer, Intersex, and Questioning
MAGU	Malawi Assemblies of God University
MCSA	Methodist Church of Southern Africa
MDiv	Master of Divinity
MIC	Mission Initiated Church
MISA	Mission Shaped Introduction Africa
MTh	Master of Theology
NA	Nostra Aetate
NDR	Netherdutch Reformed
NetACT	Network for African Congregational Theology
NGO	Non-Governmental Organisation
NIV	New International Version
NLT	New Living Translation
NRF	National Research Foundation
NRM	New Religious Movements
NWU	North-West University
OCMS	Oxford Centre for Mission Studies
OECD	Organisation for Economic Co-operation and Development
PEN	Participate. Envision. Navigate

PhD	Doctor of Philosophy
QLFS	Quarterly Labour Force Survey
RASC	Reformed African Spiritual Churches
RCC	Roman Catholic Church
ReDi	International Society for the Research and Study of Diaconia and Christian Social Practice
RSA	Republic of South Africa
SAMS	South African Missiological Society
SC	Sacrosanctum Concilium
SDG	Sustainable Development Goal
SSA	Sub-Sahara Africa
StatsSA	Statistics South Africa
TRC	Truth and Reconciliation Commission
TTL	Together Towards Life
UCC	United Congregational Church
UCT	University of Cape Town
UFS	University of Free State
UNDESA	United Nations Department of Economic and Social Affairs
UNISA	University of South Africa
UPCSA	Uniting Presbyterian Church in Southern Africa
UR	Unitatis Redintegration
URCSA	Uniting Reformed Church in Southern Africa
USA	United States of America
UWC	University of Western Cape
WCC	World Council of Churches
WCRC	World Communion of Reformed Churches
YMCA	Young Men's Christian Association

List of Contributors

Annette Potgieter
School of Theology and Ministry
Hugenote College
Wellington
South Africa
Research Associate at Stellenbosch University
Email: annettepotgieter1@gmail.com
ORCID: https://orcid.org/0000-0002-5987-4912

Annette Potgieter has been a theology lecturer at the School of Theology and Ministry at Hugenote College since 2020. She completed her Dr. Theol. (Cum Laude) at Humboldt Universität zu Berlin. She has also obtained the following degrees: M.Th. New Testament (Cum Laude), M.A. Ancient Languages and Cultures (Cum Laude) and M.Div. (Cum Laude), BA Hons Ancient Languages and Cultures (Cum Laude), and B.Th. (Cum Laude) at the University of Pretoria. Her research interests are metaphor theory, spatiality, and early Christian literature and related texts. Potgieter has received various accolades including the Vice-Chancellor's and Principal's Award for the best graduate student, the Anton Rupert Scholarship in 2010, and the prestigious Skye Scholarship in 2015. In 2016 she won the Desmond Tutu-Gerrit Brand prize for the best theology debut book for *Jong teoloë praat saam…oor God, gemeentes en geloof*. Potgieter also served as a minister in the Netherdutch Church, Tuine, between 2018 and 2019.

Buhle Mpofu
Department of Practical Theology and Mission Studies,
Faculty of Theology and Religion, University of Pretoria,
Pretoria, South Africa
Email: buhle.mpofu@up.ac.za
ORCID: http://orcid.org/0000-0002-6833-0810

Buhle Mpofu received theological training at the University of KwaZulu Natal and Stellenbosch University and obtained the following qualifications: BA Theology (2003), BTH Hons (2006), MPhil (2010) and PhD in Practical Theology and Systematic Studies (2016).

List of Contributors

Christo Lombaard
Department of Practical Theology and Mission Studies
Faculty of Theology and Religion
University of Pretoria
Pretoria
South Africa
Email: CJS.@up.ac.za
ORCID: https://orcid.org/0000-0003-0019-4717

Professor Christo Lombaard has been the Head of the Department of Practical Theology & Mission Studies, in the Faculty of Theology & Religion at the University of Pretoria since March 2021 (after 15 years at the University of South Africa [UNISA] as Research Professor of Christian Spirituality). His research specialisms include Biblical Spirituality (combining aspects of Spirituality Studies with especially Old Testament texts), Post-Secularity (as faith-positive world trend) and Theological Education. He holds two doctorates: a PhD in Communication Studies (North-West University [NWU], Potchefstroom campus, specialising in Religious Communications) and a DD in Theology (University of Pretoria, specialising in Old Testament Studies). He is a South African National Research Foundation (NRF) rated scholar and a regular contributor to conferences across the globe. His most accessible publication is *The Old Testament and Christian Spirituality* (Atlanta, GA: Society of Biblical Literature, 2012), which was awarded the 2013 Krister Stendahl scholarship medal by the Graduate Theological Foundation, United States of America (USA). (This volume may be downloaded for free at www.sbl-site.org/assets/pdfs/pubs/IVBS-lombaard2012.pdf).

Dons Kritzinger
Retired from Department of Missiology
Faculty of Theology
University of Pretoria
Pretoria
South Africa
Email: dons.kritzinger@gmail.com
ORCID: https://orcid.org/0000-0001-8539-6275

Professor (Emeritus) J.J. (Dons) Kritzinger studied Mathematics and afterwards Theology at the University of Pretoria where he was awarded the DD in Science of Mission in 1973. After some years as a pastor in a traditional rural black community, he was appointed as the assistant to Prof David Bosch at the University of South

Africa (UNISA) and later moved to the University of Pretoria where he became a researcher and Director of the Institute for Missiological and Ecumenical Research (IMER). In the following 20 years, he led a number of research projects from which followed quite a number of research papers, books, and numerous articles in more popular but also accredited journals. He retired at the end of 2002.

Ernst M. Conradie
Department of Religion and Theology
University of the Western Cape
South Africa
Email: econradie@uwc.ac.za
ORCID: 0000-0002-0020-6952

Ernst Conradie is Senior Professor in the Department of Religion and Theology at the University of the Western Cape (UWC) where he teaches Systematic Theology and Ethics. His work is in the intersection between ecotheology, systematic theology and ecumenical theology. His most recent monographs are *The Earth in God's Economy* (LIT Verlag, 2015), *Redeeming Sin? Social Diagnostics amid Ecological Destruction* (Lexington Books, 2017), and *Secular Discourse on Sin in the Anthropocene: What's Wrong with the World?* (Lexington Books, 2020). He is currently working on a series of edited volumes entitled *An Earthed Faith: Telling the Story amid the 'Anthropocene'* published by Aosis and Wipf & Stock.

Gideon van der Watt
Faculty of Theology and Religion
University of the Free State (UFS)
Email: Gideonvanderwatt5@gmail.com
ORCID: 0000 0002-5993-636X

Gideon van der Watt holds a MTh in New Testament Studies from Stellenbosch University and a DTh in Missiology and Mission History from the Faculty of Theology and Religion of the University of the Free State (UFS), where he has been a part time lecturer for many years. During his career, stretching over 40 years, he served as missionary, minister, and mission administrator in the Dutch Reformed Family of Churches. He is currently the Editor of Christian Literature Fund, pastor in the Evangelical Lutheran Church, and research fellow of the Faculty of Theology and Religion (UFS).

Johannes Knoetze
Department of Practical Theology and Mission Studies
Faculty of Theology and Religion
University of Pretoria
Pretoria
South Africa
Email: Johannes.Knoetze@up.ac.za
ORCID: https://orcid.org/0000-0002-2342-2527

Professor Johannes J. Knoetze received theological training at the University of Pretoria and obtained the following qualifications: BA Theology (1988), BD Theology (1991), and Doctoral Divinitatis (DD) in Missiology (2002). From 1992 to 2011, he was a full-time minister in the Dutch Reformed Church of Southern Africa (DRCSA). In 2012, he was appointed as Senior Lecturer in the Department of Theology in the Faculty of Human and Social Sciences at the Mahikeng Campus of the North-West University (NWU). At the end of 2016, he was promoted to Associate Professor in the same department working in the Faculty of Theology at the NWU until August 2020. In September 2020, he joined the Faculty of Theology and Religion at the University of Pretoria as Associate Professor in Practical Theology and Mission Studies. He has published various articles in different accredited journals, as well as chapters in peer-reviewed books. His research focuses include missional diaconate in Africa, the millennial (emerging adults) population, and the alleviation of poverty. He acts as an external examiner for different universities, as well as a reviewer for international academic journals in his field of research. Knoetze is a member of the following associations: South African Missiological Society (SAMS), Society for Practical Theology in South Africa, International Association of Missiological Studies, World Reformed Fellowship, and International Society for the Research and Study of Diaconia and Christian Social Practice (ReDi). He also serves as a board member of NetACT (Network for African Congregational Theology) and as a member of the Moderamen of the General Synod of the DRCSA.

Harvey C. Kwiyani
Church Mission Society
Oxford
England
Email: hkwiyani@churchmissionsociety.org
ORCID: https://orcid.org/0000-0003-2221-319X

Harvey C. Kwiyani obtained his PhD in Mission and Leadership at Luther Seminary in St Paul, Minnesota, United States of America (USA). He holds a BEd (Mathematics) from Chancellor College of the University of Malawi, a BTh (London), and a MA (Missions) from the University of Wales.

Jacques Beukes
Department of Practical Theology and Mission Studies
Faculty of Theology and Religion
University of Pretoria
Pretoria
South Africa
Email: jacques.beukes@up.ac.za
ORCID: https://orcid.org/0000-0003-4319-2439

Jacques Beukes completed his BTh (2003), MDiv (2004), Licentiate (2005), and PhD (2014) at the University of Stellenbosch. He was appointed as Lecturer and Research Coordinator at Hugenote College in 2008. Since then, he has lectured in both fields of Theology and Community Development. In 2013 he was appointed at Hugenote College as Lecturer in Theology; (ii) Programme/Course Developer, and (iii) Student Counsellor (Chaplain). During this time, he has lectured in Practical Theology, Youth Ministry, Development Studies, Community Development, and Missiology. In 2019, he was appointed as a Senior Lecturer in Practical Theology at the University of Pretoria, and he lectures in Youth and Children Ministry, Congregational Studies, Theology and Development, Community Development, and Diakonia. He has published various peer-reviewed articles in accredited journals as well as chapters in peer-reviewed books. His conference contributions include keynote addresses, and various national and international conference presentations. He is also a member of several academic societies both locally and internationally, as well as an Editorial Board Member of the international peer-reviewed journal, *Religion & Development.*, and an Executive Board Member of the International Society for the Research and Study of Diaconia and Christian Social Practice (ReDi). Beukes is an ordained reverend in the Uniting Reformed Church in Southern Africa (URCSA).

List of Contributors

Johannes N.J. Kritzinger
Department of Christian Spirituality, Church History and Missiology
University of South Africa
Pretoria
South Africa
Email: kritzjnj@icon co.za
ORCID: https://orcid.org/0000-0001-5233-131X

Professor Emeritus Johannes N.J. (Klippies) Kritzinger obtained qualifications at the University of Pretoria (BA, 1970 and BD, 1973), and at the University of South Africa (DTh in Missiology, 1988).

Jones Hamburu Mawerenga
Department of Theology and Religious Studies
Faculty of Humanities
University of Malawi

Research Fellow: Department of Practical Theology and Mission Studies
Faculty of Theology and Religion
University of Pretoria
South Africa
Email: jmawerenga@unima.ac.mw
ORCID: 0000-003-4439-6142

Jones Hamburu Mawerenga holds a BA Theology obtained in 2003 from the Global University, USA; MA Theology obtained in 2008 from the Global School of Theology, Republic of South Africa (RSA); and a PhD in Theology and Religious Studies obtained in 2017 from Mzuzu University, Malawi. He is currently a lecturer in Systematic Theology and Christian Ethics at the University of Malawi. He is the author of two books: *The Homosexuality Debate in Malawi* (2018) and *Systematic Theology* (2019). He has also published the following journal articles: 'We are Human, Just Like You: Albinism in Malawi – Implications for Security' (2021); 'Rethinking Ecclesiology and the COVID-19 Pandemic in Malawi' (2021); 'Theological Education and the COVID-19 Pandemic in Sub-Saharan Africa: A Malawian Perspective' (2022).

Mission the "labour room" of theology

Maniraj Sukdaven
Department of Religion
University of Pretoria
South Africa
Email: sukdavenm@gmail.com
ORCID: https://orcid.org/0000-0001-8693-8961

Professor Maniraj Sukdaven has been a full-time lecturer since September 2006. He holds a BTheol degree from the University of KwaZulu Natal in South Africa, and an MA (Missiology) and a PhD (Religion Studies) from the University of the Free State. He began his academic career at the University of the Free State in Bloemfontein, South Africa, in 2006. His final position at this university was as the Head of Department for Religion Studies in the Faculty of Theology where he lectured on subjects in Christian missions and religion. He was since head-hunted to join the Faculty of Theology at the University of Pretoria and was employed as a senior lecturer in the Department of Science of Religion and Missiology in July 2014. In 2020 he was promoted to Associate Professor and in 2021 received an award as a C2-rated scholar from the NRF of South Africa. He was concurrently appointed as the Adjunct Professor at the University of Tehran in 2020 in the Faculty of Islamic Studies. With this appointment he became the first Christian professor in the history of the University of Tehran. In as far as his contribution to the academia is concerned, he has successfully supervised nine Masters and nine PhD students thus far. Again, history was made by successfully supervising the first Muslim PhD graduate at the Faculty of Theology and Religion at the University of Pretoria. In addition to co-publishing three books, he has published numerous academic articles in accredited journals as well as chapters in books. In addition to receiving countless invitations to present lectures internationally, and be a guest speaker at conferences, he has also been appointed on expert panels, and been interviewed on national and international radio stations and television.

Marina Ngursangzeli Behera
Oxford Centre for Mission Studies
Oxford
United Kingdom
Email: mbehera@ocms.ac.uk
ORCID: https://orcid.org/0000-0001-7612-6863

Dr Marina Ngursangzeli Behera is originally from Mizoram, one of the North Eastern states in India and belongs to the Presbyterian Church of Mizoram. She currently serves as a Research tutor and is in charge of the MPhil stage at the Oxford

Centre for Mission Studies (OCMS), Oxford, United Kingdom. She earned her degrees from Bishops College, Kolkata (BD), MTh from the North India Institute of Post Graduate Theological Studies, and her doctorate from the Federated Faculty for Research in Religion and Culture at Kottayam, all under the Senate of Serampore College, West Bengal in India. She taught History of Christianity at the United Theological College, Bengaluru, (2005 to 2012), and served as Professor of Ecumenical Missiology at the Ecumenical Institute, Chateau de Bossey, which is attached to the University of Geneva (2012–2016). She is currently the editor of the OCMS peer-reviewed academic journal, *Transformation*, and has edited several books and published papers.

Marinda van Niekerk
Research Fellow: Department of Practical Theology and Mission Studies
Faculty of Theology and Religion
University of Pretoria
South Africa
Email: marinda@pen.org.za
ORCID: 0000-0001-5902-972X

Dr Marinda van Niekerk received theological training at the University of Pretoria and obtained the following qualifications: BA Theology (1988), B.Div Theology (1991), M.Div in 2000, and Doctor of Philosophy (PhD) in Practical Theology with a focus on Narrative Therapy (2004). Marinda was ordained as a minister in the DRCSA in 1995. She is currently connected to the Dutch Reformed Congregation Ooskerk. She was one of the founding members of the non-governmental organisation (NGO) called PEN (Participate Envision Navigate) in 1992 and became the Chief Executive Officer (CEO) in 2010. She finished an Advanced Health Management Certificate with the Foundation for Professional Development in 2016. Her PhD was published by the Vrije Universiteit Amsterdam, and she has published various articles in different accredited journals. Marinda served and is currently serving on different boards of NGOs. Her areas of expertise and\or interest include urban theology, gender issues, and social entrepreneurship.

Martin Badenhorst
Department of Theology
St Augustine College of South Africa
Johannesburg
South Africa
Email: m.badenhorst@staugustine.ac.za
ORCID: https://orcid.org/0000-0001-9347-4587

Marthinus Samuel Badenhorst received theological training at St Joseph's Scholasticate, Cedara Natal, achieving a BTh from the Pontifical Urban University, Rome, Italy in 1990. A member of the Order of Preachers (Dominicans) in the Roman Catholic Church, he was ordained to the priesthood in 1990. He entered pastoral ministry in Welkom in the Free State (1991). He obtained the STL (Licentiate in Sacred Theology) from the Pontifical University of St Thomas in Urbe (PUST or Angelicum) in 2000. He was a member of the Historical Institute of the Order of Preachers during his term of study in Rome, Italy, and also gained further pastoral experience in the UK, Canada, and Germany. In 2001, he was appointed lecturer in Theology at St Joseph's Theological Institute and also worked to achieve that institute's civil recognition from the Department of Education. He served as Head of Theology for a term and as Prior of the local Dominican community. He became a part-time lecturer at St Augustine College of South Africa in 2004. In 2012 he returned to pastoral ministry in Welkom, and then later to Springs in Gauteng. Currently he is resident chaplain at St Mary's Old Age Home while continuing his work at St Augustine College. He has contributed to peer-reviewed books, accredited journals, and regularly presents material for leadership groups in the Catholic Church in Southern Africa on diverse aspects of theology and contemporary questions. His primary focus is Old Testament, and his areas of work include Ecumenism, World Religions, and Christian Spirituality of the medieval period.

Nadine Bowers Du Toit
Department of Practical Theology and Missiology
Faculty of Theology
University of Stellenbosch
Stellenbosch
South Africa
Email: nbowers@sun.ac.za
ORCID: https://orcid.org/0000-0002-0601-2622

Nadine Bowers Du Toit is an Associate Professor of Theology and Development (Department of Practical Theology & Missiology) at the Faculty of Theology, University of Stellenbosch, and the Director of the Unit for Religious and Development Research. Her research and publications over the past 20 years have focused on the role of faith communities in addressing issues of social injustice and poverty, with a particular focus on local congregations and grassroots faith-based actors. Nadine is often invited to address churches and other faith-based actors with regards to issues of poverty and inequality. In addition to serving on the board of two non-governmental faith-based organisations, she is also the Vice President of the International Academy of Practical Theology.

Nelus Niemandt
Rector Hugenote College
Research Fellow: Department of Practical theology and Mission Studies
Faculty of Theology and Religion
University of Pretoria
South Africa
Email: niemandtn@hugenote.com
ORCID: 0000-0002-8178-5393

Professor Nelus (C.J.P.) Niemandt studied Theology at the University of Pretoria and obtained the following qualifications: BA (1978), BD Theology (Cum Laude) (1981), Postgraduate Diploma in Theology (Cum Laude) (1982), and a DD (Doctorate in Theology) (1997) with a dissertation on Ethics and Multiculturality. Currently, he is the Rector and Chief Executive Officer of Hugenote College, a private tertiary educational institution in South Africa. Previously, he was a pastor in the Dutch Reformed Church (DRC), and served for 13 years at the University of Pretoria, eventually as Head of Department and Professor in the Faculty of Theology and Religion. He is emeritus Professor in Missiology and is also a research associate of the Faculty of Theology and Religion. He has been a visiting academic and scholar at world renowned universities, including Princeton Theological Seminary, Edinburgh University, and Radboud University (The Netherlands). He is a well published academic author with more than 80 publications, and is also an NRF-rated researcher in South Africa. Niemandt has also presented more than a hundred papers at national and international conferences. Additionally, he has supervised more than 80 postgraduate researchers, including nearly 30 PhD students. He serves on the boards of various academic journals. He is a well-known church leader in South Africa and served as moderator of the Highveld Synod of the DRC, as well as two terms as moderator of the National Synod of the DRC. He served on the National Religious Leaders forum and was patron of the South African Church Leaders Indaba. He did research on leadership and published a monograph on 'Missional Leadership'.

Nicolaas J. Mostert
Director: Partners in Mission, Dutch Reformed Church Free State Synod
Department of Practical and Mission Theology
Faculty of Theology and Religion
University of the Free State
Bloemfontein
South Africa
Email: missio@ngkvs.co.za

Dr Nicolaas J. Mostert received theological training at the University of the Free State and obtained the following qualifications: BA Theology (1988) and BTh (1991). He completed a MTh in Practical Theology in 2002 at the University of Stellenbosch and a Doctoral in Theology (DTh) in Practical Theology in 2019. He started his ministry in Zambia as a pastor and part-time lecturer at Justo Mwale University. Serving in various congregations in South Africa, he become the Director for Partners in Mission in 2020. He is also the Executive Director of NetACT.

List of Contributors

Peter White
Department of Practical Theology and Missiology
Faculty of Theology
Stellenbosch University
Stellenbosch
South Africa
Email: pwhite@sun.ac.za
ORCID: https://orcid.org/0000-0002-8177-140X

Dr Peter White is a Senior Lecturer in the Department of Practical Theology and Missiology at Stellenbosch University. He holds a PhD in Science of Religion and Missiology. He specialises in African Pentecostalism, Missiology, and Religious Studies. He teaches courses in African Theologies of Religions, Missiology, and African Pentecostalism. He is a NRF-rated Researcher – C2.

Piet Meiring
Faculty of Theology
University of Pretoria
Pretoria
South Africa
E-mail address: pgjmeiring@gmail.com
ORCID: https://orcid.org/0000-0003-4108-0425

Professor Piet Meiring was born in Johannesburg (South Africa) in 1941. He studied at the University of Pretoria, as well as at the Free University, Amsterdam (Netherlands). He was ordained to the ministry of the DRC in 1968 and served in two congregations in Pretoria. His academic career includes the chair in Missiology and Church History, University of the North (Turfloop), a part-time lectureship at UNISA, and (since 1988) the chair in Science of Religion and Science of Mission at the Theological Faculty, University of Pretoria. In 1996 he was appointed to serve on the South African Truth and Reconciliation Commission (TRC). Although he retired in 2010, he is still actively engaged in writing and researching. Meiring has over the years been invited to speak to hundreds of audiences, in South Africa as well as abroad, on missiological, ecumenical, and developmental issues, as well as on the truth and reconciliation process in South Africa. Additionally, he has been involved in reconciliation initiatives in several countries, including Indonesia, Israel, Palestine, Ireland, Northern Ireland, England, The Netherlands, Switzerland,

Fiji, Rwanda, India, Sri Lanka, and Canada. He has published widely, academic as well as popular books, and has contributed numerous peer-reviewed articles and chapters in books, locally as well as internationally. He is married to Linda, and together they enjoy a full life with their children and eighteen grandchildren.

Sunday Bobai Agang
Department of Systematic Theology
Faculty of Theology, Ethics, and Public Theology
ECWA Theological Seminary Kagoro
Nigeria
Email: sunday.agang1@jets.edu.ng or sundayagang1@gmail.com

Professor Agang loves the Lord. He has been thoroughly trained educationally and professionally as a theologian in the fields of Theology, Ethics, and Public Policy. His scholarly and academic outputs demonstrate the depth of his training and education in these fields. This background has made him a renowned scholar and authority in addressing contemporary theological, ethical, socio-political, missiological, cultural, economic, policy and religious issues in Nigeria and worldwide. His publications show that he has had a solid theological foundation with which he has ably addressed contemporary issues theologically and professionally. Professor Agang has great knowledge of his academic and professional fields as demonstrated in his academic, scholarly, and social and spiritual research and writings. It is very clear that he has emerged as an outstanding African theologian and scholar, and that now he can be rated as being among the great African theologians. His latest publications – *African Public Theology; God of the Remnant: The Plight of Minority Ethnic Groups in Africa;* and *Endangered Moral Values: Nigeria's Search for Love, Truth, Justice and Intimacy* – demonstrate good academic and theological maturity in addressing and evaluating both national and international issues.

Foreword

I am honoured to have been asked by the editor of this book to write the opening reflection for this piece of work whose title is a double meaning. The 'labour room' can either be the place where birth is given, or it can designate a room where work is done. The underlying message of the proposed title is, however, that mission is the space in which theology is conceived, nurtured, and forged, even though it may be developed, systematised, and then proclaimed in other spaces. Let us explore the link between this underlying assumption and the labour room.

Starting with the labour room as the place where birth is given reminds us that a new life is a miracle. A woman gives birth. A human being which has been conceived and nurtured for months leaves the protective womb and enters the world. Whatever control we imagine to have about our life, giving birth is a process in which the body goes into labour under pain, bleeding, and with the risk of losing two lives. If all goes well, a new human embodiment comes into the world which nevertheless depends on the woman giving birth, on her feeding and protection after birth, and on the accompaniment and commitment of human fellowship which a child needs to develop and come of age.

The reality is that all over the world, women give birth in the most unlikely and unbelievable spaces. Whatever the circumstances, blessed are those who can rely on the solidarity and care of other women in this vulnerable moment. The space and the circumstances in which a woman gives birth to a child can also give hints to the story which lies behind her becoming a child bearer – is it a story of love and care, or a story of violence, or of exploited ignorance? Is it the story of a fulfilment of hopes or of despair and worry about an uncertain future? Does the arrival of the new life happen in a welcoming community, or is it an act suffered by a neglected and abandoned woman?

The metaphor of the labour space is perhaps the best transition from giving birth to a child to the context in which mission gives birth to theology. Thinking of all the unlikely places where birth labour happens, we can naturally imagine how a child is born under sophisticated and highly qualified medical care and the best possible conditions in which human knowledge and medical technology take control and minimise every possible risk. In an analogous thinking, we can well imagine theology being done in a comfortable environment and thoroughly developed with access to all possible resources, pushing research beyond the existing boundaries and coming eventually to the light of day in the form of a well written book. The analogy indicates that theology and mission, having been birthed under such conditions, run the risk of being most effective in a comparable comfortable context. This means they run the risk of becoming abstract in their meaning and of being far away from more risky and down to earth life conditions, and therefore inadequate and ineffective in spaces that differ sharply from comfortable environments. Those who accept the message of such a comfort theology would first have to produce the conditions under which it could become a viable mission. Otherwise, they will need to rework it substantially and critically in order for it to be able to speak to people living in spaces defined by more severe circumstances and precarious conditions.

The hint to the many unbelievable spaces where birth is given can be taken as a reminder that mission emerges in many different spaces, including those much less comfortable, more dangerous, and riskier than a library. Put simply, the basic concept of the *missio Dei* is God entering his creation, becoming human and relentlessly pursing his mission. One of the images that the Bible offers us for this moment is the one of a child entering the world in the manger. In the birth narrative we do not learn much about Mary's labour, how fast or easy or how complicated and painful it was for her body to bring this child into the world. If we take seriously that God wants to become fully human, we can safely assume it happened with as much pain as other births. Luke 2:7 says that Mary laid him in a manger, 'because there was no place for them in the inn'. The labour room for God's entry was definitely not the safest and cleanest place. It was at the margins of what people imagine to be a safe and comfort zone.

Another well-known image of how God enters this world is the hymn in Philippians 2 which mentions that he 'emptied himself, taking the form of a slave, being born in human likeness'. Again, a reference to an uneasy and miserable beginning of a life which informed the later ministry of Jesus Christ, taking on consciously the human form of a servant.

Bethlehem as the ascribed birthplace and the manger as the labour room are references to the fact that God's presence, and hence his mission, occur in unexpected, unlikely, and endangered places. Theology must not only reflect these various and precarious circumstances but must also account for the fact that mission emerges in a multitude of places of which the majority are uncomfortable places marked by danger and by the ensuing vulnerability of the people living there. This includes the possibility that mission must develop and happen under the risk of failing. Joining into the *missio Dei* is definitely not a guarantee for success, even though the promise of the fullness of life is inherent in every moment of the journey.

Mission as the labour room or workspace of theology reminds us that it is not theology that gives birth to mission. Mission is an emergent phenomenon which engenders theology and is in need of a theological reflection of these beginnings. Mission needs theology to become intercommunicative as a common reflection in the Christian community, both in the historical depth and in the synchronic breadth of the God event. Such a theology needs to collect the many stories and reflections about God's will to be in the world and to transform the lives of people. Otherwise, mission could remain a solitary event, similar to the many women who have given birth of whom no one has heard.

Marina Behera
Oxford Centre for Mission Studies

Introduction

This edited volume offers a critical engagement with mission history and mission understandings from different contexts in Southern Africa as an introduction to mission studies. As the book originates from South Africa, it is presented from a South African perspective, although some contributors are situated in other countries on the African continent. The common denominator, however, is that all the contributors are, in some way or another, involved in mission in Africa, either as an academic at a theological institution or as a mission practitioner within a specific denomination.

Written in a clear, concise and understandable style, this book will appeal to a wide audience. The main contribution of this collaborative work is to be sought in the insights it offers on three main areas of mission:

- Section A gives a historical, denominational, and current overview of mission in Africa. These chapters give attention to the following: Biblical, historical, systematic foundations, new relevant documents, and some practical implications in Africa.
- Section B focuses on current theological understandings of the origin of mission, the changing contexts of mission, and the importance of mission studies in the theological curriculum, especially in Africa in the 21st century.
- Section C looks at the 'how' of mission, particularly different figures of mission, under the title: 'Mission as … or mission in the context of…'.

The book not only discusses issues regarding missiology in the Southern African context, but also gives some solutions to assist ministers in their practical ministry. Thus, in this sense, it is not only an academic book, but also a wonderful resource as it provides practitioners and missiologists with practical guidance for their current and future mission endeavours.

The book presents the original and innovative research of scholars involved in mission, as it is grounded in the respective fields of practice of each contributor. It contributes to a better understanding of the complex African mission landscape, a complex landscape that is experiencing even greater challenges since the dawn of COVID-19, which is noted in some of the research findings.

Methodologically, the work draws on a combination of methods, including critical literature studies and empirical work, as indicated in the various chapters.

The 21 incisive chapters of this book will be of great interest to academics, practitioners, and scholars in the fields of theology, religion, and mission studies who seek a broader overview of what mission in Africa entails.

No part of the book was plagiarised from any other publication, nor published elsewhere before.

Johannes J. Knoetze
Department of Practical Theology and Mission Studies,
Faculty of Theology and Religion,
University of Pretoria,
Pretoria,
South Africa.

SECTION A

UNDERSTANDINGS/THEOLOGIES OF MISSION IN AFRICA

Chapter 1

Protestant Mission in Africa – A Historical Perspective on Translating the Gospel

Gideon van der Watt

The importance of studying African mission history

Africa is hosting a significant share of the world's 2.2 billion Christians. It represents a remarkable shift in gravity of Christianity. This shift from the North and West to the Global South occurred mainly during the latter half of the 20th century. In 1910, sub-Sahara Africa's (SSA) share in World Christianity was only 9%; today it is more than 63% – about one in every four Christians live in SSA (Pew Research Centre 2011:11). SSA became one of the most dynamic centres of Christianity, not only in terms of numbers, but also characterised by what is often called the 'changing' or 'new faces' of majority Christianity (Jenkins 2006:4; Sanneh & Carpenter 2005:3-18). African Christianity could well be the representative Christianity of the 21st century, determining its course (Walls 2005:85).

Reflecting on how Christianity took root and developed in Africa, i.e., a proper historical perspective of mission within the African context, is indispensable for a theological understanding of the existence of Christianity in Africa and current missiological challenges of the church. Theology, and therefore missiology, cannot but be contextual, thus familiarising itself also with mission history.

The concept 'mission' implies the church's participation in and the community's response to the comprehensive *missio Dei*. Mission has a trinitarian foundation (i.e., *missio Trinitatis*), with God as the sole subject of mission. God, however, invites us, the church, to participate in God's mission to the world, or to observe what God is doing and then witness to it. The focus of mission history is therefore the attempt, from an historical perspective, to discover and reflect on God's incarnational saving grace as well as the response by the church and community in a particular context to God's mission. To put it differently, mission history discerns the historical process of the translation (*incarnation*) of the gospel into new contexts. According to Andrew

Walls (2004:26), the Christian faith rests on the divine act of translation: 'the Word became flesh, and dwelt among us' (Jn 1:14) – a process that is and should be continued in changing contexts if Christianity is to survive. This also explains the successive nature of the expansion of Christianity, the recent shift from the North to the South, for instance.

Mission history needs to be *social* mission history; it is much more than describing the role of individuals (for instance, missionaries), outstanding events, or the contribution of 'sending' agencies (so-called sending churches or mission societies). It should also focus on the meaningful response to the gospel in particular socio-cultural contexts, the gospel's incarnational transformation of societies, the mutuality and reciprocity between the gospel, mission, and context (society). The history of mission in Africa, for example, should therefore not 'be narrated primarily from the vantage point of Western missionaries. It should rather reflect the creative reception and incarnation of the gospel in the various regions and disenfranchised communities of Africa' (Saayman 1995:199).

'Mission history' or the 'history of Christian missions', as theological disciplines, should be seen as a distinct and particular focus within church history, but it is also practiced within the framework of general ('secular') history. 'History of Christianity', on the other hand, has a wider focus than specifically mission history.

Apart from numerous histories focussing on a definite mission activity, a society, a denomination, or a particular context, various scholars wrote comprehensive mission histories during the last century. They approached the task from different angles. It is important to take note of some of these seminal contributions. Prof Johannes du Plessis' *A History of Christian Missions in South Africa* (1911/1965) is an early and extensive history from the perspective of various mission societies operating during the 19th century in the larger Southern African context. The first volume of Kenneth Scott Latourette's monumental *A History of the Expansion of Christianity* appeared in 1937 and the seventh was completed in 1945. It was in 1955 summarised and compiled into one volume, *A History of Christianity*. In the chapter on 'The penetration of Madagascar and Africa South of the Sahara' (1955:1302ff), Latourette was quite aware of the detrimental collaboration between mission and colonialism, but he also underlined the benevolent facets of the missionary enterprise: the fight against slavery, the translation of the gospel in various African languages, and the contribution towards education, medicine, etc. He was deliberately not writing church history, but Christian history in relation to human history as a whole, applying the criteria of Christian action, signs of the kingdom of God, and people's response to the gospel (cf. the validation of Latourette in Walls 2005:4-26). Following in Latourette's footsteps, are: *A History of Christian Missions* by Stephen Neill (1964/1975), *The Planting of Christianity in Africa* (4 volumes) by C.P. Groves (1958–2002), the *World Christian Encyclopaedia: A Comparative Study of Churches and Religions in the Modern World, AD 1900–2000* by David Barrett (ed.1982/2019), and Adrian Hastings (editor) *A World History of Christianity in Africa* (1979/2000).

Recent publications ventured to shift the focus towards an African church (mission) history in its own right. These include, amongst others, works by Hildebrandt (1981/1990), Isichei (1995), Sundkler and Steed (2000), and Kalu (2005). Paas (2016) links the European church history to the African church history. Kalu, on the other hand, deliberately avoided writing from an institutional, denominational, or missionary point of departure; he narrated an 'African story', stressing the continuity of African Christianity with the Traditional African Religions (cf. Paas 2016:28). Andrew Walls wrote two seminal books, *The Missionary Movement in Christian History – studies in the transmission of Faith* (1996/2004) and *The Cross-Cultural Process in Christian History* (2002/2005), focussing on historical processes of the gospel's incarnation within (translation into) African culture. In this regard he had been working together with important African scholars who also focussed on the African response to the gospel, like Lamin Sanneh (1989, 2005, 2008) and Kwame Bediako – see his *Christianity in Africa: The Renewal of Non-Western Religion* (1996).

The four phases of Christian (mission) history in Africa

The origins and growth of Christianity can be divided in four distinctive but overlapping waves: firstly, an early wave in North Africa; secondly, a wave of Roman Catholic penetration of especially coastal areas from 1400–1800; thirdly, Protestant mission endeavours during the 19th and 20th centuries; and fourthly, the current era characterised by independent churches and movements. It is vital to briefly summarise all four waves, but the focus will be on the era of Protestant missions.

Early Christianity in Egypt, North Africa and Ethiopia

Christianity's roots in Africa go back to the very early years of Christianity itself (Fatokun 2005:357–363). The successive Greek- and Roman Empires covered most of the coastal areas of the Mediterranean Sea, including Egypt and North Africa. Greek and Coptic cultures dominated Egypt, while Latin and Berber cultures were most influential in North Africa.

Probably one of the first places in Africa the gospel went to, was the Kingdom of Nubia, including Kush (today's Sudan), where the 'treasurer of Ethiopia' returned after his conversion (Acts 8:26–39).

The Coptic church of Egypt claimed its origins to the missionary endeavours of the apostle Thomas and the evangelist Mark in the 1st century AD. Alexandria, the thriving commercial metropolis, became a significant centre of early Christianity. Christianity in Egypt rapidly grew during the 3rd century, especially due to the conversion of Jewish communities, the persecution by Roman authorities (*martyrdom* as test of authenticity) and the translation of the Bible in different Coptic dialects. Christian growth was also stimulated by the leadership and teaching of early church fathers like Clement of Alexandria (†215), Origen (†254), and Athanasius (†373), who all had a profound influence on theological developments within Christianity as a whole.

During the 3rd century, Christian monasticism originated in Egypt. The Desert Fathers were early Christian hermits who practiced asceticism in the Egyptian desert. Following the example of Jesus' life, those early monks devoted themselves to vows of austerity and self-denial, contemplative prayer, and service to others as an act of solidarity with the poor and in opposition to what they considered institutionalised injustices of self-indulgence in the church. They made a huge impact on developments within the later expansion of Christianity through monastic orders. The most prominent Desert Father was St Anthony of Egypt (†356). Despite the Islamic dominance throughout many ages, the Coptic church developed into a distinct expression of Christianity and prevailed until this day.

The Latinised North Africa, with Carthage (near modern Tunis) as the centre, and the ancient Numidia (Tunisia, Algeria, Morocco) were all part of the Roman Empire. The theological school of Carthage produced influential theologians constituting the cradle of theological developments in the Latin world. They were the likes of Tertullian (†225), Cyprian (†258) and a most prominent scholar like Augustine (†430) – the zenith and culmination of early Western theology (Neill 1975:37; Paas 2016:53). Due to internal struggles and the conquering of these regions by Islam, Christianity in North Africa almost completely disappeared by the 7th century. It also never succeeded in bringing the faith southwards, across the Sahara.

Early in the 4th century, two young laymen of Tyre, Aedesius and Frumentius, travelled to the kingdom of Axum (Ethiopia) and started witnessing to the gospel there. The Ethiopian king Ezana was converted and became one of the great Christian kings of Africa. Frumentius was eventually consecrated Bishop of the Ethiopian church – with the title of Abba Salã (father of peace). Due to Islamic rule, Christianity in Nubia (Sudan) disappeared early on. However, the Ethiopian church grew and has had, together with the Coptic church, a significant impact on the African Christian identity. Andrew Walls (2005:91) wrote:

> Ethiopia stands for Africa Indigenously Christian; Africa *primordially* Christian; for a Christianity that was established in Africa not only before the white people came, but before Islam came; for a Christianity that has been continuously in Africa far longer than it has in Scotland, and infinitely longer than it has in the United States (italics in the original).

Roman Catholic penetration of coastal Africa 1400-1800

When Portugal, under Prince Henry the Navigator, embarked on discovering and conquering 'new territories' by pioneer seafarers like Bartholomew Dias and Vasco da Gama, inroads for Roman Catholic missions along the West Coast of Africa were established. It was based at Portuguese trading posts. Henry's plan to enter Africa was aimed at defeating Islam and establishing Christianity in terms of the papal decree called *Padroado*, which granted the King of Portugal all rights to economic, military, and evangelistic activities in the new areas controlled by the Portuguese. These mission endeavours unfortunately could also not escape getting associated with the slave trade across the Atlantic (MacCulloch 2009:709). However, the Roman Catholic Church grew steadily all across the South Western African coast as well as the South Eastern coast and from there inlands. The steady growth was also due to the Catholic Church's honest endeavour to accommodate the African culture, the ordination of African priests and bishops as well as diaconal and educational involvement. In subsequent ages the Roman Catholic Church spread all across Africa. More about the Roman Catholic mission into Africa will follow in the next chapter.

The Protestant approach to mission

The unique approach of Protestant mission

When, in 1517, Martin Luther nailed his Ninety-Five Theses to the Castle Church door in Wittenberg (MacCulloch 2003:123ff), he protested publicly against the then Roman Catholic Church's practise of Indulgences. This act of Luther ushered in a new era of Protestantism, which, despite some continuities with the Roman Catholic Church, represented a radical break with the medieval Roman Catholic Church, the entire edifice of Thomas Aquinas' Scholasticism and a particular Roman Catholic mission approach. Core truths rediscovered and built on during the Reformation, consequently resulted in a unique Protestant missionary approach. Bosch underlines five unique features (Bosch 1991:241ff; cf. Latourette 1955:836–839), namely:

1. The article on justification by faith (Rom 1:17) became pivotal in a new missionary approach. God, in his sovereign grace (*sola gratia*) took the initiative to forgive, justify and save fallen human beings through his Son Jesus Christ. This article could serve as an urgent motivation for mission, but it could also paralyse efforts, because it could lead to the excuse: 'God will take initiative, it is not for us'.

2. Flowing from this first principle, is the view that all creatures are sinners and can do nothing to redeem or convert themselves (not through their own reason or will, by the church itself or by coercion in whatever form). It was not so

much about the many sins of individuals, but about the essential sinfulness of humanity. Only God, through Jesus Christ's crucifixion and resurrection, can save humans from their wretchedness. The lost state of the unbelievers should therefore urge the church into missionary action. This pessimistic view of humanity could, however, also hamper mission initiative – it was often argued that only God in his providential election can do anything to the wretchedness of people.

3. The Reformation stressed the subjective dimension of salvation. It was about a personal quest of an individual – Luther's search 'Where do I find a merciful God?' – and a subjective experience of being saved. However, this emphasis could also lead to overstressing individualism instead of recognising the importance of being part of a community (the collective facet of salvation).

4. Luther's emphasis on the priesthood of all believers meant a direct relationship between the believer and God, which is not necessarily mediated only through a priest or the official church. Every believer therefore has a calling to serve God. But the priesthood of believers also meant that each could go his or her own way, thus causing schisms.

5. The centrality of Scripture, prevailing over the sacraments, became a profound characteristic of Protestant mission praxis and theology. Mission was primarily seen as preaching the Word, and not the free dispensing of baptism. But the focus on the Word also harboured the danger of biblicism and fundamentalism.

Initial hesitancy

Reformers are often criticised on the grounds that they have initially been indifferent, even hostile to mission. Since the commencement of the Reformation in the early 16th century, nearly two centuries passed before any meaningful attempt at mission outreach across the borders of Protestant countries were made (Neill 1975:220ff; Bosch 1991:243ff). Protestants were rather engaged in battles for their own survival; the reformation of the church itself; as well as endless internal disputes and divisions. They were not, like the Iberian (Roman Catholic) countries, in touch with the wider world outside Europe. The principle of *cuius regio, eius religio* (territorial Christianity, determined by rulers) influenced their hesitancy to cross borders. The Protestants also lacked the efficacy of Roman Catholic monasticism (monastic orders) as a missionary vehicle. The interpretation of some foundational theological principles, like a fervent eschatological expectation; the conviction of providential election (and rejection); the primary emphasis on what God has done in Christ rather than what humans can do to bring about salvation; and a belief that the 'Great Commission' of Matthew 28:19–20 has already been fulfilled by the apostles, also played a role in Protestantism's early hesitancy to embark on mission endeavours (cf. Verkuyl 1975:34ff; Bevans & Schroeder 2004:195ff; Paas 2016:256).

It is on the other hand not proper to judge the Reformers by definitions of what mission entailed during the 19th century – the so-called great missionary era. Luther, for instance, provided the church with important guidelines and principles for mission. Mission was, in essence, something God does (the later principle of *missio Dei*) through churches in their own context. Faith was for Luther not something passive; it was a living, restless thing, seeking to spread the gospel through words and deeds. Calvin and his successors were even more explicit in expressing the importance of mission, the believers' calling to transform this world according to biblical principles and being missional within the European context. But, despite these theological points of departure, not much happened until the early 19th century.

Early initiatives by Pietists

A breakthrough in the Lutheran and Reformed orthodoxy's dogmatic dreariness and lacklustre approach to missions came with the origins of Pietism and later with the evangelical awakening. The first identifiable sign of this new movement was the book by Philip Jakob Spener (1635–1705) called *Pia Desideria* (1675). The 'desires' of this movement could be summarised as: a demand for personal conversion; joy of the (subjective) experience of one's own salvation; striving for a disciplined and holy life rather than sound doctrine; longing for a close-knit fellowship (*ecclesiola in ecclesia*) rather than sterile and authoritative ecclesial structures; and enthusiasm for the proclamation of the gospel to all (Neill 1975:228ff; Bosch 1991:252ff; Paas 2016:251ff). In some instances, however, Pietism led to mystical extremism. Coworkers of Spener, and important leaders in this movement, were August Hermann Franke (1663–1727) a German Lutheran scholar who established several institutions, including a university at Halle, and Count Nikolaus Ludwig von Zinzendorf (1700–1760) who established the Moravian community (Brethren) at Hernnhut. The Moravian brothers were known for their deep devotion to the crucified Redeemer (a preoccupation with the wounds of the Slaughtered Lamb), pious hymn singing and missionary passion. Pietism has had an abiding significance for the development of the Protestant missionary idea. Mission could no longer be seen as the duty of colonial governments; it became the enterprise of ordinary Christians; it crossed national borders, and it illustrated total dedication (Bosch 1991:255). Pietism could also be seen as an effort to regain what the Protestant Reformation lost in terms of Monasticism (MacCulloch 2009:738).

The Moravians embarked on a first missionary attempt to Africa when, in 1737, a layperson George Schmidt established the Genadendal-mission amongst the Khoisan people in the South-Western Cape (Du Plessis 1965:50-60; Paas 2016:257;

Elphick 2012:13). He could unfortunately only work for a few years before he was banned by the Dutch colonial authorities, on request of the DRC.

Evangelical revivals ushered in the era of missionary societies
Pietism, as mainly a feature within the Lutheran tradition, was followed by more or less similar movements in other regions: the English and Scottish Puritanism, the Dutch *Further Reformation* (*Nadere Reformatie*), English Methodist Revival (John [1703-1791] and Charles [1707-1788] Wesley's Armenian stream and George Whitefield's [1714-1770] more Calvinistic version) and the American Great Awakening in which John Elliot (1604-1690) and later on Jonathan Edwards (1703-1758) played leading roles.

In his pneumatology, Calvin put a special emphasis on the Holy Spirit's role in not only renewing the human soul, the inner life, but also the Spirit's activity of renewing the 'face of the earth'. This led to a remarkable blend of soteriological and theocratic elements (Bosch 1991:256) in these movements. A missionary awakening in the Protestant churches was stimulated. Gisbertius Voetius (1589-1676), a leading theologian in the *Further Reformation* during the Dutch Golden Age of scientific, artistic and commercial domination – especially in commerce with countries abroad, became the first Protestant missiologist. The foundation of mission is primarily theological – flowing from the very heart of God – the origin of a principle that later became known as the *missio Dei*. Voetius also formulated the threefold goal of mission as the conversion of the Gentiles, the planting of churches, and the glory and manifestation of God's grace. He saw mission as the task of the church, and not of any other agencies (Bosch 1991:257; Van der Watt 2019).

But despite Voetius' emphasis on the church's role as the only legitimate vehicle of mission, the evangelical revival movements led to the activity of individuals or the establishment of mission societies (associations), rather than missionary motion by churches.

The era of Protestant mission societies (the Great Missionary Era of Protestantism) commenced in all earnest with the publication of ex-cobbler and Baptist minister, William Carey's (1761-1834) book in 1792: *An Enquiry into the Obligations of Christians to Use Means for the Conversion of the Heathens* and the founding of the *English Baptist Missionary Society* (1792). It was followed by several other mission societies that one after the other entered mission fields in Africa: The *London Missionary Society* (1795), which started as a non-denominational institution, but later on associated closely with the English Congregational Church; the Anglican *Church Missionary Society* (1799), the Wesleyan Mission Society (1813), the *Basel Mission* (1815) from Switzerland, the *Berlin Society* (1824), the *Paris Mission Society* (1822), and a host of others, also from Sweden, Finland, Norway, etc. (Neill 1975:252; Paas 2016:257). The South African Missionary society, in association with the London Missionary Society, was already established in 1799 (Du Plessis 1965:91ff).

The founding of mission societies released new energy and a rapid geographical expansion of Christianity followed, especially into Africa. The growth was remarkable. In South Africa, for example, no fewer than 385 mission stations were established by 1884, by more than fifteen official mission societies (Elphick 2012:17). The early missionaries sent out by mission societies worked as pioneering individuals, or small groups; they were driven by an intense sense of calling and a zeal for the conversion of people (individuals); they believed that the gospel affirmed that Africans were potential brothers and sisters in Christ. They were mostly uneducated laymen focussing primarily on preaching (stressing the importance of confession of sin, conversion, accepting Jesus as Saviour, holy living, and an intimate relationship with Christ), but also on the transfer of basic handicrafts; they worked on invitation of tribal rulers and identified with the plight of the people they were sent to; they learned the indigenous languages, presented basic education, started translating the Bible and attempted to accommodate some of the existing cultural customs – even immersing themselves into the existing cultural practices. 'They believed that African languages were the most appropriate instruments of evangelization and that African preachers were the most effective heralds of God's word' (Elphick 2012:17). They often collided with colonists and colonial governments. They also often sacrificed their lives in the process.

A seminal example of these early missionaries was Dr Johannes Theodorus van der Kemp (1747–1811), who was sent out by the London Missionary Society in 1799 to commence work amongst the South African Khoisan in the Eastern Cape region (Du Plessis 1965:99, 129ff). Van der Kemp was originally from The Netherlands. He studied medicine at Edinburgh and only came to South Africa in his later age, after his wife's tragic death, leading to his profound conversion experience. He was influenced by the Moravians. Van der Kemp was intelligent, a devout Christian who preferred to live a simple life, identifying with the people amongst whom he worked – he married an indigenous wife. He believed in the equality of believers across racial boundaries; he therefore often collided with white settlers and the colonial government. He trained and inspired several Khoikhoi missionaries who made a significant contribution in the expansion of Christianity in Southern Africa (Neill 1975:311ff; Paas 2016:48).

Another example – probably a fair representative of many of his contemporaries – is Robert Moffat (1795–1883). He was sent out by the London Missionary Society and worked amongst the Bechuana tribe since 1821. With the help of Tswana co-workers, he translated the Bible into Setswana in 1843 – the earliest translation into an indigenous language in SSA (Du Plessis 1965:163; Neill 1975:312ff). In this endeavour, he searched for a proper translation of the name of God into Setswana.

He decided on the existing Setswana name 'Modimo'. This translation implied that God existed in the Tswana traditional faith all along. However, Modimo was never understood by Africans as a personal being or even Supreme Being, but rather as a vital force, the source of all life – the presence of divinity in all life and all things. According to Setiloane, it was this linkage with the familiar, pre-Christian understanding of God that caused the missionary enterprise to succeed in Africa (Setiloane 1986:21-28). It reminds one of Paul's approach in his speech to the Athenian Greeks in Acts 17:24-28 – mission is a contextual translation (or recognition) of the God who has been there even before the missionaries came!

Protestant missions and slavery

Since the late 15th century, when the Iberian powers laid a triangular connection between Europe, Africa and the America's, the Atlantic slave trade became a dominant and tragic feature of not only Western African history, but as Protestants and Muslims (and some African tribal authorities themselves) joined in this cruel trade, it spread across the whole of the African continent. However, during the 19th century, anti-slavery became an important dimension of the early Protestant missionary era. The origins of the missionary movement in Britain, for instance, coincided with growing public campaigns against the Atlantic slave trade (Walls 2005:95) – see for instance the role of the English parliamentarian, and strong supporter of the Protestant missionary movement, William Wilberforce (1759–1833), in the eventual acceptance of the Slavery Abolition Act of 1833.

About 1 100 Afro-American slaves who fought in the American War of Independence managed to return to Sierra Leone in 1792, bringing with them their Protestant churches and preachers. Slaves from ships intercepted at sea en route for the Americas and brought back by the British navy to Sierra Leone also converted to Christianity and became a strong force in the indigenous missionary movement, reaching out to a wider region in West Africa. Sierra Leone, populated by freed slaves from many origins, became an important country for Protestant missions. In 1823 the Church Missionary Society (CMS) sent twelve missionaries to Sierra Leone. Within 18 months, 10 of them died of fever, yet the CMS's mission to Sierra Leone did not stop – they were constrained by the love of Christ and prepared to make sacrifices (Bosch 1991:287).

On a slave ship heading for the Americas and intersected by the British in 1822, was a man called Ajayi, born in Yorubaland in Nigeria. He was converted and was trained at the Christian Institution, which later developed into the well-known Fourah Bay College. He eventually undertook further training in Britain. He was ordained in 1843 as an Anglican minister to commence the first indigenous mission of the CMS in Sierra Leone. He took the name of Samuel Ajayi Crowther (1809–1891) and soon afterwards started a mission to the Yoruba People in

Nigeria. Crowther studied indigenous languages – which he considered more than a mechanical process but an essential and dynamic translation of the gospel into the vernacular culture and building the indigenous church in Western Africa (Sanneh 1989:165). He was ordained as the first African Bishop of the Anglican Church. This was in line with the policies of Henry Venn, the director of the CMS, who strove for the ideal of self-governing, self-supporting, self-propagating churches with a fully indigenous pastorate. Crowther was a devout leader who did much to expand Christianity in the region; unfortunately, in later years, the old bishop was brushed aside by a younger generation of European missionaries – the European Protestant missionary approach changed during the peak time of colonialism (Walls 2005:155-164; Etherington 2012:199).

David Livingstone (1813–1873), a physician from a hardy clan of Scotsmen, who was sent out by the London Missionary Society, arrived in Africa in 1841. He was married to Robert Moffat's daughter and worked for 10 years as a missionary in Botswana, but then his drive towards exploring the heartland of Africa and his obsession with discovering the sources of the Nile River took over his life. He was convinced that these traveling expeditions could be helpful in bringing an end to the East African Arab–Swahili slave trade. His subsequent exploration of the central African watershed opened the heart of Africa to 'Commerce, Civilisation and Christianity', which he believed could be a cure for Africa's open wounds of slavery. His well-documented travel explorations were the culmination of the classic period of European geographical discovery and colonial penetration of Africa. At the same time, his missionary travels; his public speeches of appeal to British students – *'Do you carry on the work that I have begun. I leave it with you'*; the publication of his book *Missionary Travels and Researches in South Africa* in 1857, his 'disappearance'; his eventual death and the burial of his heart in Africa – and subsequent glorification as a posthumous British national hero in 1874 – led to the founding of several major central African Christian missionary initiatives from different Protestant denominations, especially the various university missions. His legacy was carried forward in the era of the European 'Scramble for Africa' (Latourette 1955:1308; Neill 1975:314-316, 325).

Protestant missions influenced by the Enlightenment

Western Christianity, but especially the Protestant mission of the 19th and 20th century, were profoundly influenced by the Enlightenment (Bosch 1991:274). During the enlightenment or 'modern' era, forcefully commencing in the 17th century Europe, the autonomy of human reason (rationalism) broke free from the shackles of the mediaeval concepts of the authority of God, church, and nobles. It was believed that human reason could boldly occupy and subdue the whole earth. Progress, development, and modernisation became leitmotivs. Knowledge was seen to be factual, and religion (God) was shifted to the realm of values, which were seen as subjective beliefs. It led to the separation of the spiritual (religious) and secular worlds. The emancipated, autonomous individual took centre stage.

This led to the Western imperial outreach ... and missions. The manifold fruits of the modern Western world had to be shared with Africa, which was perceived to still dwell in darkness (Bosch 1991:289). Missionaries – especially a 'second generation' since the middle of the 19th century – often could not escape the notion of the cultural superiority of the Western civilisation, which they understood to be aligned with Christianity and which they had the right to impose on the 'uncivilised' African culture. They were convinced that Christian 'civilisation' could rescue people – that was their Macedonian calling into Africa.

Missionaries therefore often approached their tasks in what we would today call a paternalistic way: they planted churches that looked exactly like those they knew in Europe; they focused on individual conversion, and at the mission stations the converts were isolated and cut off from their traditional communities and customs; they embarked on developmental projects such as education and the transfer of agricultural and handicraft skills; they introduced 'Western medicine'; and they were very hesitant to accommodate traditional African medicine, customs and beliefs. They considered themselves 'trustees' guiding the growth of the young churches, cautious not to transfer too much responsibility too early to emerging African leaders. To the missionaries – often lowly educated craftsmen – it was the obvious way to give effect to their benevolent calling. Bringing the 'fruits' of Western civilisation has often been exactly what was expected from them by the forceful rulers like Moshoeshoe, Lobengula, and Mizilikazi, who invited them and under whose protection and rule they worked (Walls 2005:96). But despite the fault lines in their approach, they succeeded in winning Africans to the Christian faith, they brought them into churches, and began recruiting and training Africans to take over the ministry (Latourette 1955:1305). Within their historical context, their contributions should therefore be judged more favourably (Prill 2019:81–98).

Lamin Sanneh considered the missionaries' work of translating the Bible – actually translating the faith (cf. Walls 2004:28, 47) – into the pluralistic vernaculars to be their greatest contribution. It produced grammars and dictionaries, and it created space for local coverts to assist and therefore influence the translation process itself. It became a vehicle of indigenous cultural development and the basis of establishing churches. The translated Bibles gave words and concepts to be used in allowing the gospel to be incarnated into the African context and culture ... to support a later phase of decolonisation (Sanneh & Carpenter 2005:214; Sanneh 1989:105ff) and eventually creating the 'new faces' of current African Christianity.

Western education also became a most noticeable aspect of missions in Africa. Through the provision of education, establishing mission schools, enhancing the theological training of ministers in theological seminars and eventually even universities, and by allowing indigenous leadership within church structures, the missionary movement impacted the lives of a host of new African leaders in their struggle for decolonisation and building independent countries. This included the likes of Jomo Kenyatta, Kwame Nkrumah, Julius Nyerere, Robert Mugabe, Albert Luthuli, and Nelson Mandela (Walls 2005:103-106; Etherington 2012:202).

Protestant missions collaborate with colonialism

The 'colonial idea' is very old and predated the Christian era. Since the 15th century, Catholic countries embarked on colonising parts of Africa. Since the early 19th century, the European Protestant countries commenced with colonising African countries, one after the other. The 'scramble for Africa' reached its peak in the infamous Berlin Conference of 1884–1885, also known as the Congo Conference, where new borders were drawn for the African continent, countries divided and defined, and a consensus reached on which European country could accept colonial rule over which African country. Although it has been a secular process, it coincided and often followed in the wake of and was intimately linked to the pioneering missionary enterprises into Africa. Colonial governments understood the importance of the missionary contribution to the 'successes' of colonial rule, and vice versa: missionaries genuinely considered the colonial rule of their own home country to be the most beneficial option for their missionary enterprise. Bosch quoted the harsh words by the pioneer Rhenish missionary C.H. Hahn (1818–1895) who worked as a leading missionary in German West Africa (today's Namibia): 'Even when the Whites subjugate and enslave other peoples, they still offer them so incomparable much that even the harshest fate the enslaved have to endure may often be called a fortuitous turn of events' (Bosch 1991:305). Even where missionaries criticised colonial rule, or collided with colonial authorities in taking sides with the people amongst whom they worked, they rarely questioned the legitimacy of colonial rule itself.

In his seminal book *The Equality of Believers, Protestant Missionaries and the Racial Politics of South Africa* (2012), Richard Elphick described how missionaries, while accepting the egalitarian message of the equality of believers in the spiritual realm, nevertheless could actively participate in enforcing the inequality of races in the social construct of segregated communities. The role of specifically Protestant missionaries in eventually providing the biblical justification for apartheid, is well documented (Elphick 2012:238ff). However, a number of missionaries and African church leaders from the erstwhile Protestant mission churches also played a significant role in dismantling apartheid during the latter part of the 20th century.

The reception of the gospel in Africa

In his book *Missionary Movement in Christian History* (2004:86), the well-known scholar in African Christianity, Andrew Walls, wrote that 'Modern African Christianity is not only the result of [missionary] movements among Africans, but it has been principally sustained by Africans, and is to a surprising extent the result of African initiatives'. Unordained lay preachers, catechists, teachers, elders, and especially also faithful women played a crucial role in establishing the Protestant Churches in Africa – the role of what Sanneh called 'indigenous agency', translating the faith for their own context (Sanneh 1989:164ff). Many of them began witnessing to the gospel even before the white missionaries arrived in a particular area. They often even sacrificed much more than the missionaries; they mostly had to break completely with their cultural roots and social connectedness; they were despised by members of their communities; their contribution was not always appreciated; sometimes they were even maltreated by the missionaries themselves. They were often caught between their loyalty and love for Christ and the church they served on the one hand, and, on the other hand, their own people's legitimate struggle for cultural, economic, and political independence and resistance to white domination. They were not very 'learned', but often gave proof of exceptional spiritual maturity, commitment to their calling and love for their Saviour. The overwhelming consensus is that African Christianity spread through the agency of African Christians. The special contribution of missionaries was not the 'accomplishment of conversion but the methods they devised to assist the development of indigenous churches and preaching networks' (Etherington 2012:200)

There are many concrete examples of evangelists preceding the missionaries in opening up mission fields, or working alongside them in commencing with the work. The stories of the first black ministers who have been ordained in the respective churches, deserve much more recognition. There are remarkable stories of lay people who literally carried missionaries and their wives in a *machila* (hammock slung on a pole used for carrying passengers in many parts of Africa) into the mission field. There were those who served as translators, cooks, teachers, catechists, builders, etc. There are many instances of successive generations of a particular family who served the kingdom of God in an exceptional way. In many instances, tribal chiefs also played a major role in inviting missionaries to start work amongst their subjects. They protected the missionaries and opened doors for the gospel to take root among their people.

The era of decolonisation, independence and ecumenism – new mission paradigms

During the 17th century, especially since the 1950s and 1960s, a new era in the formation of African Christianity dawned – and era of churches becoming independent from the sending institutions, the formation of ecumenical relations, and the rapid growth of neo-Pentecostal churches that characterised the new face of Christianity in the Global South. This ushered in new approaches to mission, a focus on the immediate challenges within the African context.

Since the beginning of the 20th century, African churches were coming of age. An indigenous leadership was developing, and slowly the Western cloak of the missionaries' church was shed. The process of the translation of the gospel into the African context enhanced rapidly. This coincided with, on the one hand, the decolonisation process as countries became independent. But on the other hand, this enhanced process of 'translation' (or incarnation) also happened simultaneously with what Thabo Mbeki (a former South African president) called an African cultural renaissance – an awakened sense of the importance of African roots, African history, African arts and traditional values (Walls 2005:107), resulting in a growing resistance to the churches as moulded by the Protestant missionaries.

Independent churches, movements and neo-Pentecostalism

The planted 'mission churches' became independent churches, gaining autonomy from the sending churches or institutions, and consciously building denominational structures and African leadership capacity. In their new understanding of mission, the independent churches and growing African theologies take the African cultural, socio-economic and political situation seriously. A focus on growing their own denomination, even to the extent of denominationalism, became an important feature of the mainline Protestant churches – denominations are for instance defined and celebrated by members wearing particular uniforms. Christianity increased and spread exponentially after the churches became independent. During the 1970s some churches even called for a Moratorium of Missions, because they considered the presence of missionaries to hamper their growth towards independence and contextualisation. The relationship between missions/sending churches and the independent African churches changed into partnerships, mainly focussing on collaboration in the fields of theological training and the production of literature.

But independence also led to the multiplying of religious schisms and fragmentations – charismatic leaders often choose to establish their own denominations. Since the early 20th century, literally thousands of independent African Initiated Churches (AIC) mushroomed all across the continent. In resistance to the mission churches' inherited legacy still characterised by Western and Enlightenment influences, these churches deliberately reincorporated a spectrum of traditional African beliefs and practices into their ministries (Sundkler 1976:17; Oduro, Pretorius, Nussbaum & Born 2008:9). They focus on the immediate, concrete experience of being cleansed, healed, or delivered from malignant spirits; they erase the Western divide between a natural and supernatural world; through rituals and prayer they access the vital force in all living and diseased beings and objects, and they strive for a moral life in terms of Christian (mostly Old Testament) and traditional African values. They often use 'Ethiopian' in their church's name to stress that an African Christianity can exist without the mediation of Western missionaries; other groupings developed more into prophetic-healing or Zionist churches (Ngong 2012:214), translating the concept Zion into a longing for typically African spaces and spirituality, a 'quest for belonging' (Daneel 1987:18). Odoro et al (2008) characterized it as "mission the African way".

Another important feature of the movement towards independence is the advent of 'neo-independent churches', mostly called 'ministries', 'fellowship' or 'faith missions' that are operating independently of institutional oversight. Their focus is on 'being born again', the deliverance from every kind of malevolent spiritual forces, physical healing, and well-being or abundant life (John 10:10), mostly understood in material terms (Ngong 2012:209).

Since the 1970s, Pentecostal (neo-Pentecostal) and Charismatic movements have been the fastest growing religious endeavour in Africa, representing a new and important strand of African Christianity (Ojo 2012:295-296). They are characterised by the following features: the experience (manifestation) of the presence of the Holy Spirit (baptism in the Spirit, speaking in tongues, and miracles); they are mostly led by solitary leaders (using various terms in defining their exalted status, like apostle, prophet, man of God, etc); they practice prophecy as the ability to have foreknowledge; they focus on the empowerment of believers for upward social mobility – a breakthrough in peoples' economic or social life; they image prosperity and they are making skilful use of modern media to communicate their message and market their ministries. Of great importance is their claim to access and mediate supernatural power. Ojo (2012:295-308) convincingly argues that these neo-Pentecostal and Charismatic movements are not merely an import from America or imitation of the Prosperity Faith teachers and televangelists, but that they rather have a distinct African indigenous origin. This represents an African contextual translation of the gospel (i.e. mission) in which the traditional African cosmology of evil, healing and power are central to the beliefs of neo-Pentecostal and Charismatic movements in Africa.

The neo-Pentecostal churches and Charismatic movements of Africa gained strong political influence – several prominent political leaders in African are devoted members of this movement. The neo-Pentecostal churches also embarked on significant missions into a secularised Europe, reversing the direction of the mission outreach of pervious centuries. In many European cities, the Pentecostal and Charismatic mega churches are the biggest and most vibrant, not only consisting of migrant members, but also a growing number of local European members. The movement also has a profound influence within the spirituality and ministry of mainline Protestant churches in Africa.

Current challenges and the need for an ecumenical African public theology

The continent of Africa faces many challenges: socio-economic issues, political instability, corrupt and authoritative leadership, tribal and religious violence, poverty and under development, ecological degradation and natural disasters, moral decay – Africa is plagued by an 'Afro-pessimism' and is still caught in a slavery of fear (Agang, Forster & Hendriks 2020:9). These seemingly unresolvable problems persist relentlessly, despite the fact that a very large percentage of the SSA population claims to be Christian. Are the African churches and the African theology failing the continent? Is there truth in the saying that African Christianity is flowing like a very wide, but shallow, river? In an important new publication (Agang et al. 2020), several African scholars engage with this question, and plea for what they call a proper and effective public theology as part of the church's mission – 'a Christian theology that is concerned with how all aspects of human knowledge, understanding and faith in God can translate into a deep moral commitment to building a better society, one which is strong in faith, love, justice and wisdom' (Agang et al. 2020:8), a theology that may once again help Christian leaders and followers to rediscover their identity and purpose in all spheres of life. The focus of the African church's mission should therefore shift to the new contextual or missional challenges the African churches are facing: a contribution to the development of an African Christian leadership in general (Priest & Barine 2017) and in particular an efficient and sustainable theological training based on new contextual curricula for training church leaders (apart from academical knowledge, it should also focus on transformative missional leadership and spiritual formation); sustainable ministerial and institutional renewal; missional transformation of churches, focussing on congregations; conflict resolution and dealing with violence; gender issues and human dignity; community development, diaconal services and poverty/disaster relief; the church's prophetic voice regarding economic and environmental justice; the Christian response to fundamentalist Islamic threats, etc. Church and theology should engage in missional transformation – participation in God's mission (*missio Dei*) to the African context (cf. Ngong 2012:216).

A contextual mission approach or public theology also entails that churches take hands in partnerships and regain an active participation in the different ecumenical structures. Since the Edinburgh Missionary Conference of 1910 (in a sense the culmination of the 19th century Protestant missionary era expressed in the optimistic and bold slogan: 'evangelising the whole world in this generation'), many factors in the Protestant world (especially two world wars) lead to the decline of the Western Christian witness. Being in the centre of gravity of a new majority Christianity, Africa needs to also strengthen its ecumenical voice in the world. Ecumenical structures in Africa, on the national, regional and continental level, need to be revived, focusing on the theological importance of unity, justice and mission (Pillay 2015:635ff) and jointly engaging the challenges of this continent. An important example of this is the role African theologians played in formulating the significant Accra declaration issued by the World Communion of Reformed Churches focussing on the church's role in engaging with the increasing global economic injustice and ecological destruction (Smit 2009). Another example is the *Arusha Call to Discipleship* (2018) formulated by the WCC Conference on World Mission and Evangelism. Drawing particular inspiration from African contexts and spiritualities, it rediscovered what it means to be "missionary disciples". (Ross 2020:11-13) Similar initiatives are being taken by the All Africa Conference of Churches (AACC) in terms of the church's role in helping to reach the developmental goals for the continent set by the African Union's document *Agenda 2063: The Africa we want* and translating it into the 'Africa God wants' (Agang et al. 2020:401ff; cf. Sakupapa 2018).

Conclusion

African Christianity, which has its origin in the very early days of Christianity itself, and has been so profoundly influenced by an alien religious enterprise – the Protestant mission of the nineteenth and 20th century – developed over time into a primarily African enterprise. A contextual understanding of mission remains a potent force in the African religious, social, and political life. This new centre of Christianity, presenting a new face of Christianity, should continue to interact with and impact Christians on other continents, reversing the direction of the previous two centuries' mission by continuously translating the gospel into a changing world.

References

Agang, S.B., Forster, D.A. & Hendriks, H.J., 2020, *African public theology*, Langham Publishing, Carlisle.
Barrett, D., (ed.), 1982, *World Christian Encyclopedia: A comparative survey of churches and religions in the modern world, A.D. 1900–2000*, Oxford University Press, Nairobi.
Bediako, K., 1996, *Christianity in Africa: The Renewal of Non-Western Religion*, Edinburgh University Press, Edinburgh.
Bevans, S.B. & Schroeder, R.P., 2004, *Constants in context – A theology of mission for today*, Orbis Books, Maryknoll, New York.
Bosch, D.J., 1991, *Transforming Mission – Paradigm shifts in theology of mission*, Orbis Books, New York.
Daneel, I., 1987, *Quest for Belonging*, Mambo Press, Zimbabwe.
Du Plessis, J., 1911/1965, *A history of Christian missions in South Africa*, C. Struik, Cape Town.

Elphick, R., 2012, *The equality of believers – Protestant missionaries and the racial politics of South Africa*, University of Virginia Press, Charlottesville.

Etherington, N., 2012, 'Christian missions in Africa', in E.K. Bongmba (ed.), *The Wiley-Blackwell companion to African religions* (pp. 198-207), Wiley Blackwell, UK.

Fatokun, S.A., 2005, 'Christianity in Africa: a historical appraisal', *Verbum et Ecclesia* 26(2).

Groves, C.P., 1958-2002, *The planting of Christianity in Africa, 4 Volumes*, Lutterworth, London.

Hastings, A., 1979/2000, *A world history of Christianity in Africa*, Eerdmans.

Hildebrandt, J., 1981/1990, *History of the church in Africa, A survey*, African Christian Press, Achimota, Ghana.

Isichei, E., 1995, *A history of Christianity in Africa: From antiquity to the present*, SPCK, London.

Jenkins, P., 2006, *The new faces of Christianity – Believing the Bible in the Global South*, Oxford University Press, New York.

Kalu, O.U., 2005, *African Christianity: An African story*, University of Pretoria, Pretoria.

Latourette, K.S., 1955, *A history of Christianity*, Eyre and Spottiswoode Limited, London.

MacCulloch, D., 2003, *Reformation Europe's house divided 1490–1700*, Penguin Books.

MacCulloch, D., 2009, *A history of Christianity*, Penguin Books.

Neill, S., 1964/1975, *A history of Christian missions*, Penguin Books.

Ngong, D.T., 2012, 'Christianity in Africa', in E.K. Bongmba (ed.), *The Wiley-Blackwell companion to African religions*, (pp. 208-219), Wiley Blackwell, UK.

Oduro, T., Pretorius, H., Nussbaum, S. & Born, B., 1984/2008, *Mission in an African way – A practical introduction to African Instituted Churches and their sense of mission*, Wellington BM & CLF.

Ojo, M.A., 2012, 'Pentecostal and Charismatic movements in modern Africa', in E.K. Bongmba (ed.), *The Wiley-Blackwell companion to African religions*, (pp. 295-309), Wiley Blackwell, UK.

Paas, S., 2016, *Christianity in Eurafrica – A history of the church in Africa*, CLF, Wellington.

Pew Research Centre, 2011, Global Christianity – A report on the size and distribution of the world's Christian population, viewed 6/08/2022, from https://www.pewresearch.org/religion/wp-content/uploads/sites/7/2011/12/-Christianity-fullreport-web.pdf.

Pillay, J., 2015, *Ecumenism in Africa – Theological, contextual, and institutional challenges*, Geneva: World Council of Churches, John Wiley & Sons Ltd.

Priest, R.J. & Barine, K., 2017, *African Christian leadership – Realities, opportunities, and impact*, Orbis Books, New York.

Prill, T., 2019, 'Ambassadors of Christ or agents of colonialism? Protestant missionaries in Africa and their critics', *Scottish Bulletin of Evangelical Theology* 37(1), 81-99.

Ross, K.R., 2020, *Mission Rediscovered: Transforming Disciples – A Commentary on the Arusha Call to Discipleship*, World Council of Churches

Saayman, W., 1995, 'Christian mission history in South Africa', *Missionalia* 23(2), 184-200.

Sakupapa, T.C., 2018, The ecumenical movement and development: The case of ALL Africa Conference of Churches (AACC), 1963-2000 (part 1)', *Studia Historiae Ecclesiasticae* 44(3). https://dx.doi.org/10.25159/24124265/4593

Sanneh, L., 1989, *Translating the message – The missionary impact on culture*, Orbis Books, New York.

Sanneh, L. & Carpenter, J.A., 2005, *The changing face of Christianity – Africa, the West, and the world*, Oxford University Press, New York.

Sanneh, L., 2008, *Disciples of all nations – Pillars of world Christianity*, Oxford University Press.

Setiloane, G.M., 1986, *African theology, An introduction*, Skotaville, Johannesburg.

Smit D.J., 2009, 'Covenanting for justice'? On the Accra Document, Reformed theology and Reformed ecclesiology', *HTS Teologiese Studies/Theological Studies* 56(1), a279. https://doi.org/10.4102/hts.v65i1.279.

Sundkler, G.M., 1948/1976, *Bantu prophets in South Africa*, The International African Institute.

Sundkler, G.M. & Steed, C., 2000, *A history of the Church in Africa*, Cambridge UP, Cambridge.

Van der Watt, G., 2019, 'Gisbertus Voetius (1589–1676): Some perspectives on his influence on developments in the South African Dutch Reformed Church's missiology and mission practice', *Die Skriflig/In Luce Verbi*, https://doi.org/10.4102/ids.v53i3.2449.

Verkuyl, J., 1975, *Inleiding in de Nieuwere Zendingswetenschap*, Uitgeversmaatscappij J.H. Kok, The Netherlands: Kampen.

Walls, A.F., 2004, *The missionary movement in Christian history – Studies in the Transmission of Faith*, Edinburgh: T&T Clark.

Walls, A.F., 2005, *The cross-cultural process in Christian history*, Edinburgh: T&T Clark.

Chapter 2

Catholic Mission: A Theological and Historical Survey

Martin Badenhorst

[M]ission is, quite simply, the participation of Christians in the liberating mission of Jesus, wagering on a future that verifiable experience seems to belie. It is the good news of God's love, incarnated in the witness of a community, for the sake of the world (Bosch 2011:532).

Introduction

As with most Christian communities, the Roman Catholic Church (RCC) regards the Great Commission of Matthew 24:14 as foundational. The Lord's own command is carried out through the history of the Church, always in a context. The sense of mission as well as insight into its method also unfolds in the scriptural narrative. Abraham's history with God starts with a command to go (Gen 12:1). There is also a developing sense that the people are not only sent to different places, but they also have a purpose to witness and call, as we find the great songs of God's universal reign in Isaiah (cf. 66:18ff.). The prophetic ministry in Israel describes the task of shepherding as witnessing to God, especially in the development of the symbol in Jeremiah and Ezekiel (cf. Jer 23:3; Ezek 34:1ff.). The Lord's own ministry is seen in fulfilment of these aspects. Mark points to him ministering in the region of the Decapolis where there is a non-Judahite population, as witnessed by swineherding (Mk 5:1ff). John's Gospel makes special emphasis of Jesus' role as the fulfilment of the shepherding promise found in the prophets (Jn 10:1ff).

Another aspect of the biblical foundation of mission found in the life of the Lord are the silent years. Luke makes mention of the young Jesus in the temple, questioning, listening and conversing. Jesus spent years listening to the human condition and the people of his own time, before embarking on his active mission (Lk 2:46). This serves as a model for the best engagement with a society. Furthermore, the missionary history of the apostles, especially Luke's description of Paul's mission and that witnessed to in Paul's own writings, gives us further insight into the whole missionary task of the Christian community. Paul's mission on the Areopagus illustrates the aspect of listening (maybe not well enough) and responding to a society from within the framework of that society (Acts 17:15-33). Moreover, proclamation of the Word is an element of a broader sense of mission. Additionally, physical and emotional relief, as described in the tasks of the shepherd in Scripture, also forms an integral way of mission. Mission is practiced by the building of hospitals, care homes, the provision of education, and other elements of empowerment. Finally, as a core value of mission is the building of a community centred on the gospel. Community supports an experience of the presence of the kingdom of God in society. The body of Christ is an invitation to experience something that human endeavour itself cannot supply. This kingdom community can only be established by a faithful cooperation with the Spirit of God, who is the primary Evangelist.

The church's mission is to represent salvation to the world. On her historical journey the church moves ever closer to her final promise, the full restoration of all creation to the community of Divine Persons – Father, Son, and Spirit. Through the Christian presence in the world, all people may experience something of that future, though not yet the fulness of that future. The church's social action supports the movement of all peoples, Christian believers and other believers alike, towards societies which reflect the delight and intercommunion of the Divine Persons. Bringing healing, instruction in the wonder of creation, and political action toward the common good are essential components of proclamation.

The three distinct periods of mission

As we focus on the context of mission in Africa, we may, in a broad sense, discern three distinct missionary periods.

Firstly, we have the Apostolic period. The Book of Acts narrates Phillip baptising the eunuch in the court of Candace (Acts 8:26-38). It is from this encounter that the Coptic family of churches trace part of their heritage. Later tradition places the evangelist Mark in Alexandria. The bishops of Alexandria then receive patriarchal dignity for the Orthodox Churches in Africa. This fruitful period gives rise to many African theologians (e.g. Tertullian, Cyprian, and Augustine, among others). As the Christian community continues its theological growth, the early period is also rife with disagreement and heresy. The African churches in particular were regarded as Monophysite and separated from European/Near Eastern Christianity after the Council of Chalcedon in 451. Further separation took place after Islam became the ruling religious and social structure in North Africa between AD 647 and 709. The Christian communities were then no longer in communication with the body of Christianity in Europe and Asia Minor.

The second period started with the rise of the European explorers and the establishment of European colonies. The period also coincided with the European Reformation and an element of ecclesiastical and political rivalry entered into the missionary endeavour. In 1622 the RCC established a Dicastery (organisational department assisting the Pope) to oversee missionary endeavours in this context of a divided Christianity. At the time it was named *Sacra Congregatio de Propaganda Fide* (Sacred Congregation for the Propagation of the Faith), popularly known as the *Propaganda Fide*. It was renamed in 1967 to the Congregation for the Evangelization of Peoples (CEP). In 1627 a special college for missionary training was established in Rome, the *Pontificio Collegio Urbano de Propaganda Fide*, popularly known as the Urbanianum. Until 2005 all philosophical the theological academic training of aspirant clergy in South Africa was overseen by the Urbanianum. The African history of this period saw the conversion of Congolese and Angolan peoples starting in 1491. Missionary activity in Mozambique was established in 1500. In 1560 the area now known as Zimbabwe received missionaries. Socio-political changes and upheavals in Europe resulted in a pause of Catholic missionary activities from around 1775, which was exacerbated by the French Revolution in 1789 and the following era of European secularisation.

The third phase of missionary activity finds its roots in the ecclesiastical response to secularisation and the establishment of missionary families of priests and women's religious communities. The most significant of these for Southern Africa is the Missionary Oblates of Mary Immaculate (OMI), founded by St Eugene de Mazenod in 1826.

Catholic mission in the context of British colonies was controlled by the Penal Laws of England which limited Catholic church membership and social participation. The most significant repeals were in 1829 (the Catholic Emancipation Act) and 1832 (the Roman Catholic Charities Act). This allowed greater freedom to Catholic clergy and pastoral agents (such as the religious sisters). They could move beyond the confines of faithful Catholics in service of the colonial government to reach out to the indigenous populations in various regions. Some stability arose in terms of colonial spheres of influence with the Berlin Conference of 1884–1885. There were, however, devastating consequences for indigenous populations affected by this colonial imposition.

In so far as the structures of the Roman Catholic confession are concerned, Southern Africa remains a missionary territory and is not acknowledged as a mature, self-sufficient local church. This implies that local church structures work with the central government of the RCC through the CEP and not directly with various Roman offices of administration. For instance, the appointment of bishops, and the consultative process leading towards such appointment, is handled via the CEP. For the churches regarded as mature and self-sufficient, the process is coordinated by the Congregation for Bishops.

Central to the social context for mission in this era is the role of slavery. Within the apostolic period, slavery was a universal social institution, and although early church theologians did condemn the institution, it endured. During the second and third periods of mission, with regard to Africa, slavery was still present as a social and economic institution and various theological, moral, and social discourses eventually effected change and abolition. Forms of slavery are as diverse as they are morally reprehensible. Sufficient for this context is that the final conclusion of the theological and moral journey of the RCC, with regard to slavery, is summed up in the documents of the Second Vatican Council, also called Vatican II (1962–1965) – the document *Gaudium et Spes* (GS) (§ 27 and §29) places slavery with those acts of human exploitation which are a 'supreme dishonour' to the Creator.

The African mission in the 19th century

A particular missionary model emerged in the 19th century, that of the adventurer. The missionary is seen as an heroic figure battling the forces of the dark continent to win victory for the faith. This notion is seen in much of the correspondence of the era, sometimes embroidered so as to win greater financial support for the mission. So we read, in the correspondence of François-René de Chateaubriand (1768–1848), Catholic activist and French ambassador to the Papal States (please note a trigger warning regarding derogatory language and concepts):

> Here is one of those great and new ideas which belong only to the Christian religion. The idolatrous cults have not known the divine enthusiasm which animates the apostle of the gospel. The ancient philosophers themselves never left the avenues of Academe and the delights of Athens on a sublime impulse to humanize the Savage, to instruct the ignorant, to heal the sick, to clothe the poor and to sow concord and peace among hostile nations: this is what the religious Christians have done and still do every day. The seas, the storms, the ice of the pole, the fire of the tropics, nothing stops them: they live with the Eskimos in their sealskins; they feed on whale oil with the Greenlanders; they traverse the wildernesses with the Tartars and the Iroquois; they mount the Arab's dromedary or follow the wandering Kaffir (de Chateaubriand and White, 1884) in his blazing deserts; the Chinese, the Japanese and the Indian have become their neophytes; there is no island or reef in the Ocean which has been able to escape their zeal; and just as once

there were not enough kingdoms for the ambition of Alexander, now the earth is too small for their charity.

When regenerated Europe had no more to offer the preachers of the faith than a family of brothers, they turned their eyes to the regions where souls were still languishing in the darkness of idolatry. They were touched with compassion at seeing the human degradation; they were urged on by the desire to shed their blood for the salvation of these strangers. They had to penetrate profound forests, cross impassable swamps, ford dangerous rivers, climb inaccessible rocks; they had to face cruel, superstitious and jealous nations; they had to surmount the ignorance of barbarism in some and in others the prejudices of civilization. All these obstacles could not stop them ... (De Chateaubriand & White, 1884, Part IV, Book 4, Chapter I).

By the end of the period, similar views remained as we see in the writing of the Catholic missionary, Louis-Eugène Louvet, 1895 (please note a trigger warning):

The black population of southern Africa comprises three distinct races. The Kaffirs (infidels) deserve their name perfectly. Of all the African races, the Kaffirs are the most difficult to convert. They are characterised by a profound religious indifference and an abject materialism. Our freethinkers, always in search of atheistic populations, might perhaps find among them the ideal of which they dream. The Kaffir tribes split into two great branches, the Basutos and the Zulus. The Basutos appear more susceptible to being won over to European civilization; the Zulus, who are treacherous, fierce and untamed, have so far rejected all the approaches of the English. But both are equally enemies of work: dissolute, deceitful, liars and thieves. Any idea of morality would seem to be extinct in the conscience of the Kaffir: when accused he boldly persists in denial until one has been able to convict him, caught out, he shows neither shame nor repentance...

The Hottentots used to live in the plains of the Cape. Driven back first by the Dutch and then by the English, they are dragging the débris of their tribes over southern Africa ... everywhere strangers, everywhere miserable and rejected. Their customs are very dissolute, but they have a more submissive and timid nature than the Kaffirs, and in this respect at least they would be more accessible than the latter to the approaches of Christian civilization.

The Bushmen are the pariahs of southern Africa. Forced back into the deserts and caves in the mountains, they live without clothing and without any other means of subsistence than theft. The other Blacks chase them like wild beasts ... If Christianity does not come promptly to raise them from their abject state and civilize them, in a century this unfortunate race will have disappeared from African soil.

> This is the ungrateful material on which Catholic missionaries in southern Africa have been working for fifty years. That readily explains the slowness of their progress and the complete failure of the Protestant missions. Idleness, and the custom of stealing which goes with it, together with polygamy, are the two main obstacles to the conversion of the Blacks. Unfortunately, the testimonies of Protestant travellers have taught us that these evil natural dispositions have been kept alive by the Protestant missions, jealous of being able to send their subscribers each year a list of their alleged converts (cited by Comby 1996:143).

Charles Martial Allemand Lavigerie was bishop of Algiers (later a Cardinal) and in 1868 founded the Missionaries of Africa. In an address to a missionary conference in 1878, he states:

> In speaking of the material education of our young Blacks, I have said that they should be African. But on the other hand their religious education must be essentially apostolic. There are in fact two ways of making men like us. The first is to make them like us outwardly. That is the human approach, the approach of the philanthropic civilizers, those who say, as was related at the Conference of Brussels, that to change the Africans it is enough to teach them the arts and crafts of Europe. It is to believe that when they are housed, clothed, fed as we are, they will have changed their nature. But they will only have changed their garb. Their heart will be just as barbarian, even more so; for it will also have been corrupted and will apply to its corruption what it has learned of the secrets of our luxury and our softness.
>
> The apostle ... becomes a barbarian with the barbarians, as he becomes a Greek with the Greeks. This is what the apostles did, and we do not see any of them trying first to change the material customs of the peoples. They sought to change their hearts, and once these hearts were changed, they renewed the world ... (cited by Comby 1996:133).
>
> The statement 'men [sic] like us' is telling in this context. It shows that the distinctions between European culture and the challenge of the gospel were not yet fully realised.

The African mission in the 20th century

Even as the colonial boundaries in Africa were set by the Conference of Berlin in 1885, they did not remain in place. The Treaty of Versailles after the First World War (1919) removed German colonial possessions and redistributed them. At the same time there was an exponential increase in conversions in the Catholic missionary field.

The growth was not entirely the result of coming to the faith, but it went hand-in-hand with cultural imperialism and the notion of either imposing or aspiring to European culture. As seen with Lavigerie, missionaries played a role, either consciously or unconsciously, in uprooting indigenous cultures and imposing the ideal of a Christian Europe. In Rwanda, as narrated by José Hamim Kagabo (1983:53), the German colonial administration had largely protected the indigenous social institutions of Rwanda. After the Treaty of Versailles at the end of the First World War, Belgium became the protectorate of the region now known as Rwanda and Burundi. By 1930 the new colonial administration had deposed, and exiled to their Congolese territories, King Yuhi V. Musinga. He had been perceived as hostile to the European and Belgium cultural and religious domination. The governor, Pierre Ryckmans, installed the baptised son of the deposed king, to whom he was also godparent, Mutara III Rudahigwa, as the new monarch. After this, the number of converts grew explosively and the religious/political influence of the RCC culminated in the dedication of the country to Christ the King in 1946.

This was as much a gesture seeking political favour from the coloniser as it may have been an expression of faith. The ancillary role of these mass conversions and public gestures of religious identity was to counteract Muslim activity in the regions. This period also saw an upsurge in the number of independent churches, which placed its own challenge at the door of missionary activity.

The Second World War and its effects resulted in the process of decolonisation throughout the world. The approach to diverse cultures and a growing realisation of their inherent value started to shape the way the RCC approached local cultures. This is seen clearly in John XXIII's encyclical, *Princeps Pastorum*, of November 28, 1959:

> We Ourselves have already expressed Our thoughts on this matter as follows: "Wherever artistic and philosophical values exist which are capable of enriching the culture of the human race, the Church fosters and supports these labors of the spirit. On the other hand, the Church, as you know, does not identify itself with any one culture, not even with European and Western civilization, although the history of the Church is closely intertwined with it; for the mission entrusted to the Church pertains chiefly to other matters,

that is, to matters which are concerned with religion and the eternal salvation of men. The Church, however, which is so full of youthful vigor and is constantly renewed by the breath of the Holy Spirit, is willing, at all times, to recognize, welcome, and even assimilate anything that redounds to the honor of the human mind and heart, whether or not it originates in parts of the world washed by the Mediterranean Sea, which, from the beginning of time, had been destined by God's Providence to be the cradle of the Church".

John XXIII insisted that the establishment of a local hierarchy with local leadership was the ideal to which the Church should move. He also recommended the adaptation of sacraments to the local culture and equivalent cultural practices (specifically mentioning Confirmation in the context of coming-of-age rites in world cultures).

Vatican II had as a guiding principle, *ressourscement*, a return to the sources, specifically of Scripture and the Apostolic era, and discerning the accretions of human society from the development of faith as guided by the Holy Spirit. The Council applied this principle to the missionary activity of the Church in a number of its documents. It prepared several documents dealing with the Church's activity in various facets of its life, each of which has missionary implications. *Sacrosanctum Concilium* (SC) deals with the liturgy, *Nostra Aetate* (NA) deals with other religions, *Ad Gentes* (AG) deals specifically with mission, *Unitatis Redintegration* (UR) with ecumenism, *Lumen Gentium* (LG) with the church herself, GS with the church's relationship to the modern world, and *Dignitatis Humanæ* (DH) with pressing questions of human dignity. Together these documents explore the relation of humanity to God and propose tools of discernment when evaluating religious and cultural practices in the process of the Church engaging in various cultures and religious contexts.

It is particularly the document on the Church's missionary activity (AG) which offers the greatest synthesis of methods and approaches. The first major point the document makes is that the church is a 'sacrament of salvation' to all peoples. It is the very nature of the church to be missionary, and the church goes to peoples to bring enlightenment and healing to their religious quests (§3), even though those religious quests may lead people to God.

The purpose of mission is to establish local churches with their own governance (§6) through the process of bringing the gospel to people. In this activity, Christians are to, above all else, lead through example (§11). The giving of this example embraces the appreciation of the culture being approached, an understanding of the society being reached, and a sense of identifying with the people to be evangelised.

Mission, thus, needs to be prepared through knowledge and respect for the existing social and religious structures in human societies. Not only are individuals brought to Christ, but communities are built to be the place where people belong. With proper checks and balances, the building of Christian congregations can be done in cooperation with other Christians so that the One Lord may be honoured in the work of many Christian paths.

As soon as possible, local clergy are to be formed and local expressions of religious life encouraged. This leads on to the fact that the establishment of a truly local church, drawing from the richness of the whole church and contributing to the richness of a particular culture to the church, is the goal of missionary activity. The establishment of a local church depends on a mature Christian laity (§21), so that the establishment of a church is not simply the presence of a local clergy.

An important aspect of being a local church is the incorporation of aspects of local cultures and societies. The document encourages theological speculation in this area (§22). In addition to giving attention to the training of missionaries (clerical and lay), it demands of a future missionary the spirit of innovation and openness toward the receiving culture and its spiritual traditions (§23-27). The document concludes with exhortations to all members of the church – bishops, priests, clergy, and laity – to take up their particular role and make a contribution to the fulfilment of the church's universal mission.

The post-conciliar era of the 20th century

The reception of a Council unfolds in terms of decades and centuries. The details arising from Vatican II are still in the process of unfolding. Statistics may offer a snapshot of the complexities. Africa saw an increase in Catholics from 2 million in 1900 to 140 million in 2000, a 6 900% increase. The population increase over a similar period (1980–2000) was 457% or 145 to 807 million. Representation in the hierarchy of the Church also changed significantly over the period.

At Vatican I (1878–1879) there were 8 bishops from Africa, none of whom were indigenous, out of 558 bishops present at the beginning, representing 1.4% of the assembly (Hennesey 1969:496); at Vatican II there were 298 bishops from Africa present out of about 2 500 bishops (11.9%) (Wilde 2007:12); while in 2019 there were 715 bishops in Africa out of 5 377 worldwide (13.3%) (Segretario di Stato Vaticano 2021).

In terms of the missionary approach as built on Vatican II there are significant milestones. Pope Paul VI, in his encyclical, *Populorum Progressio*, of 1967, ties integral human development to the theological enterprise of mission (see especially §12). Human development is expression of the shepherding mission of Christ. The Pope is also careful to make a distinction between technological development and integral human development. Technology is not the measure of progress, human wholeness and responsibility is, so we read in §41:

The developing nations must choose wisely from among the things that are offered to them. They must test and reject false values that would tarnish a truly human way of life, while accepting noble and useful values in order to develop them in their own distinctive way, along with their own indigenous heritage.

This leads to a methodology of mission summed up in the Pastoral Guide of 1989, issued by the CEP (§11):

> The gospel transcends all cultures and is identified with none of them (cf. Jn 18:36). However, the Kingdom announced by the gospel is lived by people who are deeply bound to a culture, and the construction of this Kingdom cannot but take account of cultural elements. This important area has a deep significance for missionary evangelization, as it has an obvious link with the incarnation of the Word. The Church has not only the simple task of evangelizing cultures, i.e. promoting and welcoming all the resources, the richness and customs of the nations, in the measure in which they are good; it also has the task of bringing the Good News to all groups of peoples, to transform them from within, and purify them from negative elements, both old and new, so that the gospel message may be expressed in a new and authentic way.

The missionary imperative of the Church formed an important part of the continental synods held during the 1990s. Each of these synods of bishops resulted in an apostolic exhortation. The Synod for Africa was held in 1994, and the exhortation, *Ecclesia in Africa*, was published under Pope John Paul II on 14 September 1995. The regional synods were to prepare the Church for mission in the third millennium. The role of African Traditional Religions (ATRs) had moved to the fore in the time after Vatican II. Theological contemplation was struggling with the criteria for discerning the prevenient grace of God in the religious conceptualisations of indigenous peoples. In this process the notion of mission as incarnation was contemplated, as it is in *Ecclesia in Africa* (§87).

> Inculturation, through which the faith penetrates the life of individuals and their primary communities, is also a path to holiness. Just as in the Incarnation

Christ assumed human nature in everything but sin, analogously through inculturation the Christian message assimilates the values of the society to which it is proclaimed, rejecting whatever is marked by sin. To the extent that an ecclesial community can integrate the positive values of a specific culture, inculturation becomes an instrument by which the community opens itself to the riches of Christian holiness. An inculturation wisely carried out purifies and elevates the cultures of the various peoples.

The third millennium

At the dawn of the third Christian millennium, the Congregation for the Doctrine of the Faith, under the leadership of Cardinal Joseph Ratzinger, issued a corrective document, *Dominus Iesus* (DI). It was a response to theological questions which had arisen in regard to the relationship to other religions and the diversity of Christian confessions. In many ways it is a check and balance against unwise assimilations of cultural and religious practices and opinions which may be characterised as syncretism. It is an internal disciplinary document of the Church, which was often misunderstood. It remains a matter of some controversy because of what emerges in its anthropology.

It may be somewhat audacious to state that the greatest religious differences are matters of anthropology, and not theology. *DI* shows that there is substance to this assertion. Since the Reformation there have been distinct anthropologies at work within Christian confessions. There is an elevated view based on the total redemption of the human person through the cross and resurrection of Christ Jesus. There is also a more cautious view which assumes that human nature retains its sinful corruption, even as the possibility for redemption is created by the cross and resurrection of Christ Jesus. The elevated view is common among the Roman Catholic and Orthodox family of Churches, and the cautious view is more a hallmark of the approach described by John Calvin and the communities associated with his reform.

In the political realm, these views are represented by varied notions regarding the meaning and need for a social contract. As described by Thomas Hobbes (1588–1679), the social contract is that which limits the intrinsic miserable state of the human person by forcing the subduing of the inherent instinct to violence. The counterpoint to this is the view championed by Jean Jacques Rousseaux (1712–1778) of the nobility of the human person, where the social contract limits some freedoms for the common good. However, for Rousseaux, the institutions which arise become corrupt and have distressing effects on human freedom and goodness.

Upon reflection, one may see that these perspectives play a role in the missionary endeavour of the 19th and following centuries. Usually those on the receiving end of mission are the violent savages, while those bringing European culture are the enlightened, free individuals. Furthermore, DI appears to reflect a more negative anthropology than the one traditionally expressed in the RCC. The document describes a distinction between faith and belief. *Faith* is seen as submission of the will and intellect to the God who reveals (§7). Such a submission is, itself, the fruit of grace. There is a relationship described by the word 'faith'; firstly, a trust in God, and then trusting what God reveals because of the fundamental trust in God. Faith gives us the tools to penetrate the mystery of God (since God reveals) and to understand that mystery in a coherent fashion. *Belief*, on the other hand, 'is that sum of experience and thought that constitutes the human treasury of wisdom and religious aspiration, which man [sic] in his search for truth has conceived and acted upon in his relationship to God and the Absolute' (DI §7). Belief is still on the way to God, and lacks the element of assent to God. This is not very far from a contemporary Calvinist analysis as presented by Karl Barth (1975:341):

> It is the *Deus revelatus* who is the *Deus absconditus*, the God to whom there is no path nor bridge, concerning whom we could not say nor have to say a single word if He did not of His own initiative meet us as the *Deus revelatus* (italics in the original).

Belief discovers things about God, in human terms, but belief can never be revelation proper, because revelation is totally dependent on God revealing what cannot be known by a human search alone (this position was also articulated at Vatican I, and quoted in Vatican II, GS §59).

Acknowledging that human religion is the sum of limited thought and experience of God, how much of what other religions assert has the quality of revelation? DI would relate all that is good and in harmony with the Christian revelation to Christ as revelation. It is as if the act of God's revelation in time and space (both of which, of their nature, place limitations of what can be apprehended by humanity), creates echoes within the human spirit, echoes reflecting, though more vaguely, that which God reveals in Jesus Christ. Human reason may lead a people to a point where they acknowledge a God who reveals, but the content of that revelation is always sheer grace. They can know that God reveals, but without the Triune God, no one can know what God reveals. This distinction between faith and belief then underpins the document in its further expression. It does not offer too much of an analysis of the nuances of the distinction, but works with the fact of the distinction.

Can people outside of Christianity come to believe in the Christian God through their own systems? The answer would be, 'not fully'. The notions of creation, rebirth, and resurrection do exist in other religions, both current and those which have passed into history. Since they do not fully encounter the Risen Christ, the creative Logos, who spoke forth the universe, they are provisional – not God's final word in the person of Christ.

Before the Jubilee year, various regional synods used the term 'seeds of the Gospel' for the good found in non-Christian religions. Similarly, DI also addresses the ecumenical dimension. It proposes that Christianity currently consists of three groupings, namely: the RCC, other churches, and ecclesial communities.

The church of Christ, the sacraments, structure and continuity with Christ, as Christ willed them, subsists most clearly in the RCC. Other communities who contain these elements, with the exception of unity with the Bishop of Rome, are churches. All other communities who retain only partial elements of the sacraments, structure and continuity with Christ, are ecclesial, or 'church like' communities. So, the church of Christ requires not only faith in continuity with the history of Christianity, but an historical continuity with Christ. That historical continuity is also a structural continuity. This is the point at which the revelation can most loudly be heard, where the vision of the God who reveals God's self in Jesus Christ may be seen.

This point has raised a great number of objections since the publication of DI. The objections rest on the implied arrogance of the scandal-ridden RCC proclaiming itself as existing as God wills a church to exist.

The second African synod and Africae Munus

In 2009 a second African synod was celebrated and the following Apostolic exhortation, *Africae Munus* (AM), was published in November 2011 under Pope Benedict XVI. It appears that there has been some movement over the period between DI and AM, since the theological approach of both have Joseph Ratzinger as their author.

> It is imperative therefore to make a commitment to transmit the values that the Creator has instilled in the hearts of Africans since the dawn of time. These have served as a matrix for fashioning societies marked by a degree of harmony, since they embody traditional formulae for peaceful coexistence. These positive elements therefore need to be emphasized, lit up from within (cf. Jn 8:12), so that Christians may truly receive the message of Christ, and in this way God's light may shine before the eyes of all (AM §39).

This comes close to acknowledging an element of revelation in the cultural history of African societies. However, in §92–93 reference is made to ATR and witchcraft. This tends to impose abstraction, distinction and value judgement on what is essentially a coherent system of practice and belief, which of itself does not contain those distinctions or value judgements. The question of divided loyalties arises and is a present problem in South Africa, in particular where some people in Christian ministry are, simultaneously, practicing ministry within their traditional belief systems.

The African experience

Even as the goals of a local church, characterised by local leadership and learning from local cultures with local liturgical expressions, has been promoted with increasing vigour since the pontificate of Pius XII (1939–1958), the experience of specifically black African Catholics has not been entirely consistent with the theological paradigm. The unfortunate alliance of colonial power and missionary endeavour has characterised Christianity as part of the European colonial project.

The 'othering' of African peoples to incite donor contributions from the developed world to the developing African context still exists (cf. Pels 1989). It is sometimes encouraged by indigenous African clergy fundraising from the developed world. Thus, African clergy and African members of institutes of consecrated life represent 'progress' made by the 'other', if only enough financial resources were available.

This view remains problematic because, 'despite the interesting aspects contained in the Roman policy towards the mission fields, the policy was formulated in Europe, the mission station were not consulted about what they wanted, and the people who implemented it were of European descent' (Mukuka 2000:295). Even the process of the African synods was largely according to an agenda determined by offices in Rome, and articulated by Pontiffs and theological advisors of European descent. The early history of indigenous African clergy in South Africa highlights this problem, as Makuka (2000:295) reports:

> The view which comes up frequently in the written sources is that the early black priests were not ready to be priests, but we have discovered that, in fact, there was a constant struggle between the missionaries and the black priests over "cultural signifiers" which these priests made sense of their lives as priests and as Africans. In this case, questions like, who was to be in charge? Whose culture were the priests supposed to follow? Did becoming a Catholic priest mean, one had to totally alienate oneself from one's cultural background and world-view?

This remains an unresolved problem within the RCC for African priests and laity alike. There is perception of 'otherness' because, even as the population base of Catholicism has moved from developed to the developing world, 'the whole cultural ethos of the Church is still Euro-centric. The agenda the church tries to set and achieve is still very much determined by the whites' (Mukuka 2000:299).

These experiences highlight the problem that there is still a clear distinction between the missionary and the mission of the church. As the incarnational paradigm takes greater shape in the articulation of the theology of mission, so too the long process of listening to and becoming centred in a new cultural matrix will need greater attention. Ultimately this is the great missionary lesson taught by Jesus Christ, the Word Incarnate, who listened in the silence of an ordinary life before spending a fraction of his earthly journey engaging in mission. As articulated by Ilo (2017:70), 'The most difficult theological and pastoral task is to take a step into a place where we have never gone before and, in these uncharted territories, to engage and be open to new moments of revelation dictated by the movement of the Spirit in history'.

References

Barth, K., 1975, *Church dogmatics*, T. & T. Clark, Edinburgh.

Benedict XVI, Pope, 2011, *Africae Munus: Post-synodal apostolic exhortation*, Pauline Publications, Nairobi.

Bosch, D.J., 2011/1991, *Transforming mission: Paradigm shifts in theology of mission*, Orbis Books, Maryknoll, New York.

Comby, J., 1996, *How to understand the history of Christian mission*, SCM Press, London.

De Chateaubriand, F.R., 1884, *The genius of Christianity*, or the spirit and beauty of the Christian religion, transl. Charles I. White, John Murphey & Company, Baltimore.

Hennesey, J., 1969, 'National traditions and The First Vatican Council', *Archivum Historiae Pontificiae* 7, 491–512.

Ilo, S.C., 2017, 'Contested Moral Issues in Contemporary African Catholicism: Theological Proposals for a Hermeneutics of Multiplicity and Inclusion', *Journal of Global Catholicism* 1(2), 50–73.

John XXIII, Pope, 1959, Princeps Pastorum [Encyclical Letter], viewed 13 March 2022, from https://www.vatican.va/content/john-xxiii/en/encyclicals/documents/hf_j-xxiii_enc_28111959_princeps.html

John Paul II, Pope, 1995, Ecclesia in Africa: *Post-synodal apostolic exhortation*, Pauline Publications, Nairobi.

Kagabo, J., 1983, *L'Islam et les "Swahili" au Rwanda*, Ecole des Hautes Etudes en Sciences Sociales, Paris.

Mukuka, G.S., 2000, 'The establishment of the black Catholic clergy in South Africa from 1887 To 1957', PHD thesis, University of KwaZulu-Natal.

Paul VI, Pope, 1967, Populorum Progressio [Encyclical Letter], viewed 13 March 2022, from https://www.vatican.va/content/paul-vi/en/encyclicals/documents/hf_p-vi_enc_26031967_populorum.html

Pels, P., 1989, 'Africa Christo! The use of photographs in Dutch Catholic mission propaganda, 1946-1960', *Critique of Anthropology*, 9(1), 33–47. Doi: 10.1177/0308275X8900900104

Ratzinger, J., 2000, *Dominus Iesus*, viewed 13 March 2022, from https://www.vatican.va/roman_curia/congregations/cfaith/documents/rc_con_cfaith_doc_20000806_dominus-iesus_en.html

Second Vatican Council, 1965, *Gaudium et Spes* (GS), viewed 13 March 2022, from https://www.vatican.va/archive/hist_councils/ii_vatican_council/documents/vat-ii_const_19651207_gaudium-et-spes_en.html

Segretario di Stato Vaticano, 2021, *Annuario pontificio*, Città del Vaticano, Tipografia Poliglotta Vaticana.

Wilde, M., 2007, 'Who wanted what and why at the Second Vatican Council? Toward a general theory of religious change', *Sociologica: Italian Journal of Sociology*, 1. doi: 10.2383/24194

Chapter 3

Together Towards Life and Mission: African Pentecostals' Participation in the *Missio Dei* [1]

Peter White

Introduction

This chapter takes inspiration from the ecumenical document: 'Together Towards Life: Mission and Evangelism in Changing Landscapes' (TTL) (ed. Keum 2013). The concept 'together towards life and mission' is used in this chapter as a missional theory of the universal church's participation in the *missio Dei*. This missional participation is a life-giving journey required of every denomination and local church.

Scholars have engaged the TTL document from various perspectives. Kim (2014) discusses the document from a historical perspective. In her analysis, she unpacks the phrase 'Together towards Life'. In explaining the word 'together', Kim (2014:7) submits that 'because Life is for all and because the whole *oikoumene* is interconnected in God's web of life', our participation in the *missio Dei* should be approached from the perspective of togetherness (unity, diversity, uniqueness, and tolerance). Furthermore, the word 'towards' used in the title of the document 'expresses our orientation to Life, our expectation and hope in Christ' (Kim 2014:7). These, therefore, suggest that our mission thinking is still in process and that our mission activities are evolving in changing landscapes.

In 2015 Niemandt published two articles using *Together towards Life* as one of the key reference materials. The first one was on eco-mission.

---

[1] The chapter is an updated version of a conference paper presented on Missional Church: African Pentecostal Perspectives, at a missional church conference organised by the General Synod of the Dutch Reformed Church in South Africa on 29 September 2021.

This article was a response to the TTL call for mission towards the creation of God (Niemandt 2015a). His second article analyses the 2013 policy decisions by the General Synod of the Dutch Reformed Church (DRC) on the missional nature of the church in the light of the new mission affirmation of the World Council of Churches (WCC). He noted that the DRC finds itself, together with a broader ecumenical community, on a journey towards life. It does have an appropriate basis for good governance in church and society (Niemandt 2015b:1). In addition, Knoetze (2015) capitalised on the term 'unreached territories' in the TTL document (WCC 2013:52) and argued that the church must focus on marginalised children as 'unreached territories'. He therefore used this concept to develop African child theology.

Although the TTL document has created room for the Pentecostal Pneuma theology (WCC 2013:53-73), there is however no academic engagement of the document from a Pentecostal perspective. This chapter therefore focuses on how African Pentecostal churches have and are participating in this call for a united mission in their journey with other churches. In view of the focus of the chapter, I use the concept 'together towards life and mission' to project the idea of ecumenical recognition of the voice of various church traditions in this journey and call for missional togetherness. In the latter, we are required to learn from one another in our vulnerabilities and imperfect nature of each church tradition and theology.

The discussion in this chapter is approached from the perspective of the pneumatic statement, 'Life in the Holy Spirit is the essence of mission, the core of why we do what we do and how we live our lives'. The discussion is approached with the undertone of the four main headings as outlined by the WCC (2013:53-73), namely: Spirit of Mission: Breath of Life; Spirit of Liberation: Mission from the Margins; Spirit of Community: Church on the Move; and Spirit of Pentecost: Good News for All.

To help the readers appreciate the Pentecostal tradition and be able to differentiate it from the Neo-Prophetic churches, this chapter will start with an overview of Pentecostalism in Africa. Thereafter, the focus will shift to Classical and Neo-Pentecostal praxis, followed by a discussion on the contextual influence on theology and mission praxis, and its effect on experience in the context of Pentecostal theology, particularly the Faith and Hope Gospel, as well as African Pentecostals' expressions of missional ecclesiology. These discussions are aimed at helping the readers of this chapter to appreciate how African Pentecostals are participating in the 'life-giving' mission of God.

Overview of Pentecostalism in Africa

In African Christian historiography, African Pentecostal churches are the second stream of African Christianity. It emerged as a protest against the syncretic practices of some of the African Initiated Churches (AICs). Anderson (2003:178) refers to this category of churches as 'African Initiated Churches of the Spirit' or, in other words, 'churches of the spirit'. Ayegboyin and Ademola Ishola (1997) confirmed that quite a number of the leaders of indigenous churches prefer to identify themselves with the designation – African Spirit Churches or churches of the spirit. These types of churches are known as *Aladura* in Nigeria, 'spiritual churches or *sunsum sore*' in Ghana, and 'prophet-healing churches' in most other parts of Africa (The Editors of Encyclopaedia Britannica 2012). In South Africa, AICs are classified based on their designated identity: Ethiopian Movement of AICs, Messianic Movement of AICs, and Spirit-Type Movement of AICs (Ngada & Mofokeng 2001:4).

Pentecostalism is defined as a stream of Christianity that emphasises personal salvation in Christ as a transformative experience wrought by the Holy Spirit (Asamoah-Gyadu 2005:12). The term 'African Pentecostalism' is used generally to cover churches and denominations that are pneumatic in orientation in Africa (Wariboko 2017:2). The growth of the Pentecostal movement worldwide was estimated at 63 million adherents in 1970 to about 683 million in 2018, this figure is predicted to increase to 796 million by 2025 (Johnson, Zurlo, Hickman & Crossing 2018:24). The population of Pentecostals in Africa in 2015 was estimated at 203 million, constituting 35.32% of the continent's Christian population of about 575 million, and 17.11% of the total continent's population of 1.19 billion (ed. Johnson & Zurlo 2016).

Pentecostalism emerged in Africa through two main streams – Pentecostal churches founded by foreign Pentecostal missionaries and Pentecostal churches founded by indigenous Africans. In spite of their origin, Pentecostal churches can be grouped into two main categories: Classical/mainline and Neo-Pentecostal/Charismatic. The praxis of the Neo-Pentecostal/Charismatic churches were influenced by American Pentecostal liberal theology on the charismata.

Classical Pentecostal churches are the traditional mainline Pentecostal churches that follow the ethos, dogmas, and praxis of the proponents of the Azusa Street revival. Notable among them are: International Pentecostal Holiness Church, International Church of the Foursquare Gospel, Assemblies of God, the Apostolic Faith Mission, Full Gospel Church of God, The Apostolic Church, Christ Apostolic Church, The Church of Pentecost, Christ Apostolic Church International, and The Redeemed Christian Church of God (Melton 2014). The majority of the Classical Pentecostal churches have a structured leadership and administrative setup. They also have well-written church constitutions and church polity.

The Neo-Pentecostal churches, on the other hand, are independent churches that came into existence after the charismatic renewal of the 1960s and 1970s both within and outside the mainline Protestant churches (Menzies & Menzies 2000:38–41). They are sometimes referred to as the third wave of African Christianity. They emerged in a time of economic and social difficulty in many African nations. And as a result, their message was, and by and large still is, a focused reflection of the economic and social realities of the time, with some carrying their socio-economic-based messages into the realm of liberation theology (Larbi 2001:86).

Asamoah-Gyadu identifies the following as key among the characteristics of Neo-Pentecostal churches:

> A specific focus on youth, lay-oriented leadership, ecclesiastic office based on a person's charismatic gifts, innovative use of modern media technology, mostly urban-centred congregations, a relaxed and fashion-conscious dress code for members, absence of religious symbolism in places of worship, English as a principal mode of communication, a reflection of the modern outlook, and portrayal of an international image. Their main target groups are students and professionals (Asamoah-Gyadu 2005:31–32).

Characteristically, Classical/mainline Pentecostal churches and Neo-Pentecostal/Charismatic churches have common beliefs and practices but differ in their leadership and administrative structures.

Having established the two main Pentecostal traditions, it would be good to briefly discuss the Neo-Prophetic churches. This will help to differentiate them from the Pentecostal tradition and avoid the confusion of referring to them as Pentecostals.

The Neo-Prophetic churches

The Neo-Prophetic churches are the fourth wave of African Christianity. The Neo-Prophetic churches are those whose ethos, style, and emphasis are supposedly Pentecostal yet depart from mainstream Pentecostal traditions to syncretistic Christianity. Their beliefs and practices are fused with psycho-theology rather than biblical theology. The following are some of the views of scholars on their characteristics and the 'prophets' who lead these churches:

- They claim to have been called by God, who, through the Holy Spirit, reveals secrets and provides solutions to their constituents' problems.
- They combine the Bible and the African concept of traditional mediation to access divine power for human benefit (Akrong 2001:18).

- They operate in the context of healing centres, deliverance centres, or prayer camps (Omenyo & Atiamo 2006:59).
- They utilise 'healing agents' such as consecrated water, anointing oil, miraculous materials, and the paying of money for special miracles (Larbi 2001:32).
- Their praxis is in the context of commercialisation of the gospel.
- They are often seen by their followers as spiritual heroes and don't eschew hero worship.
- They usually have no proper succession plan.
- They sometimes see their churches as family property.
- They also amass wealth from their congregants and live flamboyant lifestyles.

In the light of the above characteristics, Neo-Prophetic churches do not fall under the theological praxis and dogma of traditional Pentecostal churches. Their features represent Reformed African Spiritual Churches (RASC). African Spiritual Churches are the early manifestations of African Christianity.

Contextual influence on theology and mission praxis

There is no thing as perfect theology. No matter the church tradition and theological orientation, every theology is influenced by culture, church traditions, and human philosophies. This therefore makes theology contextual rather than a single subject. Furthermore, there is no theology in a vacuum, every theology is born out of a context and human experience in their journey and participation in the *missio Dei* (Pobee 1991:985; Bevans 2004:5-6; Wilson 1997:1-6).

Bevans and Schroeder (2004:35-72) shared a similar view in their discussion of the six constants of mission (Christology, ecclesiology, eschatology, salvation, anthropology, and human culture). They argued that although the constants are always present in every mission theology, their interpretations are sometimes influenced by contexts – culture, church traditions, human philosophies, and experience. Pelser's study on the different ecclesiologies found in the New Testament clearly indicated the diversity of ecclesiologies distinguishable in the New Testament. His conclusion was that it is impossible to speak of 'the church' as if there is only one model of the church present in the New Testament (Pelser 1995:647–673). By implication, I am comfortable to submit that the church is both universal and contextual. The universal nature of the church is expressed through the *ecumenical perspective*, and the *contextual dimension* of every church is influenced by culture, church dogma, polity, and experience.

In view of the above, I want us to appreciate the fact that there is no perfect theology since our theological orientation is influenced by many factors. In view of this, we are all on a journey with the Triune God to help us fulfil his missional agenda in our context.

The above discussion on the context/nature of theology makes room for me to now narrow the subsequent discussions on Pentecostal theology and praxis in their life-giving journey and mission. I will now zoom in on experience in the context of Pentecostal theology, particularly the Faith and Hope Gospel (also known as 'prosperity theology'), and finally, conclude with African Pentecostals' expressions of missional ecclesiology.

Experience in the context of Pentecostal theology – the Faith and Hope Gospel

A commonly held view among Pentecostal practitioners is that Pentecostal theology is based on subjective or personal experience. Though this claim is true, it should not give room for undermining Pentecostal theological expressions. Nel (2020:202) submits that 'experience plays the bigger role in Pentecostal Theology. When Pentecostals get involved in theological endeavours, the implication is that it would be introduced by an experiential encounter with God'.

Biblical history has taught us that, in both the Old and New Testaments, people walked and related to God based on their previous experiences with him. This is why in the context of the Jewish tradition or the Old Testament narratives, the patriarchs, priests, prophets, and kings constantly remind the Israelites of God's covenant with them as well as his promises. This clearly establishes the fact that human experience cannot be taken away from theological discourses. Ruether (1986:12) argues that human experience is the starting point as well as the ending point of the hermeneutical circle.

As stated by Cox (1995:4–5):

> The first Pentecost event in Acts 2 serves as inspiration for people who are discontented with the way the religion or the world, in general is going. In order to find solutions to their challenges, they turn to Pentecostalism because it is packed with promise … it is about the experience of God, not about abstract religious ideas, and it presents a God who is ever ready and caring to attend to human needs through the power of the Holy Spirit.

In the New Testament, the early church apostles and elders presented their theology and gospel based on their experiences with Jesus Christ. The apostle John made this clear when he wrote:

> That which was from the beginning, which we have **heard**, which we have **seen with our eyes**, which we have looked upon, and **our hands have handled**, concerning the Word of life. The life was manifested, and **we have seen**, and **bear witness**, and declare to you that eternal life which was with the Father and was manifested to us, **that which we have seen and heard we declare to you**, that you also may have fellowship with us; and truly our fellowship *is* with the Father and with His Son Jesus Christ. And these things we write to you that your joy may be full (1 John 1:1–4, NKJV, italics in the original and bold is added).

Theology without experience would be a mere academic exercise. Just like any contemporary theology, Pentecostal theology emerged out of contextual experiences of people in their walk with God (Pobee 1991:985; Bevans 2004:5–6; Wilson 1997:1–6). Such experiences provide a form to their spirituality and determine how they interpret the Bible. In the process, they reinterpret biblical events to fit into their existential reality and explain the meaning of what happens in their lives from such parallels (Nel 2021:2).

This is however not to say that those experiences should become static or the yardstick for every event. God is sovereign and his sovereignty influences the dynamic nature of theology at every point in time. Furthermore, experience should not become the platform for abuse, as it has been used by some Neo-Pentecostal and Neo-Prophetic churches in many African communities. The same view was expressed by Nel (2021:5) when he wrote that 'experience and its accompanying affections are necessarily individualist and subjectivist, even in communal experiences within groups, necessitating measures to prevent subjectivist and ideological misinterpretation'.

Having stated the above, it should be noted that the existing liberation theologies and the economic and social hardships that people endured in the late 19th and early 20th centuries in various contexts, led to the development of prosperity theology, which is referred to as the Gospel of Faith and Hope in this chapter. Arguing from the perspective of human experiences, Nel (2020:xiii) noted that the role played by the African traditional notion of prosperity, which is embedded in the African worldview and African Traditional Religions (ATRs), and its appeal to the deep longings of every human heart for peace, health, happiness, wealth and prosperity, is one of the three factors for prosperity theology in African Christianity.

Referring to prosperity theology as the Faith and Hope Gospel is to establish the fact that the gospel of Jesus Christ is a gospel that stirs faith and brings hope to humanity. The Faith and Hope Gospel is defined as the gospel that addresses the spiritual, emotional, social and material needs of people by using Scriptures that bring hope and cause people to exercise their faith for breakthrough and transformation in their lives. The practitioners and adherents of the Faith and Hope Gospel are encouraged to look beyond their circumstances and believe in God for miracles. Their followers are encouraged to have hope and exercise their faith in every situation (White & Akins 2021:257).

According to Asamoah-Gyadu (2006:3):

> What people consider important in theology are the things that address their religious needs …. In continuity with the African religious paradigm, Pentecostal/charismatic Christianity has proven successful in Africa because of its openness to the supernatural and through its interventionist and oral theological forms that resonate with traditional African piety. He further noted that Pentecostal theology is expressed in three ways: Transformation, empowerment, and **successful implementation of a healing and deliverance ministry.**

Remarking on the interpretation of Scripture by advocates of prosperity, Asamoah-Gyadu (2009:1) was emphatic that the gospel of Jesus Christ, with its promises of liberation, deliverance, forgiveness, grace and restoration, certainly cannot be a gospel of poverty. Nevertheless, the Scriptures neither glorify poverty nor greed. Scripture consistently cautions about the pursuit of worldly interests that could swage people's godly values. For him, biblical interpretations that invoke justification of physical substance and wealth creation are of dire consequences to Christ's warnings on wealth possession.

African Pentecostals' expressions of missional ecclesiology

Missional ecclesiology is a specific focus within missiology that studies the doctrine or understanding of the church from a missiological perspective. It endeavours to reflect on and make sense of what is happening in Christian churches (Niemandt 2020:13). A missional church is fundamentally and comprehensively defined by its calling and sending, its purpose to serve God's healing purposes for all the world as God's witnessing people to all the world (Guder 2015:122).

African Pentecostals' expression of missional ecclesiology started with a shift from sophisticated theological and mission theories to ethno-cultural missional praxis that depicts grassroot theology and ecclesia with strong emphasis on the pneumatic manifestations. This point of departure in African Pentecostal's missional orientation, manifests in their missional ecclesiological theology and praxis in three major ways, namely: emphasis on the Holy Spirit is the power for mission; expression of missional grassroot ecclesiology and liturgy; and an unstructured church planting approach.

Emphasis on the pneumatological dimension of mission

The reaffirmation of the importance of the Holy Spirit for mission theology in the ecumenical events is an important element in the emerging missional ecclesiology as a result of a Trinitarian understanding of the divine reality – the *missio Dei* (Niemandt 2020:24).

According to Bevans (2004:293):

> The church will live out its mission worthily if it allies itself with and is transformed by the Spirit's power. If the Spirit is the first way that God sends and is sent, the Spirit's activity becomes the foundation of the church's own missionary nature. If the church is to express its nature, it must, first of all, discern the Spirit's activity.

Taking inspiration from Jesus' command to the disciples and the event of the outpouring of the Holy Spirit on the day of Pentecost in the Acts of the Apostles (Acts 1:8; Acts 2:1–3), African Pentecostals believe that in order for the church to be vibrant in mission and its activities, it requires the presence, empowerment, and leading of the Holy Spirit (WCC 2013:53–58).

Although Pentecostals believe in the doctrine of the Trinity and adopt a Trinitarian understanding of the divine reality, they emphasise the pneumatological perspective of mission. This view was shared by Bosch (1991:517) when he wrote: 'Life in the Holy Spirit is the essence of mission'. He further noted that the Holy Spirit is the 'agent' of Trinitarian mission, and the era of the Spirit is the era of the church (p. 517). Skreslet (2012:loc 1760) noted that 'The explosive growth of Pentecostalism in the twentieth century has raised the profile of pneumatology within mission, not only with respect to mission theology but throughout the field'.

African Pentecostal churches are mostly of the view that one is required to keep praying with a discerning heart to know what God wants them to do in a particular context (White & Niemandt 2015). This approach is described by Kim (2009:1) as joining in with the Spirit to identify where God is at work in a particular context.

Expression of missional grassroot ecclesiology and liturgy

African Pentecostals' missional ecclesiology is expressed through their intentional desire to promote grassroot ecclesiology and liturgy. It is a known fact that Western missionaries have contributed significantly to the social and educational development in many African communities. However, they did not make such an impact in the religious sphere, as they failed to address the traditional worldview of Africans (White 2017:1). In view of this limitation, the majority of African Christians in the Western missionaries' churches became dissatisfied with how theology was translated in their local contexts.

In his reflections on a missional ecclesiology for Africa, Henry (2018:1) proposes an African missional identity that is contextual, and yet true to the gospel, rather than the classical Western mission model. Reppenhagen (2010:169) refers to this approach as the translatability of the gospel. According to him, 'Just as the gospel is inherently translatable into every context, the church is inherently translatable. The translatability of the gospel into a new context is understood as an incarnational process' (Reppenhagen 2010:169). In a similar vein, Newbigin (1989:152) argues that:

> If the gospel is to be understood, if it is to be received as something which communicates truth about the real human situation, if it is, as we say, to "make sense," it has to be communicated in the language of those to whom it is addressed and has to be clothed in symbols which are meaningful to them.

In the light of the above, African Pentecostals are reading, interpreting, and understanding the Scriptures in their own cultural contexts and engendering domesticated theologies (Wariboko 2017:5). The domesticated theological approach foregrounded the Faith and Hope Gospel, which encompasses prosperity theology; the democratisation of gifts and ministry; priesthood for all; the practice of exorcism, deliverance from demonic attacks and influences in one's life; and vibrant singing, drumming, dancing, and making a joyful noise unto the Lord.

Unstructured church planting approach

As part of the missional ecclesiology of African Pentecostal churches, Pentecostals see church planting as a major missional call, and therefore approach church planning from the view of everywhere to everywhere. This approach addresses the TLL's call for mission to the margins (WCC 2013:52-53). Pentecostals are always of the view that, wherever there are people, church planting is possible. This approach to church planting is based on Jesus' statement: '[W]here two or three are gathered together in my name, there am I in the midst of them' (Matt 18:20).

They usually start as house fellowship, or Bible study, or a prayer group, and grow spontaneously through invitation to friends and evangelism. Due to this approach to church planting, some of them assume natural leadership responsibility in the group without any hint of a formal approach to church leadership training and theological education. Only few of them have structured leadership and administration structures. Although this approach to church planting and mission is cost-effective, it sometimes leads to lack of proper theological training and orientation, no leadership succession plan, as well as lack of transparency and accountability.

Conclusion

Our journey and participation in the life-giving mission of God is a journey of unity, diversity, and tolerance. In this journey, we are required to acknowledge the uniqueness of various church traditions. The WCC calls this journey and participation in the *missio Dei* – together towards life. In their view, this missional togetherness should take cognisance of the changing dynamics in the world. The changing dynamics, therefore, calls for an opportunity for spiritual discernment in various contexts by joining in with the Holy Spirit to know what God is doing in our context, and then doing same.

This chapter, in the light of the above, used the concept 'together towards life and mission' to propound a missional discourse on how African Pentecostal churches have and are contextually participating in the *missio Dei*. The chapter started with a brief background of African Pentecostalism, as well as looked at how different the Pentecostal tradition is from the Neo-Prophetic churches/movements. The discussion then moved on to the contextual influence on theology and mission praxis. Under this sub-heading, it was argued that every theology is influenced by context – culture, church traditions, and human philosophies. The contextual influences are some of the factors that lead to uniqueness and diversity in various church traditions in their participation in the *missio Dei*. Thereafter, the conversation narrowed to African Pentecostals' theology and missional praxis. This was approached by reviewing the importance of experience in the context of Pentecostal theology, particularly the Faith and Hope Gospel (prosperity theology). The chapter concluded by outlining African Pentecostals' expressions of missional ecclesiology.

References

Akrong, A, 2001. 'Salvation in African Christianity', *Legon Journal of the Humanities* 12, 1–29.

Anderson, A, 2003, 'African Initiated Churches of the Spirit and Pneumatology', *Word & World: Theology for Christian Ministry* 23(2), 178–186.

Asamoah-Gyadu, J.K., 2005, *African charismatics: A study of independent indigenous Pentecostal movements in Ghana*, E.J. Brill, Leiden, Netherlands.

Asamoah-Gyadu, J.K., 2006, *African Pentecostal/charismatic Christianity: An overview*, viewed 8 August 2021, from https://lausanneworldpulse.com/themedarticles-php/464/08-2006.

Asamoah-Gyadu, J.K., 2009, 'Did Jesus wear designer robes?', *Christianity Today* (November 2009), 38–41.

Ayegboyin, D., & Ademola Ishola, S., 1997, *African Indigenous Churches: Some problems of terminology*. Institute of Religious Research, viewed 8 August 2021, from https://irr.org/african-indigenous-churches-chapter-one.

Bevans, S., 2004, *Models of contextual theology*, revised and expanded edition, Orbis Books, Maryknoll, N.Y.

Bevans, S., & Schroeder R.P., 2004, *Constants in context: A theology of mission for today*, Orbis Books, Maryknoll, N.Y.

Bosch, D.J., 1991, *Transforming mission*, Orbis Books, Maryknoll, N.Y.

Cox, H., 1995, *Fire from heaven: The rise of Pentecostal spirituality and reshaping of religion in the twenty-first century*, Addison-Wesley Reading, MA.

Flett, J.G., 2010, *The witness of God: The Trinity, missio Dei, Karl Barth and the nature of Christian community*, Kindle edition, Eerdmans, Grand Rapids, MI.

Guder, D.L., 2015, *Called to witness: Doing missional theology* (The Gospel and Our Culture Series [GOCS]), Eerdmans, Grand Rapids.

Henry, D., 2018, 'Missional postures and practices for South African Baptist churches', *Verbum et Ecclesia* 39(1), a1817. https://doi. org/10.4102/ve.v39i1.1817.

Johnson, T.M., & Zurlo, G.A., eds., 2016, *World Christian database*, Brill, Leiden/Boston.

Johnson, T.M., Zurlo, G.A., Hickman, A.W., & Crossing, P.F., 2018, 'More African Christians and counting martyrs', *International Bulletin of Mission Research* 42(1), 20–28.

Keum, J. (ed.), 2013, *Together towards life: Mission and evangelism in changing landscapes*, WCC Publications, Geneva.

Kim, K., 2009, *Joining in with the Spirit. Connecting world church and local mission*, Epworth, London.

Kim, K., 2014, 'Together towards Life: Mission and Evangelism in Changing Landscapes', Paper presented at MISAL, London, May 2014.

Knoetze, H, 2015, 'Together towards Life and Evangelii Gaudium: Implications for African Child Theology today', *Missionalia* 43(2), 218–231.

Larbi, E.K., 2001, *Pentecostalism: The eddies of Ghanaian Christianity*, Blessed Publications, Accra.

Melton, J.G., 2014, 'Pentecostalism', in *Encyclopaedia Britannica*, viewed 8 December 2021, from https://www.britannica.com/topic/Pentecostalism.

Menzies, W., & Menzies, P.R., 2000, *Spirit and power: Foundations of Pentecostal experience*, Zondervan, Grand Rapids, MI.

Nel, M., 2020, *The prosperity gospel in Africa: An African Pentecostal hermeneutical consideration*, Wipf and Stock Publishers, Eugene.

Nel, M., 2021, 'Defining elements and challenges of a Pentecostal hermeneutics of experience', *HTS Teologiese Studies/Theological Studies* 77(2), a6622. https://doi.org/10.4102/hts.v77i2.6622.

Newbigin, L., 1989, *The gospel in a pluralist society*, Eerdmans, Grand Rapids.

Ngada, N.H., & Mofokeng, K.E., 2001, *African Christian witness*, Cluster Publications, Pietermaritzburg, RSA.

Niemandt, C.J.P., 2015a, 'Ecodomy in mission: The ecological crisis in the light of recent ecumenical statements', *Verbum et Ecclesia* 36(3), Art. #1437, 8 pages. http://dx.doi.org/10.4102/ve.v36i3.1437.

Niemandt, C.J.P., 2015b, 'Together towards life and mission: A basis for good governance in church and society today', *Verbum et Ecclesia* 36(1), Art. #1361, 10 pages. http://dx.doi.org/10.4102/ve.v36i1.1361.

Niemandt, C.J.P., 2020, *Missional leadership*, AOSIS, Durbanville, Cape Town.

Omenyo, C.N., & Atiamo, O.A., 2006, 'Claiming religious space: The case of Neo-Prophetism in Ghana', *Ghana Bulletin of Theology* 1(1), 59.

Pelser, G.M.M., 1995, 'Die kerk in die Nuwe Testament', *HTS Teologiese Studies/Theological Studies* 51(3), 645–676. http://dx.doi.org/10.4102/hts.v51i3.1421.

Pobee, J.S., 1991, 'Theology, Contextual', in N. Lossky, J.M. Bonino, J. Pobee & G. Wainwright (eds,), *Dictionary of the Ecumenical Movement*, p. 985, WCC, Geneva.

Reppenhagen, M., 2010, 'The missional church and the "Homo Areligiosus"', in V. Mortenson & A.Ø. Nielsen (eds), *Walk humbly with the Lord. Church and mission engaging plurality*, pp. 167–183, Eerdmans, Grand Rapids.

Reuther, R.R., 1986, *Sexism and God talk: Toward a feminist theology*, SCM Press, London.

Skreslet, S.H., 2012, *Comprehending mission. The questions, methods, themes, problems, and prospects of missiology*, Kindle version, Orbis Books, Maryknoll, N.Y.

The Editors of Encyclopaedia Britannica, 2012, 'Zionist church', in *Encyclopaedia Britannica*, viewed 8 August 2021, from https://www.britannica.com/topic/Zionist-church.

Wariboko, N., 2017, 'Pentecostalism in Africa', in *Oxford Research Encyclopedias*, https://doi.org/10.1093/acrefore/9780190277734.013.120

White, P., 2017, 'Decolonising Western missionaries' mission theology and practice in Ghanaian church history: A Pentecostal approach', *In die Skriflig/ In Luce Verbi* 51(1), a2233.

White, P. and Aikins, P.R. 2021. Name it, claim it, grab it: African Neo-Pentecostal faith and hope gospel. *Journal of Pentecostal Theology* (Brill), volume 30, issue 2, pp. 263-281.

White, P., & Niemandt, C.J.P., 2015, 'The missional role of the Holy Spirit: Ghanaian Pentecostals' view and practice', *In die Skriflig/In Luce Verbi* 49(1), Art. #1987, 7 pages. http:// dx.doi.org/10.4102/ids. v49i1.1987.

Wilson, R.F., 1997, 'Contextual theology and global Baptist', In D. Carro & F. Richard (eds.), *Contemporary gospel accents: Doing theology in Africa, Asia, Southeast Asia and Latin America*. Mercer University Press, Macon, GA.

World Council of Churches (WCC), 2013, *Together towards Life: Mission and evangelism in changing landscapes*, in World Council of Churches, *Resource book WCC 10th Assembly, Busan 2013*, pp. 51–76, WCC Publications, Geneva.

Chapter 4

African Independent Churches: *Izandla Ziyagezana* – Hands Wash Each Other

Johannes Knoetze

Introduction

John Pobee (quoted in Oduro, Pretorius, Nussbaum & Born 2008:9) said:

> ... the AICs [African Independent Churches] represent a central development of Christianity in the Africa of the 20th century. This indicates that the landscape of world Christianity is changing. There is no way we can talk of world Christianity, much less Christianity in Africa, without talking about the genre of the AICs.

It is well accepted that the church in the Global South is growing faster than anywhere else in the world. The emphasis when talking about the church in Africa is among the following three strands: mainline missionary churches, the Pentecostal churches, and the African Independent Churches. Of this growing church in the South, a large part is in Africa and amongst the African Independent/Indigenous/Initiated/Instituted Churches (AICs) (Chitando 2005:1). However, some mainline missionary churches[1] from the West and the North still do not view some of the AICs as Christian churches. Dealing with Christianity in Africa, some may ask, must we accept them as Christians? A wise pastor responds with an African proverb: 'He who has never travelled thinks his mother is the best cook' (Oduro et al. 2008:1).

---

[1] While the term 'mainline' has enjoyed currency, other labels have also been applied. These include: 'mission', 'traditional', 'orthodox', 'historic', and 'established' churches (Chitando 2005:5).

The Western missionaries did wonderful work in spreading the gospel in Africa, but today it is well known that they were not the main messengers of the gospel in Africa. 'Most Africans became Christians because they heard the preaching of the Good News by their fellow Africans and because they saw how this faith changed the lives of their fellow Africans' (Oduro et al. 2008:3). In hindsight, the missionaries' paternalistic ways of doing mission, giving converts everything, they needed at mission stations, including little responsibility and freedom, impacted the African society negatively. This mission policy undermined the traditional and societal rules, including unity and authority, and since the little groups of converts did not live amongst their own people, these converts became more dependent on missionaries for clothes, food, and housing, etcetera. This led to anger and resentment amongst some traditional rulers and communities which around the 1800s lead to the establishment of AICs.

The AICs may be divided into two main groups, namely: the Ethiopian churches, and the Zion churches. The Ethiopian churches are those churches which mainly grew out of the mainline missionary churches and reacted against the white man's monopoly in these churches. 'They stress the slogan "Africa for the Africans," and they had an important role in fighting White colonial power' (Da Silva 1993:939). The name of this group of churches refers to the kingdom of Ethiopia, a stronghold of African Christianity, as these churches view religion as a means to seek political independence.

The Zion churches are churches who mainly grew from the African traditions. These churches stress, for example, the work of the Spirit, speaking in tongues, and healing. As such, these churches are antagonistic toward Western medicine and education, including theological education. Other names used by the AICs themselves are: '"spiritual churches" (Ghana), "churches of the Spirit" (southern Africa), "Zionist churches" or "Apostolic churches" (southern Africa) and "aladura" or "praying churches" (Nigeria)' (Oduro et al. 2008:28). A question arises when we engage with the different AICs. Must we refer to Christianity in Africa or African Christianity? The AICs are part and parcel of Christianity in Africa – the history of Christianity in Africa and how it developed. But the AICs are also all about the being of African Christianity. Walls (1996:3) describes it as '…African Christianity is undoubtedly *African* religion, as developed by Africans and shaped by the concerns and agendas of Africa; it is no pale copy of an institution existing somewhere else'.

Since there are literally thousands of New Religious Movements (NRM) in Africa described as independent, separatist, and indigenous churches, we need to define our understanding of these churches. 'Separatist churches' refer to African churches that separate themselves from the missionary churches. 'Independent churches' refer to churches that are free from outside influence, are self-governed, and have their own organisation, structure, doctrines, and liturgy. 'Indigenous churches' have a more geographical and racial connotation. However, these movements are described, it needs to be noted that not all NRM are churches of Jesus Christ. Therefore, we will work with the definition of an AIC as propounded in Oduro et al. (2008:10):

> We start off by noting that the AICs "represent a wide spectrum of religious understanding and practise, ranging from groups only one step removed from traditional African religious reality to Christ-centered, Spirit-led, biblically oriented communities of faith".

Another description of the AICs by the Reformed World (as quoted in Oduro et al. 2008:10) is as follows:

> Any African founded church which believes in Jesus Christ as Saviour, the Holy Trinity (the Father, the Son, and the Holy Spirit as one God) and Christian Doctrine as founded in the Holy Bible (Old Testament and New Testament).

In this chapter we will work with these understandings of what the AICs are, although there are still other NRM which might view themselves as an AIC. Oduro et al. (2008:11) suggest that there are more than 10 000 different AIC denominations across the continent of Africa, and then go on to mention the largest groups:

- The Aladura group of churches in Nigeria
- The Harrist Church, mostly in Ivory Coast
- The Kimbanguist Church, mostly in the Democratic Republic of the Congo
- The Roho churches in Kenya
- The Zion Christian Church, mostly in South Africa
- St. John's Apostolic Faith Mission Church, mostly in South Africa

Although some of the AICs have millions of members, other churches might be a house church with only a priest and where most of the members of the AIC are from the same household.

Socio-historical background

Although the African church in the 2nd and 3rd centuries produced influential theologians like Clement of Alexandria, Origen, Tertullian, and Cyprian, it was the efforts of missionaries in the 19th century from North America and Europe that incited the growth of Christianity in sub-Sahara African (Chitando 2005:5).

African people are well-known for their spirituality. Spirituality is understood in the context of this chapter as the attitudes, beliefs, and practices which help African people to connect with God and/or the spiritual world. Turaki (1997:54) says the spirit world defines the African worldview and life. As such, many Africans, even some of those who have embraced Christianity or Islam, accept that their lives are controlled by 'pervasive, hidden, unexplainable, unpredictable and powerful spirits' (Van der Walt 2003:62). Since the mainline missionary churches fail to attend to the spiritual needs of African people, many Africans are for example unaccepting of Western medicine. However, the AICs share their understanding of evil with the African Traditional Religions (ATR), but they offer a different solution (Oduro et al. 2008:26).

Closely related to African spirituality is ATR which many Westerners might call "pagan" beliefs and practices. These might include the belief in spirits and witches. Witches, and some spirits are evil, and may cause disaster, sickness, and death. Oduro et al. (2008:21) states that African fears grow out of an African worldview, and the main purpose of African (Traditional) religion is to link the world of the dead with the world of the living and ensure harmony within the community. Like Christianity, African religions are about relationships, but in ATR it is not only about relationships in this world but includes the relationship between the human (seen) world and the spirit (unseen) world, like the nature spirits and the living spirits, as well as the spirits of the living dead. In Christianity, it is about the relationship between God and humans, humans and humanity, and humans with creation.

It is in this regard that the AICs have managed to connect the Christian message of love and redemption with the real (spiritual) needs of Africans. The AICs managed to attend to the following three important elements of the African spiritual worldview, which the missionary churches mostly ignored or negatively reacted to, namely: ancestors, magic, and impurity, and as such proclaimed the Good News of Jesus Christ effectively. The message of the missionary churches focused on the salvation of the soul but were silent about spiritual needs from the African worldview. The missionaries also attended to physical needs, poverty, health, and literacy, but in a way that was strange to Africa's understanding and societal needs. In many instances, the missionary churches did not attend to unfair political structures and, as such, did not hold any hope for Africans.

The attraction and the persuasion of the AICs are in nothing else than the very being, expression, and manifestation of a specific faith community. It is the way in which the gospel of salvation and liberation is concretely translated into everyday living through the physical and visible activities of the people which represents credibility and belief. It is first and foremost about belonging. Within the AICs:

> ... *the gospel is related much more realistically to the whole of human life than often happens in the historic churches* ... salvation is experienced in terms of the protection of God's Spirit against such powers and not necessarily as deliverance from sin (Oduro et al. 2008:27, emphasis in the original).

The importance of the Bible

The Bible is central to the ministry of the AICs, and in many AICs the Old Testament (Jewish Bible) forms the foundation of their beliefs (Mbiti 2004). The biblical figure of Moses is very important as a leader, liberator, and lawgiver. Moses also gives detailed descriptions of taboos regarding food and sex. Mbiti (2004) argues in some specific areas of the AICs life the Jewish Bible is their only Bible, when the New Testament is treated or regarded as one of its component books.

As the missionaries from North America and Europe focussed more on the 'soul salvation' of the African people, I suppose they made more use of the New Testament in their ministry. This message of Jesus was in many instances strange to Africa. Nürnberger (2007:57-62) discussed for example the role and views of ancestors and their authoritative role in the Bible and the African society. So, when Africans were able to read the Bible in their own languages, they could identify with the Jewish people in the Jewish Bible, since there were many contact points with ATR in relation to taboos, laws, and social struggles. Many Africans experience this as a contrary image to what the missionaries and colonial powers projected about them. Within the pages of the Jewish Bible the AICs find identifications and empathy with the Scriptures, in such a way that they will value and defend the Bible's authority without any compromise. Many Africans experienced that the colonialists and some missionaries treated them as 'no people', disregarding their culture and beliefs; but reading the Jewish Bible, they found they have now become 'the people of the Bible'.

Since there are hundreds of African creation stories telling how God created all things, the African people could identify themselves immediately with Adam and Eve at the beginning. As such the most common name for God is 'Creator'. According to Mbiti (2004:222), the AICs only believe in one Creator of the universe, namely, God, and in that sense, they are profoundly monotheistic. It is argued that the New Testament does not provide the same universal place of identity as founded in Genesis 1, where it is about all people and all things. '... the New Testament is a book about one person, Jesus Christ, even if through him and in him "all things were made" (John 1:3), and all things will eschatologically cohere in him (Ephesians 1:10)' (Mbiti 2004:223).

Being aware of the importance of the Bible within the AICs, it is imperative to realise that Africa has more of an oral culture than a written culture. From this understanding we need to realise that the spoken word is rather accepted than the written word. This is true not only because there is a lack of written and printed books in the AICs, but also because of the socio-political context which led to a low literacy in the AICs. An archbishop explains: 'We were not able to go to school. We had to look after the cattle' (Oduro et al. 2008:112). As such the Bible is used as a source in the AICs but it is not the only source of revelation. 'In fact, personal revelation is at least as important as the text of the Bible' (Oduro et al. 2008:113), and this is where prophecy plays an important role in the AICs. The prophet is viewed as a go-between the unseen and the seen, between God and the congregation, which might include healing, passing on of a message, and so on. 'One is said to prophesy when one passes on to other revelations or "messages" based on what has been said or heard through the special work of the Spirit' (2008:114). Prophesying is usually part of the worship service. Oduro et al. (2008:114-115) give the following witness:

> Here in Zion it is permitted that if I see something in someone that could injure her and of which she is unaware, I am free to stop the service and ask to purify whatever I see. You explain the matter ... and then we pray together that the person will see what the matter is, even if it is something bad. For instance, if I see through the Holy Spirit of God that you will have or already have a difficulty, the problem will there and then be disclosed to me ... Zionist churches work in this way, but the mainline churches, although they do have the Spirit of God, have confidence in prayer alone.

When prophesying is handled in this way in the worship service, the will of God through prophecy is added to the revelation of the will of God through the Bible.

The Bible is also used for therapeutical purposes; for this use, the texts come exclusively from the Jewish Bible. As such the Psalms are used amongst the AICS to promote matters of health and general welfare, but they also use the Bible for protection in three ways: 'As charms, potent words and medicine for protection' (Mbiti 2004:233). Two important doctrines that play a central role in the life of many AICs are puritanical ethics and the refusal of magic and witchcraft.

Worship services and Liturgy

Many AICs do not have any church buildings. In cities many worships in 'left-over spaces', while most AICs worship in nature, next to rivers, under a large tree, on mountains, or in an open field. Many African tribes also have sacred places where they prefer to worship since they believe it to be the place where God reveals himself. Examples are the Matoba hills for the Bavenda in South Africa, and Mount Kenya for the Gikuyu and Meru people of Kenya.

Worship services almost always start with prayer, or rather a prayer session. During this time, everyone kneels and will pray out loud to God according to whatever is on his or her heart, whether needs, praise, confession, or whatever else. When the people have quietened down, someone will start reciting the Lord's Prayer and everyone will follow as they pray together for God's kingdom to come. A worship service is almost certain to last more than three hours. In most instances, members take off their shoes and wear their uniforms before they participate in the service. Uniforms are not only to identify with a specific group in the AICs, but are also used to protect members against attacks and strengthen their faith. There are also rituals to bless the uniform before it is worn. Ephesians 6:10-18, which is about putting on the full armour of God, is often read on these occasions to defeat the forces of Satan.

AICs also use different objects (as tools) during their worship services to strengthen their faith, especially during certain rituals and or healing practices. As indicated earlier, the Bible is also used by some in this respect. For example, when they pray for a sick person, they might put the Bible on the person, or on the sick body part while they are praying. Water also plays an important role in the AICs, since all people know that no life can exist without water, and water also purifies. Some spiritual churches are also referred to as 'water churches'. Water may be used as a 'blessing'. In this case, water will be prayed over and then during or at the end of the service given to members to drink to help them to be healed, protected, and purified as a sign that the Spirit is present and working. On particular occasions, water is used specifically for purification. Members will either take a bath, or be sprinkled or splashed with water, depending on the issue at hand. In some instances, water is also used with other elements like salt, vinegar, milk, or ashes to cause vomiting. This is also related to cleaning or driving out evil forces. As mentioned, ashes are also used in cleaning and healing ceremonies. The ashes are usually from burning different parts of plants, trees, and even sacrificed animals. The AICs use Bible texts like Exodus 15:22-26; Numbers 19:9, 17-18, and Hebrews 9:13 to indicate ashes as a gift from God for healing and purifying. Other elements used are olive oil and lavender water.

Ropes, cords, strings, and belts are also used in worship and healing as the prophet or healer is directed by the Spirit through a dream or a vision. 'It is common practices to dip these cords in water or oil that has been prayed over. In doing so these cords become objects of power that are able to protect and strengthen...' (Oduro et al. 2008:82).

Additionally, there are different views about sacrifices within the AICs. While in some AICs sacrifices of cows, goats, chickens, or doves are part of the worship services, other AICs are totally against any sacrifices. Yet there are still other AICs that allow their members traditional sacrifices at their homes while the church does not get involved.

Within their worship services the AICs celebrate life in the Spirit; whether it is through birth rituals, initiations, weddings, or other major events, they rejoice in dance and song with their minds and their bodies. Their songs and musical instruments are all African, and from Africa, accompanied by handclapping and dancing. Dancing is regarded as an essential means of expressing joy in Christ. Singing, dancing, clapping, jumping, and praying are activities used to invite the Spirit to work in the congregation. During worship services where these activities take place, some might be possessed by the Holy Spirit. Oduro et al. (2008:92) describe Spirit possession as follows:

> When people are possessed by the Holy Spirit, they may "speak in tongues" ..., their bodies may jerk in strange ways and they may fall to the ground, cry or laugh, whistle, belch or make other sounds. During such experiences, the Spirit of God may reveal words, phrases, or even whole songs to individual members.

Da Silva (1993) describes the AICs strong faith in God and in the power of the Holy Spirit as a result of their fight against the spiritual world and their obsession with worship. Although they believe in the Trinity – Father, Son, and Spirit – the Holy Spirit has primacy in their faith. As they do not have a highly developed theology, they interpret the Bible literally, and some view the Bible as an object received directly from heaven. With the literal interpretation of the Bible and the focus on the power of the Spirit, the healing ministry is possibly the major feature of the AICs. In a worship service where their spiritual and physical needs are attended to, people experience the AICs as a caring community where they feel they belong.

Healing

Many African nations are still at a level of "disease care", struggling to provide basic health services (Kajang 2020:189). The concept of health has many definitions, the definition for health in this chapter is: "A healthy individual is someone who enjoys life and experiences well-being" (Kajang 2020:191).

There are many taboos governing traditional African life, safeguarding or producing many values of life in African culture. When the West came into contact with these taboos via the missionaries or economic activities, they disregarded and condemned them as well as other cultural traditions. The African people experience this as an onslaught on their way of life, their culture, and worldview. However, the AICs have rediscovered many of these taboos in the Jewish Bible and reinstate and model them in their faith (Mbiti 2004:223). Hence, healing and prophecy go hand in hand and are central to the ministry of the AICs, as can be seen in the following witness.

AIC pastor Lesego Mannathoko stood up slowly. She shared her experience of her physical illness and her efforts to find healing. She had been searching for help from both Western doctors and traditional healers but found none. Until one day ... as she walked by the St. Faith Holy Church in Francistown, Botswana, she heard singing. She felt like she had to enter the church. Without knowing how it happened, she found herself inside the building, standing in the middle of the congregation. As they sang a hymn of praise to God, they danced in a circle around her, and she felt the healing presence of God. She experienced the love and compassion of God through the congregation. Then she heard a message from God, calling her to hand her life over to the Lord Jesus. She was told that she should stop trying so hard to earn blessings from God and simply invite him into her life and let him take over (Oduro et al. 2008:72).

The above witness is not strange to the members of the AICs; many joined the church because they have experienced healing, not only physical healing but also spiritual healing. People are joining the AICs because they experience a sense of belonging where the believers engage with the Spirit to help those who are in need, whether it is with finances, or witchcraft, or sickness, it does not matter. The AICs are following Bosch's (1991:399) argument that Christians need to 'minister to people in their total need, that we should involve individual as well as society, soul and body, present and future in our ministry of salvation'.

The AICs in South Africa are calling for holistic healing; healing and general welfare are therefore not confined to individuals, but also relates to society. As many of the AICs worship in nature, and as they see the importance of land in God's promises, especially in the Jewish Bible, the AICs show practical association with the concept of the land (Mbiti 2004:237). Reading the Bible, they understand that God heals the land when people repent from their sins. Looking at South Africa suffering from poverty, oppression, discrimination, and corruption, our country needs healing and cleansing. 'The hands of some of our rulers are red with blood and our people are terribly bruised and wounded. They need healing ... Our people, our parliament and our nation are still very much in need of cleansing and holistic healing' (Mbiti 2004:234). African people's religion, identity and well-being are closely tied to the land, and the AICs were also affected by the history of South Africa as indicated in the following story.

> The AICs in South Africa recall with deep sorrow what happened early in the past century and was to be repeated later in different forms. The account tells that in 1914 the Rev. Enoch Mgjima "seceded from the Methodist Church to establish a group called the Israelites ... He owned a large area of land known as Ntabelanga or Bulhoek in the district of Queenstown. Many of the members of his church, the Israelites, lived on this land. Here they began to worship God according to their own traditions just as the Israelites of the Bible had done in their time. But in terms of the 1913 Land Act, Ntabelanga was not part of the 13% of South Africa, which Africans were allowed to own ... The Land Act turned Ntabelanga into a white area. Rev. Mgijima and his Israelites were told to move. They refused, claiming that God had given them this land and the white government had no right to take it away from them. The government insisted and asked the missionary Churches to support them because the Israelites were religious fanatics, they said." The government "sent in its troops from Pretoria. On 24th May 1921 they came and massacred these Christian heroes. Hundreds were killed and many more injured in what became known as the Bulhoek Massacre. The Israelites lost their land and the lives of many of their members, but they survived as a church" (Mbiti 2004:236).

It is important to realise that land restitution is (South) Africa is not only a political matter but also a spiritual matter, and that society needs the input of the AICs.

Present situation/calling

Ghana was the first sub-Sahara African country to gain independence in 1957 under the leadership of Kwame Nkrumah. As with many African countries that followed, political independence did not mean economic independence or prosperity. After an initial euphoric period, the political, social, and economic situation in almost all independent African countries deteriorated. This led to the migration of Africans from many African countries to other African countries and other continents in the hope for a better future. Consequently, African Christianity in all its different expressions found itself in diaspora all over the world. 'The creativity and diversities of expression of this versatile Christian movement from Africa have successfully redefined the glocal outlook of African Christianity in the West and Latin America' (Adedibu 2018:2). Many of the IACs as part of African Christianity also managed to reinvent themselves on other continents amongst African migrants. However,

> the importance of the primal worldview in relation to healing and wholeness is central to the holistic notion of these churches in development. ... The AICs provide not only religious spaces in Britain but also spaces for sociocultural enactment of home away from home in their former country of origin in Diaspora (Adedibu 2018:4).

In this regard, African Christianity, and more specifically the AICs, are indeed influencing world Christianity.

The holistic ministry of the AICs today also includes socio-economic involvement and development of communities. As examples, some AICs have started their own early childhood development centres (crèches), some have even started their own schools, and some give bursaries to students. Adedibu (2018:15) indicates that African Christianity, in this case independent African churches have established 24 Christian universities in Nigeria alone, and there are many more all over Africa. However, Ndukwe (2011:46) remarks that "The ethnic or tribal factor has been an obstacle in the mission of the church and has greatly effected its true growth especially in the post-missionary era"

Conclusion

This chapter began by reflecting on the words of Prof Pobee, that nobody may talk about Christianity without taking into account the role of the AICs. This will be even more important when we talk about mission and mission studies in Africa. From this chapter it is clear that the AICs are a major role player in all aspects of the African continent, whether it is religious, political, social or economic. One of the biggest tasks of the AICs is to address the important challenges of Africa with a united voice, not only in Africa but also in world Christianity.

References

Adedibu, B.A., 2018, 'The changing faces of African Independent Churches as development actors across borders', *HTS Teologiese Studies/Theological Studies* 74(1), 4740. https://doi.org/10.4102/hts.v74i1.4740

Bosch, D.J., 1991, *Transforming mission: Paradigm shifts in theology of mission*, Orbis Books, Maryknoll, NY.

Chitando, E., 2005, 'Naming the phenomena: The challenge of Africa Independent Churches', *Studia Historiae Ecclesiasticae*, 31(1), 85-110.

Da Silva, J.A., 1993, 'African Independent Churches. Origin and development', *Anthropos* 88, 393-402.

Kajang, D.R., 2020, Health, in Agang, S.B. (ed), *African Public Theology*, HippoBooks: Bukuru, Nigeria

Mbiti, J.S., 2004, 'The role of the Jewish Bible in the African Independent churches', *International Review of Mission*, 93(369), 219-237.

Ndukwe, O., 2011, *Among the nations: Rebranding the Christian church for a disappointed world*, Agbotech: Enugu, Nigeria

Nürnberger, K., 2007, *The living dead and the living God. Christ and the ancestors in a changing Africa*, CB Powell Bible Centre; Pretoria

Oduro, T., Pretorius, H., Nussbaum, S. & Born, B., 2008, *Mission in an African way. A practical introduction to African Instituted Churches and their sense of mission*, Christian Literature Fund, Wellington, South Africa.

Turaki, Y., 1997, *Tribal gods of Africa; ethnicity, racism, tribalism and the Gospel of Christ*, The Association of Evangelicals in Africa, Nairobi, Kenya.

Van der Walt, B.J., 2003, *Understanding and rebuilding Africa. From desperation today to expectation for tomorrow*, Printing Things, Potchefstroom, South Africa.

Walls, A.F., 1996, 'Introduction: African Christianity in the history of religions', in C. Fyfe & A. Walls (eds.), *Christianity in Africa in the 1990s*, pp. 1-16, Centre of African Studies, Edinburgh.

Chapter 5

Decolonisation of Christian Mission in Africa: Towards a Missiology of Reconstruction

Buhle Mpofu

Introduction

It is now widely accepted by scholars that Christian mission has been a product of various encounters between indigenous communities and missionaries who travelled around the world alongside traders and colonial administrators. The close link between the expansion of colonialism and the spread of Christianity needs to be interrogated within the context of decolonising contemporary mission as it spurns from the extension of power by the powerful states over the weaker nations whose values and cultures were considered less civilised. Consequently, indigenous knowledge systems and values were undermined at the expense of Western culture in such a way that conversion to Christianity was equated to embracing Western cultural values. The Eurocentric approach to Christian mission has encountered major correctives with the rise of African Independent Churches (AICs) as some African Christians search for contextually relevant theological and missional expressions grounded on African identity. These developments have inspired African scholars to explore theologies of African Christianity as a means to ensure the indigenisation of Christianity through inculturation theology (for examples, see Muzorewa 1985; Schineller 1990; Martey 1993; Osei-Bonsu 2005).

These African theologies were an attempt to decolonise the Western centred mission theology and ensure an inclusive approach that will embrace African identity and values. There is a need for an African approach to understand the biblical foundations and historical developments of mission. Christopher Wright (2010) understands mission to be an 'invitation' of the people of God to 'participate' in his mission towards the 'redemption of all creation'. For Wright (2010), salvation and redemption are not just intended for humans alone, but for 'all of God's creation'. This definition of mission is significant in that it helps us appreciate and embrace the holistic approach to mission as seeking redemption of God's creation by 'finding out what the Holy Spirit is doing and joining in'. This is the fundamental approach which was inspired by *Transforming mission* (Bosch 1991), and later informed *Together towards life, mission and evangelism towards changing landscapes* (ed. Keum 2013) and other scholars who have highlighted 'Mission of the Spirit' (Bevans 2014) to underscore the significance of the role of the Holy Spirit in the events which shaped current trends in mission.

Theology and mission cannot be articulated in a vacuum; they happen in a context. It is a context which accords meaning and relevance to all theological and missional activities. Consequently, the nature and practice of theology in Africa needs to be discussed within a framework of African realities, opportunities, and challenges. This is to say, in order to understand the way mission is done in Africa, we need to explore and appreciate the political, social, cultural and economic realities that have shaped and informed the lives of the African people in their diversity. More importantly, we have to acknowledge that African people have a history of colonial oppression, domination and subjugation at the hands of the powerful Western nations whose cultures, values and knowledge systems were violently imposed on them. These colonial legacies have inflicted enduring trauma even within the context of Christian mission. Bell Hooks (1992:3) referred to Stuart Hall (1990) to highlight that we can properly understand the traumatic character of the colonial experiences by recognising the connection between domination and representation:

> The ways in which black people, black experiences, were positioned and subjected in the dominant regimes of representation were the effects of a critical exercise of cultural power and normalization. Not only, in Said's "orientalist" sense, were we constructed as different and other within the categories of knowledge of the West by those regimes. They had the power to make us see and experience ourselves as "Other" ... It is one thing to position a subject or set of peoples as the Other of a dominant discourse. It is quite another thing to subject them to that "knowledge", not only as a matter of imposed will and domination, but by the power of inner compulsion and subjective conformation to the norm.

That the field of representation remains a place of struggle is most evident when we critically examine contemporary representations of blackness and black people in society is clearly reflected in racial tensions and inequalities that are still prevalent in contemporary South African society. Doing theology and missional practices on spirituality remain contested areas in which Western dominance is still visible in African religious practices where Eurocentric liturgy inherited from missionaries is dominant. There remain huge deficiencies in theological articulations, and some sections of the African indigenous churches have radically rejected theologies that ignore the 'political, socio-cultural and economic realities that shape the outlook of the African people' as exemplified in the works of scholars such as Kasali (2003:2).

Identifying the problem

Mission and theology need to consistently evolve and transform relative to changing landscapes, and this change has been recently necessitated by the impact of COVID-19 disruptions which affected all aspects of lives globally. Bosch held the view that the church was essential to Christian mission[1], and for him, the church had become marginalised as the true *missio Dei* took place in the world, as expressed in the phrase 'the world sets the agenda'. Therefore, in order for the mission of the church to be relevant, there is a need for the contextualisation of missional theology 'from below', an approach which Bosch (1991) considered to be mission from the underside of history. The main source of contextual theology and mission is the social sciences, and the main interlocutor should be the poor or the culturally marginalised. Given that the African communities were historically marginalised during the colonial period, the social sciences and the lived realities of the poor become a central aspect of contextual mission. Such a task will require approaches that are contextualised through decolonisation of theology and missional discourses. For example, in a contribution titled, 'Liturgy as a form of identity: An investigation into the lived experiences of African migrants within the transnational spaces of worship in Johannesburg', Mpofu (2018b:118) concluded that:

> ... the lived experiences of African migrants in selected congregations of the UPCSA [Uniting Presbyterian Church in Southern Africa] congregations ... have been suppressed by the Eurocentric values that are still dominantly preserved in worship styles of the former white congregations ... [and argued that] African songs, languages and cultural values should be allowed to thrive in transnational worship spaces as they are intrinsically linked with worship and liturgy, which constitute the essential elements required for the preservation of identity among African migrants.

---

[1] For more details, see Bosch, 1991, *Transforming Mission*, p. 416; see also p. 386.

This chapter will proceed as follows: First, I will discuss the contextualisation of mission as understood by David Bosch (1991) and define the concept of decolonisation in order to underline the exploration of thinking contextually as a means to decolonise mission in the African context. The chapter later unpacks the significance of Mugambi's theology of reconstruction as an example of the reconstruction of mission through reclaiming black identity and black spirituality, with emphasis on the significance of taking gender and the experiences of women and children seriously, and Afrocentrism and African theologies of identity as essential processes that are central to the decolonisation of mission in Africa.

Bosch on the contextualisation of mission

As I have already indicated that theology need to consistently evolve and transform relative to changing landscapes, the same should be expected of mission. In his seminal work, *Transforming mission: Paradigm shifts in theology of mission,* David Bosch (1991:126) rightly identified the different paradigms of mission from the early church through to what he refers to as 'the emerging ecumenical paradigm', namely:

1. The apocalyptic paradigm of primitive Christianity
2. The Hellenistic paradigm of the patristic period
3. The medieval Roman Catholic paradigm
4. The Protestant (Reformation) paradigm
5. The modern Enlightenment paradigm, and
6. The emerging ecumenical paradigm, which is of particular interest and relevance to this study.

Bosch was convinced that the 21st century would see new developments that would push the church to seek a new paradigm, what he called the 'emerging ecumenical paradigm', and attributed these developments to the following factors:

a. The West losing its dominance in the world – the current (2022) war in Ukraine is a demonstration of a possible shift in political power.

b. Unjust structures of oppression and exploitation being challenged today as never before in human history. This is evidenced by global protests which have become a popular phenomenon.

c. Western technology and the development agenda being suspect. Some countries treat technology with suspicion as it is used to control and dominate the weaker states.

d. The need to work for peace and justice given the reality that for the first time in human history we are capable of wiping out humankind. This is clear in the nuclear threats posed by Russia and North Korea.

e. European theologies can no longer claim superiority over other parts of the world given that culture shapes the human voice that answers the voice of Christ. We are now seeing a growth in contextual theologies throughout the previously Western-dominated contexts such as Africa and Asia.

f. Freedom of religion is now considered a human right, forcing Christians to re-evaluate their attitude toward and understanding of other faiths.

Therefore, thinking contextually is an integral component of doing mission in the African context and there is a need for continuous dialogue on decolonising theology and mission in order to make it relevant within the African context. In explaining mission from the perspective of contextualisation, Bosch (1991) highlighted the following:[2]

1. Mission as contextualisation is an affirmation that God has turned toward the world [...] where the hungry, poor, sick, exploited and marginalised are [located]. So the church in mission must take sides, for life against death, for justice against the oppression. The identity of all Christians is in the cross of Christ and they find their relevance in the hope of those who suffer and are oppressed, and by mediating hope for liberation and salvation to them.

2. Mission as contextualisation involves the construction of a variety of local theologies, but we have to be careful of relativism; in contextualisation, we have a dialectic relationship between theology and culture. Every *theologia localis* should therefore challenge and fecundate the *theologia oecumenica* and broaden the perspective of the former;

3. There is a danger of absolutism of contextualisation. This means universalising one's own theological position, making it applicable to everybody and demanding others to submit to it;

4. We have to look at this entire issue from yet another angle, that of 'reading the signs of the times'. It is about how we have to interpret the 'signs of the times' – the text from the Bible in our present context;

---

[2] Adapted from A. Sihite, n.d., Book review of *Transforming mission: Paradigm shifts in theology of mission*, by D. Bosch, *Asian History, Christianity and the Future of Ecumenical Movement in Asia*, viewed 14 April 2022, from https://www.academia.edu/9617434/-David_Bosh_Book_Chapter_Report_Contextualization.

5. In spite of the undeniably crucial nature and role of the context, it cannot be taken as the sole and basic authority for theological reflection. Contextualisation is a praxis that can mean too many things. As a praxis, it needs *theoria*. *Theoria* is sufficiently true and praxis ought to be carried out in its service;

6. Contextualisation is more than a problem of the relationship between praxis and theory;

7. The best model of contextual theology succeeds in holding together in creative tension *theoria*, praxis and *poiesis* (or faith, hope and love). This is a way of defining the missionary nature of Christian faith which seeks to combine these three dimensions.

Defining decolonisation

In explaining the decolonisation of theory and practice, a website[3] devoted to developing racial equity tools defines *decolonisation* as the act of '"writing back" against the ongoing colonialism and colonial mentalities that permeate all institutions and systems of government ...', while Tuck and Yang (2012:1) have warned of the 'unsettling' realities of the decolonisation metaphorisation by reminding us that,

> Decolonization brings about the repatriation of Indigenous land and life; it is not a metaphor for other things we want to do to improve our societies and schools ... As important as their goals may be, social justice, critical methodologies, or approaches that decenter settler perspectives have objectives that may be incommensurable with decolonization. Because settler colonialism is built upon an entangled triad structure of settler-native-slave, the decolonial desires of white, nonwhite, immigrant, postcolonial, and oppressed people, can similarly be entangled in resettlement, reoccupation, and reinhabitation that actually further settler colonialism. The metaphorization of decolonization makes possible a set of evasions, or "settler moves to innocence", that problematically attempt to reconcile settler guilt and complicity, and rescue settler futurity.

---

[3] Racial Equity Tools, (n.d.), *Decolonising theory and Practice*, viewed 18 November 2021, from https://www.racialequitytools.org/resources/fundamentals/core-concepts/decolonization-theory-and-practice

These observations highlight some of my concerns with the debate on decolonisation, namely. that decolonisation 'is not a metaphor for other things we want to do to improve our societies and schools', as we have seen in some circles in society where the metaphor has been blindly applied to bundle all frustrations and failures of African leadership as if we should not hold them accountable for corruption and poor administration of resources. Contrary to this self-destructive approach, this contribution adds to the voices that demand an indigenous framework and a grounded on indigenous sovereignty, and indigenous ways of thinking as an integral part of (re)building a culture that is able to interrogate the legacies of colonialism and contribute to new narratives that counter the mainstream framing of colonial history and depict African epistemologies as inferior to Western dominant ideologies.

Postcolonial scholars have been pre-occupied with the idea of decolonisation although the concept recently gained momentum. This was evident in the seminal work from Edward Said's *Orientalism* (1979) which focused on unmasking the way in which Western discourse historically sought [and continues] to 'control, manipulate, even to incorporate' the oriental 'other' (Said 1979:13). Frantz Fanon (1925 to 1961) is also widely known for his classic analyses of colonialism and advancing the notion of decolonisation. For example, his work, *The wretched of the earth* influenced African and African American social movements and has been widely praised, but it is most certainly not a work free of controversy (Fairchild 1994:191). Fanon's view of the necessity of violence as part of the anticolonial struggle has been a particular topic of contention for critics, commonly leading to accusations of 'barbarism and terrorism' (Smith 1973:32).

Thinking contextually in decolonising mission

One way in which we can decolonise mission in Africa is to think contextually and theologically. Such an approach stimulates the development of theologies from below – informed by the experiences of the poor and not imposed from the academia. The opening line of the article by Joshua Paul Smith in the book *How to think theologically*[4] introduces an interesting analysis, 'To be Christian at all is to be a theologian. There are no exceptions'. This is particularly interesting in our African context. The concept of 'being a Christian theologian' is interesting in that it underscores the reality that regardless of our academic knowledge and endeavours,

---

4   See J.P. Smith, n.d., *How to Think theologically: Part 4 Final theological reflection*, viewed 14 December 2021, from https://joshuapaulsmith.wordpress.com/tag/how-to-think-theologically/

experience is a major factor in all theological articulations. For him, 'Theological reflection is insufficient if it is done in isolation. Theological reflection occurs in the context of community. Because it is communal, it is also collaborative and dialogical' (Smith 2013:120).

In the first instance, Joshua Paul Smith (2013) introduced the concept of 'faith seeking understanding', but highlights the impact on an embedded theology, that regardless of what we claim, we all have an embedded theology. Explaining this concept, Smith (2013:16) writes, '[A]ll of our theological thinking is somewhat defined by the parameters of our upbringing, social context, and biblical/theological preconceptions …[and our] understanding of faith […] emerges from a process of carefully reflecting upon embedded theological convictions' and calls for a deliberative theology which seeks that we set aside our biases and preconceived thoughts so that we practice a conscientious theology. In analysing deliberative theology, Smith (2013) brings about the concept of belief, questioning what one believes, reconciling our beliefs with other beliefs and whether our beliefs are sufficient to help us respond to all the theological questions confronting us. He highlighted the foundations and pillars of theological reflection: experience, reason, tradition, and Scripture. Basically, we all have a particular understanding of theology from our individual and personal experiences, our embedded theology, and from our personal choice, and there must be a balance of these aspects so that we avoid too much reliance on a singular aspect, in that 'Too much emphasis on experience leads to extreme subjectivism, while too much emphasis on reason can cause one to cynically deny mystery. Too much tradition leads to empty, passionless theology (and worship), while too much scripture can lead one into "bibliolatry"' (Smith 2013:3). Therefore, thinking contextually and reflecting theologically are essential components which need to be balanced alongside resources for theological reflection; experience, reason and tradition should be an integral part of decolonising mission without falling into the traps of 'subjectivism', 'cynicism' and 'bibliolatry'.

It is not the intention of this contribution to carry out a comprehensive investigation of African scholarly works on the decolonisation of Christian theology and mission; such a study deserves a deeper analysis. However, by identifying the above scholarly attempts, it is important to emphasise that very few attempts were made by early missionaries to understand local indigenous practices, particularly with the culturally rich and diverse African context. These misconceptions and omissions were clearly evident in the accounts of the early missionaries such as that captured in a report by Wilkingson (1898: n.p.):

Mission the "labour room" of theology

> ... Their bottomless superstitions, their vile habits and heathen customs – their system of polygamy and witchcraft – their incessant beer-drinks and heathen dances which are attended by unspeakable abominations – these present a terrible barrier to the spread of Christianity and civilization ...

If anything, these reports were judgemental and negatively portrayed Africans as barbaric and humanly impaired. Therefore, there is a need to interrogate contemporary mission approaches and to establish the degree to which these *'vile habits'* and *'heathen customs'* impacted on the understanding of God's mission within the contemporary church in Africa. Although it is possible to isolate discourses of oppressor-oppressed from those of the missionary-indigenous community encounters, it is now widely accepted that the symbols of Christian mission cannot be isolated from those of Western civilisation. This needs ongoing interrogation, given the continued influence and impact of Western culture on indigenous communities. There are scholars who have underscored the significance of symbols, images, and sayings from the stories of encounters between missionaries and indigenous communities in Christian theology, among them De Gruchy and Villa-Vicencio (1994:37) who observed that,

> Scripture and tradition are essential elements of any Christian theology. Without the stories, symbols, images, and sayings linked to the origin of Christian understandings of the world, and without the subsequent history of those who have sought to demonstrate in word and deed what difference these understandings make in life, there is no Christian identity at all and thus no need for Christian theology.

Therefore, part of this contribution is an attempt to outline some of the African symbols and images that intersect with Christian mission with a view to clarifying some of the so-called 'vile habits' and 'heathen customs' within the context of decolonising the missional understanding of the church in Africa.

Mugambi: Towards a reconstruction of mission and redefining theology

Decolonising mission in the African context will require that we redefine theology. In his description of what theology is, Douglas J. Hall (2003) begins by telling us what theology is not, citing that in order to effectively define what something is, it always helps to first define what it isn't. The author in the first instance introduces a concept which is prevalent in several mainline and/or protestant churches today, stating that first theology is not a doctrine, but doctrine is part of theology and theological understanding – Christian theology. 'Theology is something that we make up as we go along, simply spinning it out entelechy. We are the inheritors of a very long and complex history of doctrine' (Hall 2003:174). The author also states that theology is not a biblical study and knowledge, which may be a foreign concept or shocking thought for many in our church today. The three pillars of theological reflection are tradition, Scripture, and reason. Hall (2003) adds that theology is not the articulation or sharing of 'religious experience'. Theology is not to be equated with ethical reflection, sensibility, and action. Noting that 'the purpose of Christian ethics, is not to reflect but to engage from a perspective that belongs centrally to our confession of faith' (2003:176).

This contribution considers decolonisation as an important aspect of the theology of reconstruction advanced by Mugambi and others. The discourse on decolonisation is one of the major focus areas for scholars engaged in narratives aimed at addressing the injustices of the past in former colonised states. A number of eminent African scholars have argued for the decolonial epistemic perspective in African Christian theology, and Maluleke (1997:5) cautioned that African theologians should pay attention to 'the ground already captured' in African theological discourse before hastily crafting new proposals. This contribution calls for renewed efforts and acknowledges that there is a number of prominent theologians who have articulated the need for an African grounded Christian theology, among them John Mbiti (1931–2019), Kwame Bediako (1945–2008), Jesse Mugambi (b. 6 Feb 1947), and Mercy Oduyoye (b. 1934), to name a few. In particular, Mugambi and others have articulated a theology of reconstruction as part of decolonising Christian mission and theology.

Mugambi's African Theology of Reconstruction, or ATOR as it is abbreviated, is contextually informed by Pan-Africanisms and boldly affirms the challenges that confound the African continent, concurring that 'beyond a mere celebration of the defeat of these ills, reconstruction theology challenges the church in Africa to actively promote human rights, social justice, peace, and reconciliation in the midst of the atrocities bedevilling the African continent' (Tarus & Lowery 2017:315). This resonates not only with the current conditions of the African continent but also reflects the challenges of poverty and inequality in the post-apartheid South Africa. These socio-economic structural challenges were exposed by the COVID-19 pandemic. The pandemic also exposed the limitations of current missional practices within the church and calls for an urgent reconstruction of society, economy, and church missional activities. It was therefore timely that Mugambi called on the church to continually reconstruct and respond to the difficult questions on identity, as he proposed four levels of reconstruction which I find relevant and useful for the current challenges experienced by the church, namely: personal reconstruction, cultural reconstruction, ecclesial reconstruction, and socio-economic reconstruction.

Mugambi (2010:71) defined the theology of reconstruction as that theology which 'provides conceptual tools in anticipation of the new society that results from successful struggles for liberation'. Since the struggle for liberation is a process, it necessarily overlaps with social construction. According to Mugambi (1995:72), reconstruction theologians practice theological introspection through self-criticism and self-reflection. He convincingly argued that the gospel will only be valid in Africa to the extent that it helps Africans to relate with their context. For him, the Good News should address all forms of dehumanisation towards total liberation. Therefore, based on this approach, future Christian missionary enterprise will not only focus on the failures of the past, but it will also move African communities toward liberation. In order to achieve such liberation, self-criticism will be an important task of reconstruction. Although a number of scholars have critiqued Mugambi's concept of a theology of reconstruction, contending that it borders on giving false hope to African people given the extreme levels of poverty and inequalities in Africa, there are scholars who have creatively engaged his concept of reconstruction to challenge corruption and leadership failures as part of self-critical engagement.

Similarly, Tinyiko Maluleke interestingly critiqued his theology of reconstruction, challenging the shape of the reconstruction paradigm and arguing that its potential for effectively replacing the inculturation-liberation paradigms remains unclear. In this contribution I argue that, although not without limitations, this theology of reconstruction is potentially effective in decolonising and reconstructing mission within the African context. Some important aspects on decolonising mission will require paying attention to blackness, understanding African traditional spirituality, and paying attention to Afrocentrism in identity theologies.

Women and children: Reclaiming blackness and the significance of African spirituality

Decolonising mission in Africa will also mean restoration and the reclaiming of black identity as part of 'overcoming theological voicelessness…' (Kritzinger 2014:1) for African communities whose voices and experiences have been undermined by powerful Western notions. Given the apartheid and colonial legacies of segregation, it is important that we pay attention to voices on the margins of society. Recently, most black communities have been inspired to reclaim their space in the global arena by the Black Lives Matter movement whose discourse on the struggles of black people is grounded on the recognition that the coloniality of power remains deeply entrenched in new forms of oppression. These tendencies are evident in perceptions that portray black Africans as unable to think, something we inherited and imbedded in centuries of colonial literature which 'had the power to make us see and experience ourselves as the "other"... of a dominant discourse' (Hooks 1992:92). While this is true for all black people who have been rendered unthinking, it is especially so for black women who were marginalised in accessing colonial education due to patriarchal practices which privileged boys and disadvantaged girls who were confined to domestic roles such as cooking and cleaning as a means to prepare them for marriage. Therefore, decolonised mission should take the experiences of women and children seriously. For example, in 'Women and the project of decolonization in contemporary Africa: Are gender considerations de rigueur?', Ipadeola (2020:1) 'faults the current decolonization project because of the lacuna of not mainstreaming gender considerations in the agitations for decolonizing Africa'.

In restoring black identity and the dignity of women, gender has been one of the important interventions for most African communities. There are even scholarships that prioritise women and girls as part of a long-term strategy to address patriarchal imbalances and empower women. White supremacy benefitted greatly from the marginalisation of black women in that poor levels of education among women ensures cheap labour, as the majority of African women are exploited in the global markets where they work as domestic workers, cleaners, and provide services at restaurants and bars. To this day, there are fewer educated women than men, and this epistemic violence is a result of the marginalisation of black women, who in some circles have been labelled as 'voiceless'. Such labelling is a convenient explanation for this violent injustice, as we have been reminded in the profound words of Indian author Arundhati (2018:1): '[T]here is really no such thing as the voiceless. There are only the deliberately silenced, or the preferably unheard'. Therefore, we need to be revolutionary and intentional about listening to the 'deliberately silenced and preferably unheard' as a means to restore the human dignity of women and decolonise mission interventions by placing them at the centre of Christian mission.

I am aware that this is separate discipline in theological studies. It is important to briefly highlight that there are some aspects of African traditional practices that cannot be isolated from African mission. As Pobee (1976:1) earlier cautioned,

> Africa is a vast continent [and] … presents an abundance and pluralism of cultures and peoples … The result is that African culture has not been static. And so the question is how traditional is traditional and how indigenous is indigenous? Suffice it to say here that by traditional we understand what is aboriginal, natural or fundamental.

The plurality of the African cultures needs to be treated with caution. The many tribal and ethnical groupings present a diverse landscape rich in creativity, and 'untribing' Africa becomes a decolonising factor so that we think beyond tribal situated knowledge, towards a universally compatible African spirituality and mission. This is particularly important because colonisers and missionaries used tribal divisions and colonial borders to divide African people. Traditions involve a 'temporal process (*traditio*) of handing down valued material' (Bronner 2011:40). According to Balke (2011:24), traditions tend not to determine the duration of their past presence, and they tend to transfigure their moment of foundation and bridge the difference between continuity and discontinuity. In this sense, traditions are often understood to stand in opposition to progress, innovation, and most pointedly, modernity (Bronner 2011:47). But contrary to this understanding, and from a perspective outside of a given tradition, traditions are necessarily innovative themselves (MacIntyre 2007:222) by the very act of constituting something that is to be preserved in the future and which is legitimised with reference to an allegedly superior past.

The encounters of missionaries and indigenous people brought together Western and African traditions in a manner that saw African traditions replaced with Eurocentric values and missionaries sought to bring civilisation. Given that traditions aim at producing a sense of belonging, the colonial project achieved civilisation through different forms of institutionalisation, targeting tribal groupings and occasionally disrupting traditional structures through counter revolution movements. It was this approach which imposed Christianity as spiritual 'epistemicide', premised on cultural revolution, as it prejudiced the need for conversion. To accept the gospel of Jesus Christ meant being civilised. This Christianisation project was based on the perceptions of the colonisers who had military power and domination.

In describing the power structures of the imperial forces, Maldonado-Torres (2014:254) describes coloniality as follows:

Coloniality as a power structure, an epochal condition, and epistemological design, lies at the centre of the present world order that Ramón Grosfoguel correctly described as a racially hierarchised, imperialistic, colonialist, Euro-American-centric, Christian-centric, hetero-normative, patriarchal, violent and modern world order that emerged since the so-called "discovery" of the "New World" by Christopher Columbus.

Afrocentrism and African theologies of identity

African identity and cohesion are central to the decolonisation of African mission. Mpofu (2018) highlighted how the mission of the church can be hostile towards perceived 'strangers' as some local South Africans use degrading names, such as '*makwerekwere*', to refer to foreign migrants who cannot speak the local languages and challenged the colonial mentality that uses colonial borders to divide Africans and cast them as rivals. Addressing Afro-xenophobia remains one of the important aspects for the debates which will ensure the recovery of African dignity at the face of Eurocentrism and neo-colonialism. Simphiwe Sesanti (2016) has underscored the significance of tapping into (subjugated) African knowledge as essential to dismantling neo-colonialism in education and some spheres of society. For him, Afrocentrism is the absolute key for this important task and the universal, historical and unbroken African culture is 'central' to an Afrocentric education. Afrocentricity, he contends, is 'a philosophical perspective associated with the discovery, location, and actualizing of African agency within the context of history and culture … a quality of thought and practice rooted in the cultural and human interests of African people' (Sesanti 2016:35). Afrocentricity is interested in what Africans traditionally regarded as best in education before colonial invasion (Sesanti 2016:35).

Although not without some criticism, Mugambi's work on identity also resonates with African realities and challenged a number of presuppositions, biases and preconceived notions about Africans. His focus on identities, and particularly African identities with a special focus on our identities as African Christians, demonstrated how the question of identity is not unique to Africa for Africans; however, it is more complex for Christian Africans who not only wrestle with the question of ethnicity but wrestle with the question of religion and Christianity. Church history teaches us that missionary efforts from the West have been linked to colonialism and therefore African theologians continue to seek ways to define African Christian identity in the post-colonial context. Mugambi articulated the concept of 'recreation', arguing that African theology, and by implication African Christianity and mission, should be reconstructing itself.

However, the major limitation of which has been identified by theologians and scholars who have critiqued Mugambi's concept of a theology of reconstruction such as Maluleke (1997), is that it borders on giving false hope to African people. Although laudable, the huge gap of inequalities between the rich and the poor, increasing levels of poverty, and corruption which continues to ravage Africa, have been cited as some of the major constraints to this approach. The question of whether it is possible to reconstruct self, culture, the church, and our socio-economic situation under the current circumstances has been raised. Some theologians have also questioned whether it is possible to completely deconstruct, or can the ideas and ideologies of colonialism be used in the process of reconstruction, or do we seek a complete overhaul? For example, feminist theologian, Musa Dube has essentially 'poured water' on Mugambi's theology of reconstruction stating, '… his theology of reconstruction is founded on sand as long as it does not address major oppressive issues of both globalisation and patriarchy' (Gathogo 2006:2).

Indeed, these are genuine concerns and as another theologian, Joseph Wandera (2002), was also quite critical of Jesse Mugambi's work, stating that 'There is still so much deconstruction to be done before reconstruction can start' (Gathogo 2006:3). In the same manner, Tinyiko Maluleke, and ardent supporter of Mugambi, critiques his theology of reconstruction by saying that the shape of the reconstruction paradigm and its potential for effectively replacing the inculturation-liberation paradigms remains unclear, and thus poses the question of whether Mugambi's proposal is progressive or is it new. Although criticised, Mugambi's ATOR gained support from several theologians, and for me it presents a helpful proposal towards the debate on the decolonisation of theology and mission in Africa.

Conclusion

Development of theology should be continuous. Theology has constantly evolved, and so should missiology, with new concepts and new themes constantly being introduced. This has rightfully brought about contextual theologies, born out of the realisation that there is a need to contextualise theology to suit a particular situation or time. Accordingly, this has gave rise to the likes of feminist theology, queer theology, and African theology. For example, in the 12th century, theology became an academic discipline formalised by the awarding of degrees to theology students. History has informed contextual theology, with different centuries facing diverse challenges and developments. The context of the first and second century was different from that of contemporary society, whereas in the former there was a need for a structured message, which gave rise to redemption theology, the decolonisation of African institutions after independence in the 20th century triggered questions around African heritage, and this gave birth to African theology which prompted the rise of African indigenous churches.

Whereas the corruption in the church in 1517 meant that the church was seeking spiritual renewal, the acceptance of female ordination in most denominations in the 21st century has given rise to a theology concerned with addressing gender and sexuality challenges of the past, the oppression of women, and the socio-political situation of the 21st century has brought about an awakening against gender oppression. Black theology is characterised by a thoroughgoing diversity in its history, context, content, and expression. Although it originated in the United States of America (USA), it now exists in many countries, including South Africa. In the latter where 'it established itself in the mid-1970s, it was defined by opposition to apartheid, a system of White rule premised on the separation of the races in which Blacks were deprived of power and regarded as inferior to Whites' (McFarland, Ferguson, Kilby & Torrance 2011:66). This clearly teaches us that the mission of the church and the gospel message shouldn't be concerned only with doctrines but should evolve as situations and circumstances change. This is what is at the heart of transforming mission towards changing landscapes, a vision well-articulated by the World Council of Churches (WCC) (ed. Keum 2013).

Therefore, decolonising mission in the African context will require taking every voice seriously and acknowledging previously disadvantaged and marginalised communities whose voice and participation in God's mission has been overlooked. It is also important to consider what Indian author and activist, Arundhati (2018:2) has emphatically reminded us, that: 'There is really no such thing as the voiceless. There are only the deliberately silenced, or the preferably unheard'. Doing theology from the margins locates our theological articulations contextually and highlights our responsibility to hear the deliberately silenced and preferably unheard, and provides us with an opportunity to locate biblical scholarship at the centre of their lives – this is an important task for us as the emerging generation of researchers and scholars – to ensure that the 'silenced and preferably unheard' are listened to.

Here are some important points to consider in doing contextual theology towards decolonising mission in Africa:

1. Who are the key players, and whose voice is dominant in missiology and theological interpretations and discourses – are women, youth, the disabled, children, and the poor at the centre?

2. Centrality of Scripture and the agency of the Holy Spirit – mission as finding out (discerning) where the Holy Spirit is at work and joining in – kenotic engagement/dialogue. [Supremacy of Scripture and salvation/Lordship of Christ as a foundation to build on]

3. Social analysis, interdisciplinarity, and community well-being; poverty, crime, violence and more.

4. Re-reading the Bible from the margins of society to address contextual issues
5. Allowing for creative dialogue between contextual realities and biblical interpretation

References

Arundhati R., 2018, *The deliberately silenced and preferably unheard*, viewed 09 September 2021, from: https://www.girlsglobe.org/2018/08/10/the-deliberately-silenced-and-preferably- unheard/?doing_wp_cron=1630847541.1168539524078369140625.

Balke, F., 2011, 'Gründungserzählungen', in H. Maye & L. Scholz (eds.), *Einführung in die Kulturwissenschaft*, pp. 23-48, München.

Bevans, S., 2014, 'Mission of the Spirit', *International Review of Mission* 103(1), 30-33.

Bosch, D.J., 1991, *Transforming mission: Paradigm shifts in theology of mission*, Orbis Books, Maryknoll, NY.

Bronner, S.J., 2011, *Explaining traditions: Folk behavior in modern culture*, University Press of Kentucky, Lexington.

De Gruchy, J. and Villa-Vicencio C. (ed.), 1994, *Doing Theology in Context, South African Perspectives;* Orbis Books, New York

Fanon, F., 2001, *The wretched of the earth*, transl. C. Farrington, Penguin, London.

Fairchild, H.H., 1994, 'Frantz Fanon's *The Wretched of the Earth* in contemporary perspective', *Journal of Black Studies* 25(2), 191-199.

Gathogo, J.M., 2006, 'Jesse Mugambi's pedigree: formative factors', *Studia Historiae Ecclesiasticae* XXXII(2), 173-205.

Hall, D.J., 2003, 'What is theology?' *Cross Currents* 53(2), 171-184.

Hooks, B., 1992, *Black looks: Race and representation*, Boston, South End Press.

Ipadeola, A.P., 2020, 'Women and the project of decolonization in contemporary Africa: Are gender considerations de rigueur?', *Culture and Dialogue* 8(1), 43-58. https://doi.org/10.1163/24683949-12340074.

Kasali, D.M., 2003, Doing Theology in Africa. A paper delivered at Wheaton graduate school, Nov 5, viewed 04 September 2021, from https://congoinitiative.org/wp-content/uploads/2015/11/Kasali-Theology-in-Africa.pdf.

Keum, J. (ed.), 2013, *Together towards life: Mission and evangelism in changing landscapes*, WCC Publications, Geneva.

Kritzinger, J., 2014, 'Overcoming theological voicelessness in the new millennium', *Missionalia: Southern African Journal of Missiology* 40(3), 233-250.

Maldonado-Torres, N., 2014, 'Race, religion, and ethics in the modern/colonial world', *Journal of Religious Ethics* 42(4), 691-711.

Maluleke, T.S., 1997, 'Half a century of African Christian theologies', *Journal of Theology for Southern Africa* 99, 4-23.

Martey, E., 1993, *African theology: Inculturation and liberation*, Orbis Books, Maryknoll.

McFarland, I., Ferguson, D.S.A., Kilby, K., & Torrance, I.R., 2011, *The Cambridge Dictionary of Christian Theology*, Cambridge University Press, Cambridge.

MacIntyre, A., 2007, *After virtue: A study in moral theory*, 3rd edn., University of Notre Dame, Indiana.

Mpofu, B., 2018a, 'Church as hostile, host or home: Perspectives on the experiences of African migrants in South Africa', *Alternation Journal* 22 (Special Edition: Religion and Migration in Africa and the African Diaspora), 103-118.

Mpofu, B., 2018b, 'Liturgy and migration: A missiological critique into the lived experiences of African migrants within the transnational spaces of worship in Johannesburg', in L.C. Siwila & R. Hewitt (eds.), *Liturgy and identity: African religio-cultural and ecumenical perspectives*, Cluster Publications.

Mugambi, J.N.K., 1995, *From liberation to reconstruction: African Christian theology after the Cold War*, East African Educational Publishers, Nairobi.

Mugambi, J.N.K., 2010, 'African theologies of reconstruction', in D. Patte (ed.), *The Cambridge Dictionary of Christianity*, Cambridge University Press, Cambridge, New York.

Muzorewa, G.H., 1985, *The origins and development of African theology*, Orbis Books, Maryknoll.

Osei-Bonsu, J., 2005, *The inculturation of Christianity in Africa: Antecedence and guidelines from the New Testament and the Early Church*, Peter Lang, Frankfurt.

Pobee, J. S., 1976, Aspects of African Traditional Religion, *Sociological Analysis* 37, 1-18.

Racial Equity Tools, (n.d.), *Decolonising theory and Practice*, viewed 18 November 2021, from https://www.racialequitytools.org/resources/fundamentals/core-concepts/decol-onization-theory-and-practice.

Said, E.W., 1979, *Orientalist*, Vintage Books, New York.

Schineller, P.S.J., 1990, *A handbook on inculturation*, Paulist Press, New York.

Sesanti, S., 2016, Afrocentric education for an African renaissance: Philosophical underpinnings', *New Agenda: South African Journal of Social and Economic Policy* 62 (2016), 34–40.

Sihite, A., n.d., Book review of *Transforming mission: Paradigm shifts in theology of mission*, by D. Bosch, *Asian History, Christianity and the Future of Ecumenical Movement in Asia*, viewed 14 April 2022, from https://www.academia.edu/9617434/-David_Bosh_Book_Chapter_Report_Contextualization.

Smith, J.P., 2013, 'How to Think theologically: Part 4 Final theological reflection', viewed 14 December 2021, from https://joshuapaulsmith.wordpress.com/tag/how-to-think-theologically/.

Smith, R.C., 1973, 'Fanon and the Concept of Colonial Violence', *Black World/Negro Digest* 22(7), 23-33.

Tarus, D. & Lowery, S., 2017, 'African theologies of identity and community: The contributions of John Mbiti, Jesse Mugambi, Vincent Mulago, and Kwame Bediako', *Open Theology* 3(1), 305-320.

Tuck, E. & Yang, K.W., 2012, 'Decolonization is not a metaphor', *Indigeneity, Education & Society* 1(1), 1-40.

Wandera, J., 2002, *The voice magazine: A journal of St Paul's United Theological College*, Vol. 1, Limuru, Kenya.

Wilkinson, H., 1898, From Namaqualand to Pondoland. *Cape Town: The Methodist Churchman* 3(75), 357.

Wright, C.J. H., 2010, *The Mission of God's People*, Zondervan, Grand Rapids.

SECTION B

WHAT IS MISSION?

Chapter 6

Whose Mission? The Mission of God

Piet Meiring

Introduction

For more than two thousand years, missionaries have travelled across the world, telling people of God's love and inviting them to accept Jesus Christ as their Saviour and Master. For many believers it was the most natural thing on earth to do. Once you have met the Lord, you wanted to share him with others. Churches accepted it as their God-given responsibility to join in the mission, establishing churches – communities of believers – across the globe.

But sometimes we need to take a step backwards and ask ourselves: What are we doing? Why are we doing it? More important even, Whose mission is it? What is the content of our mission? These are the questions we want to address in this chapter.

Different role players

Who is responsible for mission? Who has been given the primary task of sharing the good news of the gospel of God's love and salvation to the world? Strange as it may seem, in the past, different answers were given to these questions. Throughout the centuries many agents of mission have stepped to the fore.

In the time of the Early Church, mission was **mostly spontaneous** (see also Bevans &Schroeder 2006:10ff, Neill1975:26ff, Wright 2010:35ff). Jesus had sent his apostles to be his ambassadors, to carry the gospel to all the nations, baptising them and teaching them (Mt 28:19) to be his witnesses in Jerusalem, Judea, and Samaria, and to the ends of the earth (Acts 1:8). The disciples, obedient to the Lord's command, did move out, sharing the news of the crucified and resurrected Lord to all. Soon Paul was called to follow suit, and in his wake numerous co-workers and missionaries travelled far and wide, planting churches across the reaches of the Roman Empire. Many of the names of the early missionaries were recorded in the New Testament and the annals of the Early Church. The majority of the names, however, were never recorded. Women and men, often young people, could not keep the news to themselves. Driven by the power of the Holy Spirit, the expansion of the church simply 'happened'. In the short space of three centuries, Christianity became the official religion of the Roman Empire. The emperor confessed his faith in Jesus and accepted his responsibility to proclaim the gospel of Christ to all under his reign.

In the centuries that followed, the Christian mission went hand in hand with the expansion of the Christian State (the so-called *Corpus Christianum*). **The state saw itself as the primary agent of mission.** The goals of the church and of the state converged: the conversion of the non-Christian tribes, leading them into the community of believers. Sometimes the process went smoothly and by persuasion, while at other times the opposite was the case and violent means were employed. During the Middle Ages in European history, Christian rulers first brought the Germanic tribes in northern and eastern Europe, and then to the Vikings of the far north, and subsequently to the Saracens of the Middle East, under the authority of the Word of God, and the Bishop of Rome.

This period was followed by the **colonial era,** when Western powers extended their influence across the oceans of the earth, subjugating millions of Africans, Native Americans and Asians to their rule. In 1493 Pope Alexander VI divided the non-Western world between the two great Christian powers, Spain and Portugal. From then on, Spain would have the responsibility of 'Christianising' the Americas (with the exception of Brazil), while Portugal was made responsible for the whole of Asia, Africa and Brazil. Together with the *conquistadores* (conquerors), Catholic priests and missionaries would bear the standard of Christendom, often leaving a trail of murder and bloodshed behind them.

It was however not only the Roman Catholic countries that used state power to bring the gospel to the nations. When **Protestant countries** in other parts of Europe became colonial powers as well, they too viewed mission in the same light. When, in 1706, two pioneering Danish missionaries, Ziegenbalg and Plütschau, departed to Tranquebar in India, it was under the auspices of King Frederik IV of Denmark. For the next two and a half centuries this became the norm. Every state that considered itself to be a Christian state was automatically deemed responsible for expanding Christendom.

At other times in history, European governments opted to take a back seat, allowing **other organisations, even trading companies,** to take the initiative of conducting trade and establishing trade centres in the New World. One famous example is when the Dutch government decided not to establish its own colonies on the islands that today are known as Indonesia. Instead, they gave a charter to a trade company, the Dutch East India Company, to settle on the islands and to conduct trade, to build the necessary infrastructure, and to support missionaries in their work among the local people. The trading company not only paid the salaries of the missionaries and pastors, but also subsidised the building of schools and hospitals, and even established the first Protestant missionary seminary in history, the *Seminarium Indicum*, in the Dutch city of Leiden.

There were other role players as well. Since early in the 13th century when the two famous Catholic Orders were established (the Franciscan Order and the Dominican Order), **missionary orders and organisations** took responsibility for missionary work, often in collaboration with, but sometimes also in defiance of, the official church. Up to today, Catholic missions in the world heavily depend upon the orders.

The 19th century, in Protestant circles, is regarded as the 'Great Century' of missions. Large numbers of missionaries, women and men, travelled across the globe, bringing the gospel of Christ to millions in six continents, sent by numerous **interchurch and parachurch missionary societies**. When the official church declined to become involved, William Carey founded the Baptist Missionary Society to equip and send missionaries to India. In its wake, numerous societies in Great Britain, Germany, Holland, Scandinavia, America, as well as South Africa, were established. While the churches of the day kept aloof of missions, the missionary societies gladly accepted the responsibility to share the gospel. Even today many missionary societies continue to play a huge role. New societies are still being found, not only in the West but also in Third World countries.

Just over a hundred years ago a significant shift took place, when at the World Missionary Conference in Edinburgh (1910) Christians from all over the globe gathered to discuss their mutual responsibility to share the gospel with the world. Acknowledging the role played in the past by all the previous agents of mission, the delegates however were unanimous that **the church itself** needed to take responsibility for missions, that the entire church should be regarded as a missionary organisation. The delegates stressed that the life of the church depended on its missionary character. Since 1910, at virtually every ecumenical gathering, it has been reiterated: mission belongs to the church; mission is the *essence* of the church. This insight brought new energy to mission across the globe. Denominations and local congregations accepted their responsibilities. It was no longer only up to individuals, volunteers, and missionary organisations to carry the banner of the gospel. The whole church, the body of Christ, was on the move.

But this, too, is not the final answer to our question: Who is ultimately responsible for mission? The answer is rather amazing: the mission does not belong to individuals, rulers, missionary orders and organisations, it does not even belong to the church. Mission belongs to God! The triune God, Father, Son and Holy Spirit, is the real, and first, Missionary.

God's mission: The *missio Dei*

It was the famous German theologian Karl Barth, who, addressing a missionary conference almost a century ago (1932), told his audience that if you really want to know what mission entails, if you need to discover *who* the real initiator of mission is, you need to revisit what the Bible teaches us about God, about the being and the work of the triune God, Father, Son and Spirit. Mission, Barth said, is not primarily *our* activity, it is *God's* activity.

Mission conferences and ecumenical statements in the decades that followed embraced this insight enthusiastically. Virtually all Christian traditions – Protestant, Catholic, Orthodox, and Charismatic – nowadays align themselves with this position. In our time the phrases *missio Dei* (the mission of God) or *missio Dei Trinitatis* (the mission of the triune God) are used widely. But what, exactly, do we mean by that?[1]

Mission, the Bible teaches us, isn't some kind of human achievement, but a gift from God himself. The Father, Son and Spirit are continuously in relationship with One another, They reach out to each Other in eternal and perfect love. But God also pours his love out into the world. He reaches out to us, to his creation! *God is a sending/missional God.* The very life of God is a process of sending and being sent: the Father loved the world (creation) so much that He sent His only begotten Son to bring new life and hope; the Son then sent the Holy Spirit to accompany and empower the church; and the Father, Son and Holy Spirit sent (and are still sending) the church into the world (*missio ecclesiae*). Thus, it is not only a case of God *doing* the sending, but of God, in His very essence, *being* a sending/missional God. In the same way that we say, 'God is love', we can also say, 'God is mission'. The mission statement of a South African denomination states it aptly:

> Mission is the salvific act of the Triune God – Father, Son and Holy Spirit – towards the world, through which He gathers to Himself a community by way of His Word and the Spirit from the entirety of humankind (Kerkorde van die N G Kerk, 2007, Artikel 53:23, my translation).

According to the Scriptures, *God is the One that always takes the initiative* – the Father reaches out in love to humankind and sends his Son. The Son came to earth

---

[1] For a comprehensive discussion on the topic, see Dutch Reformed Church, 2013, *Framework Document on the Missional Nature and Calling of the D R Church*. See also book by Burger, Marais and Mouton, 2020, *Cultivating Missional Change. The Future of Missional Churches and Missional Theology*

as the First to be sent to proclaim God's salvific plan, as well as to set it into motion. When Jesus' work here was finished, both he and the Father sent the Holy Spirit to the world as an affirmation of God's salvific work.

All of the above means that the triune God is the exact opposite of a community that only exists to serve itself and its own needs – from before the beginning of time, *God – Father, Son and Spirit – has been a holy community focused outward.* For this reason, Christian mission should be the proclamation of the Kingdom of the Father, where life is shared with all through the sacrificial love of the Son, and from where it is witnessed to all those around it through the Spirit. The church's calling can be described as being the body of people sent by God as part of his mission. In all of its thinking and endeavours, the church at its very core is supposed to be directed outward and always moving in the direction of the world.

The mission of the church: The *missio ecclesiae*

If mission is understood as God's activity – what then of us? Does the *missio Dei* exclude the mission of the church (*missio ecclesiae*)? To the contrary. We are invited to join God in his mission. 'As the Father sent Me, so I send you', Jesus told his disciples on the day of his resurrection (Jn 20:21). The Book of Acts underscores the commission of the church. On ascending into heaven, Jesus said to his disciples: 'When the Holy Spirit comes about you, you will be filled with power, and you will be my witnesses in Jerusalem, in all Judea and Samaria, and to the ends of the earth' (Acts 1:8). Sent by the Father and the Son, and empowered by the Holy Spirit – that is the church!

The church, in itself the direct *result* of God's mission, is invited to become his co-worker on earth, a participant in his mission. The deepest reason for the existence of the church, is exactly this: to be part of God's work in the world. It is important to reiterate that the church is not the primary agent in the implementation of this mission – the fact that God chooses to involve the church in his *missio Dei*, does not mean that this mission has now been delivered into the hands of the church or that it has become dependent upon the church's obedience, dedication, understanding and faithfulness. To the contrary. *God is busy with his work* on earth! That means that not even an unfaithful, disloyal church can foil or frustrate God's mission.

But we do have a high calling. Through Christ the church is not only connected to the triune God, but also to his work on six continents. We believe that the church belongs to God alone, and therefore exists in covenant with him alone. The church is the people of God, the body of Christ and the temple of the Holy Spirit. Everything that the church is and does – its identity, mission, and ministry – is dependent upon this relationship. Sent by God, following Christ and by the power of his Spirit, we are called to obedience, and to dedicate ourselves to discerning the will of God through his Word with willing spirits, in order to be able to live out his will in the challenging and complex world we find ourselves in. The church must be a *missional church.*[2] Everything it is, everything it does, and everything it confesses, revolves around the fact that the church is sent by God and used by God in his mission.

Implications for the church

All of the above has huge implications for the church. If the church primarily exists within the *missio Dei*, if it wants to be a missional church, it means, *inter alia*:

- *The focus of the church is on the triune God.* The essence of a missional church is doxology – to worship God. The church knows and loves God as Father, Son and Holy Spirit, and its primary focus is to share in God's mission. The focus is not on the church's own survival.
- *The church may never back down on its calling.* It is participating in God's work till the end of time. The church is an 'expecting community' sharing a message of hope in a world full of despair, preparing the world for the final triumph of God.
- *The church has to live its own message of love.* It has to be a 'sign' of God's Kingdom, affording the world a foretaste of God's healing sovereignty.
- *The church has to incarnate the gospel.* The essence and nature of being church is determined in relation to the context in which the congregation finds itself, as well as the context of the community to which the church is called. The church transforms the community and brings about change. Through the power of the Holy Spirit and the gospel message, the church changes the community (context) – and, in return, the church is changed by the community (context).
- *The church practices a kenotic existence,* emptying itself, giving itself up totally. The church moves to the 'ends of the earth', to places and networks where the gospel has not been heard, often into dangerous situations, where a heavy price may be asked. Mission often means 'emptying yourself, taking on the very nature of a servant, obedient to death' (Phil 2:7).
- The church also has a *solemn duty towards creation*, a mission with a definite ecological dimension. God is Creator, the source and sustainer of all that exits; we need to share God's love and care for creation.

---

2 A note: During the 1960s and 1970s when the missionary nature of the church was rediscovered, the terms 'missionary church' and 'missionary message' were used in ecumenical circles. In the recent past, with many new publications on the subject, the terms 'missional church' and 'missional message' are preferred. See the seminal book by Guder, D.L.,1998, Missional Church – *A Vision for the Sending of the Church in North America*, and a followup publication: Van Gelder C., and Zscheile D.J. 2011, *The Missional Church in Perspective*.

Denominations or local congregations?

When we speak about the church, another question arises: Do we refer to denominations or to local congregations? Obviously, everything we have said above applies to denominations and large church structures, but we should never lose sight of the fact that the church primarily exists at the local level. The beautiful images used to describe the church in the New Testament ('the people of God', 'the chosen race', 'royal priesthood', 'body of Christ', 'household of God', 'letter from Christ', 'light', 'salt, etcetera) apply in the first instance to the local congregation. Paul's letters were directed at local groups of believers. Denominations, synods, dioceses, and presbyteries are important – but the real challenge is at the local level. It is here, at the level of the local church, that the church maintains contact with the world. The church and world are constantly rubbing shoulders everywhere, but it is particularly at the grassroots level that Christians come into daily contact with the beliefs, praxis, and needs of the non-Christian world. Hence, the main field of mission is not somewhere far away or among some strange peoples, but in the daily life of the church and its members.

Dimensions, intentions and structures

A missional congregation that accepts its responsibility to join God in his mission in the world has an awe-inspiring mandate: to represent the triune God in the community that the church is serving. It has to proclaim the gospel of grace in its teaching and preaching. It has to serve the community in a myriad of ways: caring for the poor, reaching out to the sick, embracing the vulnerable and the weak, standing against injustice, campaigning for reconciliation and healing in the community, and taking care of the environment. It has to nurture the community of believers, establishing and building young churches where there were none. This means that every single decision taken in the church, every act by the church leaders and the members, every service of worship, every sermon, must be undertaken in the light of its missional calling. Everything we do or don't do must have a *missional dimension*. Outsiders take note of what is happening in the church; they listen to the 'music' that in many ways spills through the windows, and are attracted and impressed – or repelled.

But we need more than that. The congregation also needs a *missional intention*, specific acts, a special programme, directing the congregation in its outreach to the world. The budget of the church must reflect its missional commitment, every activity in the church must be challenged. Does the allocation of the finances and the facilities of the church, the daily schedules of the pastors and leaders, show the church's orientation to the world? Or is the lion's share of income and time spent on its own needs and concerns? Does the weekly programme indicate that reaching outward enjoys a high priority? To have a missional dimension is of utmost importance, but equally important are specific plans and projects, special people set aside to drive the missional intention of the church.

Although it is vitally important, it is not sufficient for the church only to have the intention to be of service to the world. A missional congregation must be enabled and empowered to develop *missional structures* to convert its intention into practical commitment.

The church, especially local churches, all too often show a tragic inability to practice what it preaches, unable to guide its members on the way of becoming active participants in God's work in the world. Age-old church traditions and structures, developed over centuries, should be re-examined. Are they helping or hindering the proclamation of the gospel? In recent years, in Europe, many have bewailed the 'social imprisonment of the church'. While some structures and traditions have withstood the test of time and are of great value to us today, others have become stultified, blocking the church's outreach to the world. In some studies, these structures are referred to as 'heretical structures'. Heretic preachers with a heretical message, through history, make it impossible for men and women to meet the Lord Jesus as Saviour. Heretical structures are guilty of the same iniquity, making it impossible for the good news to flow from the church to the world. The Protestant slogan *Ecclesia Reformata semper reformanda* ('a Reformed church must always be willing to reform') needs to be remembered, also when the structures of the church are re-evaluated. Missional denominations and missional congregations need flexible structures, adapted to the needs of the people we serve, and to the context in which we find ourselves.

In the past the various geographical and sociological situations in which the church existed were carefully studied, and the parochial churches were structured accordingly. In the same way, today, the various geographical and sociological situations must guide us in devising equally varied structures for the people we serve.

Moreover, people live concurrently on several levels, and they have to be reached and offered refuge at each of these levels. A salient point, often made in the Bible, is that outsiders should largely determine the 'internal' affairs of the church, not so much through active participation but through their reaction to what these practices and structures communicate to them. The missional structure of the congregation goes far beyond the simple question of whether it possesses a functioning mission committee; it is rather a question of the entire existence of the church, of the overall image that it presents to those on the outside.

A missional ministry

What does all the above say about the members of the church, and of the ministry of the congregation? Traditionally, in Protestant circles, we tended to see the church as a double-storied house. The top floor belongs to the minister and the clergy, and the bottom floor to the members, to the laity in the pews. According to this view, only a small, privileged group of believers, are ordained into the ministry. They are called to minister on behalf of the congregation. The ordinary members are considered to be laity, the uninitiated, with little or no responsibility in the church.

The Bible, however, uses the word 'ministry' in its original sense of *service*, clearly stating that the ministry belongs to the whole church, to every member of the congregation. A better picture is that of God on the top floor, reaching out to all of us on the ground floor, to every member of the body of Christ. All of us are called and equipped to serve God, one another, and the world. According to Paul, the Lord did give special ministers to the church – apostles, prophets, evangelists, pastors, and teachers – but with the express aim to equip all the saints (members) for their ministry, of building up the church (Eph 4:11). Paul's image of the church being the body of Christ, leads us to the conclusion that all of us, all the members of the body, are equally responsible for the mission of the church in the world.

This view of the ministry of the church is inspiring, but it contains a number of serious implications for us as well:

- The first implication is that the existing pattern whereby the work of the church was often confined to a few paid workers, needs to be revised. Not only is the task far too great for a few individuals, there is ample proof that excessive reliance on these paid officials is the main reason why 'God's chosen people' have become 'God's frozen people'!

- The second implication is that the body image is of equal importance: Each member has a unique contribution to make to the functioning of the church, a factor that the church has to recognise and allow for in its structures.

- The third implication is that the minister who traditionally presented a one-man/-woman show, now consciously assumes the biblical role of 'enabler' (Eph 4:12). His/her educative task will receive more attention and more appreciation in the missional congregation.

- The fourth implication is greater emphasis on teamwork in the congregation. The church is a body, an organism, in which all parts cohere and all limbs function in unison. Hence, 'The Spirit of the Lord is upon me, because He has anointed me to preach the good news to the poor. He has sent me to proclaim freedom for the prisoners, and recovery of sight for the blind, to release the oppressed, to proclaim the year of the Lord's favor' (Lk 4:18ff). The congregation must become oriented to 'body life'.

Missionaries, a vanishing species?

Does all of this mean that missionaries have become obsolete, that they are a vanishing species? If every member of a missional congregation assumes his or her responsibility, do we still need the missionaries of old? For centuries they were the ambassadors of Jesus, the men and women at the cutting edge of mission, who, constrained by the love of Jesus, travelled far and wide to carry the gospel to the ends of the earth – often at a great cost to themselves and their loved ones.

But do they still have a place in our world, and in our mission? Over the past decades a serious debate has ensued on the issue of missionaries. Sharp criticism was voiced by many Christians in Africa, Asia, and the Americas. Sometimes it had to do not so much with the missionaries themselves, but with the circumstances in which they operated: representatives of a foreign culture, of 'older churches' in the West, coming from the ranks of the 'haves' of the world, ministering to the millions of abject poor 'have-nots'. Often the antagonism had to do with colonialism. Missionaries in Asia and Africa were seen as symbols of former injustices. At times missionaries were regarded as a threat to local leaders, denying them the opportunity to assume responsibility. In the 1970s the Kenyan church leader John Gatu called for a 'moratorium' on missionaries in Africa.

And yet, the vast majority of churches in the world have come to the defence of missionaries. At the Pan African Leadership Assembly in Nairobi (December 1976) one African church leader after the other brought homage to them. 'I do not believe that Christians in Africa have done enough to thank the Lord for the missionaries who brought the Gospel of Jesus Christ to our continent', the Ghanaian theologian Gottfried Osei-Mensah said. 'The graves of many missionaries, men as well as women, are to be found all over Africa, silent witnesses of the cost of spreading the Good News. By dying, they introduced us to life in Christ' (Meiring 1977:50-51, my translation).

Missionaries, God's special envoys, will always have a part to play, but then in a new role, not as leaders, but as servants. Not to tell people what they ought to do, but to be with them, to serve the Lord with them, to minister to them, to visit the sick and to help the poor, to sing God's praises in their tongues, to dance with them and to pray with them – these missionaries, will continue to be needed and respected and loved.

Missional congregations, local churches, need missionaries as well: to inspire them and to inform them, to open the world for them and to help them focus on their tasks. Every congregation needs its missionary or missionaries, not to relieve the local Christians of their responsibilities, but to be their representatives in areas and contexts where they themselves are unable to visit. By interesting themselves in the work of the missionaries, by praying for them and contributing to their work, by serving as a home base where they feel welcome when on furlough, the local congregation becomes co-workers of God and of the missionaries in the field.

There are different categories of missionaries today, namely:

- *Missionary theologians,* highly skilled and trained in theology and linguistics, will always be in demand. The intricate problems to be faced in the mission field, the challenges of Bible translation, reacting to the needs of the young churches, call for well qualified theologians, the best that the church can make available.
- *Career missionaries,* men and women who dedicate themselves to a full-time, life-long ministry. They do not need a theology degree, but a heart full of love for the Lord and for their co-workers in the communities they are serving.
- *Tent-making missionaries* have become a favourite option in missions today: professional people offering their skills to the local church and the mission; self-employed missionaries who are able to maintain themselves in the field; students willing to spend a year or two abroad; retired men and women who want to serve the Lord in a new way.
- *Short-term missionaries* have become increasingly important to churches and missionary organisations. Where in the past long-term missionaries were in the majority, most sending churches and mission organisations today rely heavily on highly enthusiastic and usually very able short-termers.

Unity and mission: 'Father, I pray that they may be one...'

The unity of the church is a *sine qua non* for the mission of the church. If Christians do not stand together, if they do not present a united front to the world, if they do not speak with one voice, their message will scarcely be heard or understood. Believers who take the *missio Dei* and the *missio ecclesiae* seriously, are equally serious about the unity of the church – and extremely anxious and concerned about the disunity among Christians.

The night before his death, Jesus called his disciples to him, to join him at the table where he was to take the bread and wine in his hands, passing it to his friends: His body, his blood! During the meal Jesus got up, took off his outer clothing, poured water into a basin and began to wash his disciples' feet. 'A new command I give you', said Jesus. 'Love one another as I have loved you. By this all men will know that you are my disciples, if you love one another' (Jn 13:34f).

Later that night, just before he departed from the table on his way to Gethsemane and to the cross, Jesus prayed for his friends. John 17, Jesus' prayer, even after twenty centuries, touches one's heart deeply and profoundly – especially when we read that Jesus not only remembered his disciples in his prayer, but us as well:

> My prayer is not for them alone. I pray also for those who will believe in Me through their message, that all of them may be one, Father, just as You are in Me and I am in You. May they also be in Us so that the world may believe that You have sent Me. I have given them the glory that You gave me, that they may we one as We are one (Jn 17:20ff).

Why is the unity of the church so important? Why is our confession of the 'one church, the community of believers' at the core of our faith? There are four reasons:

- *Our confession of the triune God is at stake.* A disunited church, Christians who squabble and tear the church apart, deny their faith in the One God – Father, Son and Spirit. During the Reformation when Christian communities broke ranks with one another, John Calvin was extremely perturbed. A disunited church is tearing the body of Christ, our Lord Jesus, into pieces, he protested. At the start of this chapter, when we discussed the mystery of the *missio Dei,* we said that in a wonderful way we, the church, are invited into the life of the Trinity, to become part of the relationship of love, that binds the Father, Son and Spirit together. Try to imagine what this means to us, members of a missional church, that by loving one another, washing each other's feet, we are drawn into the heart of God! And try to imagine, as well, what we miss if we lose our unity.

- *Our survival as the church, as the body of Christ, is at stake.* Jesus knew his friends well: Peter with his loud mouth, James and John with their short fuses, Matthew the tax collector, Thomas who found it hard to believe, and Simon the Zealot who carried a dagger under his cloak. He heard them squabble, and he witnessed their private jealousies. At the table Jesus did the near impossible, binding them together in love, washing their feet, setting an example. By their love, they will be known to be his disciples. A house that is divided will fall, but brothers and sisters embracing one another will prevail against all odds.

- *Our own understanding of our message is at stake.* Christians need to be united into one family, not only to stand together against the enemy, but to come to know the riches of their faith, to discover together what God has in stall for us. Paul, in his famous payer for his brothers and sisters in Ephesus, asks God that they, 'being rooted and established in the love of Christ, may have power, *together with all the saints,* to grasp how wide and long, and high and deep is the love of Christ' (Eph 3:17f). Without one another, without all the saints, we will not survive, and we will not grasp the full meaning and the depth of our message to the world.

Mission the "labour room" of theology

- *Our witness to the world is at stake.* Jesus prayed: 'Father, I pray that they may be one, so that the world may believe that You have sent Me' (Jn 17:21). We have said it over and over in this chapter. To be the church of Christ, to be part of his body, the church needs to be a missional church. The reason for the church's existence is to be a witness to the world. But a divided church has little to say. How can we speak of the love of Christ if we do not experience it ourselves? How can we bring a message of reconciliation if we are disunited, or unreconciled, among ourselves? It is often pointed out by church historians, that the extraordinary rapid growth of the Early Church was not in the first instance because of the preaching of the apostles and their followers, but because of the love that the Christians had for one another. Jews and gentiles, slaves and masters, men and women, rich and poor, privileged and marginalised, embraced one another. Walls of separation were broken down. If this can happen, if enemies can become brothers and sisters, I want to be part of that! This is what we dearly need in our fractured, divided, violent world of today: the message of God's love. But we must do more than speak about it, we must embody our message.

Christians in our day have come to understand the importance of the unity of the church. There were times when many, also sending churches and missionaries themselves, made light of the disunity of the church. In the mission field, missionaries often competed with missionaries from other denominations or societies. Did it help to convince the people they served of their message of love? Obviously not!

The 20th century, in Christian circles, is dubbed the 'ecumenical century', the age when Christians started to move towards one another again, to heal the rifts of the past as well as the many misunderstandings between denominations. The World Council of Churches was formed, together with other ecumenical bodies. Protestant, Orthodox, Catholic and Pentecostal Christians rediscovered one another again, finding that what they have in common far outweighs their differences.

The reason? During the 19th century great numbers of missionaries were sent into the world. In the mission fields they realised how confusing the many churches competing with one another, the opposing messages, were to the indigenous people. Whom should they believe? Whose gospel was the 'purest'?

Moreover, the missionaries realised how much they needed one another. In the field, often in times of crisis and danger, it did not seem to matter so much if you were Methodist or Reformed, or Lutheran, Baptist, or Pentecostal. In the home countries the churches may want to keep apart and play on their differences and old prejudices, but in the field where the gospel of love needed to be spread, they needed one another. They realised that the disunity of the church was a *skandalon*, an obstacle to the gospel, and started to campaign to bring churches together again. The ecumenical movement was born out of the missionary movement. At the first great World Missionary Conference at Edinburgh (1910), an urgent plea for church unity was made. The seeds for the ecumenical movement were sown.

Unity in a missional church is not an option – it is a must!

The dimensions of our mission: Kerygma, diakonia, koinonia, leitourgia

The last question we need to ask is: What is on the agenda for the church? What does the *missio ecclesiae* entail? In his Great Commandment, Jesus sent his apostles to the nations to 'make disciples', to 'teach' and to 'preach', and to 'baptize' (Mt 28:19). Over the years, Jesus' agenda was developed into numerous programmes: evangelisation, outreaches, campaigns, Bible translation, catechism classes, schools, medical services, clinics, hospitals, orphanages, and agricultural schemes, etcetera. In his groundbreaking *Transforming Mission*, the South African missiologist David Bosch counted no less that thirteen different elements of the missionary paradigm of our day (1991:368-510).

If we see our mission as following Jesus' mission, we get a clear picture of our own task. 'As the Father has sent Me, I am sending you', Jesus told his disciples (Jn 20:21). In Luke 4 Jesus addresses the people of Nazareth, his hometown. He explained to them his mission, why the Father had sent him to the world. Opening the scroll handed to him, the Book of Isaiah, Chapter 61, Jesus read:

> The Spirit of the Lord is upon me, because He has anointed me to preach the good news to the poor. He has sent me to proclaim freedom for the prisoners, and recovery of sight for the blind, to release the oppressed, to proclaim the year of the Lord's favour (Luke 4:18ff).

Luke tells us what happened next:

> Then He [Jesus] rolled up the scroll, gave it back to the attendant and sat down. The eyes of everyone in the synagogue were fastened on Him, and He began by saying to them: Today, this scripture is fulfilled in your hearing (Lk 4:20f).

Taking his cue from this, the evangelist Luke, in his Gospel, takes us upon a journey, following Jesus on the way of his mission, calling his disciples and moulding them into a new community, preaching about the kingdom of God, calling people to repent, reaching out to the hungry and the poor, healing the sick, liberating the oppressed, praising God with them for his mercy and love.

Following in our Lord's footsteps, our mission has four dimensions, namely: preaching and teaching, taking care of the suffering, building a new community, and praising God. Very often the fourfold tasks – or, put better, the four dimensions – of the *mission ecclesiae* is defined by using four Greek words: *kerygma, diakonia, koinonia,* and *leitourgia*.

The kerygmatic dimension

The Greek word *kerygma* can best be translated as 'proclamation', and is usually in the New Testament linked to the gospel or to good news. The kerygmatic dimension of mission therefore refers to all the various forms of the ministry of the word in mission: preaching, witnessing, evangelising, discussions, providing literature, Bible translation, catechism, theological education, etcetera. The content of the kerygma is always the good news that God, the Creator of the universe, has personally intervened in human history. He has done this by sending his Son, by the ministry of Jesus of Nazareth, who is the Lord of history, Saviour and Liberator.

The kerygmatic dimension of our mission calls for a special kind of commitment: to speak, evangelise, conduct campaigns, write, translate, to teach new members of the church in such a way that they really understand the message and the implications of the message. This means that the missionary should understand the context of the people, adopt as far as humanly possible their culture, study their history and traditions, sharing their hopes and their fears. It also means that the missionary should from time-to-time refrain from speaking and become a silent listener. A seasoned missionary in West Africa said: 'The Lord provides us for our ministry with *two* ears and *one* mouth. You have to listen twice, before you speak once!'

At the core of the kerygmatic dimension is inter-faith dialogue, the serious, patient, respectful and always hopeful, conversation with believers from other faiths. To listen to your partner telling his/her story, explaining their deepest convictions and experiences, and then, in turn, sharing your story, the good news of Jesus Christ, with him/her, is an incredible privilege and a joy.

Lastly, the effectiveness of the message has everything to do with the messenger himself or herself. The good news is shared not only by the words of the missionary, but by his/her attitude, integrity, and honesty. Far too often our message of love and grace is cancelled by our attitude, by our example. Our message needs to be lived!

The Apostle Paul knew this, often calling on his fellow Christians not only to listen to his words, but to emulate his example. A modern-day Paul, an African pastor in Zimbabwe, wrote his testimony on the wall of his hut in large letters for all to see (Meiring 2016:24):

I'm part of the fellowship of the unashamed. I have stepped over the line, the decision has been made: I'm a disciple of Jesus!
I won't look back, let up, slow down, back away or be still.
My past is redeemed, my present makes sense, my future is secure.

I no longer need to be praised, regarded or rewarded.
My face is set, my gait is fast, my goal is heaven, my road is narrow, my way is rough, my companions are few, my Guide reliable.

I cannot be bought, compromised, detoured, lured away, turned back, deluded or delayed. I will not flinch in the face of sacrifice, hesitate in the presence of the enemy, ponder at the pool of popularity or meander in the maze of mediocrity.

I am a disciple of Jesus.
I must go on till He comes and will work till He stops me.
When He comes for His own, He will have no problem recognizing me.

The diaconal dimension

The Greek word *diakonia* can be translated as 'service' or 'ministry'. The diaconal dimension of our mission therefore refers to the various forms of ministry and service in which the Christian community in imitation of Jesus, who was among as One who serves, puts itself at the service of the world. Following Jesus' mission, the church is called upon to reach out to the poor, to proclaim freedom for the prisoners, and recovery of sight for the blind, to release the oppressed, to proclaim the year of the Lord's favour.

The diaconal ministry of the church encompasses all the charitable services the community needs: hospitals and clinics, medical services, programmes to help the poor and to alleviate their plight, children's homes and orphanages, schools for the blind and the deaf, taking care of the aged, welcoming women, and girls, in need.

The history of mission is filled with examples of diaconal service. Soon after a missionary or a group of missionaries arrived at the scene, they did not only erect churches, but proceeded to build hospitals, clinics, schools, everything necessary to provide for the needs of the community. In missionary circles, in the past, a distinction was often made: the *main service* of the mission was preaching the word, the most important building on the mission station being the church. The diaconal service – the clinics and hospitals, the schools, and the orphanages – were considered to be the *auxiliary service* of the mission and of lesser importance. Fortunately, in our time, we have come to realise that the distinction was wrong: the diaconal service is of equal importance to the kerygmatic service. Jesus made no distinction between preaching the gospel and reaching out to those in need. He spoke of God's love and he demonstrated his love – all part of the same message. Where across Africa men and women reach out to the poor and the needy and the marginalised, it is not an extra, an auxiliary service to our mission, but the love of God in action!

The diaconal service goes beyond taking care of the needy and the suffering. It has to address the reasons for the pain and suffering. Campaigning for justice in society, standing up for those who need a champion, against all forms of gender-based violence and xenophobia, working to correct the structural imbalances and injustices that cause sickness, poverty and oppression, is part and parcel of the missional calling of the church. It may land the church and mission into hot water, into conflict with the powers that be, as was the case with Jesus. We need to courageously and wisely follow his example. We dare to stand up, not because we are just another pressure group or labour union or political party, we do it for our Lord. We do not subscribe to a political agenda; we speak because of our vision of God's salvation. David Bosch (1991:400) wrote:

> Those who know that God one day will wipe away all tears will not accept with resignation the tears of those who suffer and are oppressed now. Anyone who knows that one day there will be no more disease can and must actively anticipate the conquest of disease in individuals and society now. Anyone who believes that the enemy of God and humans will be vanquished will already oppose him now in his machinations in family and society. For all of this has to do with salvation.

The koinonial (fellowship) dimension

The Greek word *koinonia* is best translated 'fellowship', and in our instance, 'the fellowship of believers', the 'new community founded by Jesus'. Central to the mission of Jesus was to call his disciples and to mould them into a unique community. He spent much of his time speaking to them, teaching them, nurturing them to become the first church, his representative, his body, upon the earth. The apostles followed his lead and wherever they went, when people responded to their message, the believers were gathered together into a community of faith, into the church. In a similar fashion, missionaries over the centuries saw it as an essential task to plant churches and to nurture new Christians into the fellowship of Christ. In Protestant circles it was always maintained that mission had a threefold goal, namely: the glory and manifestation of God's love, the conversion of the gentiles, *and the planting of the church.*

Planting his church, is what Jesus did. And following our missional mandate, that is what is required of us: gathering new believers into the fellowship of disciples, teaching them to understand, nurturing leadership, helping them in any possible way to plant and develop their church. The young churches need not to be carbon copies of the 'home churches'. Instead, they need to be vibrant, dynamic churches, best suited to grow within their own context, facing the problems of their people, to take care of the congregants – and above all, to become mature missional churches themselves, reaching out to the world with the love of Christ.

In a very real sense of the word, the church itself becomes part of its message. By breaking all barriers between people, by creating a community where love and reconciliation reigns, where people truly reach out and take care of one another, creates a living advertisement of the gospel.

The missional church, carrying out its calling, needs to become a church-with-others, walking the way with the young church, sharing with them, suffering with them, and putting its resources to the use of the young church. In return, the 'older church' will receive much from the 'younger church': inspiration, enthusiasm, and a new understanding of our faith.

Finally, any congregation opting to be part of the missional church, needs to take a long, hard, look at itself. Is it a welcoming church, with open arms and a heart full of love for the outsiders? Is it a church where the destitute find refuge, where the marginalised and forgotten are embraced?

A very shocking story was told recently, that makes one think. I do hope it is fictional and that it did not really happen, but the message should be clear:

> In our town a peculiar thing happened the other day. It was mid-winter, and early on a Sunday morning, the sexton of our church made a disconcerting discovery: a man, destitute and in rags, on his back, on the steps of the church. Moving closer the sexton found that the man was dead. He had bandages on his leg and he was emaciated, with rags to keep out the cold of winter. When he had a last meal, was anybody's guess. The sexton quickly called for help and removed the dead man to the local mortuary.
>
> The next evening the church council was called for an urgent meeting. What were they to do? What was the message of the man on the steps of their church to the congregation? How should they prepare themselves for a future repeat?
>
> The elders and deacons, after a long discussion, found a solution to the satisfaction of all. Money needed to be made available to erect a proper fence around the church!

The liturgical dimension

Leitourgia was the term used by the Greeks for the public service that people rendered to the community. A wealthy man, for instance, would carry the cost of building a theatre, or staging a big public event. His *leitourgia* was recognised and praised by all. In the Christian church the term is employed to denote our service to God, especially through worship.

Mission in the first and final instance is about glorifying God. Mission is above all to worship God and to glorify his Name. This service, our *leitourgia*, can be rendered to God directly by worshipping Him in payer and praise, or it can be rendered indirectly by serving the people around you. When Paul called upon the Church in Corinth to give generously to fellow Christians in need, he wrote: 'This service that you perform is not only supplying the needs of God's people but is also overflowing in many expressions of thanks to God. Because of the service … men will praise God' (2 Cor 9:12f).

Diaconal service and liturgical service can be distinguished, but never separated. Whereas diaconal service is the essential expression of the sacrificial compassion and solidarity of Christians with suffering or oppressed human beings, liturgical service is the expression of the Christian desire to praise and worship God for who he is. It is in this respect that Paul's characterisation of himself as God's *leitourgos* to the gentiles (Rom 15:16) is important to us. For the apostle, the most elemental reason for proclaiming the gospel to all was not just his concern for the lost, nor was it primarily because of the obligation he had to God, it was rather a sense of privilege. Christian mission is therefore an inherent dimension of our worship of God, praising him for who he is.

The liturgical dimension of mission serves to place each of the other three dimensions in perspective. We proclaim our message not because we know better than others; we serve not because we are more privileged; we have fellowship not in order to patronise, we do all of this – gladly – because the greatness of God's love leaves us no other option.

A costly calling: The blood of the martyrs is the seed of the church

Following Christ is a costly calling. For Jesus, obedient to his Father's mission, it meant suffering and dying on the cross. He had to give his life away for the salvation of humankind. Similarly, if we want to follow Christ, the cost may be high. Dietrich Bonhoeffer, who suffered a martyr's death at the hands of the Nazi's at the end of World War Two, used to say: 'When Christ bids you to follow Him, He invites you to die with him' (Bonhoeffer 1963:99).

This was always the case. In the Early Church many died for confessing Christ. The Greek word for 'witness' is *martyria*. So many men and women gave up their lives for the gospel that the word *martyria* became the word for suffering and dying, as if being a witness for Christ naturally meant accepting a martyr's death. The enemies of the gospel thought that suffering and martyrdom will be the end of the church. But the opposite happened. The faith and courage of the early Christians, their willingness to follow Christ all the way, made a huge impression, and persuaded many to accept the Lord themselves. A famous North African church leader and theologian, Tertullian from Carthage (AD 160–220), coined the phrase: 'The blood of the martyrs is the seed of the Church' (Cross 1957:1335).

It is still happening today. The history of the African church is also the history of suffering. It relates the stories of men and women who travelled far into the continent, facing all sorts of adversaries: threats, illness, hunger, loneliness, and much more. And it contains the stories of martyrs who willingly gave their lives to the Lord. There are many accounts of ordinary men and women, often young Christians, who died a martyr's death. Some of the stories reached the outer world. At the entrance to Westminster Abbey in London, a statue was erected to remember the life and death of Archbishop Janani Luwum of Uganda, murdered by Idi Amin. Next to Luwum's statue is that of the young South African maiden Manche Masemola who was killed by her own father because of her faith. They are but two of many. Martyrs' stories are found all over Africa. Every community and every church are blessed by witnesses who did not refrain from putting all they had on the line, from paying the price, even to the point of suffering a martyr's death.

In conclusion: The Mission and the mission

The story of this chapter was about God's Mission and our mission, about the supreme Missionary and about us, missionaries, sent by him as co-workers in his field. It was also the story of the church, the missional church, that realises that the only reason for its existence is to carry the gospel of love to the world. We listened to the Lord praying that the church may be one, for the world to believe that the Father had sent him to the world.

We finally discussed the content of our mission, or better put, the four dimensions of our mission. So, what does it mean to belong to the missional church? What do missionaries do? Why are they willing to pay the price of being witnesses?

They serve to manifest the glory and greatness of God's grace. They call people to conversion and to faith in Christ. They reach out to those in need. They plant churches. There is no single way to do this. The multifaceted nature of Christian witness and mission was described in a document published by the World Council of Churches in 1959 (quoted by Bosch 1980: 228-229):

> The Church has borne witness in different times and places in different ways. This is important. There are cases when dynamic action in society is called

for; there are others when a word must be spoken; others when the behavior of Christians to one another is the telling witness. On still other occasions the simple presence of the worshipping community or person is the witness. The different dimensions of witness to the one Lord are always a matter of concrete obedience. To take them in isolation from one another is to distort the Gospel.

At the General Assembly of the *World Council of Churches*, at Busan, South Korea (November 2015), the following declaration was accepted:

Mission begins in the heart of the Triune God, from where it overflows onto humankind and the whole entirety of creation.

God is a sending/missional God Who sent His Son into the world and Who is still calling all the people who belong to Him and equipping them to be a community of hope.

References

Bevans, S.B. & Schroeder, R.P. 2006, *Constants in Context – A Theology of Mission for Today*, New York: Orbis

Bonhoeffer, Dietrich, 1963, *The Cost of Discipleship*, Macmillan: New York.

Bosch, D. J., 1980, *Witness to the World*, Atlanta: John Knox.

Bosch, D.J., 1991, *Transforming mission: Paradigm shifts in theology of mission*, Orbis Books, Maryknoll, New York.

Cross, F. L. (ed) 1957, *The Oxford Dictionary of the Christian Church*, London: Oxford University Press.

Guder, D.L. (ed) 1998, *Missional Church – A Vision for the Sending of the Church in North America*. Grond Rapids, Michigan: Eerdmans.

Meiring, Piet, 1977, *Die Kerk op Pad na 2000*, Tafelberg-Uitgewers, Cape Town.

Meiring, Piet, 2016, *In die Voetspore van Jesus*, CUM-Uitgewers, Vereeniging.

Nederduitse Gereformeerde Kerk (Dutch Reformed Church), 2007, *Die Kerkorde van die Nederduitse Greformeerde Kerk*, Bybelmedia, Wellington.

Nederduitse Gereformeerde Kerk (Dutch Reformed Church), 2013, *Framework Document on the Missional Nature and calling of the Dutch Reformed Church*, General Synod of the DRC, Pretoria.

Neill, S., 1975, *A History of Christian Missions*, UK, Penguin Books

Van Gelder, C., & Zscheile, DJ. 2011, *The Missional Church in Perspective – Mapping Trends and Shaping the Conversation*, Grand Rapids: Baker Books

Wright, C.H.J., 2010, The *Mission of God's People – A Biblical Theology of the Church's Mission*, Langham Partnership International

Chapter 7

Mission – Where?

Dons Kritzinger

The question of context

A young Christian feels in her bones that the Lord has called her to become a missionary (or to involve herself in mission). The question is: where? Naturally, the first and obvious answer is: 'Right here'. There is no doubt that any Christian and church grouping is needed in the mission of God in the context where they are, because of the needs all around. Somebody might then rightly argue that there is probably a greater need elsewhere. Our church is present here, and lots of other Christians, but what about those places where people haven't even heard of Jesus? This kind of debate always takes place in the missional church: the balance between the 'here' and the 'there'. Yes, there is mostly agreement – after some debate – that it is not either/or but both/and, but then what? See, it is necessary to address these practical questions about the 'where' of mission – Where should I get involved?

However, maybe even more important is the underlying questions of how to look at the world. How must we bring everything that we have learnt about mission in the previous chapters to these questions about the 'where'? We can say that up to now we have dwelt on the TEXT – how to understand the subject which is mission – but it is just as important also to dwell on the CONTEXT (see Ott, Strauss and Tennent 2010:265ff). Which factors should we look at when we look around us? How can we get to understand the context?

This chapter is about understanding the context of mission. The story is well known: an advertising board proclaimed: "Jesus is the answer!", but someone wrote next it: "Yes, but what is the question?" The work of mission always takes place in a specific place. What are the questions, the challenges, the needs, right there?[1]

---

[1] For a description of the challenges within the African context, see the recently published book by various African scholars: Agang, Forster & Hendriks, 2020, *African Public Theology*, HippoBooks, Langham. The 2013 declaration by the World Council of Churches *Together towards Life: Mission and Evangelism in Changing Landscapes* also focus on different contexts for mission

Mission the "labour room" of theology

Contextual analysis

Before we begin to the enumerate the important aspects of the missionary challenges present in the world at large – as well as in our local contexts – we can do well by systematising the way we should look at any context.

Traditionally we tended to define the question about 'where' in terms of what or who to be reached, the places where we should become involved, like: the religions of the world, the continents or countries to be reached, the main socio-economic blocs (First World, Third World), and so forth. We thought we should reach out to the Hindus, Muslims, Buddhists, or Traditionalists in the world, and then determine statistically where we would find those people, and then go there. Or someone would feel called to Africa, or a specific country like (say) Sudan, and subsequently focus on that country. Others decided to concentrate on areas where there are socio-economic needs or disasters like famine, war, or endemic poverty. But in time we have realised that it is necessary to be much more focused.

The general situation (like the Muslim world) may be of use as a background, but if we look closer, we see that in each of these categories there are tremendous varieties. The Muslims of Saudi Arabia are very different from those in Iran, and again very different from those in South Africa or Kenya. And are the Muslims of the Western Cape really the same as those in KwaZulu Natal?

In a single country there are so many different communities that you can certainly not (in mission terms) simply think in terms of a country as a whole. And are the problems and realities of your own town or city the same as another? What are the things that we must look out for when we would like to understand a place or a community from a mission perspective? Yes, there are instruments and approaches that can be used to analyse a community in order to understand what is going on there. Most of these are from a sociological or anthropological angle. We should make use of these because they are usually well thought through and have a history of usefulness. However, from the missiological side there will mostly be a specific focus which may ask for some unique aspects. We must explore these in this chapter.

It is important to remember how we have defined our understanding of mission. It is multi-faceted and holistic. Mission is interested in the total life of not only people, but the whole of God's creation. It has to do with God's involvement with his good creation. And we are called to follow God in his concern and care for his world and especially his relationship with his image bearers. It can also be said that mission is need-oriented. Where there is a need, the church should respond, but in such a way that the real needs are addressed. Also, these needs may be on different levels, not only on the spiritual level.

We therefore propose a wholistic (looking at the whole of reality) and systematic view of the context, incorporating at least the following five dimensions: (a) the religious dimension, (b) the social dimension (realities), (c) the economic dimension (factors), (d) the political dimension, and (e) the environmental dimension (aspects). Through a grid like this we will probably get closer to seeing the whole picture and the unfinished task.[2] However, we will have to look at all these from a historical perspective. It is not enough to take a snapshot view. Life is dynamic, so we will always have to take cognisance of the before and after of the snapshot: what went before and where is it going.

The religious dimension

Religious affiliation

An important starting point is to look at the **religious affiliation** of the people in any place. When we talk of a religion, we should realise that we are not only talking about the so-called world religions, but any religious worldview. It may also be a traditional, local religion. Now: is there a dominant religion, or a wide variety of religious groupings in that area (or country)? It will make a world of difference for the Christian who feels called to work there if by far the majority of the people see themselves as Muslims (or Hindus, or Buddhists, etc.). This could even be the reason why these Christian feels called to work there. This is not the place to dwell on the Christian's approach to people of the various religions, but we need to be reminded that for a religious person religion is part and parcel of his or her worldview. Their outlook is determined by the way they look at reality. They may not understand the intricacies of their religion, but it is part of their personality, their being. So, respect is expected.

It will make quite a difference if the adherents of the majority religion are intolerant towards a Christian witness, or neutral. The government may even have laws against what they understand as proselytising, even if the Christian is there for business or humanitarian work. There is a whole list of countries today that don't allow Christian evangelism. The Christian will have to be extremely wise in his or her actions in that country, and will definitely have to first win the acceptance of the people (and leaders).

---

[2] To a large extent the following approach is based on the author's decade long research into the 'Unfinished Task of Mission in South Africa'. This project culminated in 34 booklets (of 3 300 pages), mostly in Afrikaans, but was condensed in the publication *The South African Context for Mission* (Lux Verbi, 1989). In the heart of the book is a description of 12 typical South African scenarios. Although the information of which this book is based is dated, it may still be regarded as an example of the following method.

Or the community may be pluralistic in term of religious orientation. The majority of the people may even be agnostic, atheistic or nominal adherents of whatever religion. This will make it easy (in a sense) for the outsider to function as a Christian (and even missionary), but without saying that success will be easier to attain. The challenges will be different, even if the government or leaders are tolerant.

It is also still possible that the missionary arrives in a community where the general culture is that of a traditional religion. Such a community is usually relatively open, but wary. Here the missionary should be aware not to repeat all the mistakes of the missionaries of the previous centuries when they had a negative view of the worldview of the traditional folk and simply tried to change it to their own (mostly Western) worldview. Too often they only succeeded to break down the intricate net of the traditional culture with their stronger (Western) cultural trappings without succeeding to let the gospel bring the necessary changes (see Newbigin 1989).

It should be clear that, in terms of religious affiliation, a given community will be somewhere on the spectrum between a closed, hostile one or an open, welcoming community. Each community will be different, and it will be the task of the missionary to understand it. It will to a large extent determine how he or she will have to go about.

The unfortunate fact is that by far the majority of people in the world – and especially those who are identified as 'unreached' – live in countries that do not welcome Christian missionaries (to put it mildly).[3] This shouldn't mean that all efforts to reach those will have to be put on hold.

Christian denominational make-up

In reality, most missionaries (or cross-cultural workers) work in areas or countries that have a considerable number, or even majority of, (nominal) Christians.[4] Very few work among the so-called unreached peoples without any contact with Christian communities. (We are not here going to debate this reality, whether it is acceptable or not. We just state it as a fact). In such a place it will be of utmost importance to get to know and take cognisance of the fact of the Christian denominational make-up.

---

[3] See, for example, https://www.pewresearch.org/religion/2021/09/30/globally-social-hostilities-related-to-religion-decline-in-2019-while-government-restrictions-remain-at-highest-levels/ where the Pew Research Centre described the situation in 2019.

[4] It is estimated that 85% of missionaries (even cross-cultural missionaries) work in nominally Christian communities.

Too often we find that an enthusiastic Christian comes to a community and starts work without any reference to the local setup in terms of churches. There are probably long-established churches in the community. There may be a wide variety of churches on the spectrum from so-called mainline churches, 'mission' churches, Pentecostal, charismatic, Zionist, and Apostolic churches. What would this 'missionary' intend doing if he or she is not joining the combined effort to identify specific needs or gaps in the ministry of the churches? There may be already a network of cooperating churches, but this missionary or evangelist is not interested to join them. This is sad. It is important to see your work in relation to others. No one should work without brotherly relations with other Christians. It may even become clear that you are not really necessary in this situation. The missionary who ignores the other churches must not be surprised if he or she is not welcomed!

In an evangelised community there is always much more work to be done (in the light of the broad definition of what mission entails), but it should not be done as a loner as if there are no Christians in the community. It is important to find out about the Christian community. One can begin by researching the local statistical or census records. In many cases this may not be available, but sometimes one may be surprised about what can be unearthed. But in any case, it will need footwork. Make contact with Christian leaders, and in time a picture will be formed.

Which are the churches that are present in the community? Which seem to be the strong churches, those with the largest numbers? They may be the older ones which were traditionally setting the tone. Are there dynamic new churches which are growing and attracting new members from the non-Christians (or other churches)? They are important. And what about those churches which are often regarded as somewhat syncretistic, those which are close to the more traditional worldview of people, and who are different from the typical Western oriented Christians? Get to know the total Christian community in its variety. The missionary may certainly feel more at home with some churches, but must refrain from writing off the others.

And very important, what are the relationships between these different churches? In the worst-case scenario, they are not acting as family (brothers and sisters) but rather as competitors with no love lost. Or they may just ignore the others and carry on as if there are no other churches. Hopefully there are in the Christian community initiatives like ministers' fraternals or the like. Find out about such organisations, make contact, and in such a way become part of the Christian scene.

The goal of this kind of research into the Christian setup would be, on the one hand, to find a place within the community and, secondly, to identify gaps where the witness of the church as a whole could be strengthened. It is the one church as the body of Christ which should work together in their ministry.

General religious atmosphere
Apart from the specifics of the religious make-up of the community, there is the general religious atmosphere. In the modern world many societies tend to move towards secularism. It means that the spiritual and religious dimension of the people's lives seem to be less important to them than before. People may profess to be Christians, Muslims, or Hindus (to name the largest religious groupings), but in practice they are agnostic or atheistic, they are nominal. Religion is not really important to them. Their worldview tends to be scientific and sceptical about the role of a god in their world. The efforts of a Christian missionary are viewed much different here than in a society where the religious fervour is high. And this last scenario is the other end of the spectrum. Here everything religious attracts much attention and almost everyone is emotionally involved. A missionary will here be viewed with suspicion and maybe hate. It is important to be able to gauge the general religious atmosphere and carefully work within it.

The social dimension

It almost goes without saying that the social situation of people to a large extent determines how receptive they may be for the gospel message. The saying that people can't hear the gospel on an empty stomach is not too far from the truth. The social context cannot be ignored by the missionary. It should be researched, analysed, and understood, not only for the successful communication of the gospel message, but also to understand where the good news of the gospel must lead to social action.

A good but superficial beginning is to gather **demographic data** on the community. Many countries have good and regular censuses which bring together mountains of data about the population of the whole country, but usually also make it available for smaller geographical areas. But apart from that there is also the information that municipalities gather. And it may just be that other people have done this research before you, and you can make use of what is published.

The first important factor which classifies a community is the **rural-urban divide**. But also, here we have to understand a spectrum ranging from peripheral rural areas with traditional communities with subsistence farming, through intensive or extensive agricultural areas around rural towns, then semi-urban areas, suburbs of different kinds, up to the central cities. Each of these situations are unique.

Mission is in the business of communication. Therefore, it is very important to know which **languages** are spoken. Is there a *lingua franca*, a common language spoken by most people, or not? What are the home languages of the people? It gives an idea of the **ethnic composition** of the community. But also, which further social sub-cultures can be identified in the community?

The demographic statistics (the term *demo-graphic* means per definition a description of the people) usually provide breakdowns in terms of gender, age groupings, and registered births and deaths. Other social indicators that are enumerated are the number and kinds of housing and households, state of and highest level of schooling of the people, employment and unemployment, and even the spread of income. This statistical information paints a broad picture of a society and provides background to more specific knowledge.

The more specific aspects should be researched on the ground. In the first instance one would like to get an idea of the stability or instability of **family life**. What kind of families are there: extended, traditional, or modern atomistic families with few (or no) children? How general is single-parent families? And absent fathers? Do the young people marry, and at what age? What about teenage pregnancies? Is it allowed, discouraged, or even encouraged? And the new and very relevant issue of gender? Is homophobia present?

This is closely aligned to the question of **housing**. Is it a rural area with family compounds, and enough space to accommodate also the next generation? Or maybe a stable urban area, suburban, with good housing? Or is it an area (which is becoming more common) of informal settlement (often called squatters because of its unplanned or even illegal state) where mainly newly arrived people from rural areas settle? It is well known that **urbanisation** is one of the most important socio-economic realities all over the world. And especially in the developing world it usually goes together with inadequate or insufficient housing for new arrivals. Cities in general cannot cope with the influx of people; as a result, informal shacks are erected without any planning, and without services such as water, electricity, sewage, and the like. Consequently, unhygienic and unhealthy, dangerous circumstances are the order of the day. But it is not only the new arrivals from the rural areas who put a strain on the possibility of housing, but also those arrivals through the cradle are adding to the backlog. Most housing, even in one or two-room shacks, have extended families living in them. The overcrowding and the kind of housing – or lack of it – has an enormous impact on the family. It also plays a significant role in the health of the people. It is not possible for the people in such a situation to sustain a healthy and stable family life. Children are born already doomed because of the social condition. Childcare during the important first year's leaves much to be desired, especially if young mothers conceive outside safe family structures.

Urbanisation and the housing crisis also bring with it other social effects. Two of them are the endemic problem of **drugs** and the related scourge of **gangs and violence**. Alcoholism is the order of the day. Not all urban communities are plagued by these asocial habits, but it is unfortunately too common. Unfortunately, much of the violence, driven by alcohol, is even in the home. And on the street, it is the gang killings. People live in fear because they are not safe anywhere. These are all part of the crime scene. Not all crime is violent, but it is very difficult if your belongings are not safe, especially when you have very little. The presence of these social ills will not only present mission with serious foci, but will also provide endless troubles. But their presence or not is one of the most important social factors to influence the role of the church. The community cannot really be reached without an understanding of these issues.

The housing crisis of urbanisation is also an important factor influencing the **health care** of the community. Overcrowding has and is still causing the spread of diseases and pandemics like HIV/AIDS and, more recently, COVID-19. Health services cannot cope. In the shanty towns there are usually no facilities for healthy sport activities, and it leads to unhealthy street life. The presence of physical health services or not is a significant element of the social environment that is important for the missionary to understand. It is an essential element of the health of a community.

The same goes for the availability of **education**. Are there enough and quality schools? Is there ample provision of Early Childhood Development (ECD) centres? We know the importance of stimulation and care for the under six-year-old children. What are the challenges relating to education in the community? What about school dropouts? Why do children drop out from school? Are there training possibilities and work opportunities for school leavers? What can you find out about the quality and work ethic of the teaching staff? Are the things taught in school relevant for life? To what extent is what the children experience education, or only schooling? These and other questions should be addressed by the researcher in the intensive immersion in the community.

Other structural issues that are important for an understanding of the community are things like **racism, discrimination,** and **xenophobia**. To what extent is this community, or sections within this community, the victim of all kinds of discrimination? We have already mentioned the fact that some people don't have access to good housing and services. Some of it may be the result of the urbanisation that overwhelms the planners, but often there is also discrimination involved. Worldwide there are refugees fleeing from oppressive situations or wars and find that they are not welcome elsewhere. Some groups are targeted by governments or factions which cause them to flee. It may be racism or tribalism or simply historical issues which cause people to become refugees or migrants. In many communities there are individuals or groups of immigrants. They moved there for different reasons, often just to look for a better future. Are they welcomed, or do they suffer under xenophobia, where they are hated and feared? Many of them are victimised for no other reason than they are foreigners.

These are some of the social aspects that need to be taken into account in an analysis of a context.

The economic realities

A third dimension that must come into play when analysing a context is that of the economic realities which are experienced in that community (see also Myers 2012). As already mentioned, there may be census data available which give an economic overview of the general situation in the country, region, or even in this smaller geographic area. Research will establish whether there is such valuable data available, or maybe even studies that have already analysed the data.

The background will be provided by the **general economic policies** of the government. Are we looking at a centrally planned socialist or communist economy or a more capitalistic one? We know that there are presently probably no pure socialist or capitalistic countries around, but every country is somewhere on the spectrum between these extremes. Where more or less on the spectrum do we find this community? This economic policy is just one element of the reality that forms a society. Together with the social aspects (and even the political factors which will be addressed in a following paragraph), a grid will form which is often described as the socio-economic reality; no single perspective or vantage point can describe the whole situation, but they intersect and intertwine, so that they together provide insight into the community.

The situation of the community on the **centre-periphery** spectrum will explain quite a lot. In any country there is a centre (or a few centres) of economic activity, and from there outwards are widening circles towards the poorer periphery. The centres house the financial and industrial hubs, the powerhouses. The majority of work or career opportunities are there, and therefore also the concentration of workers and the highest population. It is also from the centre that the media spreads information, the entertainment, and the cultural changes. Moreover, from the centre radiates the transport network, the national roads and rail lines. Into the centre come the electricity power lines, the water and oil pipelines, and everything necessary to keep the industry going. And from the centre flow the manufactured products countrywide and worldwide, but also the affluent and waste produced by industries and population densities.

At the outer periphery are people. They suffer because of the lack of employment opportunities, and a lower quality of general services, especially health and education. To a large extent the outer periphery is only providing cheap unskilled labour to the centres. Yes, the periphery is attractive as the place of open spaces and nature reserves to be enjoyed mainly by the people of the centres who feel the need and have the money to get 'out there'. The people living there just look on when the well-heeled come to enjoy their natural resources, without having an idea how it is to live there. The people in the outer periphery are mostly involved in subsistence farming, if at all. Often, they just depend on the money which is sent home from the cities.

An inner periphery (economically speaking) is where there are other primary industries: commercial agriculture, and mining. In those areas there are larger and smaller towns which are dependent on the people who are involved in the agricultural and mining activities in their vicinity. On a lower economic level these towns are in turn also centres, because the people on the farms and at the mines are dependent on the basic services they provide. These therefore also experience (to a lesser extent) the urbanisation problems of the cities, because people move there from the farms: housing shortages, social ills, and the security issues coupled with joblessness and discrimination. The difference is that they don't have the tax base to be able to solve the problems.

Where on this centre-periphery spectrum is this community that the missionary wants to get involved in? Is it in a city or rural area? Is it in a town or a traditional subsistent area? Or does it find itself in an industrial area? Is it a working-class community, or maybe in a tree-lined, affluent suburban area? Economically speaking there are many different human contexts on this spectrum.

The kind of economic activity that is prevalent also puts a stamp on a community. Are the people with employment generally in government service as clerks or other administrative positions, or are they non-skilled or lower skilled workers? Are they in highly qualified positions in the so-called Fourth Industrial Revolution of the modern information technology (IT) industry or in primary industries like agriculture and mining? Or are the majority in this community those who search in vain for a job, or have even lost hope to find one?

In any country there are rich and poor people. Incomes vary widely. Some have actually too many luxuries, and others next to nothing. It is general that there are such **structural inequalities** present. Often the majority of the population in a country are poor, even absolutely poor, living below the breadline. Sometimes poverty has to do with the accident of where the person is in terms of the centre and periphery. There is just not so much money going around in the periphery. But usually the inequality is historic, because of the lack of opportunities people had, causing different levels of schooling and training. Unfortunately, the gap between the salaries of the managers and the workers are usually huge, even though they work equally well and hard. The capitalist system is known for this kind of inequality, that the rich get richer and the poor poorer. It is especially the unschooled or less educated workers who have the greatest problem. It is difficult to find work, especially in an underperforming economy, or they are paid extremely low wages (which they accept because they have no choice). And many of those poor are migrants or refugees who are willing to work for a pittance because they are without any security. No wonder that crime becomes a tempting alternative for people without any hope of making a living. But there are also other kinds of discrimination that may cause inequalities. Women, for instance, are usually paid less than men, and they have a ceiling on their upward mobility. And generally, it may also be racism or tribalism that keeps people down.

All these are called structural discrimination.

Although the missionary must be willing to fit into any community on the economic scale, it will always be the poor who should receive priority attention. This much was already established in the previous chapters of this book. But the point of this paragraph is that the missionary context is also strongly influenced by the economic situation of the place. It cannot and should not be ignored.

The political realities

We know that the root of the word 'politics' has to do with the running of a city (*polis* in Greek). Politics has to do with every aspect of life in a community, whether it is the social, economic, or even religious aspect of life. Some people are in formal political roles, whether on a national, regional, or local level. But on the other hand, it must be acknowledged that every citizen is a politician in a sense, doing political things, because we live in community. We must not confuse this understanding of politics with 'party politics'. Often, we complain about politics being 'dirty', and politicians being 'liars', but that has to do with the practical machinations of the struggle for power. Party politics is the organised politics in a democratic government system. Some may never want to be a member of a political party, and prefer to remain independent, but all of us are involved in political thought and decisions.

We are all impacted by the **political system** in which we live. Some countries are ruled according to a communist policy where the state has the first and last say. The citizens are only free to the extent that they fall in with the central regulations. However, most countries in the modern world regard themselves as democracies, where the people (*demos* in Greek) vote for the leaders or representatives in government whose decisions are then supposed to reflect the will of the people. However, to a greater or lesser degree we must confess that democracies are not so democratic; the politicians are not always serving the people who have elected them. In short, the point we are trying to make is that the political system has a huge influence on the life of the people.

Even in a period where the move towards democracy and freedom is regarded as necessary in practice, it seems as if, in a growing number of cases, there is a close relationship between **religion and state**. Especially in the Muslim majority states the tendency is to declare the state as a Muslim state, and to declare *shariah* (Islamic) law as the system of law. Some Buddhist majority nations do the same, as does India with its majority of Hindus. On the other hand, there are a (diminishing) number of (Western) countries where certain Christian churches or groupings have a strong influence in government. It is not necessary to spell out how different the Christian ministry will be in these diverse political scenarios. One has to understand the political climate which shapes the Christian approach accordingly.

Some countries are **corrupt**. The political system of a country will also determine the economy because politics and economics are like two sides of a coin. So if the political leaders are corrupt, it will work through to the economic life. There is a saying that goes: 'power corrupts; and absolute power corrupts absolutely'. In a really corrupt society, this way of operating works down from the top levels to every small local community. Because the politics of government is unfortunately a power game, the risk of corruption is always there, also in democratic countries. But the point of this all is that corruption in government – from national to local – has a great impact on the livelihood as well as morality of a community. How does a witness for Christ function in such a context?

The governments of many countries are regarded as **illegitimate** by the majority of the citizens, or by the outside world. It may have come into power through a coup, or it represents only a minority ethnic group. One can expect pressure from (parts of) the international community on such a state, pressure that may also hurt the general population. There will always be local demonstrations against such a government, and these uprisings will often be crushed through violence from the side of the state. There will be pressure on individuals to take sides, and tensions will build up in communities. How does the Christian witness position him or herself here in the light of Romans 13?

Racism and discrimination lodge in the heart of people, this we know. But it is often also imbedded in the structure of a society. Is the political system in this case racist? And what about other kinds of discrimination: gender, ethnicity, language? The Christian witness cannot accept unrighteous discrimination against people, but how to minister to the rulers (local and national) in this regard will ask for much wisdom.

The more racist a country and its population are, the more unsatisfied the population will be with the government, and the more restlessness there will be. How **safe** is a country for its people? To what extent is crime under control? There are countries, and especially metropolitan areas where people don't feel safe, and not without reason. It is not only your property which may be under siege, but also your life. How is the police force? Also corrupt?

The above is dealing with unsatisfaction and restlessness which has its origin within communities. Criminal elements also begin to play a political role and contribute to an unsafe situation. But in many cases a country and its communities suffer from forms of insurrection. Daily we hear of terrorist attacks in many different places. All this puts pressure on a community, and may make it very difficult for a Christian witness.

One political issue which has recently become a very thorny issue is that of **refugees and migrants**. Sometimes people are fleeing faction wars and violence and become refugees in another region of their country (**internally displaced**), or they have to stream across the border to a neighbouring country (**internationally**

displaced people). They often have to leave everything behind, and are in dire need of food, clothing and shelter. This places an enormous burden on the receiving country, with the result that governments understandably are not too positive towards these people. They are sometimes seriously discriminated against, or sent back. This political nettle is very difficult to solve. Some leaders courageously welcome the immigrants, and often have to deal with negative political results. Others are hardliners and close their eye to the needs of the people and face criticism because of that.

Other people cannot be defined as refugees but, to a large extent, their situation is just as bad. They move from their places of abode where they have no future, to other parts of the world where they hope to find better possibilities. Sometimes streams of migrants merge and become a very visible problem, especially for better-off countries. However, these migrants are just the latest form of the movement of peoples that is as old as humanity itself. But it doesn't take away the fact that it causes great difficulties for receiving governments. There is pressure from the citizens who feel culturally and economically endangered; there may even be episodes of xenophobia and violence against these needy people. How governments and communities handle these issues will become an important factor in colouring the political context.

The environmental restraints

In our understanding of mission, we take for granted that God is involved with the whole of his creation. The church and the missionary should likewise take the welfare of creation seriously in their actions. To this end there is strong and growing theology to support this involvement with the environment. It will therefore be important to study the health or ill health of the context where the missionary is called to. Not only the human aspects of the context, namely the religious, social, economic and political dimensions should be analysed, but also the environmental.

Very few contexts where people are living are pristine. But how degraded is this environment where we (want to) labour? Is it degraded because of **pollution**? What kind of pollution? Is it **littering** on the ground, the streams or ocean, or is the water quality unhealthy, or is the air quality dangerous? All this seriously impacts on the well-being of the inhabitants. Moreover, what could be the reasons for the degraded environment? Is it human carelessness and lack of a sound theology or is it just the result of unbridled growth and consumption? Why is this specific environment like it is?

Let us start with the **mentality** of the people. Is it OK for them just to throw things away when their user value is over? The packet is empty, the bottle or tin has served its purpose, so throw it away (or just leave it there). Someone else will (maybe) pick it up. All this litter eventually clogs and pollutes the streams, and ultimately, the ocean.

Maybe it is not a case of a bad mentality. It may be that there are no (or not enough) containers to chuck it in, or the municipality and local government aren't doing what they are supposed to do: to remove the waste to a safe place? And what kind of a home or shack does this person live in, and where? Is it a case of lack of basic environmental and hygienic education or maybe other serious issues causing the spread of rubbish?

We all know how serious the problem of plastic pollution is. But what about the abundance of paper and cardboard used for packaging? Is all this necessary? Furthermore, we must remember that all this plastic and paper packaging comes from natural resources that are in many cases not renewable. There is a general mentality of overdoing the packaging, to say nothing about the cheap products that are meant to be thrown away after a short while. In a sense we should realise that the people only provide the hands which pollute, but behind them are the producers and the advertisers who cause all the useless products to find their way into people's hands. There is a more serious problem imbedded in the mentality of the economic system.

Is there a **recycling** drive in the community? This will say much about the health of the community. It is important to remember the mantra of the recycling industry: 'Reduce ... re-use ... recycle'. The recycling comes at the end; the other two habits are even more important: reduce your impact on the environment by using less, and using items for longer.

Is there a **theology** of environmental care around, whether it is the Christian one, or the Buddhist or traditional approach of living in harmony with your environment? This would be something that the Christian worker could wholly embrace and assist.

But it should also be remembered that the unsightly litter in the environment may only be the tip of the iceberg. The often unseen **pollution of the air** makes life – all life – increasingly impossible, not to mention the resulting impact on weather systems. Additionally, the **pollution of the water sources** with all sorts of unhealthy and poisonous waste from households and industries is serious. We can't live without water, and our health (whether in affluent or degraded societies) is under serious threat by this kind of pollution.

And where does all this come from? Apart from ineffective government with its lack of good service delivery, it is the notion that one can continue to misuse the natural resources in the effort to have more possessions, to become affluent. It is clear that the impact of the rich, the industries, the growth mongers, on the health of the earth is much greater than that of the poor, even if the latter are more numerous.

Let's take the case of **energy use** and its impact on the environment. We all have become absolutely dependent on electricity for every aspect of our existence: cooking, heating, communication, and relaxation. In most countries electricity is generated by burning fossil fuels, especially coal, which is not only depleting non-renewable natural resources, but causing immense amounts of pollution, not only into the atmosphere, but degrading huge areas of land. Is there in this community a drive towards renewable, clean energy? And is there personal motivation to save on the use of energy? Or is this community a poor one where much of the cooking and heating is done with wood, wood that must be found (by the women) in the surrounding (and soon to be depleted) land? Depending on the situation of the community, the use of energy has a significant effect on the environment. Is the missionary willing to get involved in countering this trend in a positive and creative way?

Also, the impact of **agriculture and forestry** must be taken into account. Agriculture, especially the producing of mono-cultural crops, changes the environment almost forever. Should the missionary not (with the relevant practitioners) become involved in the search for better agriculture – meaning not only better production, but with less of an impact on the environment? There is talk about 'agriculture in God's way', and 'no tillage'. Is it something that gets attention in the community?

The environment is heavily impacted by the **population density**. Urban planning increasingly takes into account the need for open spaces for relaxation and fresh air, but also even 'urban agriculture'. A dense population cannot but put a heavy burden on the environment. Creative planning and determined motivation can make quite a difference.

The missionary should think about looking for and joining all **conservation** efforts in the community. That could become a very symbolic and profitable activity in line with the calling to be God's witness in the community. If need be, it could also develop into a role of agitation and activism for the environment.

To summarise, the health of the environment should also be on the missionary's agenda. It should be studied so that the dangers to the health of the environment are identified, and positive steps propagated. This should receive serious attention.

Specific global issues

In the section above we have already touched on most of the issues that influence the global context, but it may be worthwhile in summary form to call attention to some of these factors.

Urbanisation

Urbanisation is a worldwide phenomenon. It is closely connected with the global economy, but specifically with the economic development of each country and region. The world urbanisation growth statistics are as follows: 1960=34%, 1980 = 39%, 2000 = 47%, and 2020 = 56% of the world's population were urbanised

(World Bank open data). In 2020 about 35% of Africa's population resides in cities while almost 65% of Southern Africa residents resides in cities (Guneralp, Lwasa, Masundire, Parnell & Seto 2018:2). These percentages varies between the so-called 'developed world' (or the 'Global North) and the fast-growing percentage of urbanised citizens in the 'Global South'.

Even in the richer countries urbanisation poses enormous challenges. How can local governments (or whoever is responsible for this task) plan ahead for the influx of people from the rural areas, and make available the necessary infrastructure that this growth in population can be absorbed in a healthy way? It is an enormous task. Even in the richer countries this phenomenon often leads to great social stress and unrest. The other side of the coin is that the rural towns and the traditional communities experience a drain of especially young people. It has a deleterious effect which is often overlooked.

It goes without saying that in the poorer countries this movement to urban areas mostly gets out of hand. Cities grow in an unplanned way. Social and health services cannot cope with the enormity of the influx. The road, water, electricity, and sewage grid cannot handle the growth. The growth mostly happens on the outskirts of the city, and the social fabric comes under enormous stress.

In all cases the motivation for moving to the city is mostly economic. A person or a family hope to have a better life there. There is the possibility of work opportunities, hope for a better education for the children, and possible upward mobility. Unfortunately, the dream of most migrants to the cities isn't always realised.

Refugees and migrancy

Almost the same situation pertains in the very visible and problematic phenomenon of the movement of refugees. That which is mostly in the news is the hundreds of thousands of people who (try to) cross international boundaries from areas of conflict or desperation to countries where they hope to find refuge and a new life. Some of these refugees wish to go back to their homes when things are stabilised, and it may become possible to return. But most have given up hope. They are fleeing from death and don't expect that there is any future back home. Examples at the time of writing are the desperate refugees from Afghanistan, the refugees from the Tigray region in Ethiopia, the refugees from Myanmar to Bangladesh, as well as the millions of Syrians, Iraqis, and others from the Middle East and North Africa trying to cross the Mediterranean to Europe. And what about all those from Central America moving towards the United States of America (USA).

The millions of internally displaced people (IDP) are not so visible, but the numbers are equally staggering. Not only are all these people desperate, and in need of more or less everything, but they pose an almost insurmountable problem for those countries where they are fleeing to.

The other related phenomenon to refugees is that of migration in general. It is somewhat different, but in this 'global village' there is a tendency for people to move around. As a matter of fact, the whole world was in the distant past populated by people who started emigrating from Africa, the region where *homo sapiens* evolved! So, not all people are refugees in the technical sense of the word, but they do tend to (try to) move towards countries and places which offer greater possibilities. It is also good to realise that the most influential country in the world (the USA) is a nation of immigrants! In most countries you can find pockets of immigrants, usually in groups of their own people. Most of the immigrants eventually play a positive role in their receiving country, but for a time they encounter many obstacles, not least the fear (or hate) of foreigners.

For the church and missionaries, it is important to note the repeated reminders in the Bible that God champions the cause of the 'aliens' and all people in need (see for example Psalm 146) and that we are called to have the same spirit.

Poverty and justice issues

May we also remind the reader that the worsening gap between the rich and poor is like a dark cloud hovering over the world. It is a serious problem in probably every country on earth, but it is especially present on a global level. The international economic system is not effectively able to address this problem. In fact, many would argue that the International Monetary Fund (IMF) and other international efforts just make the problem more irreversible. This is a dark cloud because it seems so impossible to solve the problem. None of the alternative economic policies of socialism and capitalism seem to have the answer. That is why all sorts of combinations of government involvement is tried, but to no avail. This income gap plagues all contexts. Not only is it a reality within which the church must learn to function, but the witnesses of Christ should be doing their utmost to make a positive difference within this crucible.

Issues of cultural and worldview changes

Apart from the socio-economic-political realities that we summarised above, it is also important for a moment to highlight the changes in the mindsets of people. The traditional worldviews of people are being challenged by an array of strong influences brought about mainly by the media developed in the West. Television, radio, and all the modern electronic social media have an unmeasurable impact on erstwhile traditional communities. Although some fundamentalist groups (especially Muslims) try their best to stop this influence and turn back the clock, it is usually hopeless. Globalisation and secularisation storm over the whole world like a tsunami flood.

Mission the "labour room" of theology

The advent of modernism, the result of the scientific and industrial revolutions, seems impossible to stop. It has to a large extent taken over the traditional worldview and way of life. Yes, pockets of conservative resistance are everywhere to be seen, but in general the materialistic lifestyle and mentality are supplanting the spiritual or traditional religious outlook.

But even more than that, also the modernist approach is in the process of making way for the so-called post-modernism. Whereas the scientific modernist tended to be sure of everything – he/she knew and (thought to) understand everything – the post-modern person is not so sure anymore. There are too many things that go above our understanding. On the one hand, this is a positive development, a more humble attitude. But on the other hand, it is also leading to pluralism and an uncertainty of values, principles and faith. That is why there is also the development of a 'post-Christendom'.

This new worldview has a thorough going impact on the Christian mission in the world. We cannot ignore it if we are realistic. And it will have an impact on our mission.

New churches

The face of Christianity in the world has changed remarkably over the past half century or so. Whereas in the past the West (or the North) was regarded as Christian and the rest as 'mission fields'; however, this was changed by two tendencies, namely: the church (or rather Christianity) declined in the former countries and regions that were regarded as Christian; and a remarkable growth of Christian churches took place in Africa, the East, and Latin America. There are presently many more Christians in these parts of the world than in Europe and North America. As it is often said, the centre of gravity of the Christian church shifted south and east!
Another reality in today's world are the internal shifts in the ecclesial world. There was a time when the churches in the world were either national (established) churches and their offspring, or so-called mainline churches. The mainline churches were church formations like the Catholic Church (the largest single 'denomination' on earth), or the different Orthodox churches, or the traditional Protestant denominations. These churches originated in the West (or North), and planted their 'daughter churches' in the 'mission fields'. However, in the modern missionary movement of the 19th and 20th centuries, it was not so much the denominations but inter- or non-denominational mission societies that spread the gospel into Africa and elsewhere. From this work was birthed a variety of denominations who were in the first instance linked to the mission societies as their 'parents'.
This was especially the case in Africa. Apart from the Roman Catholic Church that never planted new churches, but just 'expanded' into new areas, a whole array of churches came into being. But that was just the first phase of the Christianisation

of Africa. Through the process of indigenisation or contextualisation, many new churches came into being. It is a study in itself to try to classify all these new church plants. Some of these fast-growing churches are closer to the traditional cultures, and cause some observers to warn of syncretism. Others, at the other end of the spectrum, are strongly influenced by the Pentecostal and charismatic movements and tend to be fundamentalist evangelical. And then there are all those somewhere on the spectrum. Charismatic and traditional leadership is the key to their growth. As we already mentioned earlier, for the gospel witnesses it is of utmost importance to act as part of the body of Christ in its bewildering variety. It should be remembered that a missionary is in the first instance a witness for Christ and not for a denominational or doctrinal group. A certain openness is required.

Ethical issues like race, gender, etc.

A last aspect that can be mentioned is the importance given to (relative) new ethical issues that were traditionally not given too much attention, things like the discrimination against certain ethnicities, races, women and, more recently, the gender issues. Almost nowhere else is the clash of traditionalism against modernism and liberalism more sharply and energetically defined. This has not only religious but also political and cultural overtones.

In any case, these issues are too important to ignore. What makes it more difficult, however, is that the church and its mission were traditionally not in the forefront in combating these discriminatory issues. On the contrary, the mission enterprise is often accused of being guilty in this respect. It was really with the advent of the liberationist theologies that this came to the forefront.

Looking at the world

After the above paragraphs dealing with an approach to look at the context with missionary eyes, the reader may want more specific information. However, this was not the purpose of this chapter. On the one hand, the worldwide context changes dramatically almost from day to day. By the time this book is published, the most recent published facts may already be obsolete. The reader will just have to keep up to date with developments, and there are a host of dependable news outlets and commentaries that are available for this purpose. On the other hand, we consistently iterated the fact that every micro context is different from another. It will not make sense to try and describe a few of them. It was exactly the purpose of this chapter to give the Christian worker or potential missionary the 'tools' to analyse his or her context. We hope that this will be the case.

References

Agang, S.B., Forster, D.A., Hendriks, H.J. 2020, *African Public Theology*, HippoBooks, Langham Publishing

Guneralp, B., Lwasa, S., Masundire, H., Parnell, S., & Seto, K.C., 2018, 'Urbanization in Africa: challenges and opportunities for conservation', *Environmental Research Letters* 13(2018), 015002. https://doi.org/10.1088/1748-9326/aa94fe

Kritzinger, J.J, 1989, *The South African context for mission*, Lux Verbi.

Myers, B.L. 2012, *Walking with the Poor - Principles and Practices of Transformational Development*, New York: Orbis Books

Newbigin, L., 1989, *The Gospel in a Pluralist Society*, Grand Rapids, Eerdmans

Ott, G., Strauss, S.J., Tennent, T.C., 2010, *Encountering Theology of Mission, Biblical Foundations, Historical Developments, and Contemporary Issues*, Grand Rapids, Michigan: Baker Academic.

Pew Research Center, 2021, *Globally, social hostilities related to religion decline in 2019, while government restrictions remain at highest levels*, viewed 19 May 2022, from https://www.pewresearch.org/religion/2021/09/30/globally-social-hostilities-related-to-religion-decline-in-2019-while-government-restrictions-remain-at-highest-levels/

World Bank Open Data, viewed 1 June 2022, from data.worldbank.org.

World Council of Churches, 2013, *Together towards Life: Mission and Evangelism in Changing Landscapes*, https://www.oikoumene.org/sites/default/files/Document/Together_towards_Life.pdf

Chapter 8

The Place of Missiology as a Theological Discipline in Africa

J.N.J. Kritzinger and H. Kwiyani [1]

Introduction

The teaching of missiology (or mission studies) in Africa, like in the rest of the world, has been controversial for a long time. A number of universities and seminaries across the continent have either phased out missiology or replaced it with (or absorbed it into) another discipline. This chapter contends that such strategies, as understandable as they are, have deprived academic programmes of key theological emphases and caused them to deliver ministers to African churches who are insufficiently equipped to face the challenges of a fast-changing continent. This chapter argues that there are other ways to address the legitimate concerns expressed in these moves and that it is of vital importance for theological education in Africa not only to promote critical-creative reflection on Christian mission, but for the whole curriculum to be mission-centred.

The structure of the chapter

This introductory section defines the terms 'mission' and 'missiology' and explains the sources of the chapter. The subsequent two sections discuss the place (or absence) of missiology in theological curricula at some public universities across the continent:

Missiology is removed from the curriculum
Missiology is taught, but marginalised

---

[1] The two authors met at Liverpool Hope University in the UK in 2018, where Harvey Kwiyani was attached to its Andrew Walls Centre and Klippies Kritzinger was a visiting fellow. This joint paper is the product of fruitful conversations on the challenges facing missiology in Africa.

We then respond systematically to the issues raised by the previous sections and reflect on the role of missiology in a theology curriculum, making some suggestions for the way forward.

Mission

This chapter follows David Bosch's comprehensive understanding of Christian mission, which he characterised as a multifaceted ministry, encompassing dimensions such as witness, service, healing, reconciliation, liberation, peace, evangelism, fellowship, church planting, earthkeeping, and much more (Bosch 1991:512). To overcome the paralysing polarisation between evangelism and social action, as the debate was conceived in the 1970s and 1980s, Bosch argued that evangelism should not be seen as the sum total or the heart of mission, but as an indispensable element (dimension) of a broadly inclusive set of actions and attitudes that embody God's mission.

We also follow Bosch's emphasis on the nature of mission as God's initiative and as flowing from God's trinitarian existence. The missions of churches are authentically Christian only if they are embedded in – and fundamentally shaped by – God's mission as revealed in Scripture. In other words, there are definite criteria and guidelines within which churches need to operate as they develop their embodiments of God's mission in the particular contexts in which they find themselves. The Holy Spirit, as the guiding and empowering Agent of Christian mission, works in and through human agents, shaping them into instruments of change by summoning and sanctifying all their intellectual, cultural, and spiritual resources.

Missiology

This chapter works with an understanding of missiology as the critical-creative exploration of all the activities of Christian missions for the past two millennia. Critical is understood not as criticism or rejection but as a detailed examination and careful weighing of evidence from the past and the present, while creative refers to attempts at finding credible and transformative ways of embodying the gospel for the future.

A *critical* examination of past practices would include questions of agency (who were the actors?); context analysis (how did they 'read' the context(s) in which they were trying to bring about change?); ecclesial analysis (how did they understand the church and its role?); interpreting the tradition (where did they find inspiration and authority in Scripture and history for what they were doing?); discernment for action (what kind of activities did they plan and initiate to bring about transformation?); reflexivity (did they reflect critically on their actions and learn from their experiences?); and spirituality (how did they experience the calling-sending presence of God?).

A *creative* embodiment of the gospel for the future would involve a missiology that asks the same seven questions imaginatively, but in the first person plural: Who are we (as actors)? How do we read the context? etc. We believe that the critical and creative aspects of missiology are two sides of the same coin and need to be nurtured simultaneously in the lives of students. If the critical aspect eliminates the creative, missiology can become clinical and cynical historiography or self-righteous 'missionary-bashing'. If the creative aspect eliminates the critical, missiology can become superficial activism or self-righteous triumphalism.

To conceive missiology in this way implies that there is an intricate and ongoing interplay between mission and missiology. This is best captured by using the concept *praxis* – not as a synonym for action but as a description of this ongoing mutual interaction.

Sources

Since the choice of one's interlocutors is a key aspect of every exercise in theology, we need to explain the sources we used to write this chapter. Due to the focus of the book on an African missiology, we have primarily consulted African publications and examined the positions prevailing at universities and seminaries on the continent. This needs to be qualified in two ways. Firstly, we did not attempt a comprehensive survey of the position (or absence) of missiology at all theological institutions across Africa.[2] The three approaches were identified by examining a limited number of universities, but they seemed to us representative of prevailing trends. Secondly, since there is global interaction between universities (and missiologists), these positions are also found on other continents, so we did not focus on African sources in a myopic way.

Missiology is removed from the curriculum

Background

The background to this move is the historical entanglement between mission and colonialism. It is no secret that Western mission to Latin America, Africa, and Asia coincided with the expansion of European and later American imperialism in the world. It is for this reason that missionaries have been called the 'religious arm of the colonial empires ... the ideological shock troops for the colonial invasion whose zealotry had blinded them' (Andrews 2009:663), 'the spiritual wing of

---

2 This is a potential dissertation topic for an enterprising postgraduate student.

secular imperialism' (ed. Omer-Cooper 1968), or even 'imperialism at prayer' (Sanneh 1989:88). We read of this critique of mission both in religious (Christian) and in secular post-colonial literature. While, of course, there were European missionaries in Africa in the decades before the 1880s, the era of great missionary success and impact started with the Scramble for Africa. In 'sub-Saharan Africa',[3] for example, missionaries and colonial agents generally worked hand in hand to the point that it was often said that 'there is no difference between the colonial master and the missionary'. We get similar sentiments in fictional works by African writers of the 1950s, 60s, and 70s. Whether is it *Things Fall Apart* (Achebe 1958), *The River Between* (Ngugi wa Thiong'o 1965) or, indeed, *The Poor Christ of Bomba* (Beti 1971), the stinging critique of the colonial methods of Western missionaries in Africa is loud and clear. The history of the church, whether in Nigeria, the Democratic Republic of Congo, or Malawi is a bittersweet recollection of God's kingdom taking root while being propagated by fallible and sometimes conniving Christians. More often than not, European colonial agents and missionaries collaborated to oppress African independent churches and their leaders, for instance. Stories of many African leaders including Samuel Ajayi Crowther, William Wade Harris, John Chilembwe, and Simeon Kimbangu, among many others, tell of the complex relationship between mission and colonialism. Nevertheless, the problem of colonialism and missiology goes back to the early days of European imperialism, to the late 1400s when the Portuguese and the Spanish maritime empires began to expand Europe's presence and influence to the rest of the world.

This critique of mission has become increasingly prominent in the decades following the 1970s, as postcolonial discourse emerged. This discourse sought to deconstruct the impact of colonialism. Since Christian mission was so closely associated with colonialism, at least in the eyes of the colonised, the wrongs of colonialism were also attributed to mission. A dialogue continues about the place of mission in the world today. Critics ask: Why do we need mission when it has led to colonialism? The very language of 'mission' itself is in question, with some scholars arguing that it is so irredeemably tied to Western imperialism that we must stop using it (Niringiye 2015).

In the 2010s, the discourse took a turn towards decoloniality. In this school of thought, mission is not necessarily all bad; it is acceptable if it can be uncoupled from colonialism to become an agent of decolonisation. Some have argued that it is impossible, but that is precisely what liberation theologians have done, presenting God's mission as liberating praxis of (and with) the poor and oppressed people of the Global South. Most liberation theologians did not use the term 'mission' as a key

---

[3] From a pan-African ideological perspective, the term 'sub-Saharan' creates a problematic division between the (mainly Muslim and Arab) North and the rest of the continent. However, the term seems appropriate for a chapter on the teaching of Christian theology/missiology in Africa, which applies mainly to institutions in countries with a nominal Christian majority.

category, precisely because it is so tainted with colonial associations, even if it is clear that they regarded themselves as *sent by God* to work as Christians for economic justice and holistic liberation.[4] Additionally, their liberating understanding of mission has remained marginal in African churches and universities, with the result that it has not become a dominant factor in theological curricula.

A negative view of mission understandably translates into a negative view of missiology as a theological discipline. This must also be understood in the light of the fact that most public (state-funded) universities across sub-Saharan Africa do not have faculties (or departments) of *Christian theology*. When theology courses are taught, that is done by departments of religion or religious studies, which teach various religions. This system had its origin in the process of decolonisation, when newly independent African states adopted a non-aligned policy to the teaching of religion at public universities. That was due to a number of factors: Firstly, members of different religions campaigned and struggled side by side for independence from colonial rule. The political leaders of most post-colonial African states, having been shaped by that experience, therefore adopted 'secular' constitutions, in which the state (and its educational institutions) did not identify with (or privilege) a particular religion or church, but allowed its citizens the freedom to practise the religions of their choice.

Secondly, during colonial rule there were departments of theology (or divinity) at some university colleges, which were the forerunners of public universities. However, independent African states removed such privileges at the newly established state universities, to avoid public taxes in a democratic state from being used to train (only) Christian ministers. This development is clearly expressed by the University of Ghana:

> The Department for the Study of Religions of the University of Ghana ... started as the Department of Divinity in 1948 as one of the original units of the Faculty of Arts of the then University College of the Gold Coast. Its current name was adopted in 1962 to reflect the secular and multi-religious character of the country. The change of name was also to reflect the orientation of the Department as a sub-unit of a public secular university committed to the academic rather than confessional approach to the study of religion.[5]

---

4   Kritzinger (1988) showed in his doctoral thesis 'Black Theology – challenge to mission' that South African Black Theology (as a liberation theology) presented a double challenge: *opposition to* traditional (White) Northern mission as well as *mobilisation for* liberating (Black) mission.

5   University of Ghana, Department for the Study of Religions, 2022, *History of the Department*, viewed 1 July 2022, from https://www.ug.edu.gh/religions/about/brief_history.

University of Cape Town (UCT)

UCT is a respected university on the African continent with an excellent research record, which has always had a Department of Religious Studies. During the 1970s and 1980s it was a strong and productive centre of teaching and research in Christian theology, led by scholars like John de Gruchy, Charles Villa-Vicencio, James Cochrane, and others, but that focus has shifted. The department introduces itself now as being 'committed to the open, plural, intercultural, non-confessional and interdisciplinary study of religion and religions in South Africa and the world'. The undergraduate major in Religious Studies

> looks at both mainstream religious traditions and new religious movements and examines the relationship between religion and modern society. The degree allows you to explore religious aspects of media, politics, literature and art, as well as the significance of the body, sexuality and gender in religion. It will offer insight into some of the most relevant issues concerning contemporary society such as violence, conflict and social cohesion.

The core courses of the undergraduate major in Religious Studies include the following fields of study:

> Religion and Society; Psychology and Religion; Religion, Sexuality and Gender; Religion and Politics; Religions Past and Present; Judaism, Christianity and Islam; African Religious Traditions; Religion and Media; Religion in Africa.[6]

This curriculum presents a stimulating approach to the role of religions in society and to ways of studying them. Students who are firmly committed to a specific faith

---

[6] University of Cape Town, n.d., *Faculty of Humanities, Religious Studies*, viewed 1 July 2022, from http://www.religion.uct.ac.za/sites/default/files/image_tool/images/113/Final%20ReligiousStud%2023Apr%20final.pdf.

will find these courses challenging and stimulating if they are preparing to play a constructive or transformative role in society. In other words, it will broaden and deepen their understanding of the role of religion in society, but the nature of their response will depend on the sense of mission that they bring to the study in the first place, and on the spiritual resources that inspire and guide them.

A Christian student who is committed to one or more dimension of mission in Bosch's (1991:512) definition could find help from this curriculum to be a more informed, sensitive and effective agent of change in society, but the focus is on 'creative and critical *thinking about* religion' (emphasis added) rather than on creative and critical *acting* on the basis of one's religious commitment. The student will have to bring the latter aspect to the classroom from their own convictions and from their faith community.

A curriculum like this has been influenced not only by African postcolonial or decolonial discourses, as discussed above, but also by the academic cultures of leading universities in the United States and Britain, where Religious Studies (taught in this way) has become dominant. From the viewpoint of our chapter, this approach presents the least conducive framework for promoting and mobilising Christian mission. This is not a negative judgement on the academic integrity or quality of such a Religious Studies programme, but only a view on the contribution that it can make to enhancing a critical-creative Christian missiology.

Makerere University

Makerere University in Kampala, Uganda, which is celebrating its centenary in 2022,[7] has a Department of Religious Studies in its College of Humanities and Social Sciences. It operates 'on resolutely non-sectarian principles', teaching Christianity, Islam, and African Religions, along with others (Sicherman 2002:101). Its website[8] shows that courses in Christian theology, Islamic Studies, and African Religion[9] are offered side by side, along with Hebrew, Greek and Arabic. There is no course dedicated explicitly to Christian mission, but there are modules on African church

---

[7] Makerere College, founded in 1922 as a vocational school, became Makerere University College in 1949, as a constituent college of the University of London. In 1970 it became Makerere University, an independent National University of the Republic Uganda (Magara 2009:65).

[8] Makerere University, 2020, *Bachelor of Arts (Arts)*, viewed 30 June 2022, from https://courses.mak.ac.ug/programmes/bachelor-arts-arts.

[9] One of the courses on African Religion is titled 'African True Religion', which transforms the acronym ATR (usually referring to African Traditional Religion). This is clearly a move to overcome the pejorative connotation of the term 'traditional' in the term ATR as 'backward' or 'superseded'.

history, new religious movements, and the encounter between religions, which means that some basic components of a missiological orientation are present in the curriculum.

The comment of J.N.K. Mugambi, reflecting on his experience of the late 1960s – when the late John Mbiti was the head of that department – is insightful: 'The Department of Religious Studies and Philosophy at Makerere was the only place in East Africa where these two disciplines could be "secularly" studied' (in ed. Healey 2020:407). In other words, Makerere established a tradition of scholarly teaching and research in theology that was: a) ecumenical, i.e. not confined to a particular confession; b) not limited to the training of church ministers but at producing critical, reflexive Christian intellectuals; and c) open to the exploration of Christianity as an African religion, in dialogue with the broad context of African religion, culture, and politics.

Similar to the situation at UCT, this curriculum can deepen and broaden a student's mission praxis, provided they bring a strong sense of 'sentness' into the classroom in the first place, based on their personal commitment and the support of their faith community.

Chancellor College of the University of Malawi

Chancellor College was the founding institution of the University of Malawi, which was established in 1964 in Blantyre and moved soon after that to its current location in Zomba, both cities in southern Malawi. It is home to the University of Malawi's Department of Theology and Religious Studies, a department that goes as far back as the 1970s, when the university was just taking shape. For a long time, it was the only academic department in Malawi's higher education system that offered theology and religious studies, and had to take a non-aligned approach to meet the demands of all faith traditions, especially as a public university in a 'secular' African state. It is situated close to the Zomba Theological College of the Church of Central Africa Presbyterian, with which it has a close mutual relationship. Students of theology from either institution are allowed to take courses at the other; they also have access to other resources, like the library.

Chancellor College's Department of Theology and Religious Studies states that its mission is 'to offer education that trains high-caliber academics and professionals in theological studies with various orientations so as to respond to the contemporary needs of Malawi, the region and globally'.[10] The department used to have Mission Studies as part of their curriculum. Indeed, it was a very

---

[10] University of Malawi, 2022, *Department of Theology and Religious Studies*, viewed 22 July 2022, from https://www.unima.ac.mw/departments/theology-and-religious-studies.

important part of their offering because of the legacy of Scottish missionaries in Malawi. Both Klaus Fiedler and Kenneth Ross brought their expertise in mission and church history to that department.[11] Following a great deal of reorganising and restructuring in the 1990s – something we might call 'decolonising' today – the place of Mission Studies in the curriculum was lost to other subjects, but Church History remained. Today, the department has four sections, including Church History, Biblical Studies, Systematic Theology, and Religious Studies. Mission is not included on the list of courses on offer in 2022. Courses offered by the department include Wisdom and Poetic Literature, Christian Ethics, Church History, New Religious Movements, Old Testament Prophecy and Apocalyptic Literature, New Testament Introduction, Pauline Literature, Islamic Jurisprudence, Islamic Philosophy, Phenomenology of Religion, Systematic Theology, among others.[12] It seems that Practical Theology and Missiology have been dropped and that mission history has been subsumed under church history. It is possible that an agreement was reached with Zomba Theological College that they would offer mission-related and other Practical Theology courses.[13]

Interim reflection

The change from Theology (or Divinity) to Religious Studies at Makerere University and the University of Ghana did not bring about a radical side-lining of Christian theology, but it did place it on par with (and alongside of) courses in Islamic Studies, African Religion, and other religious traditions. One could say Religious Studies conceived in that way amounts to a department of parallel (and interacting) theologies of different religions. Viewed through the lens of Bosch's (1991:512) encompassing definition of mission, as mentioned earlier, these theology courses do not mobilise students for witness, evangelism, healing, and church planting but could encourage them to engage in service, reconciliation, liberation, peace, fellowship and earthkeeping. We should therefore not speak of the disappearance of mission from such curricula, but at most of the side-lining of certain key dimensions of mission. However, the model of religious studies found

---

[11] While they are both still active in Malawi, Klaus Fiedler joined Mzuzu University (MZUNI) in the late 1990s and, with his move, the teaching of missiology became more pronounced at MZUNI as it died down at Chancellor College. Ken Ross continues to teach at the Zomba Theological College, where his courses in church history continue to include mission history, especially that of the church in Malawi.

[12] University of Malawi, 2022, *Department of Theology and Religious Studies*, viewed 22 July 2022, from https://www.unima.ac.mw/departments/theology-and-religious-studies.

[13] The website of Zomba Theological College (http://www.zombatheological.org) is under reconstruction, so we were unable to verify this.

at UCT does represent a different approach. It could challenge and empower a student actively involved in faith-based service, reconciliation, liberation, peace and earthkeeping, but the dynamics will be different from that in the previous two examples.

The removal of courses in missiology from theology and religious studies curricula at state universities across Africa is understandable, but neither universal nor inevitable. Much depends on the particular history and context of a university and a country at large. Much also depends on the content of the missiology courses and the credibility of the lecturers among their peers in other disciplines – theological and otherwise. As we will argue later in more detail, mission is central to the identity and very existence of the church, which means that its concerns cannot be removed from a theology curriculum without doing it serious damage. To argue for the inclusion of missiology in a theology curriculum at a public university may mean, however, that for the sake of credibility and viability, specific changes need to be made to the language used, the priorities exhibited, and (in many cases) the people doing the teaching.

Missiology is taught, but marginalised

A second set of options exercised by public universities is when missiology courses are retained in a theology curriculum but are marginalised. This happens in two major ways: by isolating missiology into an elective (optional) position by renaming it, or by absorbing it into another theological discipline. We look at three examples.

University of Ghana

The University College of the Gold Coast was founded in Accra in 1948 as a college linked to the University of London and in 1961, after independence, it became the University of Ghana. It has a Department for the Study of Religions in its College of Human Sciences. The developments around the teaching of theology were similar to that in East Africa, partly due to the decolonising policies of the same (British) colonial power. Their academic approach to the teaching of religions is explained as follows:

> The Department is dedicated to the promotion of the scientific study of religions but also continues with the promotion of high-quality theological education for a just, peaceful and humane society. The academic training provided by the Department is intended to equip students to understand and interpret the world and society, and to enable them respond creatively to the challenges presented by the multicultural local and global environments.

There is also a serious academic engagement with African Indigenous Religions and Cultures with the aim of making a distinctive African, and for that matter Ghanaian, contribution to religious and theological studies.[14]

At the fourth level of the BA degree, the Christian Option in the curriculum offers an elective entitled Missions (SREL461).[15] To have no courses in the first three years and one elective at level four gives some recognition to the importance of mission for theology, but does give it a marginal position. Similar to Makerere University, however, it is clear that the 'high quality theological education' offered here is ecumenical, imparting skills of contextual analysis that are aimed at transformative involvement in society and an ongoing process of Africanisation. In other words, the curriculum as a whole does have a missiological orientation, slanted towards the dimensions of service, reconciliation, liberation, peace and earthkeeping in terms of Bosch's (1991:512) definition.

Missiology becomes Intercultural Theology

Another trend that we have observed in the teaching of missiology in Africa has been a shift towards either 'Intercultural Theology' as seen in Europe (Germany and Ireland) or 'Intercultural Studies' (following some United States institutions). Along with those who have moved towards Intercultural Theology (or Studies), there are other institutions that have transformed Missiology into 'World Christianity'. Both these trends have been common in Western academic missiological circles for a few decades: Intercultural Theology at Hermannsburg in Germany, Intercultural Studies at Fuller University, and World Christianity at Edinburgh University. This shift in the Global North is often a result of a loss of confidence in mission as such – largely because of its colonial history, as explained above – or to help their alumni gain access to countries that would frown upon a degree in mission.

---

[14] University of Ghana, Department for the Study of Religions, 2022, *History of the Department*, viewed 1 July 2022, from https://www.ug.edu.gh/religions/about/brief_history.

[15] The core module at level 400 is Theology and Ethics of the Old Testament and it is accompanied by five electives: Introduction to Old Testament Prophetic and Apocalyptic Literature; Missions; Hebrew 1; The Theology of the Gospels; and Doctrine of the Early Church (University of Ghana, n.d., *Department for the Study of Religions Courses for First Semester of 2020/2021 Academic Year, Bachelor of Arts (BA)*, viewed 1 July 2022, from https://www.ug.edu.gh/religions/sites/religions/files/u8/2020-2021%20First%20Semester%20Courses-BA.pdf

Mission the "labour room" of theology

Some African universities and seminaries have also made such shifts, replacing Mission or Missiology with one of these alternatives. Among the African institutions offering World Christianity degrees is the Africa International University in Nairobi, Kenya, which offers a master's degree in Mission Studies and a PhD in World Christianity. Another important African institution that has adopted a 'Mission as intercultural theology' discourse is the Akrofi Christaller Institute for the Study of Theology, Mission, and Culture, located in Akropong, Ghana. But we want to focus more closely on the Malawi Assemblies of God University (MAGU) in Malawi, which offers a degree in Intercultural Studies.

The MAGU started out in the mid-1990s as a missions training school under the guidance of Lazarus Chakwera, who is currently the President of the Republic of Malawi. It began as the Assemblies of God School of Theology (AGST), with funding from the United States of America (USA) Assemblies of God. AGST had a mission focus right from the beginning. Chakwera had been involved in the missions work of the Africa Assemblies of God council since the 1980s. He was also, in the late 1990s, studying for his Doctor of Ministry (DMin) degree at the Trinity International University at Deerfield, Illinois, in the USA. For his DMin research project (completed in 2000), he developed a mobile mission school 'to be utilized as a means of mobilizing, training, and sending missions workers from Malawi and nearby countries to unreached peoples' in Africa and beyond (Chakwera 2000). That mission school was called The Eleventh Hour Institute (EHI). Once established, it became the focal point of the missionary ethos of the AGST, with the purpose of empowering and enabling lay Assemblies of God members (and their congregations) to engage in mission in other parts of Africa. Thus, right from its very early days, AGST had a mission focus, with the Eleventh Hours Institute being its school of missions. For almost 15 years, EHI, with the help of AGST, sent missionaries from Malawi to several other African countries (Swaziland, South Africa, Sudan, and others) as well as to France, the United Kingdom, and the USA.

In 2013, AGST received a government charter to become the Malawi Assemblies of God University. Its stated purpose is to 'provide leaders with quality, innovative, transformational and Spirit-empowered tertiary education with global relevance based on biblical principles'.[16] By becoming the MAGU, the AGST needed to adopt a liberal arts approach, while remaining a Christian university. The MAGU leaders describe it as

---

[16] Malawi Assemblies of God University (MAGU), 2018a, *Vision, Mission, Core Values*, viewed 31 July 2022, from https://magu.ac.mw/vision-mission-core-values/.

an academic community dedicated to creating and communicating knowledge, MAGUniversity provides excellent undergraduate, graduate and professional education in the Christian tradition for the glory of God and the well-being of humankind.[17]

Its vision is to be 'a world-class university, culturally relevant, offering transformational education and quality leadership that is applicable locally and globally'.[18] With the shift to becoming a university, the mission focus that the EHI brought to the AGST seems to have been lost, since they have replaced Missiology with 'Intercultural Studies'. And yet their master's programme in Intercultural Studies[19] teaches regular missiology courses in a Pentecostal mode. Courses covered include: History of the Expansion of Christianity; Paradigms for Spirit-Empowered Missions; Pentecostal Response to Islam and Animism; Trends and Issues in Missions; Missions from the Two-Thirds World; and Strategies for Cross-cultural Ministries. This is an interesting collection of modules, but their titles do not seem to reflect an academic change of direction. It seems as if Intercultural Studies is just a new name for an existing programme in Pentecostal Mission Studies, without any theological change of emphasis. It is also strange, if not offensive, for an African university to use the term 'animism' for a course on African religion.

These trends at African institutions of higher education are still evolving. It will be important to keep track of them and to enter into dialogue on them at an Africa-wide level.

University of Stellenbosch

The University of Stellenbosch arose out of a theological seminary of the Dutch Reformed Church (DRC), which was established in 1859. After the addition of an Arts department, it became Victoria College in 1886 and it got official state recognition as the University of Stellenbosch in 1918 (Coertzen 2009:9). In 1963 the Theological Seminary formally became the Faculty of Theology of the university. In other words, theological teaching has had a long and distinguished history at

---

[17] Malawi Assemblies of God University (MAGU), 2018a, *Vision, Mission, Core Values*, viewed 31 July 2022, from https://magu.ac.mw/vision-mission-core-values/.

[18] Malawi Assemblies of God University (MAGU), 2018a, *Vision, Mission, Core Values*, viewed 31 July 2022, from https://magu.ac.mw/vision-mission-core-values/.

[19] Malawi Assemblies of God University (MAGU), 2018b, *MA. Inter-cultural Studies*, viewed 31 July 2022, from https://magu.ac.mw/ma-inter-cultural-studies/.

Mission the "labour room" of theology

Stellenbosch. Courses in missiology were offered for the first time in 1914 and became firmly established since 1916 with the appointment of the well-known (and later highly controversial) Professor Johannes du Plessis (Olivier 2009:16), who published a number of influential books on mission history and mission theology (du Plessis 1911; 1912; 1929).

The ministry agenda of the DRC dominated the faculty from its inception in 1859 until around the 1990s, when other churches became significant partners too. As a result of DRC dominance, missiology was a marginal discipline in the Stellenbosch faculty, since most of the students were young white (Afrikaner) men who were preparing to become ministers in whites-only DRC congregations. The DRC judged that their students required a curriculum loaded with Greek, Hebrew, biblical studies, church history, dogmatics, and a large number of 'how to' (practical theology) courses to equip them for congregational ministry in the white community. The handful of students who 'wanted to become missionaries' did the few elective missiology subjects that were on offer. Bosch (1991:490) described the results as follows: 'Missiology became the theological institution's "department of foreign affairs", dealing with the exotic but at the same time peripheral'. That description certainly applied to Missiology's role in the Faculty of Theology at Stellenbosch University[20] during apartheid.

One symptom of that peripheral position of missiology under apartheid was the practice of Afrikaner Reformed churches to separate *evangelism* (which was what white Christians did among 'no-more-Christians' – fellow whites who had drifted away from the church) and *mission* (which is what white Christians did among 'not-yet-Christians' – primarily black people). In faculties of theology at Afrikaner universities, evangelism was taught as part of Practical Theology, while a separate department of 'Sendingwetenskap' (Science of Mission/Missiology) addressed issues of communicating the gospel outside the white community. Mission was what good white Christians did to (and for) black communities – and missiology equipped them to do that. Such an (implicitly racist) justification for a discipline of missiology cannot be justified – and has fortunately been abandoned.

The Faculty of Theology at Stellenbosch presently has a majority of black students, a significant number of black lecturers, new church partners (who recognise its degrees as part of their ministerial formation programme) and a redesigned curriculum (Combrink et al. 2009:33-51). For the purpose of our chapter, we pose the question: What position does missiology occupy in the curriculum today?

---

[20] The same can be said of the Faculties of Theology at the other Afrikaans-dominated universities (University of Pretoria, University of the Free State, Potchefstroom University of Christian Higher Education) before the 1990s.

At present, the Faculty of Theology at the University of Stellenbosch has a merged Department of Practical Theology and Missiology. Does such a merger represent a move to marginalise Missiology by absorbing it into Practical Theology? Sometimes such mergers are merely administrative in nature due to management pressure, in which case it has little effect on the functioning (and flourishing) of missiology. On the other hand, a merger could amount to marginalising and disempowering it.

Another way of looking at such a merger is to say that it is academically meaningful and necessary. Some theologians have argued that the two disciplines should merge, since their agendas in a post-apartheid and postcolonial era overlap to such an extent that it is no longer academically meaningful to keep them apart. In conversations some colleagues draw a parallel with the stereotypical relationship between sociology (studying the West) and cultural anthropology (studying the Rest). They suggest that Practical Theology has traditionally studied ministry in the West and Missiology ministry among the Rest, and that a decolonising of theology makes such a distinction redundant.

There is an element of truth in this view, but it does not present the whole picture. It may help to return to the evangelism/mission distinction mentioned above. One of the most important influences that David Bosch had in the DRC community in South Africa was to undercut that way of distinguishing between evangelism and mission. In *Witness to the World* (Bosch 1980:11-20), he contended that we should not see these terms as synonymous, nor distinguish them in terms of geography (near/far) or in terms of recipients (no more/not yet, as in the DRC tradition), but rather view mission as the wider (encompassing) concept, which includes evangelism (and much else besides). In other words, the reason why missiology should play a role in a theological curriculum is not because it emphasises particular groups of people outside 'normal' or dominant Christianity, but because it brings to the agenda a number of crucially important dimensions of theology that are usually ignored or side-lined – and that are not always addressed by practical theology.

To return to Stellenbosch, the way in which the merged department introduces itself gives an indication of its overall focus:

> In the discipline group Practical Theology and Missiology we try to understand how the Word and acts of God take shape in the words and deeds of man (sic) in the world. We try to understand *what it means to be sent out by God to the world* where we live and work. How do we *cross the boundaries* of culture, race, class, gender, place and age to reach those in need? Theology is witness and words about God. When we see and hear God, God guides us to the needs of our neighbours. What are these needs? What causes these needs? How do we deal with them? How do we equip leaders,

members, congregations, to *become involved in God's mission to the world*? In the light of these questions, Practical Theology deals with the issues of church ministry, the life of faith communities in different contexts, and the *transformative actions within society* (development). The homiletical process of the church service embedded in liturgical rituals forms the meeting point between God and humankind. We also focus on spirituality development, pastoral care, *diaconal outreach, missional involvement, inculturation*, as well as contemporary youth questions (emphasis added).[21]

When one looks at the terms that reflect a missiological emphasis (which we have italicised in the quote above), it does not seem as if missiology is being absorbed or marginalised by practical theology, but (as we argue later) the real question is whether missiology has succeeded in helping the whole faculty (and all its programmes) to embody a mission focus. Without delving into such details, this is an opportune time to move from the survey of different universities to a more systematic reflection on the role of missiology in a theology curriculum.

The role of missiology in a theology curriculum

At this point we need to repeat that the preceding survey is far from exhaustive. We did not make any reference to Roman Catholic or Orthodox theological institutions on the continent. Neither did we survey the wide range of African missiological publications in French or Portuguese. Our focus has been on institutions shaped by Protestant, Evangelical, and Pentecostal theologies – and that only in a highly selective way. We also need to underline that our comments on the different institutions are not intended as value judgements; we have chosen these institutions only to serve as examples of the trends that we picked up in our investigation. We hope that this survey will stimulate further reflection on this theme among African missiologists, which would include refining our description of these trends and perhaps identifying others.

A separate department of missiology?

We do not argue merely for the continued existence of a discipline (or department) of missiology in a theology curriculum. Our main contention is that theology has an 'innate missionary dimension', which means that all theological disciplines are

---

[21] Stellenbosch University, n.d., *Practical Theology and Missiology (PTM)*, viewed 31 July 2022, from http://www.sun.ac.za/english/faculty/theology/Pages/Practical-Theology---Missiology.aspx

expected to 'incorporate the missionary dimension into the entire field of theology' (Bosch 1991:492). Put in other words, 'Just as an unmissionary church is not a church, a theology that is not missiological ... is not theology, certainly not Christian theology' (Duraisingh, quoted in Ott 2001:208). The issue is not 'the integration of missiology *for the sake of missiology* (to satisfy the guild of missiologists); it is the recovery of the missionary dimension of theology *for the sake of theology*' (Ott 2001:208, emphasis added).

In other words, the primary responsibility of missiology is to help a theological curriculum to affirm that the church is 'missionary by its very nature' because it is not God's church that has a mission but God's mission that has a church – and that is much wider than the church (Bosch 1991:493). The fundamental calling of a theology curriculum is to inform and equip future church leaders to embody this community-directed 'sentness' and ex-centric nature of the Christian movement.

To make certain that this proposal does not suggest a takeover by missiology, the distinction between missionary *dimension* and *intention* is necessary (Bosch 1980:199; 1991:494-496). Every act of the Christian life and ministry has a mission dimension but not everything has a mission intention. Likewise, every course in a theology curriculum will have a mission dimension, even though it does not have an explicit mission intention. In this way, God's mission provides the underlying unity and logic of the curriculum, while at the same time respecting the diversity of ministries within it: 'Dimension and intention should be dynamically interrelated. The one nurtures and stimulates the other' (Bosch 1980:200).

Andrew Walls (1997:18) used the metaphor of a map to illustrate how a theological curriculum guides a church to navigate its way. And he suggested that the whole 'map' of (traditional Western) theology needs to be redrawn:

> Conventional theological education too often employs pre-Columbian maps of the church. Everyone is aware, of course, that there is a New World, that there are Christians – perhaps many Christians – beyond the Western world. But the pre-Columbian theological map that they work with prevents their giving them theological space. The map no longer reflects reality. It is little use to draw new insets to put in its corners; it will have to be thrown away. And mission studies are essential for the redrawing of the theological map (Walls 1997:18).

When Andrew Walls wrote these words 24 years ago, he was addressing theological curricula in the Global North, but the question is whether his critique does not also apply to theological curricula in Africa. Do we add small 'insets' to the corners of our curricular map – to deal with 'Third World Theologies', economic justice, eco-theology, the challenge of other faiths, decoloniality or the Fourth Industrial Revolution – while the map remains dominated by the same huge 'continents' (the sacrosanct 'fourfold pattern') of Scripture, History, Doctrine and Ministry, taught in the same way as before?

In arguing for a redrawing of the curricular map, Walls (1997:18f) went so far as to call the process a 'holy subversion', in which missiology would 'subvert the other disciplines, irritate them, force them into new channels'. In spite of his radical language, Walls was not suggesting a power game among theological disciplines but a reformation of the whole curriculum. His two main emphases were that theology in the Global North had to learn from missiology how to deal with the challenge of other religions and of 'modern Western society', which he described as 'one of the great non-Christian cultures of the world'. His point was that theology in the Global North was still being done as if living in a 'pre-Columbian' Christian society, whereas it should learn from missiologists – and from Christians in the Global South – who have grappled for centuries with living as a minority in non-Christian cultures and have 'gradually learned something of the processes of comprehending, penetrating, exploring, and translating *within* them' (Walls 1997:19, emphasis added). The question facing us now is: Are the curricula of theological institutions across Africa replicating and perpetuating the 'pre-Columbian' curricular structures of the Global North, which is often expressed by the marginalisation of missiology, or have we succeeded in adequately reforming and decolonising our curricula?

Bosch (1991:496) also used strong language to describe the challenging role of missiology within theology, calling it to be a *theologia viatorum* (a journeying theology):

> In this role, missiology acts as a gadfly in the house of theology, creating unrest and resisting complacency, opposing every ecclesiastical impulse to self-preservation, every desire to stay what we are, every inclination toward provincialism and parochialism, every fragmentation of humanity into regional or ideological blocs, every exploitation of some sectors of humanity by the powerful, every religious, ideological, or cultural imperialism, and every exaltation of the self-sufficiency of the individual over other people or over other parts of creation.

Such an 'integration' of key missiological concerns into every other theological discipline – and into the theological curriculum as a whole – would make the existence of a separate *department* of missiology theoretically unnecessary (Bosch

1991:494). Experience has shown, however, that the pressure to produce specialised research publications in their respective fields often prevents colleagues in other theological disciplines from collaborating in a shared theological curriculum for which mission provides the underlying, unifying and dynamising logic. For that reason, the existence of a separate department (or discipline group) of missiologists remains necessary, to keep on playing the 'gadfly' role (Bosch 1991:492), but without arrogance or superiority: 'Missiology's task, in free partnership with other disciplines, is to highlight theology's reference to the world' (Bosch 1991:494). The task of missiologists is to serve their colleagues (and students) by constantly reminding them that 'The whole world is a mission field' and that theology is everywhere practised in a missionary situation, so that every theological discipline should empower people for participation in God's mission.

Responding to challenges

The strong language used by Walls and Bosch to describe the role of missiology could become counterproductive if it causes missiologists to overestimate their importance and to start playing power games. It is therefore essential that missiology takes careful note of the challenges that the developments surveyed in the first part of the chapter present to its existence and function.

Religious Studies approaches

The academic discipline of Religious Studies challenges missiology (and all of theology) to justify its presence in a public university, where government subsidies sustain the programmes. To respond to this challenge, one needs to counter the widespread perception that missiology amounts to nothing more than 'training Christians to convert others and plant churches'. Courses in mission studies at public universities need to adopt an inclusive understanding of mission, as proposed by Bosch, which means that evangelism and church planting are only two dimensions of a much wider agenda of transformation. Such courses should also exhibit a critical-creative approach to each of the mission dimensions, which means that past and present practices are exposed to critical scrutiny. That scrutiny should respond firstly to the experiences of those who were the 'recipients' of mission and, together with them, reflect on more constructive ways to embody it. In other words, missiology cannot consist of 'how to' training courses in any dimension of mission. At the same time, it must be clear to any observer that the purpose of such courses is to nurture agents of transformation in society who are equipped and committed to serve transformation for the common good of society.

Another argument for missiology at a public university is that Christian mission is happening all the time in African communities, often quite irresponsibly and sometimes in shocking ways.[22] In such a context it is in the public interest that Christian missiologists are appointed at public universities to reflect on those aberrations and give concrete guidance on how they can be prevented in future. But then it must be clear that the missiology programmes are actually geared towards those public goals.[23]

In conclusion, it could also be pointed out that no university programme is presented in an 'objective' or unbiased way. It is not only missiology that 'has a mission'. The values inculcated in students by disciplines like Economics, Education and Law are not neutral; they instil and promote particular values and practices that have definite ideological ramifications, sometimes unacknowledged. The teaching of missiology at a public university is no different, but it is essential for missiologists to admit their biases and submit them to public scrutiny in the community of scholars that is a university – if they are to operate there with credibility.

African agency

One of the common features of the Religious Studies programmes we have surveyed is their emphasis on studying religions in the African context, giving close attention to African religion and Islam, and foregrounding African agency. The agency of African innovators of change must be central to the curriculum: historically, in the writing of mission history, and creatively, in planning and mobilising people for new initiatives. In this regard, the strong emphasis of Religious Studies programmes on African religion and spirituality must be a key aspect of the decolonising thrust of mission studies in Africa. The accusation that Christian mission in Africa has 'destroyed African cultures' is at least partly true – and should therefore be addressed head-on. The stress on African agency should, however, not cast a shadow over the

---

[22] In South African some disturbing abuses have taken place in mushrooming charismatic churches in poor African communities, which were widely reported in the media and have raised national concern. The Commission for Cultural, Religious and Linguistic Rights (CRL), established in terms of Article 9 of the South African Constitution, conducted a detailed investigation into such abuses and released a report (CRL 2017) which suggested that a peer review structure to ensure proper regulation of religious institutions (under the supervision of the CRL Commission) should be established, so that future abuses can be avoided (CRL 2017:42).

[23] A good example of such a response by a South African missiologist is the recent book by Prof M.S. Kgatle (2021), in which he examines the abuses occurring in 'new prophetic' Pentecostal churches and exposes them as 'cultic tendencies' that are fundamentally alien to Pentecostalism.

divine initiative. The entire enterprise of mission must be seen theologically as the work of God (*missio Dei*) through the work of African agents: 'What is urgently needed in Africa is missiological training that will liberate Africans from perceiving themselves solely as recipients of mission ... [and] prepare African Christians to be responsible and full participants in global mission' (Tiénou 1997:95). He also stresses the need to nurture 'intellectual probity' and credibility among African church leaders to overcome 'the mediocrity of the intellectual formation of African clergy' (Mbembe, quoted in Tiénou 1997:96). To achieve that, he proposes a 'multidiscipline-based missiological curriculum' that includes African history, sociology, urban studies, political thought, African philosophy, Islamics, and African literature (Tiénou 1997:98).

At this point it is also crucial to mention the agency of African women in developing a new agenda for missiology – and therefore for theology. Phiri (2009:105) has spelled out the four major challenges taken up by the Circle of Concerned African Women Theologians in relation to theological education: to redefine the identity of African women theologians; to empower more women to study theology and be on permanent staff; to 'engender' theological education by ensuring the inclusion of African women's theology in curricula; and to collaborate with African male theologians. She concludes her paper as follows:

> We need to educate the churches and theological institutions locally and globally that the community of women and men should work together to decide on the type of theology that should be taught in the theological institutions. If indeed the church acknowledges that God gives gifts to both women and men for the common good of the church, then it needs to transform itself to support in word and action the theological education of both men and women. This requires the realization that according to the signs of our times theological education should no longer be seen as training soldiers of Christ to ward of heresy, but servants of Christ willing to build a community or women and men (Phiri 2009:117).

This has huge implications for missiology and theology in Africa. To decentre the male dominance that is prevalent within African agency in missiology and theology means building a community of women and men who are committed to serve the coming of the reign of God together. Since God's mission can only be carried out by all God's people, one of the key challenges for the future is to work for the full inclusion of African women's initiatives in mission and missiology.

Counteracting triumphalism

Religious Studies models also make us acutely aware of the danger of triumphalist approaches in mission, which amount to overestimating ourselves and disrespecting others. It means making mission a power game in which we are the winners and others the losers, instead of the Lordship of Christ being manifested to us and through us. The well-known statement of David Bosch (1991:489) is as relevant as ever:

> We ... are prepared to take risks, and are anticipating surprises as the Spirit guides us into fuller understanding. This is not opting for agnosticism, but for humility. It is, however, a bold humility—or a humble boldness. We know only in part, but we do know. And we believe that the faith we profess is both true and just, and should be proclaimed. We do this, however, not as judges or lawyers, but as witnesses; not as soldiers, but as envoys of peace; not as high-pressure salespersons, but as ambassadors of the Servant Lord.

The challenge for African agents of mission is to find creative and credible ways of embodying this delicate correlation between humility and boldness – to avoid both paralysing withdrawal and arrogant imposition. There are important theological dimensions to this challenge, but also issues of gender, culture, race, class, and spirituality. Triumphalism is more likely to develop in theology curricula that unfold in comfortable isolation from the study of other religions and from the presence of followers of those ways. Since mission always has to do with encounters – between Christians and adherents of other faiths, between women and men, rich and poor, black and white – courses in missiology should not only *prepare* students for such encounters but *expose* them to actual encounters as an essential part of the journey to learn mission. Walls (1997:20) aptly observed: 'Mission studies are not simply preparation for mission; mission studies are part of mission'.

One way of counteracting triumphalism, without sacrificing boldness, is to ensure that the respectful study of other religions as living and active agents of change and renewal in society are a part of theological curricula. If this is not the case, missiology should play its 'gadfly' role to make it happen. In order to achieve that, it is helpful to be taught the beliefs and practices of other religions by proponents of those religions themselves, rather than only through Christian interpreters. An important aspect of this is to explore the views that people of other faiths have of Christianity and to respond to those views – negative, positive, or indifferent – with repentance and introspection. To develop a credible approach to African mission, we need to grow in experiencing and embodying Christianity as an African religion among other African religions.

Private Christian universities

Our section on MAGU raised the issue of private Christian universities in Africa. Our focus has been on public universities, so we only referred in passing to the theological seminaries and colleges set up by denominations to train teachers, evangelists, catechists, and ministers/priests for their growing constituencies. We did not explore the teaching of missiology at those institutions, since it is our perception that missiology is not being side-lined or eclipsed in them.[24] It may be that their missiology courses are inadequate in other ways, but that is a discussion for another chapter. The focus of this chapter is on situations in which the right of existence or the unique contribution of missiology itself is under pressure.

However, one aspect does deserve comment here. In recent years, a large number of church seminaries in African countries have been transformed into private Christian universities, offering degrees in different fields of study. Such institutions do not experience the pressure of conforming to a 'secular' state constitution, since they do not receive government subsidies. Most of them are denominational in character (or at least in origin) and their very establishment expresses a strong sense of educational mission: not leaving higher education to the state but carving out a space for Christian witness and service in the academic terrain of postcolonial African societies.

Their establishment expresses a holistic approach to knowledge, recognising that all truth is God's truth and that the false dichotomy between 'spiritual' and 'secular' must be overcome, if a mature and sustainable African Christianity is to emerge in the 21st century. Andrew Walls (1997:20) stated this well: 'Let us not fear secular learning. In the service of the Kingdom there is no secular learning; it all belongs to the Redeemer of the world'.

Due to the absence of state subsidies and to the vast poverty in African communities, such universities will understandably be financially vulnerable, but they represent a significant new arena of Christian witness and service in postcolonial Africa. In relation to them, our first question should not be: What is the content of the missiology courses they offer? Instead, we should ask: What is the overall mission of such a private Christian university and its intended impact on society? This presents an important topic for ongoing research, since the number of these universities is increasing and they present huge opportunities for holistic Christian mission but also unique challenges and problems, on which missiologists should reflect.

---

24 If this perception is wrong, we trust that other researchers will correct it by doing the research and presenting the evidence.

Conclusion

God's mission is a liberating movement. God was in Christ, moving towards us, moving into a human body, moving into neighbourhoods and communities, to embody and share freedom, dignity and justice. Whenever the church becomes a static and status-conscious club for insiders, it betrays the intention of its Founder. The inherent other-directedness of the Jesus movement is well expressed by Gutiérrez (1973:205): 'To be converted is to know and experience the fact that, contrary to the laws of physics, we can stand straight, according to the Gospel, only when our center of gravity is outside ourselves'. It is the calling of missiology, as an academic discipline within a community of theological scholarship, to keep on reminding everyone of this.

References

Achebe, C., 1958, *Things fall apart*, Heinemann, London.

Andrews, E., 2009, 'Christian missions and colonial empires reconsidered: A black evangelist in West Africa, 1766-1816', *Journal of Church and State* 51(4), 663–64.

Beti, M., 1971, *The poor Christ of Bomba*, Heinemann, London.

Bosch, D.J., 1980. *Witness to the world. The Christian mission in theological perspective*, Marshall, Morgan & Scott, London.

Bosch, D.J., 1991, *Transforming mission. Paradigm shifts in theology of mission*, Orbis Books, Maryknoll.

Chakwera, L.M., 2000, 'The development of the Eleventh Hour Institute to be utilized as a means of mobilizing, training, and sending missions workers from Malawi and nearby countries to unreached peoples', PhD thesis, Trinity International University.

Coertzen, P., 2009, 'Die ontstaanskenmerke van die Teologiese Seminarium, 1814-1909', in P. Coertzen (ed.), *Teologie Stellenbosch 150+, Die verhaal van teologiese opleiding op Stellenbosch – die mense en die gebeure*, pp. 5-13, Bybelmedia, Parow.

Combrink, H.J. Bernard et al., 2009, 'Van Seminarium na Fakulteit Teologie: Besinnig en ingrypende veranderings', in P. Coertzen (ed.), *Teologie Stellenbosch 150+, Die verhaal van teologiese opleiding op Stellenbosch – die mense en die gebeure*, pp. 33-52, Bybelmedia, Parow.

Commission for Religious, Cultural and Linguistic Rights (CRL), 2017, *Report of the hearings on the commercialisation of religion and abuse of people's belief systems*, viewed 22 July 2022, from https://www.gov.za/sites/default/files/gcis_document/201708/report-commecializationofreligionandabuseofpeoplesbelievesystems.pdf.

Du Plessis, J., 1911, *A history of Christian missions in South Africa*, Longmans, Green & Co., London.

Du Plessis, J., 1912, *The evangel in South Africa*, Cape Times Ltd Printers, Cape Town.

Du Plessis, J., 1929, *The evangelisation of pagan Africa*, J.C. Juta, Cape Town, Johannesburg.

Gutiérrez, G., 1973, *A theology of liberation*, Orbis Books, Maryknoll.

Healey, J. (ed.), 2020, 'Tribute to John S. Mbiti (30 November 1931-6 October 2019)', *Proverbium* 37, 404-424.

Kgatle, M.S., 2021, *Pentecostalism and cultism in South Africa*, Palgrave Macmillan, Cham.

Kritzinger, J.N.J., 1988, 'Black Theology – Challenge to Mission', DTh thesis, University of South Africa.

Magara, E., 2009, 'Financing a public university: Strategic directions for Makerere University in Uganda', *Journal of Higher Education in Africa* 7(3), 61–86.

Makerere University, 2020, *Bachelor of Arts (Arts)*, viewed 30 June 2022, from https://courses.mak.ac.ug/programmes/bachelor-arts-arts.

Malawi Assemblies of God University (MAGU), 2018a, *Vision, Mission, Core Values*, viewed 31 July 2022, from https://magu.ac.mw/vision-mission-core-values/.

Malawi Assemblies of God University (MAGU), 2018b, *MA. Inter-cultural Studies*, viewed 31 July 2022, from https://magu.ac.mw/ma-inter-cultural-studies/.

Ngugi wa Thiong'o, 1965, *The river between*, Heinemann, London.

Niringiye, D.Z., 2015, *The church: God's pilgrim people*, InterVarsity Press, Downers Grove, IL.

Olivier, A.R., 2009, 'Die jare van die leerstryd, 1910-1935', in P. Coertzen (ed.), *Teologie Stellenbosch 150+, Die verhaal van teologiese opleiding op Stellenbosch – die mense en die gebeure*, pp. 15-21, Bybelmedia, Parow.

Omer-Cooper, J.D., (ed.), 1968, *The making of modern Africa: The growth of African civilization*, Vol. 2, Longman, New York.

Ott, B., 2001, *Beyond fragmentation. integrating mission and theological education. A critical assessment of some recent developments in evangelical theological education*, Regnum Press, Oxford.

Phiri, I.A., 2009, 'Major challenges for African women theologians in theological education', *International Review of Mission* 98(1), 105-119.

Sanneh, L.O., 1989, *Translating the message: The missionary impact on culture*, Orbis Books, Maryknoll.

Sicherman, C., 2002, 'Makerere and the beginnings of higher education for East Africans', *Ufahamu: A Journal of African Studies* 29(1), 91-120. Doi: 10.5070/F7291016563.

Stellenbosch University, n.d., *Practical Theology and Missiology (PTM)*, viewed 31 July 2022, from http://www.sun.ac.za/english/faculty/theology/Pages/Practical-Theology---Missiology.aspx.

Tiénou, T, 1997, 'The training of missiologists for an African context', in J.D. Woodberry, C. van Engen & E.J. Elliston (eds.), *Missiological education for the twenty-first century. The book, the circle, and the sandals. Essays in honor of Paul Pierson*, pp. 93-100, Wipf & Stock Publishers, Eugene, OR.

University of Cape Town (UCT), n.d., *Faculty of Humanities, Religious Studies*, viewed 1 July 2022, from http://www.religion.uct.ac.za/sites/default/files/image_tool/images/113/Final%20ReligiousStud%2023Apr%20final.pdf.

University of Ghana, n.d., *Department for the Study of Religions Courses for First Semester of 2020/2021 Academic Year, Bachelor of Arts (BA)*, viewed 1 July 2022, from https://www.ug.edu.gh/religions/sites/religions/files/u8/2020-2021%20First%20Semester%20Courses-BA.pdf.

University of Ghana, Department for the Study of Religions, 2022, *History of the Department*, viewed 1 July 2022, from https://www.ug.edu.gh/religions/about/brief_history

University of Malawi, 2022, *Department of Theology and Religious Studies*, viewed 22 July 2022, from https://www.unima.ac.mw/departments/theology-and-religious-studies.

Walls, A., 1997, 'Missiological education in historical perspective', in J.D. Woodberry, C. van Engen & E.J. Elliston (eds.), *Missiological education for the twenty-first century. The book, the circle, and the sandals. Essays in honor of Paul Pierson*, pp. 11-22, Wipf & Stock Publishers, Eugene, OR.

Zomba Theological College, 2018, *Zomba Theological College, Until we all reach unity in the faith*, viewed 31 July 2022, from http://www.zombatheological.org.

SECTION C

THE HOW OF MISSION:
MISSION AS/IN THE CONTEXT OF...

Chapter 9

Mission in an Urbanised Context. Cities: 'Wild Spaces Within a New Frontier'

Marinda van Niekerk

Introduction

In the process of understanding the challenge and opportunity that urbanisation presents to the church to be missional in the cities of South Africa in particular, and in the broader African context and world in general, we need to have a better understanding of urbanisation. In this chapter, the monsters lurking in city slums and streets are confronted, but then we also go in search of the wells of hidden treasures that make cities the wild spaces within a new frontier. The writer is convinced that cities are wild spaces that hold within themselves the capacity to be the new frontier of missions. If we get mission right in the city, we will get it right elsewhere. In this chapter guidelines are suggested to the church to develop and grow in her mission to build the kingdom of God in an urbanised context.

To begin, let us give attention to understanding the concepts of 'urbanisation' and 'missiology'.

What is meant by 'urbanisation'?

Perhaps two definitions will suffice here. 'Urbanisation' is defined by the Editors of the Encyclopaedia Britannica (2021) as the process by which large numbers of people become permanently concentrated in relatively small areas, forming cities. The United Nations Department of Economic and Social Affairs (UNDESA) further describes urbanisation as the gradual shift of relative populations from rural to urban areas (UNDESA 2014).

Relevant statistics taken from the document titled 'Cities in the World: A new perspective on urbanisation' (Organisation for Economic Co-operation and Development [OECD]/European Commission 2020) reveal that:

Mission in an Urbanised Context

- The population of people living in cities (more than 50 000 inhabitants) has shifted from 1975 where 1.5 billion people lived in cities (37%), to 3.5 billion people living in cities in 2015 (48%), with the projection of 5 billion people who will be living in cities in 2050 (55%). Sizes of cities are growing exponentially to accommodate this movement of people as projected in Figure 1 below.
- City density has increased immensely in the last 40 years. Average population density in low-income countries is four times higher than in high-income countries.
- The urban population in South Africa has grown from 47.9% 50 years ago to 67.8% in 2021 (Knoema, 2022).

The graph presented in Figure 1 below depicts the current as well as population growth of our cities, and indicates what the projections are for the next few years.

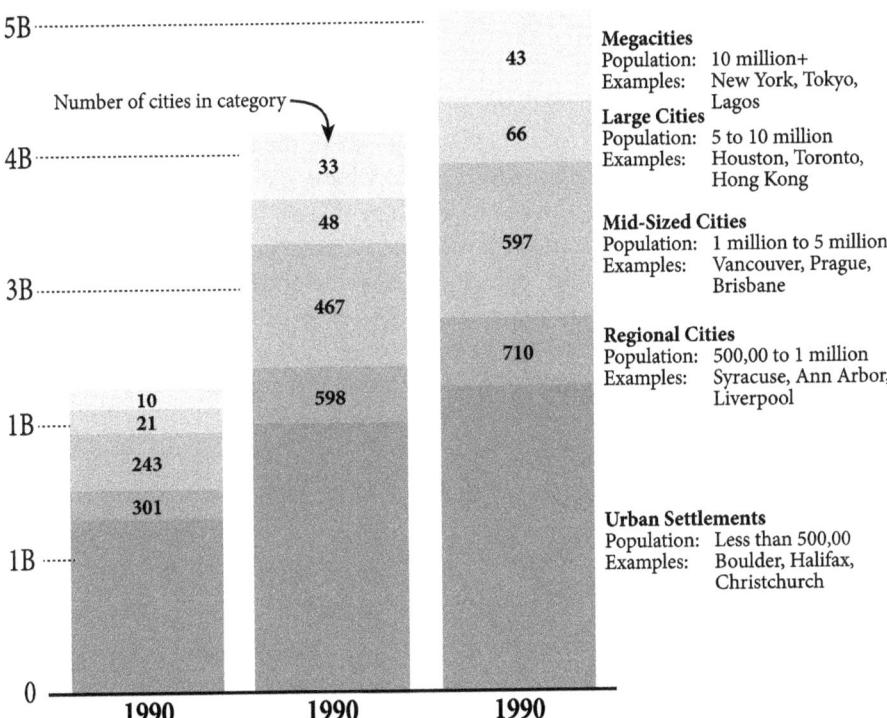

Figure 1: Global urban population, by size of city (Source: UNDESA:n.d.)

Mission the "labour room" of theology

What is meant by 'missiology' and the 'mission of the church'?

According to David Bosch (1991), the entire goal or intent of the Christian church lies in the missional heart of its existence. Bosch quotes Kasting (1969:127) who says, ›Mission ... was a fundamental expression of the life of the church. The beginnings of a missionary theology are therefore also the beginnings of Christian theology as such'.

Kravtsev (2012:8) presented a working definition that helps us in bringing missiology in context with urbanisation:

> Missiology is an academic discipline aimed at understanding and explaining the specifics of the church's missionary calling in light of the *missio Dei*. Being biblically based, it is historically informed, theologically balanced, and grounded in particular cultural contexts with the ultimate purpose of directing the practice of the Christian mission in its specific settings (italics in the original).

If we then want to talk about mission in an urban context, it should be all about the intent of the church to realise God's kingdom in the context of cities and to embrace the challenge to be church in a world where many people from different social classes come together. The way in which people are together in cities, should be influenced by the church and her theology – we must have a missional intent to be church in a way that establishes the principles of God's kingdom in the context of cities: the building of community, the political structures, the expression of human dignity through defending the rights of all people, with an emphasis on the poor and vulnerable. The mission of the church did not change over the years. Sills (2015) makes the point in his book, that the world and its challenges are fast changing, but our great commission always stays the same (Matt 28:18-20), namely, to share the love God has for the world in the most effective, modern, and wise ways needed.

Urbanisation and kingdom principles

Urbanisation and Kingdom principles: it grew from a garden and ended up in a city (or is it cities)... The story of the Bible starts in a garden and ends in a city. This is according to different writers through the years, but depicted beautifully in this Methodist hymn:

> *God has given us a book full of stories,*
> *which was made for his people of old,*
> *It begins with the tale of a garden,*
> *And ends with the city of gold.*
> (Maria Penstone 1933).

The role of cities in a biblical context is best described by Ian Paul (2017:304-319) in *The urban world and the first Christians*. He discusses the seven cities in the Book of Revelation but ends up describing the difference between the two metaphorical cities (Rome and Jerusalem) as metaphors for the space ruled by **human laws** and the city of Jerusalem, which represents **God's rule** with God's people on earth. He makes the point that disciples of Jesus will have their loyalty tested towards the two metaphorical rulers.

This provides the context to understand the shift that has taken place in understanding the choices the church and Christian believers are making up to today. The church is challenged to make a choice between serving the loyalties of cities, ruled by human design, or cities redefined as spaces that open new frontiers for mission to change the face of principalities and powers as Paul understood it. The church has her mission defined, namely, to build cities that are governed by kingdom principles, other than by rules of injustice and greed. When we consider the opportunity for being a missional church in an urban context, many issues come into play.

The call towards the urban church is reflected in several biblical stories, like the story of Babylon, the story of Jonah being called to minister to Nineveh (Jonah 1), and the stories of Paul and other apostles who ministered the gospel to people living in cities like Rome, Damascus, Antioch, Cyprus, and Cyrene.

The church in Antioch provides valuable insight into the challenges presented to the church even today. Similar issues are still being dealt with in the contemporary era, such as issues of overcoming cultural differences, racial issues, greed, idolatry, and power struggles. It also brought opportunities to develop a missional focus in the church: leadership development, compassion for the poor, and development of a missional strategy to take the gospel into the world (Greenway & Monsma 1989).

In an article J.J. Kritzinger (1995:201, italics in the original) addressed the issue of missiology and its intricate relationship with urbanisation, when he mentioned the following: 1). Missiology is concerned with the city *'because people are living there'*; 2). *'the city poses immense problems for people'* because countless people are suffering due to poverty, exploitation, etc.; and 3). *'cities represent the growing edge of the world'* meaning, the world comes to live in the city; this asks of the church to successfully build a meaningful, contributing church that influences the life of cities.

The challenge posed to modern-day churches is to have a strong enough theological foundation that can hold and carry the requirement of a missional intent that can help to build a society based on **kingdom principles**. This includes:

- Developing strong leaders who can live by their values in a world run by human laws.
- Having a true concern with justice that is strong enough to stand up to the greed-driven society in which the church should have influence.
- Helping to build and uphold governments and its leaders that will respect and uphold the value of people above power and money.
- Leaders living by a different code of integrity, accountability, and stewardship that contrasts to the societies we see around us.
- Justice for all people: the church should become safe spaces for people from all social sectors, age groups, cultures, religions, and identities (sexual or otherwise).
- A society that honours kingdom principles, and upholds basic respect for human life and human rights.
- Forming people who are 'better citizens' when they are outside of the church, than before: people who carry the need to build a society where there is mutual respect, and respect for God.

Monsters threatening the lives and livelihoods of city dwellers

This section lists some of the menaces, which I refer to as 'monsters', that are impacting on the lives of those living the city.

1. **Risks to children**

    In cities, children are exposed to a variety of risks. Children who travel alone are especially at risk of being taken (trafficked) and exploited by adults with ill intent. There is also the risk of children being lured into undesirable activities, such as criminality or substance abuse.

    Although these risks are not unique to the city, it is a matter of density and prevalence. If we consider that 90% of a child's brain develops from the age of 0–5 years, stunting is a significant risk for children who are undernourished and under-stimulated. This brings the issue of having access to quality childcare and education to the fore. If we take into account that according to Careers Portal[1]

---

[1] Careers Portal, n.d., viewed 22 May 2022, from www.careersportal.co.za

80% of Grade 4 learners in South Africa cannot understand what they read, a great catastrophe is heading our way. This heightens the crisis of education; in cities, access to quality education is a big need.

2. **Unemployment**
Currently South Africa has a 46.2% unemployment rate (under the expanded definition of unemployment), of which 66.5% is young people. Joblessness pushes families over the edge into poverty (Statistics South Africa [Stats SA] 2022). People from rural areas and other countries flock to the city with the dream to get a job. This exacerbates issues like homelessness, crime, and food-scarcity.

3. **Crime**
According to the Numbeo Crime Index of 2021, South Africa is ranked as the third most dangerous country to live in, in the world, with six cities under the 20 most dangerous cities in the world (Staff Writer, 2021). The highest crime categories are bribery and corruption. Women, especially those who often must travel alone or reach their work and homes by foot, are at greater risk of falling prey to physical attacks or rape.

On 18 Feb 2022, Minister Bheki Cele announced the latest crime statistics. According to Shange (2022), from 1 October 2021 until December 2021, 11 315 people were raped (of which 42 were men) and 2 069 people were sexually assaulted. South Africa still counts as the rape capital of the world. These crimes are committed within the boundaries of the cities of our country.

4. **Pollution**
According to a report by IQAir, 11 of Africa's most polluted cities are in South Africa (Mataranyika, 2021) mainly due to our high reliance on coal for energy. Cities are confronted with different forms of pollution: air, water, and noise. Issues of overcrowding and population density heightens these issues. Waste and waste processing are part of the challenges regarding pollution.

Stubbs (2022) says that South Africa produces more or less 122 million tons of waste per year, of which only 10% is recycled. Accordingly, 90% ends up in landfills that are nearing capacity all over South Africa. Another big issue is illegal dumping. We need to acknowledge that these are all based on old statistics. Latest numbers are not even available, which is a great concern. Waste and waste management is a monster waiting to devour health, and perpetuate global warming, food security, and many other issues. The fact that South Africa is one of the fastest urbanising countries in the world, we need to take this monster seriously going forward.

5. **Housing issues**
South Africa has about 2 700 informal settlements due to the lack of housing available in urban areas. A backlog of about two million houses is currently

experienced. According to the United Nations Human Settlements Programme, half of the world's seven billion people live in cities and one billion of those live in informal settlements. This is projected to increase to three billion by 2030. In Sub-Saharan Africa, 55% of urban dwellers live in slums (Mbanga 2020). In our experience of working in urban Tshwane, lack of proper housing can be the monster that devours health, social well-being, and family stability, and is the cause of other social ills.

6. **History: spatial development**

A lot has been written over the years about the affect apartheid laws had on spatial development and the resulting social crisis it caused to many, mostly black South Africans. The impact of being forced out of city-centres to outskirts and forming informal settlements (squatter camps) has been devastating on most levels.

People caught in poverty are up to today forced to travel long distances to work. This has an impact on family life (getting up incredibly early in the morning and coming home late at night). It impacts the risks taken in travelling and making use of public transport, which is often unsafe and unreliable. It puts the lives of especially women and children at risk. Sharing small spaces, such as in taxis, heightens the health risk of getting sick (e.g. contracting tuberculosis [TB], COVID-19, and other communicable diseases).

Although it has certain advantages to live in squatter camps, there are many disadvantages, such as overcrowding, high crime levels, low access to health care, long traveling distances, and risk of getting sick due to leaking roofs or low insulation.

7. **Political context causing lack of service delivery**

In July 2020, the highest incidence of service delivery protests (about eight a day) was experienced in South Africa. In August 2020 to January 2021, there were 900 protests held (Martin 2021), mostly service-delivery related.

In certain cities in the last few decades, unstable political conditions caused lack of service delivery in cities. There is a growing lack of servant leadership in government entities: good work ethics is becoming a scarce commodity (many examples exist like the Life Esidimeni scandal, Social Grants scandals, etc.)

8. **Food scarcity**

Especially during the hard lockdown period in 2020 due to the COVID-19 pandemic, the issue of food security for the most vulnerable people living in cities was brought to the fore. People who survived by living right on the edge of their means, suddenly were pushed under the breadline. Others who lived on the streets and made a living through hustling, lost their means to earn an income. People did not have access to a proper meal every day.

During the period of September – December 2020, 9.34 million people in South Africa (16% of the population analysed) faced high levels of acute food insecurity. In the projected period (January – March 2021), 11.8 million people (20% of the analysed population) were expected to be in crisis (Integrated Food Security Phase Classification [IPC] 2021). Children were deeply impacted by food scarcity. School feeding programmes were stopped. Young children who attended any form of day care were left without that basic food provision and care. This period emphasised the vulnerability of all poor communities regarding access to food. The smallest change in income or access to services, pushed communities over the edge.

9. **Access to healthcare for people who are poor**
Even though one of the strengths of cities is the easier access to services like health care, it becomes a liability regarding people who are poor and dependent on public services. Immigrants and refugees are even more vulnerable. Resourced people can buy all the services they need, but if you cannot afford private services, this becomes a great liability. People are queuing for long hours at public healthcare facilities. City facilities are overpopulated with little resources.

10. **Defragmented family lives**
As referred to previously, people living far from their core family structure become defragmented. The result is a lack of emotional and economic support. Men are separated from their partners and children. Children are sometimes sent to extended family in rural areas. Children are left in the care of untrained or ill-equipped caregivers who put them in harm's way. Mothers work for long hours, often at two or more jobs, to make ends meet.

11. **Migration and refugees**
Certain cities are the centre where refugees and legal and undocumented immigrants gather. Cities are known to be spaces where people can move to from impoverished rural areas to spaces where jobs are more readily available. In these cities, refugees and immigrants meet and find living spaces, still in their countries of origin, e.g. China Town, Little Amsterdam, etc. Movements are launched to mobilise local people against foreigners, mostly out of fear that the few job opportunities will be taken away by foreign nationals. People have lost their lives in recent years due to xenophobic attacks. Groups like Operation Dudula are not helping the situation.

12. **Overcrowding**
The sad reality of many people flocking to cities to find better job opportunities is that they are disillusioned. They end up in shanty towns where people are forced to live in adverse conditions that are unhygienic and overcrowded. This creates breeding grounds for social ills, health risks and high crime.

Wells of hidden treasures

Cities holds the capacity to bring hope, knowledge, access to care and capacity for growth to all humanity – if cultivated in the right way. The richness of diverse opportunities that cities bring, can provide a platform to design a 'Jerusalem' where all people can 'belong and thrive'.[2] Cities hold the treasures that need to be explored and redefined to create these spaces where everyone belongs and thrives.

1. **The prophets speak through art and music**

   The beauty of cities is that it becomes the centre stage for the artists who play the role of social prophets, to voice/paint/dance their stories and protests. Often the poets and artists are the ones who address social issues in a visual way. Someone like the well-known street artist Banksy, is a good example. His art brings political and social issues to the front. He boldly critiques social injustice and political misuse. There are countless other examples, but this provides a snapshot.

2007-08
Mona Lisa Bazooka
"In this work, Banksy plays upon one of the world's most famous paintings, The Mona Lisa (1503-4). Although in his piece, the female protagonist wears a headset while aiming a rocket launcher in his typical black and white stencil style. The piece first appeared in the Soho district of West "London. https://www.theartstory.org/artist/banksy/

Figure 2: **Mona Lisa Bazooka** (Source: The Art Story Foundation 2007)

2. **Transport and infrastructure**

   Cities provide great access to roads, buildings, gardens, water, sanitation, electricity, and healthcare services. It becomes the centre where all people flock to. Hospitals and clinics are well represented in cities, compared to in vast rural areas. Cities are the hubs of connectedness for railways and roads. Money is available to maintain infrastructure critical for any country to make economic growth possible (moving export goods to harbours, fresh produce to city centres, etc.).

---

[2] Participate. Envision. Navigate. (PEN), n.d., viewed 21 May 2022, from https://www.pen.org.za/

3. **Economic activity**
The dream of finding a job brings many migrating communities, refugees, and young people desperate for work to the cities. Cities form the hub for economic opportunity. In South Africa, the informal business sector plays a crucial role in job creation. A third of all jobs in South Africa are within the informal sector.

4. **Newly defined sense of community**
Even though people tend to stick to the known, e.g. staying in ethnically defined groups in specific areas, cities provide great spaces for people from different social and ethnic backgrounds to make new friends and find a renewed sense of belonging.

5. **Networks**
One of the hidden treasures that cities provide is access to networks: friend circles, church networks, ecumenical networks, economic connections, business opportunities provided through new connections, sports, music, art – the spaces created to build supportive networks are endless.

6. **Communication centres**
Cities provide spaces for people to come together for big sports events, for music festivals, church meetings, conferences, and shows, to mention a few examples. Printed communication like newspapers and magazines are produced in cities. TV stations and other broadcasting hubs are mostly situated in cities.

7. **Centres for learning and training**
Cities are the wells of knowledge. Universities and training colleges are mostly situated in city spaces. Skills development hubs and informal businesses flourish in the city spaces.

8. **Technology**
Technology and access to the Internet is centred in city spaces. This provides social and economic platforms to start new businesses, to build communities of care, to build social platforms for lovers to meet, for interest groups to find each other, for knowledge to be shared and trades to be taught.

9. **General well-being**
Regarding the general well-being of people living in cities, evidence from 111 countries (Gallop World Poll in OECD/European Commission 2020) shows that city residents are more satisfied with their lives than people from rural areas. This trend explains why people continue to be attracted to cities, which further drives urbanisation. In terms of general well-being, according OECD/European Commission (2020), the percentage of people who are satisfied with their lives is reflected in the following: in rural areas 16%; in towns and semi-dense areas 17%; and in cities 19%.

10. **Health**
    People living in cities are on average 6% healthier than people living in rural areas due to better access to health services (OECD/European Commission 2020).

Guidelines for local urban churches to establish kingdom principles

The opportunity cities bring to the local church, to embrace their mission as a church, is very real. The missional church in an urban context, is the church that should be relevant in the city. In that it should be a space and place of hope and courage; where people can meet and become a loving, caring community; where people mobilise to be active in the fight against injustice; and where people who are poor or marginalised are welcomed and supported. The urban church is a church that understands the kingdom principles and need to build a society where every person who is lonely, destitute or poor, can be received with love, kindness and mercy. Church is the place where people learn how to have a good relationship with people from different cultural, social, or political standings. Here, we create wild spaces for the kingdom of God to flourish and to embrace the new frontier for mission.

Practical pathways to build a missional church in an urban context

This section provides several suggestions on how to build a missional church in an urban context.

1. **Understanding the context: Mapping your environment**
   For any church in any context to have an influence and be impactful in her community, leaders must have a clear understanding of their context. The method of mapping has been developed and refined in the urban context by Rev. P.F. Smit working in the urban context of Gauteng. He and others have developed the method to move into a community with the purpose to get to understand the 'lay of the land'. In this context, mapping means that you have a structured plan to intentionally identify the following important points of interest:

   Leaders in the community
   – pimps, drug lords, church leaders, municipal leaders, community leaders.

   Schools and Early Childhood Development (ECD) centres
   – primary schools, secondary schools, or any day care centres or spaces

   Spaza shops or any other shops

   Gathering hotspots
   – trees, shebeens, clubs

   Information sharing spaces
   – a specific space where notices are shared and gossip exchanged

Transport routes
- taxi ranks, train, or bus stops

Danger zones
- drug hotspots, crime hotspots, open fields

Child facilities
- parks, streets where children play

Service delivery spaces
- municipal offices, police stations, post office, churches

With this information, understanding and insight into the community, its people and movement patterns are formed. This again provides tools to develop engagement strategies. Respect and humbleness are the building blocks for any community engagement strategy.

2. **Establish networks and partnerships: Connect with local government and community leaders**

   For a church and her leaders to be missional in an urban context, networks and partnerships are key. Community leaders are critical to get to know and to win their trust. This includes leaders from other churches, political leaders, police or councillors, people who carry influence in their communities like doctors, teachers, drug dealers, pimps, or any other influencers. With insight and goodwill of the local leadership, a congregation can play a meaningful role in building trust and earning respect in the community. Partnerships that are mutually beneficial can be a game changer in contexts of disasters or any crisis a community may experience. There are quite good examples of this: KwaZulu Natal experienced countless crises. During these times, churches, and community organisations formed the backbone of the disaster response initiatives. Organisations like the Red Cross, Doctors without Borders, Gift of the Givers, and many church-based initiatives combined with the governmental response, made a stark difference to the lives of people on the ground.

3. **Resources and resource sharing**

   It is important to plot the resources in the broader community. Part of the mapping process will be to understand who the people are that can unlock resources in your church and community. Churches who understand their missional goal, will know that they are a great resource to any community and must live in a way that they will be missed if they are not there anymore. People in distress must know what support they can expect from their local church and how to access any form of help needed.

4. **Embrace diversity**
   One of the identified risks of urbanisation can also become a huge strength, namely diversity. If a local congregation can get it right to manage diversity well (especially in a South African context), it can become a huge strength. The various forms of diversity are indispensable: Diversity in people groups, racial diversity, interest and skills diversity, and diversity in welcoming people from different social backgrounds. All of this is complex and requires wisdom and intentional planning. Managed with care, diversity can become a church's greatest asset. An approach of healthy conflict resolution is immensely helpful. Ways can be developed to engage difficult issues. If leaders can develop a way of dealing with hard issues in a direct and respectful way, it will be beneficial to make the biggest impact. Core groups to discuss different issues, can be formed. Learning communities comprised of diverse individuals with differing viewpoints can be helped to engage each other. There are many tools and courses available to help leaders in this process.

5. **Local church as the epicentre of community**
   True community is the key to authentic change and transformation. To create spaces where all people feel they are valued and can contribute in a meaningful way, is the secret key to developing a true sense of community. If people – whether old or young; black, white or brown; gay or straight; good or bad – are all equally welcomed, growth will occur, and change will take place. In building community, people get to know and understand each other's needs. Prayer and physical support groups become increasingly important. Interest groups help to serve each other and the community, e.g. business minded people, or people who share interests like cooking, painting, making music, exercising, or adventure. Teaching groups or groups for learning new skills, e.g. how to read the Bible, can be very stimulating for growth. The method of contextual Bible reading is a non-confrontational method that helps people from different knowledge levels or social backgrounds to meet each other in a safe, neutral, and welcoming space. Being the epicentre for community, includes being accessible for families in all its possible definitions. Paul first helped us to see the benefit in a family centred approach for urban ministry. Households were more extended, but often formed the base of gatherings where faith was shared and grown (Acts 16:15; Gal 6:10). People with young children, with teenagers, with grandparents in their homes, are all interest groups with specific needs. This ought to be accommodated.

6. **Power of social media and communication**
   Having confirmed that true community is the key to building a kingdom principled missional church and society, good communication skills and the ability to meet your people where they are, are critical. This includes

communicating in a fast and effective way. Social media platforms are one of these tools at the disposal of the church. As a result of the mapping exercise, leaders should learn how to best communicate in their community. In the streets of Sunnyside in Tshwane, there is a park with a specific tree where all important notices are put up. Every church should get to know and understand the best communication channels for their different social and people groups. Social media platforms, like Instagram, are an effective way to communicate to certain groups of young people. Older people might prefer paper-based communication or Facebook. Effective, simple, and clear communication is an important key to a successful ministry.

7. **Express through art, music, dance, architecture**
The growing of a culture of care and communication helps a church to engage her members and meet them where they are. Another language of urban communities is the language of art and music. To convert spaces of grime, pain, and horror into spaces of beauty and healing, is a powerful skill that needs to be enhanced and embraced by the city church. Through art, dance and music, the message of the kingdom of God can be communicated in the most powerful ways. Not the languages of condemnation that the church has become fluent in over the ages, but the language of beauty, healing, and growth. Architecture plays into this space. Converted spaces become spaces for community and engagement. In these spaces people learn to share and to care for one another. Traditional church spaces are not the only way to receive urbanised people. Spaces like sports fields, school halls or sitting rooms, can be very effective as well. Appreciation and celebration are expressed best in song, dance, and the creation of healing spaces.

8. **Ecological responsibility**
The church should be the entity that leads the world in being responsible for our natural resources. The earth is our gift that should be treasured and protected. All of God's children share this responsibility. Recycling and repurposing waste is a key solution that should be developed, especially in the urban environment. The risk pollution holds to all the earth, brings the value of stewardship to the fore. The church is co-responsible to care for the earth. It should be part of our missional calling to protect God's creation. Recycling initiatives are spearheaded by certain churches like the Dutch Reformed Church Stella Street in Pretoria. They are taking the initiative in guiding other congregations in how to do recycling in a practical and sustainable way.[3]

---

[3] Cf. Stellastraat, n.d., viewed 21 May 2022, from www.stellastraat.co.za

9. **Advocative responsibility**

Most Christian leaders do not see that they have a role to play in the arena of politics. If we consider this biblically, the church has always been in the centre of the political arena. Where there is injustice, the church has a role and a responsibility. All Christian leaders who are called to engage with injustice were encountered in their sphere of influence. Issues of injustice in our South African context can sometimes become overwhelming. There are so many forms of injustice presenting on so many levels. In our own churches, we must confront every form of injustice that creeps in. There are countless examples of people who are discriminated against for their gender, their race, or their sexual orientation. People who are poor, are exploited by people who are rich, even in our own churches. The power games played by most leaders within the church needs to be confronted and dealt with. This emphasises the need within the local church for strong mentorship programmes for young leaders. If we intentionally grow leaders who are equipped to engage in a responsible way with issues of injustice in the public arena, we are contributing to building a just society.

The church has an opportunity to engage with government on the implementation of basic human rights for all people. As already referred to, a willingness is required from the local church to engage in the political arena, especially with regards to addressing issues of injustice. This is even more evident when it comes to engaging local and\or provincial government structures to ensure that the basic rights of people (especially the poor and the vulnerable) are protected and respected.

10. **Caring for the poor, but understanding community development versus charity**

Part of our core missional response in the urban context is the fight against the injustice caused by poverty. In South Africa, most people who are caught in the cycle of poverty are stuck there because of apartheid history. Over decades a large number of black people have fallen for the lies that they are not good enough or worthy. Many white people have fallen for the lies that they are better and deserve more than people of other races. Both these lies should be confronted, and the church is uniquely positioned to engage in these conversations. This brings the issue of community development to the forefront. Previously disadvantaged areas and groups of people should be assisted to find their own strengths and supported to break out of the chains of history that have a hold over people. The theory of community development should be embraced. There will always be a place for charity work and mercy support, but that can never become the strategy of the church to engage the impact of poverty in communities. People and communities must be guided to find their inner strength to break away from the poverty mindset and the entitlement attitude that sometimes comes with it. True community development helps communities to take ownership of their own development and empowers them to be able to say: 'We did it ourselves!'

Conclusion

The aim of this chapter is to provide enough encouragement and stimulation to engage the wild spaces cities provide to conquer the cities as a new frontier for missions. Time was spent on understanding the monsters that are meant to overwhelm the church in her quest, but also to go in search of the wells of treasures cities hold to bring a fresh approach to her missional goals. May our churches flourish on this journey.

References

Bosch, D.J., 1991, *Transforming mission: Paradigm shifts in theology of mission*, Maryknoll, New York, Orbis Books.

Greenway, R.S., & Monsma, T.M., 1989, *Cities: Missions' new frontier*, Baker House Company, USA.

Integrated Food Security Phase Classification (IPC), 2021, *South Africa: Acute Food Insecurity Situation September - December 2020 and Projection for January - March 2021*, viewed 1 May 2022, from https://www.ipcinfo.org/ipc-country-analysis/details-map/en/c/1153024/

Knoema, 2022, *South Africa - Urban population as a share of total population*, viewed 13 April 2022, from https://knoema.com/atlas/South-Africa/Urban-population.

Kravtsev, A., 2012, 'What is missiology?' Research paper, Trinity Evangelical Divinity School.

Kritzinger, J.J., 1995, 'Missiology and the challenge of urbanisation in South Africa', *Missionalia* 23(2), 201-215.

Martin, G., 2021, '900 service delivery protests in South Africa over six months', *DefenceWeb*, viewed 26 April 2020, from https://www.defenceweb.co.za/featured/900-service-delivery-protests-in-south-africa-over-six-months/

Mataranyika, M., 2021, '11 out of Africa's 15 most polluted cities are all in South Africa - Report', *News24*, Nov 24.

Mbanga, S., 2020, 'Policy exists, but shacklands spring up', *Mail and Guardian*, June 29.

Organisation for Economic Co-operation and Development [OECD]/European Commission, 2020, *Cities in the world: A new perspective on urbanisation*, OECD

Urban Studies, OECD Publishing, Paris. https://www.oecd.org/publications/cities-in-the-world-d0efcbda-en.htm

OECD/European Commission (2020), Cities in the World: A New Perspective on Urbanisation, OECD Urban Studies, OECD Publishing, Paris, https://doi.org/10.1787/d0efcbda-en.

Pentsone, M.M., 1933, *God has given us a Book full of Stories*, viewed 14 April 2022, from https://hymnary.org/hymn/Meth1933/857

Shange, N., 2022, 'CRIME STATS | Dozens of men raped between October and December 2021', *Sowetan Live*, February 18.

Sills, D.M., 2015, *Changing world, unchanging mission*, IVP Books, Illinois.

Staff Writer, 2021, 'The most dangerous cities in South Africa', Bussinesstech, 20 January 20.

Statistics South Africa (StatsSA), Media release 29 March 2022, viewed 30 April 2022, from http://www.statssa.gov.za/publications/P0211/Media%20release%20QLFS%20Q4%202021.pdf

Stubbs, K., 2022, 'State of the South African waste industry', *Infrastructure News*, March 10, viewed 1 May, from https://infrastructurenews.co.za/2022/03/10/state-of-the-south-african-waste-industry/

The Art Story Foundation, 2007, *Artists: Bansky*, viewed 21 April 2022, from https://www.theartstory.org/artist/banksy/

The Editors of Encyclopaedia Britannica, 2021, Urbanisation, viewed 26 April 2022, from https://www.britannica.com/topic/urbanization.

United Nations: Department of Economic and Social Affairs (UNDESA), n.d., *World Urbanization Prospects 2018*, viewed 15 April 2022, from https://population.un.org/wup/

United Nations Department of Economic and Social Affairs (UNDESA), 2014, *World urbanization prospects: The 2014 revision*, viewed 23 April 2022, from https://population.un.org/wup/Publications/Files/WUP2014-Highlights.pdf

Walton, S., Trebilco, P.R. & Gill, D.W.J., 2017, *The Urban world and the First Christians*, Wm.B. Eerdmans Publishing, Grand Rapids, Michigan.

Chapter 10

Not the Future Leaders of Tomorrow! Youth, *Missio Dei* and the Missiological Research Agenda in (South) Africa

Jacques W. Beukes

Introduction

Despite the so-called 'new South Africa' and its promises, notably after South Africa's first democratic election in 1994, South Africa has received no favourable commitments. A severe expectation issue has evolved into a horrific culture of violent crime and property devastation (Kgatla 2016:58). South Africa has become one of the world's most impoverished nations, with pervasive poverty, persistent unemployment, and substantial inequality (Ward 2012:215; cf. Kgatla 2016:58-59). Other experts[1] concur that South Africa has an ingrained culture of violence. Poverty, unemployment, and severe socio-economic disparities with a strong tendency for exclusion and marginalisation are enabling aspects of a violent culture. The current administration has had difficulty addressing these obstacles.

In addition, as in the rest of the world (cf. Columbia Global Policy Initiative 2014:6), contemporary South African society views youths as a vulnerable and marginalised group (Department of Social Development [DSD] 2013:30; cf. Beukes & Van der Westhuizen 2016:1; cf. Swart, Vähäkangas, Rabe & Leis-Peters 2022). The three most prominent contributory variables found are poverty, unemployment, and marginalisation. This viewpoint is reinforced by a recent book by Swart et al. (2022) as well as other study results and data on young people being excluded from school, employment, and/or tertiary education options (Department of Higher Education and Training 2017). Other social issues that marginalise South African

---

[1] Such as Pelser & De Kock 2000; Meth 2006; Van Niekerk, Tonsing, Seedat, Jacobs, Ratele & McClure 2015.

youths include a high drop-out rate in educational settings; inadequate skills development; inadequate youth work services; poor health; a high HIV and AIDS prevalence; a lack of access to sporting and cultural development opportunities; a lack of social cohesion and volunteerism; and disability and exclusion (Republic of South Africa [RSA] 2015:10–15; cf. Beukes & Van der Westhuizen 2018:1). The National Youth Policy (RSA 2015:3) identifies youth as a crucial resource for social development with the capacity to function as 'key agents of social change, economic expansion, and innovation'. Numerous data indicate that youth are the most vulnerable demographic in South Africa and the rest of the globe (cf. Aziz 2020; Swart 2018; Swartz & Nyamnjoh 2018; Beukes & Van der Westhuizen 2016; R. Nel 2014; 2015; DSD 2013). Additionally, prior research studies also demonstrate that youth sometimes feel marginalised, vulnerable, and alienated inside the church and specific religious organisations (Beukes & Van der Westhuizen 2016; Voas & Watt 2014; King 2012).

Having said that, Cloete (2015:2) is of the opinion that the youth should not be disregarded or ignored, but rather included in every aspect of the ministry. According to Nel (2000:78-79), this is non-negotiable since children and youth are the duty of the church. The issue emerges, though, when we operate with a distorted present view. This view on youth ministry stems mostly from the notion that youths are tomorrow's leaders and church members (Cloete 2015:2; Nel 2000:63). If the youth are simply recognised for their potential worth in the future, they are not seen as valued members of the religious community who may make a significant contribution now. Youth involvement in decision-making and the day's agenda is important not only for creating and keeping peace, unity, reconciliation and justice, but also for changing society as a whole.

This chapter addresses the research question of why the youth discourse and youth ministry must remain a priority on the missional research agenda. To answer this topic, I will begin with a quick explanation of the *missio Dei*, followed by a contextualisation of youth in South Africa. Following that, I will examine missiological discourses, developments, trends, and trajectory; youth within mission and missiology; and youth as a research agenda based on the *missio Dei*.

A [very] brief exposition of the inclusive character of *missio Dei*

Although this book deals extensively with the notion of *missio Dei*, I still deem it important, albeit briefly, to address the inclusive nature of *missio Dei* as a basis for the remainder of this chapter. Missiology and/or Mission Studies relate to the inclusiveness of the *missio Dei*. The inclusiveness of the *missio Dei* is also examined in the works of Bevans and Schroeder (2004) and Kritzinger (2008), who both emphasise contextualisation as a suitable means for the church to participate in the inclusiveness of the *missio Dei*. Historically, the phrase *missio Dei* may be traced back to Augustine in light of the dogma of the Trinity. In 1952, however, the idea of *missio Dei* was proposed from a missiological standpoint at the Willingen Conference (Amenyedzi 2021:3). Karl Hartenstein may have created the word in his Willingen report since it was absent from the original text (Amenyedzi 2021:3). He defined mission as 'participation in the sending of the Son, in the *missio Dei*, with the inclusive aim of establishing the Lordship of Christ over the whole redeemed creation' (Engelsviken 2003:482). Knoetze (2015:5) concurs:

> *Missio Dei* is the very mission of God in creation, redemption and continual sanctification. God the Father's mission to this cosmos is through his covenant with his people. It is about the Father's unconditional love, his commitment to be the God of his people and their descendants and to bless them, so that they will be a blessing to the cosmos, as is described in his covenant (Gn 12:3) and administered in the sacraments (Baptism and Holy Communion). As *immitatio Trinitatis*, the church must show the same unconditional love commitment to families and youth (Mt 5:43–48; 18), who must realise that the covenant of the Father makes their life story part of God's story. In communion with the Trinity the ministry will at least participate in creativity, generosity, reconciliation and identity.

With this all-inclusive aspect of *missio Dei* in mind as a background, I utilise youth ministry as a research agenda in mission studies to defend youth ministry as a research focus. Young people are also a part of God's mission, which has to include all people. According to M. Nel (2015:3), to be missional, one must grasp some of Jesus' inclusive principles. All people (youth included) are the goal of *missio Dei*, according to Knoetze (2015:3), and Baron (2017:5) concurs that youth should have an equal role in questioning the *status quo* and being motivated by church activities to make a positive impact on those around them. As a result, the youth should serve as both recipients and givers of the divine mission (*missio Dei*).

Youth within (South) Africa

South Africa's youth unemployment rate is quite high (Kgatla 2016:62). Unemployment rates among 15- to 24-year-olds in South Africa are among the highest in the world, with 58% of those ages 15 to 24 either unemployed or not enrolled in higher education or training. Young people are the first to be laid off and the last to be hired when the economy is in a slump. Quarterly Labour Force Survey (QLFS) findings for the first quarter of 2020 show that employment declined by 38 000 to 16,4 million while the number of jobless individuals grew by 344 000 to

7,1 million (Statistics South Africa [StatsSA] 2020). As a consequence, the official unemployment rate climbed by 1 percentage point from the fourth quarter of 2019 to 30.1%. The rate has been stubbornly high throughout this time, with 15- to 34-year-olds being the most impacted by unemployment. In the first quarter of 2020, there were 20.4 million young people between the ages of 15 and 34. These young people represented 63.3% of the total number of jobless individuals. During the first quarter of 2020, the unemployment rate among this group was 43.2%. The youth between the ages of 15 and 24 are the most vulnerable in the South African labour market, with a 59% unemployment rate in the first quarter of 2020. The unemployment rate for graduates in this age range was 33.1% during this time, compared to 24.6% in the fourth quarter of 2019 — a rise of 8.5% from quarter to quarter (StatsSA 2020).

Similarly, the youth face several life-threatening societal issues, including adolescent pregnancy, substance abuse problems, perpetration of violence, and poor upbringing and socialisation as a result of their parents' still recovering from the scars of apartheid (Sokfa, Kaunda & Ntokozo 2015:112). While Africa has the world's greatest youth population, half of the South African population is comprised of young people (Knoetze 2017:15). Thus, if the youth are susceptible, the nation and continent are also vulnerable, and the church is likewise vulnerable. Therefore, as the place where God stands, the church is obligated to stand with those who are most vulnerable (cf. 1986 Belhar Confession, art. 4). Even though this is true for youth in South Africa and on our continent, Knoetze (2017:15) says that this group is still the least studied.

In these conditions of youth marginalisation and socio-economic and socio-political challenges, one must realise that faith in God is not the problem (cf. Knoetze 2015:2). The actual difficulty is having faith in God, believing that he is there and will, can, and wants to make a difference. What does God want from his church when 37 000 children die every day from diseases that could have been prevented or that are caused by poverty? (Knoetze 2015:2).

Youth marginalisation must be recognised as a worldwide issue. However, it is vital to comprehend what marginalisation of adolescents entails to devise creative strategies for their demarginalisation. Several factors contribute to the marginalisation of young people. The top three identified variables are poverty, unemployment, and marginalisation. The truth is that young people who do not have jobs are less able to help their country grow and have fewer chances to use their rights as citizens. They have less money to spend as buyers and less money to invest as savers. They also often do not have a 'voice' to make changes in their lives and communities. This is a clear reason why they cannot get out of the margins where they find themselves

There needs to be more than one paradigm shift. Societal paradigm shifts, cultural paradigm shifts, educational and racial paradigm shifts, faith community paradigm shifts, and academic paradigm shifts are all needed. Young people are often seen as troublemakers, rebels, and unreliable in their societies. Despite that, youth movements and activism are on the rise around the world on different issues that affect them because they want a voice. The young should be included in primary spaces, their voices should guide practice, and services should help them become more independent.

Missiological discourses, developments, trends, trajectories

In their contribution, Mangayi and Baron (2020) look at how South African missiology has changed and grown from 2010 to 2020. Mangayi and Baron (2020:8) used the published work of six South African missiologists to do their research. They found that when it comes to the question of what mission is all about, most people agree that mission should focus on people instead of institutions and programmes. This people-centred notion is an inclusive concept that includes individuals of all ages. Nonetheless, based on the cited research (cf. Mangayi & Baron 2020), the authors perceived a reluctance from contributions and praxes to propagate a 'radical-Christocentric' mission approach, which could have brought the most marginalised voices into mainstream missiological discourse in South Africa. Mangayi and Baron motivate this by saying:

> Unheard voices of marginalised groups, such as children, women, and homeless communities, are not yet taken seriously in South African missiology. For example, the focus on "children" as agents of mission as an important issue to challenge and transform the hermeneutics of mission in the future is not taken as seriously as it should be (Mangayi & Baron 2020:10).

Even though Mangayi and Baron's research of South African developments, trends, and trajectories focused on the decade 2010–2020, these two scholars acknowledge that there is a glimmer of hope in the fact that North-West University colleagues are working on missiological perspectives on issues of children and youth, including urban missions (2020:12). It is also obvious that South African academics such as Van Schalkwyk, Kgatle, Knoetze, Banda, Nel, and Baron have researched women, children, and adolescents from a missiological standpoint (Mangayi & Baron 2020:14). They add that theologians at Stellenbosch University, for instance, concentrate on how South African students will redefine their identity in a post-colonial society and that Nel (2013) is especially interested in how young people contribute to the church, especially in his denomination. He does this when he talks about what the future holds for South Africa (Mangayi & Baron 2020:12). But his work also shows how important and influential young people are in changing the church and society (Mangayi & Baron 2020:12).

Youth within mission and missiology

According to Elton (2013:67-68), from the first years of mission organisations, youth have had a substantial presence, and youth ministry has always had missional energy, but it has lacked an adequate missiological language. The re-emphasis on the importance of youth in mission can also be traced back to the evangelicals' assembly in Manila for 'Lausanne II', the World Council of Churches (WCC) conference in San Antonio in 1989, and the Salvador de Bahia 1996, to name a few (Ross, Keum, Avtzi & Hewitt 2016:126-135).

In several ways, youth ministry and mission have interacted mainly regarding mission work (Elton 2013:67). Young people migrated to the city in the early 1900s, as the population shifted from rural to urban regions. Concerned about these young individuals, the Young Men's Christian Association (YMCA) was founded to reaffirm Christian values and shield youth from the dangers of urban life (Elton 2013:67; cf. Root 2007:31). However, whereas Elton (2013:67) believes that the convergence of youth ministry and missiology has existed from the beginning, Wyngaard (2015:411) acknowledges that in every age of human history, young people seem to be the only social group that is seldom regarded seriously. Similarly, according to Baron (2017:4), the youth in the church are sometimes only good for church activities, such as participating in Sunday worship and the various ministry departments, but are sometimes intentionally overlooked in terms of being equipped for participation and mobilisation as change agents in society. Yet, it is precisely that same group that has the power to alter the course of history.

Nel (2016), in his article 'Children must be seen and heard…', deconstructs the iconic South African phrase 'children must be seen, not heard' and examines its influence on the church and missional ecclesiology. In that contribution, he argues that the:

> younger believers, irrespective of their own agency, may be seen, or better, gazed upon, targeted theologically and eventually ministered to by ever-new children's evangelism campaigns, yet they are not to speak up for themselves. Unlike what is often projected as the "angry" black theologian, or the resilient African theologian, "obsessed with their traditional rituals", the African children are often constructed as so "friendly" and "open to the

gospel" – ready for the taking. They have been (and remain still), largely, the soft targets of mission campaigns and strategies to ultimately conquer and dominate the "Dark Continent" (Nel 2016:1).

In addition, Counted (2016:91) provides a missional answer about youth from a different perspective in his work on youth identity crisis. Counted uses a missional hermeneutic to help young people deal with the crisis of figuring out who they are. I would like to briefly explain this here so that I can make my point. His missional hermeneutic for youth dealing with crises is threefold: seeing the suffering youth through the missional lens of God's story; explaining the missional purpose of the crises of youth identity; and addressing the *missio*-cultural locatedness of the youth identity crisis. This can redeem and change the youth as the people of God on a mission to the world by the example of their own lives (Counted 2016:98). This hermeneutical key would assist the youth-in-mission in submitting to the guidance of the Holy Spirit as they reinvent and reinvest themselves in the character of God as a community in transition, longing for a new future via God's mission. According to him, a missional hermeneutic view of the crisis of youth identity, first as a missional phenomenon, and second, as a unique opportunity that not only provides the foundation for embodying the *missio Dei* in our daily lives but also elucidates the nature of the missionary life as a story of God's walk with the youth from beginning to end, rather than merely their salvation. This viewpoint invites young people back to God's mission as a missional community that represents God's image before the world as they interpret the identity crisis to hear God's voice, providing them with the solutions to life's difficult problems (Counted 2016:91). This missional hermeneutic also requires youth and youth ministry workers and pastoral caregivers to read the identity crises of youth from God's viewpoint. To assist young people with their identity crisis, the first step in a missional hermeneutic of coping would be to see them as a community sent to participate in the *missio Dei*, as they are, in fact, a part of the narrative of God's mission. This first stage begins with the process of inclusion, a comprehension that incorporates the missional foundation of young people in a manner that enables them to recognise themselves in the revelatory portrayal of God's Great Communication. This inclusivity helps the youth ministry worker or pastoral caregiver direct the young's attention to God's inclusive nature and purpose, enabling the young people to perceive themselves as part of a global and interplanetary endeavour (Counted 2016:92). When young people see themselves as a part of God's plan for the world, they feel like they have a clear purpose in life.

Thus, by acknowledging the current South Africa young people find themselves in, I am still tempted to ask, so, what now? What do we want to see happen? Where are we moving towards? What do we do with all this information? How do we transform the curriculum? How do we transform faith communities? How do we transform societies? How will this book or information help in moving forward? How do we allow youth to claim their space? How do we include them in initiatives such as this book publication? Are they only research objects and subjects? Why not co-authors or sole authors? Earlier, I mentioned the paradigm shift that needs to take place in moving *from* the understanding that the youth should only be acknowledged because of their possible value for tomorrow, *towards* the understanding that they are valued members of and should make a valuable contribution today. But also, the paradigm shift from '*doing for*' to '*doing with*' towards '*doing themselves*' is needed. Hence, I want to challenge academia to set an example by implementing '*doing with*' in our academic endeavours when we write such publications. Empower young people, youth, and students to write with us. Furthermore, how or when will we integrate youth (work) and mission (studies) more seriously in our endeavours?

Youth inclusion efforts should not be limited to 'once-off' programmes and lip service; rather, young people should be integral to the process, not as objects but as key decision-makers. The notion of integrating the primary stakeholders engaged in the activity at hand is acknowledged as the key to success in practically every circumstance. For instance, we would instantly doubt the efficacy of an organisation that mainly serves people of colour if it were led by an all-white team, or if a women's rights group was led by males alone. Similarly, if we want to assure the validity of our study on youth, then we must engage young people in its conception. Equally, including young people in the change process will ensure that the choices made make sense from the standpoint of all stakeholders, including the intended beneficiaries. When youth take their place at a changing table, it shows that they are a respected and responsible citizen.

Youth social capital/potential

From the youth movement and activism regarding climate change (environmental consciousness), the Arab Spring in Egypt, and the student revolts in South Africa in 2015–2016 about student fees, it is clear that the political and socio-economic future of Africa is already determined and will be determined by the youth (cf. Knoetze 2017:16; Beukes 2021). Similarly, according to R. Nel (2015:518), the struggles of young people and students have evolved from activism against colonial racism to activism against marginalisation in a post-colonial, neoliberal society. He then frames this new activism against marginalisation as a rising dissatisfaction in a particular post-colonial setting, but more significantly, as a symbol of agency among youth and student organisations (R. Nel 2015:518). Another reason why adolescents might be considered both beneficiaries and agents of *missio Dei*.

According to Knoetze (2018:3), the contemporary youth are also the generation that has broken down the majority of prior socio-political barriers between South Africa's many demographic groupings. Depending on the geography and demographics of their locality, many of them had, for example, attended multiracial schools. However, the majority of South African millennials are members of a 'new' global culture that is tightly tied to electronic communication, the cyber world, and a secular worldview (Knoetze 2018:3). However, social media technologies are also a tool for connecting, informing, and organising social movements, which are mostly led by youth and students (R. Nel 2015:517).

As the youth see the limits of their human abilities, it is important to encourage them to have a prophetic-missional voice that reminds them that God is with them and has a purpose for them in his *missio Dei* story. Such a prophetic trigger can get rid of the feelings of nothingness and helplessness that come with marginalisation, vulnerability, feelings of exclusion, and an identity crisis. It does this by connecting the hopeless feelings of youth to a world of order that fits with God's mission (cf. Counted 2016:97).

Youth as a research agenda based on the *missio Dei*

Youth marginalisation is a big problem in South Africa and Africa as a whole. I have already talked about how the marginalised are left out of society, but they are also left out of church structures. So, the question is, how does the church interact with young people who are both inside and outside of the church's traditions and rules? Klaasen (2018:1) agrees that the church has not always helped marginalised youth become more powerful. He argues from an Anglican Church point of view while looking at the youth inside of the traditions and the norms of the church that:

> The youth occupy a traditional marginal position in the church. The church's centre is made up of decision-making bodies. These, whether they are local or diocesan, are dominated by ordination. Because very few of the youth are part of the ordained ministry, and subsequently part of the decision-making bodies, there is a clear divide between decision-makers at the centre and the youth at the margins (Klaasen 2018:1).

Yet, young people are entitled to significant involvement in mission since they have always been God's mission's main agents and beneficiaries. According to Wyngaard (2015:411), God is the one who calls and motivates the church to reach out to young people. Therefore, youth ministry or Christian youth work is founded on God's missionary character. This is founded on the *missio Dei*, which states that the mission belongs to God and not the church. This notion is seen in the work of

Mission the "labour room" of theology

Bosch (1991:390), who likewise views mission as the *missio Dei* in the sense that 'mission is a divine attribute'. God is a missionary God. The church does not have a mission to go out to the world; rather, God's mission includes the church.

A missional strategy is relevant and important in this context of youth marginalisation in South Africa. Clark (2001:80) describes the missional approach as the church community's collective commitment to caring for and reaching out to the adolescent world to incorporate them meaningfully into their fellowship. However, Klaasen (2018:4) warns that the missional approach might be misinterpreted as a 'we' and 'them' categorisation, with the 'we' group holding the centre and the 'they' group occupying the outskirts. Due to this misunderstanding of the church community, the older generation views the young as the portion of the world in need of mission. In the missional approach, the church goes beyond its members and reaches out to the rest of society (Klaasen 2018:4). Clark (2001:81) says that the community will be a part of missional youth ministry, but never for the sake of the community. Clark (2001:81) says that the goal is not just to focus on the people who are already part of a church's youth ministry programme. Instead, the theological mission of youth ministry should be to bring the gospel and the kingdom to every young person. The church needs to step up and let this theological axiom change and shape church customs and traditions (Clark 2001:81).

Ancient church-centred missiology was theologically limited in that it did not fully comprehend the breadth of missionary duty, as demonstrated by Jesus' outreach to the poor, sick, and marginalised (Amenyedzi 2021:3). Bosch (1991:393-401) emphasises mission as a mediator of salvation; this portrays mission as inclusive and holistic, as salvation is not limited to the individual's relationship with Christ, but also considers hatred, injustice, oppression, marginalisation, violence, and other forms of suffering in the world. Similarly, mission as a pursuit of justice must concentrate on the conflict inherent in expressing unconditional love in a culture rife with injustice. Salvation must be a source of pleasure and hope for everyone, particularly the marginalised in society, which includes youngsters both inside and outside the church's walls.

Regarding marginalised youths in an attempt to demarginalise them, I believe mission studies/missiology may contribute as young people investigate their experiences and everything that lies behind them in connection to God's mission in the world using a missional hermeneutic. Such a missional stance enables adolescents to rely on the promise of God's ultimate narrative to guide them back to God's image as new creatures in Christ. As a religious community assigned to fulfil the *missio Dei*, having a missional orientation for the tale of God's mission encourages youngsters to find purpose in their powerless and terrible situations. Most importantly, this would also require a deeper and more personal understanding of what *missio Dei* means and how it can change a person.

When engaging with youth, R. Nel (2015:515) employs a postcolonial missiological viewpoint. According to him, a postcolonial missiological approach begins with a dedication to God's mission, as recommended by liberation theologians, with people on the 'underside' or 'standing with...' marginalised communities in compassion and solidarity with their practise (R. Nel 2015:515). This commitment is consistent with what Bosch (1991:425) refers to as an 'intersubjective' epistemology, and it is crucial in the quest for a sensitive and creative conversation with the current cohort of younger generations, or 'catching up' with the impulses of the new period of youth challenges.

Because of this, the contribution of Counted (2016:93) is so important in proving that youth ministry should be part of the missional agenda. He thinks that by encouraging suffering youth to personalise the missional direction of God's story for their lives, they are empowered to participate in the *missio Dei* as they practise a self-hermeneutic process that becomes an embodiment of the good news they are called to proclaim (Counted 2016:93). This hermeneutical process may not completely resolve their identity crises, but it will reframe them so that the youth-in-mission's quality and character can become a reflection of what God desires. This happens when the powerful story of God's grace is told in the context of a missional community in transition. This makes it possible for young people to see themselves as part of the big story of creation and as people who are 'sent' into the world to do God's work (Guder 2004:59-73). This eye-opening picture of *missio Dei* shows how identity crises can be used to equip young people for missional purposes (Goheen 2008).

In the current situation in South Africa, and by recognising the youth's agency and potential through mission studies, young people also play an important role in preventing and resolving conflicts. They are key to the success of both peacekeeping and peacebuilding efforts. I also think that as young people become more in charge of their own learning, they can and should play a key role in helping the public understand change and getting other people involved in the process. When learners, students, and young people, in general, go from being 'objects' to being 'agents of change' in their churches, schools, universities, workplaces, and communities, they can take that new way of being and become 'ambassadors for change' or disciples, as M. Nel (2015) calls it.

The church might also begin by asking probing questions. Questions that highlight the principal missional aim of the church, which is to empower and liberate people who are oppressed and broken within the contextual community. In this sense, Counted (2016:96) poses some thought-provoking questions:

> "How does our understanding of community and family affect the way we relate with our loved ones?", "How has the circle of parental abuse and apathy become a norm in our communities and affected the way young people relate to God, self, and their social others?", and "How can the church build and encourage better family models that can encourage and strengthen secure attachment relationships between parents and their children?" These questions and many more could help the church understand the *missiological* issues related to the cultural locatedness of the youth-in-crisis and engagements of communities with the youth culture, as faith communities set the path straight for reconciliation and healing.

M. Nel (2015) believes that the church should disciple young people who will continue to disciple others. He sees that not only adults but even children are involved in the process of discipleship. However, this should be a deliberate and purposeful procedure. He emphasises that this does not imply that only lessons about God should be imparted to young people (M. Nel 2015). Baron (2017:4) agrees that the church should not ignore the young, who are an integral component of the church's mission on earth. This comparable perspective is seen in Reggie Nel's (2016) article 'Children must be seen and heard...', in which he argues from a specific (southern African) Reformed experience that:

> unless this imperial, colonial experience of African Christians and churches, including their youngest worshippers and witnesses, are taken seriously in ministries with children, and unless they are allowed to disrupt domineering practices, these imperial mission campaigns and strategies, and their concomitant theologies, will not be able to seriously address the heart of the plight of African children. (2016:1).

Similarly, in his most recent book, Malan Nel (2018) also underlines that the congregation, of which youth are an important part, is in mission. Nel is compelled by the missional dialogue to build his fundamental approach to youth ministry as a ministry to, with, and through youth with the knowledge that the congregation is in mission. For Nel (2018:11), the purpose of youth ministry is to help youth (children, adolescents, and young adults, as they are already an integral part of the faith community) become what they were created and called to be: people who are *already involved* (not future or tomorrow) in the acts of God, in the service of the communication of the gospel and in the kingdom of God that has come and will come to the world. God is approaching them and working through them. They are already doing mission work because they are important parts of the religious community (Nel 2018:11).

Hence, for the African and South African contexts, the discourses on youth within Mission Studies should not just remain on the research agenda but should be prioritised as a crucial element of God's intended mission, his *missio Dei*.

Conclusion

In this chapter, I have argued that a missional approach to youth work and youth ministry tries to position adolescents within the *missio Dei* and, by extension, the mission of the church. The missional method places the edges in continuity with the centre, and the boundaries are softened such that interactionist overlap links the margins and the centre. Youth are formed in the image of God and are located within the Triune God. In the margins, where Jesus urges the church to respond to God's mission, youth ministry occurs. Through his mission for and with them, as well as the rest of the world, the *missio Dei* to the young also serves as a reminder of God's love and presence during difficult times. I accept that youth marginalisation is a global phenomenon and that while youth have been part of the missional agenda for ages, they tend to be disregarded. Youth should be prioritised as mission agents and important beneficiaries not just for the future but, most importantly, for the now.

References

Amenyedzi, S., 2021, '"We are forgotten": The plight of persons with disability in youth ministry', *Scriptura* 120, 1–17.

Aziz, G., 2020, 'Age does not determine influence: a consideration for children in ministerial service', *HTS Teologiese Studies/Theological Studies* 76(2), a5848. https://doi.org/10.4102/hts.v76i2.5848.

Baron, E., 2017, 'The role of church youth in the transformation agenda of South African cities', *HTS Teologiese Studies/ Theological Studies* 73(3), 1–7.

Belhar Confession, 1986, 'The official English translation of the *Belhar Confession 1986* approved by the General Synod of 2008', Belhar: LUS Printers.

Beukes, J., & Van der Westhuizen, M., 2016, 'Exploring the voices of children and youth: a plea for renewal in church structures for child and youth ministries', *Stellenbosch Theological Journal (STJ)* 2(2), 111–130.

Beukes, J.W., 2021, 'Seen and heard: The youth as game-changing role-players in climate change and environmental consciousness – A South African perspective', *HTS Teologiese Studies/Theological Studies* 77(2), 1–8.

Bevans, S.B., & Schroeder, R.P., 2004, *Constants in context: A theology of mission for today*, Orbis, New York.

Bosch, D.J., 1991, *Transforming missions: Paradigm shifts in theology of missions*, Orbis, New York.

Clark, C., 2001, 'The missional approach to youth ministry', in M.H. Senter III (ed.), *Four views of youth ministry and the church; Inclusive, preparatory, missional and strategic*, pp. 77–96, Zondervan, Grand Rapids, MI.

Cloete, A., 2015, 'Creative tensions in youth ministry in a congregational context', *HTS Teologiese Studies/Theological Studies* 71(2), 1–7.

Columbia Global Policy Initiative, 2014, 'Overcoming youth marginalization conference report and policy recommendations', Conference in March 2014, Columbia Global Policy Initiative and the Office of the United Nations Secretary-General's Envoy on Youth, New York.

Counted, V., 2016, 'Missionising youth identity crisis: Towards a missional hermeneutic of coping in youth ministry practice', *Missionalia* 44(1), 85–102.

Department of Higher Education and Training, 2017, *'Fact Sheet on "NEETS" (Persons who are Not in Employment, Education or Training)'*, viewed 15 March 2017, from http://www.dhet.gov.za/Planning%20Monitoring%20 and%20Evaluation%20 Coordination/Fact-sheet-on-NEETs-Final-Version-27-Jan-2017.pdf

Department of Social Development (DSD), 2013, *'Framework for social welfare services'*, Department of Social Development, Pretoria.

Elton, T.M., 2013, 'Mergers and possibilities: The intersection of missiology and youth ministry', *Missiology* 41(1), 62–73.

Engelvisken, T., 2003, 'Missio Dei: The understanding and misunderstanding of a theological concept in European Churches and Missiology', *International Review of Missions* 92(367), 481–497.

Goheen, M.W., 2008, 'Continuing steps towards a missional hermeneutic', *Fideles: A Journal of Redeemer Pacific College* 3, 49-99.

Guder, D.L., 2004, 'Biblical formation and discipleship', in L. Barrett (ed.), *Treasure in clay jars: Patterns in missional faithfulness*, pp. 59–73, Wm. B. Eerdmans, Grand Rapids.

Kgatla, S.T., 2016, 'Church and South African realities today: Towards a relevant missiology of radical discipleship', *Stellenbosch Theological Journal (STJ)* 2(2), 57–75.

King, S., 2012, 'Youth and children's ministry', Australia: Effective Ministry, viewed 9 February 2016, from http://www.effectiveministry.org

Klaasen, J.S., 2018, 'Youth ministry at the margins and/ or centre as space of the other: Reflections on the resolutions of the Anglican dioceses in the Western Cape 2017', HTS Teologiese Studies/Theological Studies 74(3), 1–7.

Knoetze, J., 2015, 'Perspectives on family and youth ministry embedded in the missio Dei – an African perspective, In die Skriflig/In Luce Verbi 49(1), 1-9.

Knoetze, J.J., 2017, 'African millennials and missional diaconate as transformational development to God's glory', in V. Kozhuharov & J.J. Knoetze (eds.), Conversion and transformation: Children and youth in mission contexts', pp. 13–27, Christian Literature Fund, Wellington, South Africa.

Knoetze, J.J., 2018, 'Marginalised millennials: Conversation or conversion towards a Christian lifestyle in South Africa?', HTS Teologiese Studies/Theological Studies 74(3), 1–7.

Kritzinger, J.N.J., 2008, 'Faith to faith – Missiology as encounterology', Verbum et Ecclesia 29(3), 764-790.

Mangayi, L., & Baron, E., 2020, 'Ten years (2010 – 2020) of exciting Missiology in South Africa: Trends and trajectories', Scriptura 119, 1–18.

Meth, C., 2006, '"Rational ignorance" and South African poverty statistics', Africus 37(2), 81–110.

Nel, M., 2015, 'Imagine-making disciples in youth ministry ... that will make disciples', HTS Teologiese Studies/Theological Studies 71(3), 1-11.

Nel, M., 2018, Youth ministry: An inclusive missional approach, HTS Religion & Society Series, Volume 1, AOSIS, Cape Town.

Nel, M., 2000, Youth ministry: An inclusive congregational approach, Kitskopie, Pretoria.

Nel, R., 2015, 'Social media and the new struggles of young people against marginalisation: a challenge to missional ecclesiology in Southern Africa', Stellenbosch Theological Journal (STJ) 1(2), 511–530.

Nel, R., 2016, '"Children must be seen and heard" – Doing postcolonial theology with children in a (southern) African Reformed church', HTS Teologiese Studies/Theological Studies 72(1), 1–7.

Nel, R.W., 2014, 'Discerning the role of faith communities in responding to urban youth marginalisation', HTS Teologiese Studies/Theological Studies 70(3), a2743. https://doi.org/10.4102/hts.

Nel, R.W., 2013, 'Discerning an African missional ecclesiology in dialogue with two uniting youth movements', PhD thesis, Dept. of Missiology, UNISA, Pretoria.

Pelser, A., & De Kock, C., 2000, 'Violence in South Africa: A note on some trends in the 1990s', *Acta Criminologica* 13(1), 80–94.

Republic of South Africa (RSA), 2015, '*National Youth Policy 2015–2020: The authors are generation 2020. The authors don't want a hand-out, the authors want a hand up!*', The Presidency of the Republic of South Africa, Pretoria.

Root, A., 2007, '*Revisiting relational Youth Ministry: From strategy of influence to a theology of incarnation*', InterVarsity, Downers Grove, IL.

Ross, K.R., Keum, J., Avtzi, K. & Hewitt, R., 2016, '*Ecumenical missiology: changing landscapes and new conceptions of mission*', Regnum Edinburgh Centenary Series, Volume 35, Oxford.

Sokfa, F.J., Kaunda, C.J., & Ntokozo, C.M.M., 2015, 'Contesting the 'Born Free' identity: a postcolonial perspective on *Mzansi* stories', *Alternation* 14, 106–125.

Statistics South Africa (StatsSA), 2020, '*Quarterly labour force survey*', viewed 25 November 2020, from https://bit.ly/3JmODg8.

Swart, I., 2018, 'Youth marginalisation as a faith-based concern in contemporary South African society: introducing a research contribution', *HTS Teologiese Studies/Theological Studies* 74(3), a5253. https://doi.org/10.4102/hts.v74i3.5253.

Swart, I., Vähäkangas, A., Rabe, M., & Leis-Peters, A., 2022, '*Stuck in the margins? Young people and faith-based organisations in South African and Nordic localities*', Research in Contemporary Religion, Volume 31, Vandenhoeck & Ruprecht.

Swartz, S., & Nyamnjoh, A., 2018, 'Research as freedom: using a continuum of interactive, participatory and emancipatory methods for addressing youth marginality', *HTS Teologiese Studies/Theological Studies* 74(3), a5063. https://doi.org/10.4102/hts.v74i3.5063.

Van Niekerk, A., Tonsing, S., Seedat, M., Jacobs, R., Ratele, K., & McClure, R., 2015, 'The invisibility of men in South African violence prevention policy: National prioritisation, male vulnerability, and framing prevention', *Gender and Health Inequalities: Global Health Action* 8(2015), 1–10.

Voas, D., & Watt, L., 2014, '*Numerical change in church attendance: national, local and individual factors*', Essex: The Church Growth Research Programme Report on Strands 1 and 2.

Ward, C.L., 2012, 'Violence, violence prevention, and safety: A research agenda for South Africa', *Issues in Medicine* 102(4), 215–218.

Wyngaard, J., 2015, '*Missio Dei* and youth ministry: Mobilizing young people's assets and developing relationships', *Missionalia* 43(3), 410–424.

Chapter 11

Collaboration and Networking in Missions in Africa

Nico Mostert

Introduction

Visualise a typical hypothetical scenario of a young woman selling tomatoes from a stall next to the road somewhere between Nairobi and Eldoret in Kenya, or between Tete and Vila Ulongwe in Mozambique or Blantyre and Lilongwe in Malawi. A phone rings and she rummages through her things to find her phone. While a highly decorated *matatu*, or East African commuter bus, stops and the passengers disembark to buy some items for the journey, she speaks to her sister on the phone and arranges the visit of her parents. They will be travelling to the city the following day and her sister needs to pick them up at the market.

The Africa we find ourselves in has changed dramatically over the past two decades. The role of technological developments that changed the face of Africa in both urban and rural settings[1] cannot be ignored. People are no longer disconnected or excluded from what is happening in the global context; they are connected to each other and to the global community. In rural markets, one can buy cellular phones, sim cards, and solar charged radios from a street vendor. The flipside of this coin is that the world has access to Africa and its people. Reaching and connecting with people is made easier as technology is more readily available, and connectivity is broadened across the continent.

It is in this context that the church finds herself with the age-old calling of Matthew 28:19 (also referred to as the Great Commission) where preaching the gospel and the making of disciples is central to the missionary endeavour. In Africa, this calling plays out against the backdrop of a mission history stretching back more than 500 years[2] – an era which can be described as a denominational-driven

---

[1] Cf. Chakravorti and Chaturvedi (2019).
[2] Cf. Walls (1996; 2002); Pass (2016).

missional movement where the emphasis was largely placed on denominational church planting.

This suggests that it was driven mainly by Western mainline denominations each working with its own vision and mandate to evangelise Africa. It is only in the latter part of the 20th century that the Pentecostal charismatic movement gave rise to a more independent missions movement with a focus on evangelical crusades and the consequential planting of independent churches (Paas 2016:484-491).

It can be observed from mission history that this rarely points to collaboration between the parties involved. The model of a missionary (usually a family) being sent by a church or group of a specific denomination to take up residence among the targeted group, remained the prevalent methodology of missions over the past three centuries. The question remains: what will missions in Africa look like in the future? Will the church, both mainline and non-denominational, follow the proverbial age-old methodologies with the same emphasis on a denominational mission approach, or are different strategies and an even stronger kingdom-orientated approach needed for the future?

In this chapter, we will explore possible options for collaboration as a different approach to missions. By reviewing the difficulties of collaboration, the theoretical thinking on collaboration, the need for collaboration, and the possibilities as well as some practical examples of collaboration efforts, it is hoped that more of a kingdom-centred approach to missions might be achieved in future.

Why is missional collaboration so difficult?

Mandell, Keast and Chamberlain (2017:328) write the following on collaboration:

> One of the significant difficulties faced in inter-organizational collaboration is the conflict between an existing collective identity, formed with formerly autonomous organizations, and the need for a new collective identity involving interdependent organizations working towards mutual goals.

The concepts relevant to the conversation on missional collaboration are: existing collective identities, autonomous organisations, new collective identities, interdependent organisations, and working towards mutual goals.

When one reviews past and current missional practices, it is observed that these practices support the strengthening of existing denominational identities, which tend to reinforce the establishment of strong, autonomous mission organisations and just as strong local churches with the same identity. It can be said that collectively the church has a very strong and well-developed identity to function as strong autonomous denominations or groups on the continent.

However, as research indicates, this is not a prevailing trend. There are strong indications in Africa of the global tendency of declining mainline denominations.[3] In the past, mainline denominations had a strong ecumenical undertone. Therefore, some form of collaboration existed as joint agendas and member churches' participation therein were considered. But this scenario is changing as indicated by the World Council of Churches (WCC), the world's largest ecumenical movement[4].

To the contrary, the growth of Christianity in Africa can mostly be contributed to the strong growth of African Independent Churches (AICs)[5] and the Pentecostal/Charismatic awakening in African Christianity.[6] From the reviewed literature, it is evident that within this awakening, strong emphasis is placed on the term 'independent'. Given the high regard for independence, few traces are found of missional collaboration. The understanding of mission is focused more on the emotional and spiritual needs of African people.[7]

This leaves us with the conundrum of existing building blocks that contributed towards an almost impossible setting of very limited collaboration and a lack of partnership between churches in the present mission endeavour in Africa.

These building blocks, if listed, are:

a. **A missionary history of denominational church formation**
   Our mission histories of Africa depict a story of each denomination planting churches that were mirror images of themselves. It is not a history of partnership or collaboration but rather a history of individual focus and efforts to reproduce the missional (sending) church. Very few succeeded in planting churches that are truly indigenous.[8]

b. **Theological differences (Dogma)**
   This was an inevitable consequence of the mission's endeavour. The theological training that followed duplicated that of the mission church, and local established institutions continued to train along those lines, especially if they are a church-specific training institution. This history is well documented in the book, *A family of Reformed churches*, which outlines

---

3   Cf. Ferreira and Chipenyu (2021); Hofmeyr (2004).
4   Cf. Diara and Onah (2014); Kobia (2006).
5   Cf. Kealotswe (2014); Adedibu (2018).
6   Cf. Nel (2019); Wariboko (2017); Meyer (2004).
7   Cf. Thomas (1995).
8   Read the works of the late Andrew Walls in this regard.

the development of mission churches within the Reformed tradition and the subsequent theological education that supported that tradition.[9]

c. **The loss of a Kingdom vision**
Taking all this into account or rather putting all these blocks together, an argument can be put forward that African communities have a 'silo' methodology and thinking with regard to missions. The church is not collaboration- or partnership-inclined and hence our methodologies and ways of doing testify to that. A kingdom vision is different from a silo approach. It stems from the *missio Dei* of the Trinitarian God that God is by his nature invitational and cooperative. He is not the God who builds higher walls for a silo but rather a bigger table to share the abundance by inviting more to sit at the table.

New realities that call for collaboration and networking

Africa (and the church in Africa whether mainline or independent) find themselves facing new realities that demand a collaborative effort if their impact is to be addressed by the church. These realities pose a hinderance to the existing conditions of no collaboration and limited networking since these two concepts are more complex and therefore more demanding in the challenge they pose to the existence of the church in Africa. The church needs a combined or collaborative effort, not a mere silo-like, independent response. Numerous as the problems are, the following are selected as the most prevalent that will require a combined effort to address them successfully.

They are:

a. **Poverty and global economic decline that has a direct influence on Africa**
Poverty among African churches, together with corruption and the lack of development, is a direct consequence of economic decline.

b. **Reoccurring pandemics**
COVID-19 surfaced on the African continent in 2020 and together with the continuous struggle against HIV/AIDS and Ebola, once again exposed how vulnerable the people of Africa are to unknown diseases. Existing fault lines in governments and the church were rapidly and starkly exposed. These fault lines are not only found in collapsing health care services but also in our theological understanding of diseases and the interface between faith and science.[10] Some philosophers like Harari (2016) and some economists

---

[9] Cf. ed. Van der Watt and Odendaal (2022).
[10] Cf. Venter (2021); Nganwuchu, Anizoba and Molokwu (2021).

predict that we should expect more 'black swan'[11] pandemics, such as COVID-19, and that they could occur at a higher frequency rate in future.

c. **The steady rise of Islam**

The geographic spread of Islam in Africa over centuries has been well documented by scholars, indicating a movement from the North to the South (Sub-Saharan Africa) and from the traditionally Arab Eastern Africa westwards into the interior.[12] A 2017 survey introduced by Pew Research (Hackett, Cooperman & Schiller 2017) further indicates that as Christianity is growing in Africa, so is Islam. According to this research, Islamic growth is attributed to natural growth by birth. A closer look reveals that a radical strain of Islam is growing among Muslims in Africa.[13] As the theology of Islam operates with an interwoven understanding of the political, economic, legal and social life,[14] a geographic advancement combined with a natural population growth does indeed pose an imminent threat to the existence of Christianity. Glimpses of this threat can already be seen in countries like Nigeria[15] where an escalation in violent conflict is experienced.

The new (or prevailing) realities experienced in Africa, call for a different approach to missions in Africa. The extent of the realities is of such a nature that a more collaborative effort by the church in Africa should be considered. A first step would be to introduce the terms 'collaboration' and 'networking' in our ecumenical language.[16] In the current lingua of the church, these are seldom used when we refer to mission. Mandell et al. (2017:328) help by stating, 'Conversation and language are the tools through which these new collective identities are negotiated, and successful collaboration is achieved'. A better understanding of the term collaboration may open possibilities of conversation among ourselves where we can negotiate new collective identities that lie beyond our current silo-like thinking of mission.

---

[11] Based on the theory of black swan events as described by Taleb (2007) and the necessity to build a robustness towards such negative impacting events.

[12] Cf. Michalopoulos, Naghavi and Prarolo (2012); Hassan Bello (2018).

[13] Cf. Solomon (2015); Rabasa (2009).

[14] Cf. Sookhdeo (2013; 2020).

[15] Cf. Sulaiman (2016); Ojo and Lateju (2010).

[16] Mandell et al. (2017) emphasise the importance of language that it 'affords a collective act of sense-making that contributes to the richness of the shared vision and individuals' commitment to the common goals within networks'.

Different possibilities of collaboration

This brings forth the latter part of the remark by Mandell et al. (2017:328), and that is: '**[a] need for a new collective identity involving interdependent organizations working towards mutual goals**' **(emphasis added)**. If a different mission methodology is to be adopted in Africa, then a new collective identity should be cultivated. This new identity would have to be shaped by interdependency, not by silo thinking. It is proposed that the underlying thinking of any methodology should be that of collaboration or networking as a method to shape interdependency.

Moving to a very short workable definition for collaboration or networking, it can be said that it is 'the action of working with someone to produce something'. The theory of Keast and Mandell (2013) suggest three types or models of how collaboration can take place. They propose as models the concepts of cooperation, coordination, and collaboration.

A first step would be to shape new language. Cooperation, coordination and collaboration are terms not used much in missiology. Language shapes a new way of thinking. Establishing the language of collaboration and networking is suggested as a pivotal first step to shape a collective identity. A second step would be to start discussions about collaboration, cooperation and coordination. This would require the participants to 'climb' over the silo walls and get together around a table where discussions could take place.

In exploring practical ways of how collaboration and networking can take place, the following is put forward (although more proposals could certainly be added):

Cooperative networks

A cooperative relationship or network can be described as a space where participants may agree to share information, share physical space, supplement 'gaps' or identify hiatuses in a specific work field, make referrals, exchange resources, etc. The goal would be the establishment of short-term collaboration relations, often informal and largely voluntary, between organisational entities.

A network is not focussed on formal treaties and agreements but more on informal sharing, thus making a network the perfect space to start discussions and explore possibilities for cooperation. As a process, cooperation networks or relationships are essentially about considering others, initiating working relationships, compromising your silo, and being accommodating, without necessarily adjusting individual goals. Given that cooperation entails the use of very few resources, mainly information sharing, it is further characterised by low levels of intensity and smaller risk taking.

Coordinative effort

This occurçs when there is a need to better align or orchestrate people, tasks, and resources to achieve a predetermined goal. This takes shape when organisations or entities start to understand that for various reasons they are unable to achieve their goals on their own. It is a deliberate effort to lower the silo walls and to explore new ways to achieve goals in cooperation with another organisation.

Coordination requires more than information sharing and informal network relations. Here there is a deliberate move towards joint planning and policymaking, decision-making, and joint actions and programmes between organisations. Although it is more structured and formal in nature to link organisations, they remain separate from each other and coordinate work. It moves from more than mere lip service to practical initiatives that can make or contribute towards real change by coordinating efforts.

Collaborative relation

In a collaborative relation there is a shared vision, reciprocal interdependence, and deliberate building of organisational relations. When a common problem or task is identified that demands more than what one organisation can do, a collaborative relation is needed. For collaborative networks to succeed, the following factors needs to be considered:[17]

Institutional factors –
What resources are available from who? Is the structure of collaborative organisations compatible or is there a need to form new structures that will serve the collaborative relation and is there within the structures a willingness to change?

Relationship factors –
Here, open and honest communication, commitment to goals and the process, mutual trust and respect for denominational and institutional culture are crucial features.

Output factors –
What are the joint and individual objectives that need to be achieved, what are the needs and requirements of all parties concerned, and how will knowledge be transferred? In what way can the sharing of technology help to bring about hope and to foreshadow the kingdom for the people in Africa?

---

[17] Cf. Rybnicek and Königsgruber (2019).

It is evident that various possibilities exist for collaboration. Part of creating new collective identities will entail the involvement of interdependent organisations working towards mutual goals. This can be achieved via one or all three possibilities for collaboration. If we in Africa are to envision a kingdom approach that lies beyond denominational silos, either one or more of the mentioned possibilities can be used by organisations.

Practical examples of collaboration efforts

Hofmeyr (2004) indicates four instances in Africa between 1975 and 2002 where combined or collaborative efforts of the church in Africa did achieve certain goals that were pivotal to the church in Africa and Africa as a whole. These refer to the role of churches and church leaders in their struggle for independence from colonial rulers (starting in the 1950s), the combined struggle against racism and apartheid, the enculturation of African theology as an evangelism tool as Western missionaries started to withdraw, and tertiary theological education at Christian universities that began to emerge on the continent. Africa today is a different continent due to the contribution that each of these instances brought to the development of Africa.

It is worth mentioning the latter two as continuing practical examples of collaboration and the results they have produced in Africa. The rise of the AICs is, as mentioned earlier, one of the contributors to the rise of Christianity on the continent. It might not fall in the exact methodological categories of formal collaboration, but the movement has collaboratively contributed to the growth of Christianity. The second example is that of theological education in Africa, which is well documented in the *Handbook of theological education in Africa*. In section four various authors contributed by relating the story of how their respective network was formed and how it attributes to better collaboration and the goal of providing, not only as a service to the church but also as a contribution for the betterment of theological education in Africa (Hendriks 2013).

Of the four areas identified by Hofmeyr, three remain excellent areas for collaboration, namely evangelism of missions, theological education, and the combat of a growing exploitation of African people by new forms of racism and colonialism. All three can be better addressed if the church in Africa works collaboratively to grapple with them.

Conclusion

In conclusion, it can be said that there is no 'one-size-fits-all' solution. It is argued that the heritage of a strong denominational approach to missions in Africa is slowly dwindling as Africa is developing its own identity. The growth of Islam necessitates a kingdom vision on missions. As indicated, there are examples in our past where collaboration did work, and which is therefore possible in future.

Numerous good networks exist in Africa (and they in turn, are networking) as well as ecumenical movements in disciplinary fields such as theological education.[18] It is via networking that a movement can begin that will foster discussions among all who are concerned with missions in Africa. Accordingly, a 'new' language will begin to take shape among the discussants and that language will communicate a kingdom vision where interdependence through collaboration can help to bring the gospel of Christ to those who need hope.

We do have options in Africa. As technology continues to develop throughout the continent, it opens more possibilities. As the funding models for missions are changing in the Western world, it opens the door for Africa to explore different ways to make disciples and preach the gospel. We have a choice though, to follow the old pattern of operating in silos or to opt for collaboration. Arguably a different approach, but one with a kingdom vision.

References

Adedibu, B.A., 2018, 'The changing faces of African independent churches as development actors across borders', *HTS Teologiese Studies/Theological Studies* 74(1), https://doi.org/10.4102/hts.v74i1.4740.

Chakravorti, B. & Chaturvedi, R.S., 2019, 'Research: how technology could promote growth in 6 African countries', *Harvard Business Review*, https://hbr.org/2019/12/research-how-technology-could-promote-growth-in-6-african-countries.

Diara, B.C.D. & Onah, N.G., 2014, 'The phenomenal growth of Pentecostalism in the contemporary Nigerian society: A challenge to mainline churches', *Mediterranean Journal of Social Sciences* 5(6 Special Issue), 395-402. https://doi.org/10.5901/mjss.2014.v5n6p395.

Ferreira, I.W. & Chipenyu, W., 2021, 'Church decline: A comparative investigation assessing more than numbers', *In die Skriflig/In Luce Verbi* 55(1), a2645. https://doi.org/10.4102/ids.v55i1.2645

---

18 Read the story of NetACT to understand how the formation of a network helped to shape theological education within the Reformed Churches in Africa and then grew via collaboration to being one of the biggest theological networks in Africa. See H.J. Hendriks, (n.d.), *Multiplying resources and research in Africa – The NetAct Story*, viewed 30 April 2022, from https://netact.org.za/wordpress/wp-content/uploads/2016/10/Multiplying-Resources-and-Research-in-Africa-The-NetACT-Story.pdf and also H.J. Hendriks, 2012, 'Contextualising theological education in Africa by doing theology in a missional hermeneutic', *Koers – Bulletin for Christian Scholarship* 77(2), art. #56. http://dx.doi.org/10.4102/koers.v77i2.56.

Pew research., 2017, *The changing global religious landscape*, Pew Research Center. https://assets.pewresearch.org/wp-content/uploads/sites/11/2017/04/07092755/FULL-REPORT-WITH-APPENDIXES-A-AND-B-APRIL-3.pdf

Harari, Y.N., 2016, *Homo Deus: a brief history of tomorrow*, Harvil Secker, London.

Hassan Bello, A., 2018, 'Islam and cultural changes in modern Africa', *Arts & Humanities Open Access Journal* 2(1), https://doi.org/10.15406/ahoaj.2018.02.00030.

Hendriks, H.J., (n.d.), *Multiplying resources and research in Africa – The NetAct Story*, viewed 30 April 2022, from https://netact.org.za/wordpress/wp-content/uploads/2016/10/Multiplying-Resources-and-Research-in-Africa-The-NetACT-Story.pdf.

Hendriks, H.J., 2012, 'Contextualising theological education in Africa by doing theology in a missional hermeneutic', *Koers – Bulletin for Christian Scholarship* 77(2), art. #56. http://dx.doi.org/10.4102/koers.v77i2.56.

Hendriks, H.J., 2013, 'Contextualising theological education in Africa by doing theology in a missional hermeneutic', in I.A. Phiri & D. Werner (eds.), *Handbook of theological education in Africa*, pp. 818-831, Regnum Books International, Oxford.

Hofmeyr, J.W., 2004, 'Post-independent mainline churches in Africa (1975-2000)', *HTS Teologiese Studies/Theological Studies* 60(4), a637.

Kealotswe, O., 2014, 'The nature and character of the African Independent Churches in the 21st century: Their Theological and Social agenda', *Studia Historiae Ecclesiasticae* 40(2), 227-242.

Keast, R. & Mandell, M., 2013, 'Network performance: A complex interplay of form and action', *International Review of Public Administration* 18(2), 27–45.

Kobia, S., 2006, 'New visions and challenges to ecumenism in the 21st century', World Council of Churches, viewed 14 December 2021, from https://www.oikoumene.org/resources/documents/new-visions-and-challenges-to-ecumenism-in-the-21st-century

Mandell, M., Keast, R. & Chamberlain, D., 2017, 'Collaborative networks and the need for a new management language', *Public Management Review* 19(3), 326–341, https://doi.org/10.1080/14719037.2016.1209232.

Meyer, B., 2004, 'Christianity in Africa: From African Independent to Pentecostal-Charismatic Churches', *Annual Review of Anthropology* 33, 447–474, https://doi.org/10.1146/annurev.anthro.33.070203.143835.

Michalopoulos, S., Naghavi, A. & Prarolo, G., 2012, *Trade and geography in the origins and spread of Islam*, NBER Working Paper No. w18438, viewed 30 April 2022, at https://ssrn.com/abstract=2157882

Nel, M., 2019, 'The African background of Pentecostal theology: A critical perspective',

In die Skriflig/In Luce Verbi 53(4), a2418. https://doi.org/10.4102/ids.v53i4.2418.

Nganwuchu, C.G., Anizoba, E.E. & Molokwu, G.C., 2021, 'Christian theology in the era of COVID-19', *Journal of African Studies and Sustainable Development* 4(5), https://doi.org/10.13140/RG.2.2.28191.89765.

Ojo, M.A. & Lateju, F.T., 2010, 'Christian-Muslim conflicts and interfaith bridge-building efforts in Nigeria', *Review of Faith and International Affairs* 8(1), 31–38. https://doi.org/10.1080/15570271003707762.

Paas, S., 2016, *Christianity in Eurafrica - A history of the church in Europe and Africa*, Christian Literature Fund, Wellington.

Phiri, I.A. & Werner, D. (eds.), *Handbook of theological education in Africa*, Regnum Books International, Oxford.

Rabasa, A., 2009, *Radical Islam in East Africa*, Rand Corporation, Santa Monica.

Rybnicek, R. & Königsgruber, R., 2019, 'What makes industry–university collaboration succeed? A systematic review of the literature', *Journal of Business Economics* 89(2), 221–250, https://doi.org.10.1007/s11573-018-0916-6.

Solomon, H., 2015, 'Islam in Africa: From Sufi moderation to Islamist radicalization', *Journal for Contemporary History* 40(2), https://hdl.handle.net/10520/EJC182082.

Sookhdeo, P., 2013, *Understanding Islamic theology*, Isaac Publishing, McLean.

Sookhdeo, P., 2020, *Understanding living Islam: Spirituality, structures, society and sects*, Isaac Publishing, Vienna.

Sulaiman, K.-D.O., 2016, 'Religious violence in contemporary Nigeria: Implications and options for peace and stability order', *Journal for the Study of Religion* 29, 85–103.

Taleb, N., 2007, *The black swan*, Random House, New York.

Thomas, N.E., 1995, 'Images of church and mission in African Independent Churches', *Missiology: An International Review* XXIII(1), https://doi.org/10.1177/009182969502300102.

Van der Watt, G. & Odendaal, M. 2022, *A Family of Reformed Churches in Africa: Remarkable stories of God's grace*, Christian Literature Fund, Wellington.

Venter, R., 2021, 'Theology, philosophy of biology and virology: An interdisciplinary conversation in the time of COVID-19', *Verbum et Ecclesia* 42(2), a2354, https://doi.org/10.4102/ve.v42i2.2354.

Walls, A.F., 1996, *The missionary movement in Christian history*, Orbis Books, New York.

Walls, A.F., 2002, *The cross-cultural process in Christian history*, Orbis Books, New York.

Wariboko, N., 2017, 'Pentecostalism in Africa', In *Oxford Research Encyclopedia of African History*, Oxford University Press, https://doi.org/10.1093/acrefore/9780190277734.013.120.

Chapter 12

A Mission-Centred African Public Theology

Sunday Bobai Agang

"You are my witnesses," declares the LORD, "and my servant whom I have chosen, so that you may know and believe me and understand that I am he, before me no god was formed, nor will there be one after me" (Isa 43:10, NIV).

You are truly my disciples if you remain faithful to my teachings. And you will know the truth and the truth will set you free (Jn 8:31-32).

Introduction

Over the years, evangelicals have devoted their time to the reading of the Bible, and they are very good at it. However, when it comes to 'reading' society, they are less adept. Given the lack of growth, security, transformation, and development in the African continent, the African church needs to hold the reading of both the Bible and society in total balance. In other words, 'The church needs to engage with society afresh and it needs theologically educated disciples to do so; followers of Jesus Christ who see their mission as both ecclesial and societal in a globalised world' (Cartledge, in ed. Greene & Shaw 2021:1). Thus, in this chapter I explore the theme of the mission of God within the confines of public theology in Africa. I argue that Africa's public space needs the Good News of Christ Jesus. I also emphasise that the Good News can only be 'good news' if the message of the incarnate Christ is heard, believed, and understood in all of its truth.

In the context of the dark backdrop of Africa's social, economic, cultural, political and spiritual corruption, and acting with impunity, the need for the Gospel of Christ to be specifically targeted towards grasping how God is interacting with the public space in our beloved continent can never be overemphasised. Given the deep-rooted nature and scope of corruption in the African continent, it has become extremely difficult to think of any hope for Africa. But those of us who know what the Good News is capable of doing in the life of any nation, cannot give up on our society.

The Good News is good news because it rescues people from all forms of slavery to sin and death in all spheres of life. St. Paul tells us that the gospel is the power of God that saves, and makes people – men and women, young and old – right with God. This gospel is the antidote and antibody to the sinful nature, which is a threat to our human existence. We will consider some of the things we will need to hold in perfect balance to enable us to do well in our grasp of the nature and scope of the gospel.

From the outset, it is important to observe that of all there is in planet earth, nothing is worthy and capable of being compared with the Good News of Christ Jesus. The Good News is about the mission of God in the world, what St. Paul calls, 'The power of God for salvation' (Rom 1:16-17). God's incomparably great power has brought salvation to the reach of all humans – delivering them from their greatest enemy – sin and death – and making it possible for them to have right standing in God's sight. The Gospel of Christ Jesus is truly Good News! It is the whole gamut of how those who believe in the crucifixion, death, and the resurrection of Christ Jesus from the dead are translated from the kingdom of darkness into the kingdom of God's marvellous light.

No wonder there is no generation of humans in the entire history of humanity that is as fortunate as the generation(s) which now exist(s) after the incarnation. To be balanced Christians, every generation of Christians must rediscover the power of the gospel, the Good News, afresh. It was such rediscovery of the Good News in all its truth that enabled past generations of Christians to live up to the moral vision and mission of Christ, particularly as spelt out in the Sermon on the Mount (Matt 5-7). In other words, it enabled them to build their lives on a solid rock, sound biblical truths. For instance, Bosch (2007:240) points out how,

> Augustine had rediscovered Paul for the fifth century; Luther rediscovered him for the sixteenth century. And he found the central thrust of Paul's theology in Romans 1:16, where "the gospel" is described as "the power of God unto salvation to everyone who believes", and even more particularly in the next verse which reads (in the King James Version), "For therein (that is, in the gospel) is the righteousness of God revealed from faith: as it is written, The just shall live by faith".

Thus, to have the audacity to live, walk, be, believe, and bear witness to this critically important truth, requires a thinking mind, characterised by knowledge, faith, and reason, which is seeking understanding, in order to love and treasure God above all else in the whole universe. Thus, the mission of God is impossible without knowledge, belief and understanding. Without a grasp of who God is and a confirmed belief in his existence and/or an understanding of who he is as a person – 'glorious in holiness, fearful in praises, doing wonders' – we cannot be his witnesses in a broken, decaying and dying world.

African public space defined and explained

The public space in Africa needs theological education that can change and transform it into a place that benefits all people in the continent. This is because of many factors. First, our public spaces are inundated with assumptions. As such, we cannot assume what we mean by a 'public space'. The public space is a place where everybody – Christians or non-Christians – co-exist. This is where some Christians tend to believe that it is 'a-no-go-area for God'. It is assumed, like the Assyrians once thought, after Israel defeated them in the battle between King Ben-Hadad of Syria and Ahab of Israel. The Assyrians consoled themselves by believing and concluding that Israel's gods were the gods of the hills and not of the valley. The Syrians believed that if the battle was brought to the plains, they would win the battle. But, as history shows, that assumption was completely wrong. In that, when the battle was taken to the plains where the Assyrians thought Israel's gods could not come to their aid, God helped Israel to defeat them (1 Ki 19:13, 21, 23-25, 28-29). That was proof that Israel's God was not only the God of the hills, but also the God of the valley or the plains. The defeat of the Syrian army both in the plains and on the hills underscores the fact that God is everywhere – both the hills and the plains are his. Therefore, both private and public spaces of this world are his. Our mission is not limited to private life. It is to be in all spheres, professions, academic disciplines, specialisations, etc.

So, I will attempt to define what I think it is. First, a public space is a place that is open to both citizens and non-citizens, religious and non-religious. It is space that is shared by all people. In other words, it is available to all people of faith. Therefore, it can be used interchangeably with 'public sphere', 'public square', or 'marketplace', which are places where all people freely have access. Thus, a public space includes, among other places, roads, public squares, libraries, marketplaces, parks, government offices, institutions, and/or infrastructures. So as long as something is *public*, it concerns the people as a whole – it is open to or shared by all the people. Thus, no individual can legally claim what is there as their property. This includes, *inter alia*, public furniture, public money (both public incomes and expenditures), public records, public goods/services, and so on. A public space is for the common good or for human flourishing.

Second, public space has largely become a place where many people in the world, including Christians, tend to think that it is a no-go-area for God. They think like that because it is open to everybody, which then means that 'morality is not significantly important and therefore not required'. That whole philosophy or worldview of a public space distorts and evades morality and ethics. That is why corruption is unprecedented in the African society. In refusing to acknowledge God, who is the Creator of all there is, Satan takes advantage of that ignorance and causes us to serve him. As such, Satanic activities are carried out in Africa's public spaces. That is why Jesus told Judas Iscariot, the son of Simon, 'You will always have the poor among you' (Jn 12:4-8). That is so, especially in Africa where public servants who are entrusted with public money tend to become thieves of the state. That is so because of the fact that both public and private people who are entrusted with public money steal from it for their personal use. They steal what belongs to us, both you and I, and deprive us of our God-given resources for human flourishing.

The contemporary African local church has not quite grasped the mission and vision God has given it when Jesus came and told his disciples,

> I have been given all authority in heaven and on earth. Therefore, go and make disciples of all the nations, baptising them in the name of the Father and the Son and the Holy Spirit. Teach these new disciples to obey all the commands I have given you. And be sure of this: I am with you always, even to the end of the age (Matt 28:18-20, NLT).

If Jesus Christ is now the Lord of all of life in heaven and on earth, it then implies that there is no public space he is not Lord of. St. Paul puts it thus,

> Now he is far above any ruler or authority or power or leader or anything else – not only in this world but also in the world to come. God has put all things under the authority of Christ and has made him head over all things for the benefit of the church. And the church is his body; it is made full and complete by Christ, who fills all things everywhere with himself (Eph 1:21-23, NLT).

So, how can we exclude God from our public spaces in Africa?

Mission the "labour room" of theology

Thinking in terms of public space means recognising that Christ has given his body, the church, power and authority over all spheres of life and the demons and diseases that are in them (Lk 9:1-2). The church is in a public space to preach the kingdom of God to it and to heal its corrupt ways—dishonesty, lack of integrity, and lack of respect for human dignity. The salvation that the church preaches promotes, protects, and defends human dignity. Jesus, the Saviour and Lord of all spheres of life and creation, the sole owner of Africa and the church, taught, preached, worked, and lived in public (Jn 7:13, 16). Our task is to give people the food that will endure to eternity. Today, as always, we face the challenge of a world where people labour harder for the food that perishes and less for the food that endures to eternity (Jn 6:27). After all, God is a missionary God.

We need to study both the Bible and the society so that we will be able to grasp the obvious fact that, in spite of the celebrated and truly unpredicted growth of Christianity in Africa today, the African public space is increasingly becoming ungodly. Our public and private spheres or publics are both characterised by corruption, acting with impunity, injustices, lack of integrity, dehumanisation of our fellow brothers and sisters by exploitation, marginalisation, domination, etc. The source of all these evils is the human heart:

> As humans, we search for joy in all the wrong places. And what we receive is just a sporadic sampling, a fraction of the real deal, a clever counterfeit to genuine joy. We look outside, not inside. The secret to a joy-filled life is so close, so obvious, that inside is often the last place we look. We search everywhere but within (Newberry 2007:5).

This is primarily because the mind which God has given us to think like him has been distorted and corrupted to the extent that we no longer think like God thinks. One of the places where it is extremely difficult to think like God thinks is the public space, which has been taken over by secular humanists who have infiltrated our universities as well as socio-political, socio-economic, and socio-cultural life. The call for the knowledge of the role of the church in the public spaces of Africa is germane and apt. It involves thinking, reflecting, and meditating on how God thinks and reveals his character. In this regard, Thomas Newberry (2007:xv) writes,

To understand how God thinks, we must first comprehend who God is. With just a quick glimpse through the Bible, we learn the following truths about who God is:

- God is love
- God is all-powerful
- God is ever present
- God is all absolute truth
- God is holy
- God is merciful
- God is faithful
- God is compassionate
- God is just
- God is unchanging, etc.

To think like God, we must become intentional about mirroring his image in all that we do [in every sphere of life]. When it comes to theological education for public space, our thought life matters. As our minds are infused with God's thoughts, to the extent that they reflect God's being, not only will we glorify God, but we will also increase our positive influence on those we love.

> No doubt you will become a much brighter light to many whom you may never meet personally. God wants to impart his character and power through every individual. And when this happens, the world is instantly changed because those who reflect his glory impact the world (Newberry 2007:xvi).

It is therefore obvious that God saves us and leaves us on earth for the work of mission. He is a missionary Godhead.

God as a missionary God

The mission of God is basically about the fact that God is love; and because of his love, God is in the business of pursuing humans until he helps them to discover that he is love and he has poured out his love for them so that they can experience true peace, joy, justice, compassion and forgiveness, which is what the power of the gospel allows us to have access to. God pursues us and finds us because he is a missionary God. Or more succinctly put, God the Father, God the Son, and God the Holy Spirit, in short, the Godhead, is a missionary God. 'Then the man and his wife heard the sound of the LORD God as he was walking in the garden in the cool of the day, and they hid from the LORD among the trees of the garden. But the LORD God called to the man, "Where are you?"' (Gen 3:8-9). The garden used to be a place where Adam and Even enjoyed unimaginable intimacy and fellowship with God. However, since the Fall of Adam and Eve, sin has continued to dominate the entire world. As a result, the place of relaxation and rest became a place of fear and hiding. Since then, God has continued to pursue humans until he brings them to his saving knowledge, light, truth, love and justice, etc.

Mission the "labour room" of theology

The mission of God is about God's perfect purpose, plan, and continuous interaction with his entire creation. That is why some of us African public theologians define theology not only as the study of God, but also as the study of and reflection on how God interacts with his creation. Thus, it is extremely important to recognise that our understanding of mission will be incomplete if we do not have a grasp of the contribution of public theology in Africa to the mission of God and the theology of the public implication of the Christian faith. Public theology draws us to the essence of the whole gamut of the mission of God.

In this chapter, I am primarily concerned with teasing out how our reflection on the mission of God in the world can be deeply grasped so that Christians are better equipped with the truth and infused with a new moral consciousness to the extent that they can have the wherewithal to concretely demonstrate the power of God for salvation. This will include, *inter alia*, the ability to bring God's good news of reconciliation to bear on our ethnically, religiously, and politically divided society; the restoration of broken relationships and ensuring integral transformation; and the redemption of our society from its systemic injustices to one that is humane and allows for human flourishing in all spheres of life. Thus, such grasp of the Good News is what would enable us to collapse the dichotomy between the sacred and secular spheres. So, African public theology holds hope for our continent and its pursuit of Agenda 2063: The Africa We Want and God Desires.

African public theology as the mission of God

A grasp of public theology and its missional content will help us rediscover how the first century church had such a tremendous impact on its entire world. For instance, an acclaimed missiologist, David J. Bosch (2011:203), tells of how, 'In the first centuries the church indeed spread its arms widely. It did not incarnate itself only in the cultures and thought-forms of the Greeks and the Romans but also expressed itself through the liturgies of other cultures. Coptic, Syriac, Maronite, Armenian, Ethiopian, Indian, and even Chinese'. This was only possible because the early Christians collapsed the sacred-secular divide. And to a large extent, they understood theology the way I define it in this chapter. I use the term 'theology' to mean the study of God and how he has continued to interact with his entire creation, and/or the world and all creatures in it, particularly the human race. So, the chapter is advocating the need for a practical grasp of theology as the mission of God in all spheres, both private and public. Thus, African public theology itself is all-embracing. It does not have room for the assumption that certain spheres, disciplines, professions, subjects, careers, and so on, are 'a-no-go-area for God'. African public theology provides a powerful way of seeing reality which Christians need to imbibe in order to dislodge the present danger facing African and global

Christianity: the sacred-secular divide. African public theology goes to show that, 'The power of the sacred-secular divide is not that people think it's true but that it shapes their lives anyway. In fact, it has successfully shaped the culture of the global church. It's so deeply embedded in the way we do things that often we don't notice it' (ed. Greene & Shaw 2021:1-2). African public theology helps Christians to build on the fundamental truths of the Bible. God is in the business of pursuing humanity until he finds it. In other words, as God searched for Adam and Eve after the Fall, so has he continued to extend his invitation to humanity to come back to him, so that humanity will enjoy unbroken fellowship with him by not only receiving Christ through faith but also fully participating and partnering with the incarnate Christ. This way of seeing reality from God's perspective enables us to develop strength of character and confident faith in our salvation. It also enables us to trust God to help us bring our fellow men and women to a state of mind where they can grasp and receive God's outpouring of love. A clear grasp of God's unfailing love is what is actually capable of bringing the desired humane change, transformation and restoration of the human race and its environment to God's original plan and purpose as clearly teased out in Paul's Gospel. Christopher Wright has distilled what Paul taught in his Gospel, thus:

1. There is only one supreme God, who has made himself known through creation and in the story of Israel.
2. All other gods are false human constructs that do not provide for human needs and cannot achieve human salvation.
3. The one living God has sent his own Son, Jesus of Nazareth, in fulfilment of his promise to Israel.
4. Through the death and resurrection of Jesus, God has opened the way for people of all nations to find salvation, forgiveness and eternal life.
5. Through faith in Jesus, God's appointed Saviour and King, people of any nation can now belong to the redeemed people of God, and be found among the righteous when God will intervene again through Jesus in the approaching day of final judgment.
6. This conversion through repentance and faith in Jesus was all that was needed to belong to God's covenant people (Wright 2006:191-192).

Transformation is what the gospel is all about. To do this well we will need to understand the state of the church and society in the mission of God in Africa.

African public theology as good news to Africans

A broad-based understanding of the mission of God will liberate the contemporary African church from its parochial focus on raising denominational Christians instead of disciples of Christ who are equipped with the truth of God for every good work. Of course, as we pursue the goal of raising Christ's disciples, we are not ignorant of the fact that it is no longer news that the centre of Christianity's gravity has shifted to the Southern hemisphere – Africa, parts of Asia, and Latin America. This paradigm shift of Christianity to our continent puts an enormous responsibility on our various denominational theological institutions across the African continent. They can no longer afford to do theology just to fulfil their denominational vision and mission, but also to ensure that their theological education is aimed at collapsing the sacred-secular divide, which has invariably continued to cause Christians to lack the ability to turn their knowledge of God into a viable value chain: being a conduit of God's virtues of love, honesty, integrity, peace-building, and development in church and society. This is why Sunday Agang (2020:4) has argued that,

> Public theology speaks not only to pastors and church leaders but [also] to every person who claims to follow Christ. It calls on each of us to take responsibility for carrying out the three tasks that the church everywhere is called to do: 1) proclaim the word which God has spoken, 2) demonstrate the way of Christ, and 3) work hard for the healing of our nations.

In other words, the mission of African public theology is to correct the lack of a grasp of the deeper meaning of the mission of God in Africa, which has created a huge disconnect between our Christian religious vigour and the ability to translate such Christian moral and ethical passion and enthusiasm into both socio-spiritual and socio-economic value chains.

By and large, African Christians seem to deny the power of the gospel, the Good News. For example, St. Paul's grasp of the depth of the Good News helped him to say,

> For I am not ashamed of this Good News about Christ. It is the power of God at work, saving everyone who believes – the Jew first and also the Gentile. This Good News tells us how God makes us right in his sight. This is accomplished from start to finish by faith. As the Scriptures say, "It is through faith that a righteous person has life" (Rom 1:16-17, NLT).

The gospel is indeed good news! But what makes it good news?

In Scripture there is one amazing truth: The gospel is the Good News. It is the Good News because it tells of how God saves sinners and transfers them from the kingdom of darkness into his kingdom of light. Since the Good News is the power of God at work where it has genuinely been preached, taught, understood and received, it must bear fruit that will stand the test of time. That is partly what makes it good news. However, the highest, the best and final Good News, are the foundational events that make the gospel Good News. They are, 'Christ died for our sins in accordance with the Scriptures, that he was buried, that he was raised on the third day in accordance with the Scriptures' (1 Cor 15:3-4). Yes, that is true. Without this, there is no gospel or mission at all. But what must we see in those events if they are to be gospel for us? Second Corinthians chapter 4 verses 4 and 6 tell us: We must see 'the glory of Christ who is the image of God'. In other words, we must see 'the glory of God in the face of Christ'. Equally, for there to be change, transformation, and development in our society, we (Christians) must show 'the glory of Christ in our faces'. Why? Because that is what the gospel entails.

To explain further, the gospel is not just an historical event where Christ died, was buried, and rose on the third day. Thus, the gospel is incomparably good news, which is beyond our human comprehension. And we do not see the decisive good in the good news if we do not see in the events the glory of Christ who is the image of God. This points to something immensely important. We humans who have been created in the image of God are intended to radiate the glory of God in our faces wherever we find ourselves (Isa 43:7, 10). For the gospel to be truly good news in Africa's public space, the people Christians meet and socialise with in the public space must witness the radiant glory of God in our lifestyle and in our moral attitudes and behaviour. We must be the good news to our society and church. To further appreciate the fact that the gospel is good news, we need to take a look at its fruits and benefits.

The direct benefit we have in the gospel

Many Christians have a parochial understanding of the power of the gospel, the Good News of Christ. So, it is very important to notice carefully the use of the word 'gospel' in 2 Corinthians 4 verse 4: It is the 'gospel of the glory of Christ who is the image of God'. This is the gospel. The glory of Christ seen in the work of redemption is Good News. This is the highest and best and final good that makes other good things promised in the gospel good. Here are the benefits that we directly have in the gospel:

1. Justification: This is good news because it makes us stand accepted by the one whose glory we want to see, love, and serve above all things.

2. Forgiveness: This is good news because it cancels all the sins that keep me from seeing and enjoying the glory of Christ who is the image of God.
3. Removal of wrath and salvation from hell: That is good news because now in my escape from eternal misery I find eternal pleasure beholding the glory of God in the face of Christ.
4. Eternal life: This is good news because this is eternal life; Jesus said, that they know me and him who sent me.
5. And freedom from pain, sickness and conflict are good news because, in my freedom from pain, I am no longer distracted from the fullest enjoyment of the glory of Christ who is the image of God.

In other words, 2 Corinthians Chapter 4 verses 4 and 6 tell us what the highest, best, ultimate good of the good news is: the glory of God in the face of Christ, that is, the glory of Christ who is the image of God. This is a real glory, a real spiritual light that shines in his saving work, and is seen not with the physical eyes, but with the eyes of the heart (Eph 1:17f) or of the spiritual (2 Cor), and after we (Christians) have seen it with spiritual eyes, we cannot help but decisively live for his renown, joy, praise, and honour wherever we find ourselves – and then all professions, careers, tasks, jobs, businesses, all spheres of our influence, subjects of educational pursuits, and so on, will benefit from us becoming the image of God in the public space.

The mission of African public theology is largely to encourage the local church to play the role of being a catalyst of a revolution in Africa by campaigning for an African continent that is shaped by the understanding that God is the only Creator and all else is created by God, that God created all humans in his image to be like God in character virtue, morality and ethics because they are intended for his glory. Thus, our engagement in theological education in the public spaces is to call men and women back to their God-given vocation to that they will be people who are, 'Doing God's work, in God's way, for God's glory' (James Hudson Taylor).

We need an Africa that recognises that two accounts – the creation narrative in Genesis 1:26-27 and the incarnation narrative of Jesus in John 1:1, 14 – tangibly reveal God as the source of human dignity. This recognition will enable African Christians to respect, promote and defend human dignity, and create and use technology to protect human dignity as the monks did in the Middle Ages (Mangalwadi 2011). We need an African continent that recognises that nature; spirits of the living dead, of ancestors; the forests, hills, valleys, and stars in the galaxies; angels; leaders, including so-called men/women of God, are created. All of them are created and they can be studied, but they cannot in any way be feared and worshipped or be placed over and above God.

We need theological education that helps believers build not only an intellectual bank of knowledge, but also spiritual and moral character virtues, which include, among other things, development of a passion for truth and truth-telling, love, justice, peace, compassion, repentance, forgiveness, and righteousness. Therefore, engaging the public space in our theological education is critical. It will require us to pay careful as well as critical attention to the local, national, international, or global news. That is to say, we will intentionally read local, national and international newspapers, and carefully examine where the truth is said, or the truth is distorted. This approach is very necessary because we live and walk and have our being in a dark, broken, and decaying world.

God's mission in our social context

The social context that the gospel/African public theology seeks to transform is characterised by social crisis, political chaos, spiritual and economic famine, disease, civil wars, coups, dictatorships, social disorder, spiritual and economic corruption, and the unfortunate contemporary legitimisation of military regimes. These challenges seem to be the most outstanding elements of post-independence Africa. For instance, the preaching and evangelisation of the African continent actually contributed to the agitation for independence. The seed for the idea of independence was sown when the Church Missionary Society (CMS) secretary, Henry Venn, proposed that the African church needed to be infused with the idea of self-reliance: Self-propagating, Self-governing, and Self-supporting – three 'selfs'. Post-independence crises have led Kofi Adusei-Puku to observing that the mood of optimism, hope and high expectation has today been overtaken by frustration and pessimism (Adusei-Puku 993:320, in Ayittey 1999). To salvage Africa, public theology calls the Christian community back to the Bible.

The Bible as a book that has helped the West

The sources of theological education include, *inter alia*, the Bible, Christian history, traditions, and experiences. In Africa, one of the incredible blessings is that we hold the Bible in high esteem. However, we are yet to come to terms with the enormous value of the Bible. For instance, the Bible helped the West to discover human dignity in the Middle Ages. African Christians have been studying the Bible for over a century. But what has the Bible helped African Christians to discover that will help the public space and transform our society and church into humane spaces? According to Visal Mangalwadi (2011:193), in the West, 'The Bible's impact on literature made it the West's source of cultural authority'. Jesus profoundly states, 'You are truly my disciples if you remain faithful to my teachings. And you will know the truth and the truth will set you free' (Jn 8:31-32). In the Middle Ages, the monks' discovery of human dignity in the course of their comparative study of the account of the creation of man and woman in Genesis 1:26-27, and the account of the incarnation in John 1:14, led to the development of technology and science to protect human dignity. The monks' discovery led to a huge revolution of the public spaces of Europe.

The role of the mission of the church in the public space

The mission that the public space needs, which public theology promotes, is the social embodiment of the gospel of Christ Jesus. This entails a careful analysis of the context of doing the contemporary mission of God. Of course, without mincing words, the Good News has always been preached in the context of enormous social and spiritual darkness, persecution, suffering, killing and destruction of lives and property on a daily basis. (As the Scriptures say, 'For your sake we are killed every day, we are being slaughtered like sheep' [Rom 8:36]).

Jesus said, 'As long as I am in the world, I am the light of the world' (Jn 9:5). He further said, 'As the Father sent me so sent I you' (Jn 20:22-23). He also said, 'Go and make disciples of the world – teaching them to obey my teaching ...' (Matt 28:19–20). 'The church lives from something and toward something that is greater than the church itself' (Volf 1997:x). Miroslav Volf talks about the need for theological education to raise and nurture 'constructive theologians, who seek to develop an ecclesiology that will facilitate culturally appropriate – which is to say, both culturally sensitive and culturally critical – social embodiment of the Gospel' (1997: 5). He is of the opinion that, 'The costal form of the church must find its basis in its own faith rather than in its social environment. Only thus can churches function effectively as prophetic signs in their environment' (1997:15).

In terms of theological education, it means that the primary goal of theological education in Africa is the quest for the knowledge of God's truth revealed in nature and in Scriptures. Basically, Christians have two books – the Bible and the book of nature – where they acquire knowledge of God's truth (Dow 2013). The idea of theological education in the public space is not about teaching theology in our public spaces. Rather, it is about theological institutions training men and women of holistic intellectual character. Jason Baehr (from Loyola Marymount University) explains that a person's intellectual character consists of their inner attitudes and dispositions toward things like truth, knowledge, and understanding. This explanation is very important because it points to the way we can assess the kind of people that can make a difference in our public spaces. For example, do our students care about learning and knowledge? Do they desire to understand the world around them? Are they curious about why things are the way they are, about the unfolding of history and about what ultimately exists or what is ultimately good? (Dow 2013:11).

Truth matters. As such, it must not in any way be confused with remarkable intelligence and impressive academic credentials. For as Baehr argues, 'Remarkable intelligence and impressive academic credentials are no guarantee that a person will actually care about truth – or at least, care about it more than other values such as money, power, and professional prestige' (cited in Philip Dow 2013:12–13).

Theological education which prepared people like Martin Luther (the Reformer), William Wilberforce, Martin Luther King Jr., and so on, for positive interaction with the public space, is one that,

> [C]ares about and gives special attention to the intellectual dimension of personal character … A concern with truth is the very heart of virtuous intellectual character; it is what gives rise to the range of individual intellectual virtues such as reflections, attentiveness, fair-mindedness, intellectual carefulness and courage (Dow 2013:13).

In other words, to do theological education that will be relevant to the public space, is to:

> [C]are for knowledge of truth in general because God has given humanity two books: the inspired Jewish and Christian Scriptures and the "book of nature." To care about knowledge in general—including the subject matter of history, mathematics, economics, psychology, philosophy and the like—is to care about the content of this second book. Similarly, it is often said that, "All truth is God's truth," meaning that God and God alone is the ultimate source of all that is. If this is right [which I believe it is], then Christians need not limit themselves to biblical or theological knowledge. For in doing so they cut themselves off from a deeper and more profound understanding of the creation and its Creator (Dow 2013:13–14).

If African Christians want to change Africa's present socio-political and socio-economic public space or contexts, they have no option but to 'be concerned with the enterprise of education [as well as with the cultivation] of an interest in and understanding of matters of intellectual character and virtue' (Dow 2013:16).

Conclusion

God's mission within the confines of a Christian perspective on God's mission is how Christians can bring Africa true transformation. It is the pursuit of God's truth until we realise what God's mission entails: God's love, compassion, righteousness, justice, godliness, faith, self-content, gentleness and endurance, which involve hard work, doing everything humanly possible to serve God in what we do (Rom 13:6b). The church impacts and transforms the public space when she teaches her members to see all work, all study, all subjects, all professions, all disciplines, and so on, as a means to reciprocate God's love by doing his work in the way he prescribes, to achieve his intended glory (Rom 11:36). This kind of transformation is only attainable through the Holy Spirit who is to constantly be in charge of our lives and relationships with God, humans, and the environment.

Christianity helps its adherents to understand how transformation trickles down to key sectors of human life and relationships: (1) Self; (2) God; (3) fellow humans; and (4) the environment. As Christians, when transformation has holistically taken root in the public space, which is expressed in this way: 'So the word of the Lord continued to increase and prevail mightily' (Acts 19:20), there is a paradigm shift in direction and men and women in a given society resolve in the Spirit to do what is necessary for the common good of the individual members of the society.

References

Agang, S.B., 2020, 'The need for public theology in Africa', in S.B. Agang, D.A. Forster & H.H. Hendriks (eds.), pp. xxx, Chapter 1, *African public theology*, ACTS, Bukuru, Nigeria.

Ayittey, G.B.N., 1999, *Africa in chaos*, St. Martin's Griffin, New York.

Bosch, D.J., 2007, *Transforming mission: Paradigm shifts in theology of mission*, Orbis Books, Maryknoll, New York.

Dow, P.E., 2013, *Virtuous minds: Intellectual character development*, IVP Academic, Downers Grove, Illinois.

Greene, M. & Shaw, J.I., 2021, *Whole-life mission for the whole church: Overcoming the sacred-secular divide through theological education*, Langham Global Library, Carlisle, Cumbria.

Mangalwadi, V., 2011, *The book that made your world: How the Bible created the soul of Western civilization*, Thomas Nelson, Nashville.

Newberry, Thomas, 2007, *The 4.8 Principles: The Secret to a Joy-Filled Life*. Tyndale House, Chicago, Illinois.

Volf, M., 1997, *After our likeness: The church as the image of the Trinity*, Eerdmans Publishing Company, Grand Rapids.

Wright, C.J.H., 2006, *The mission of God: Unlocking the Bible's grand narrative*, InterVarsity Press, Downers Grove, Illinois.

Chapter 13

Dialogue With Other Faiths in Africa

Maniraj Sukdaven

Introduction

As of 27 October 2021, the population of Africa stands at 1 382 815 807, and in southern Africa, it stands at 67 503 634.[1] Southern Africa is constituted of the following countries: South Africa, Namibia, Botswana, Lesotho, and Swaziland. For the purpose of this chapter, Zambia, Malawi, Zimbabwe and Mozambique will be incorporated into this region. The religious breakdown of this region is as follows: Christianity 81.1%, Islam 8%, and other religions (including African Traditional Religion [ATR]) 10.9%. However, one must take precaution in accepting these figures as some who regard themselves as Christians are in fact practitioners of ATR but attend Christian services. These people could rather be described as followers of folk Christianity or a form of syncretic religion (ATR and Christianity). When one considers the religious breakdown in the southern African countries, Christianity dominates this region, followed by Islam and indigenous religions.

The question is, how do these more prominent religions relate to each other and, more specifically, because Christianity remains the dominant religion, how does Christianity specifically relate its faith to other religious beliefs and practices? In the context of this chapter, the focus will predominantly be on interreligious dialogue as a means of fostering relationships with adherents of different religions on the African continent. The history of missions on the African continent is well documented, and yet Ani (2005:142) succinctly suggests that, 'If the nineteenth century was the Century of Mission, then the twentieth Century was certainly the Century of Dialogue'. In this regard, Ani (2005:140) raises some compelling issues, such as:

> Should interreligious dialogue replace mission, or is it now a matter of mission or dialogue? Do we say that mission and dialogue should go together?

---

[1] Worldometer, n.d., *Africa population live*, viewed 27 October 2021, from https://www.worldometers.info/world-population/africa-population/.

Or when we talk of interreligious dialogue do we mean that the content of the Good News be disseminated by Dialogue? Which religion should now operate with a flair of superiority, or are all religions just equal and the same?

These questions raised by Ani need to be seriously considered and discussed in missiological circles. One cannot agree more with Orton (2016:350) that, '… improved dialogue between people identifying with different religious faiths has often been promoted as a positive way of building more cohesive communities in response to the perceived threat and conflict which can arise from such divisions'. This leads to the following questions: (1) What forms can be adopted for Christians to relate their faith? (2) How should these forms be communicated? and (3) Is Christian mission and interreligious dialogue compatible?

In this chapter I endeavour to address these three questions by, firstly, defining communication and its affiliated methods, and secondly, discussing the forms that can be adopted, together with the challenges that these forms pose for religious relations, especially Christianity and missions. The most prominent form that is espoused here is the concept of dialogue with other religions in Africa.

In order to understand the concept of dialogue, I will attempt to differentiate between different communicative methods, and to place dialogue in the correct slot amongst the communicative tools. Communicative tools consist mainly of the following: (1) communication/conversation; (2) dialogue; and (3) debate. Much of this chapter will be devoted to the dialogical tool of communication that will attempt to address some of the questions raised by Ani earlier in this chapter.

Communication

It is important to understand what is meant by communication, especially when engaging fellow human beings on matters concerning faith traditions and cultures. According to Bohm (2004:2), the meaning of the word 'communication' is 'based on the Latin *commun* and the suffix "ie" which is similar to "fie," in that it means "to make or to do." So one meaning of "to communicate" is "to make something common," i.e., to convey information or knowledge from one person to another in as accurate a way as possible'. This communicating of knowledge can take the following forms: (1) thoughts and ideas; (2) instructions, videos, and other such forms of recordings; and (3) conversations, through facial expressions, emails, WhatsApp, and various forms of texts. This list is certainly not exhaustive, as communication can include a range of tools, with dialogues and debates, which are discussed hereafter, being only two such examples. Communication as a definitive term can include one or more people, whereas conversations, dialogues, and debates include more than one person.

Before considering dialogue as a communicative tool, I want to briefly turn to debates in order to substantively reject this form of communication as it is an obstacle to interreligious relations.

Debates

A debate can be construed as a conversational contest where a view is concretised and therefore unmoving, as this view seeks to dominate in a 'power struggle' to win the contest. In such contests there is a 'pro' and 'con' side, with the aim to convince either side which is the correct view. When considering this form of communication in interreligious dialogue, one can already see conflicts arising between different religious affiliates, which can lead to disharmony, discord, and divisions. These conflicts are presently visible not only on the African continent but within the global community as well. Therefore, one tends to agree with the special report by Garfinkel (2004:2) wherein she states that, 'The notion on interfaith dialogue[2] encompasses different types of conversations, settings, goals and formats. But it is not an all-encompassing concept: interfaith dialogue is not intended to be a debate'. For the Christian to foster meaningful relations with other religions, they need to steer away from debates with other religious affiliates, as this will provide more hindrances that open doors for engagement. What about the dialogical conversational tool? Can the implementation of the dialogical conversational tool help to promote interreligious dialogue so as to enhance better relations with other religious traditions? We will now turn our attention to this form of interreligious engagement in order to understand how such a tool will assist in Christians developing a more cohesive community of different religious affiliations.

Dialogue

The word 'dialogue' comes from the Greek word *dialogos*, which is made up of a further two Greek words, viz. *dia*, meaning 'through' and not 'two', and *logos*, interpreted as 'word' or 'meaning'. Therefore, to engage in a dialogue is to engage in making meaning, with the emphasis on 'meaning'. Dialogue can take many forms, but the intended purpose is to be able to communicate, without contesting from a position of power to enforce one's own opinion, as was seen with debates. Bohm (2004:7) confirms this notion when he states that:

---

2   The terms 'interfaith dialogue' and 'interreligious dialogue' are used interchangeably, even though 'interreligious dialogue' is a more embracing term to denote all belief systems and not just faith belief systems. For further discussion please see the article by M. Sukdaven, 2019, 'Religion, religion! Wherefore art thou, religion? Enactment in interreligious encounters as walking the talk', *HTS Teologiese Studies/Theological Studies* 75(4), a5640. https://doi.org/10. 4102/hts.v75i4.5640.

> In a dialogue, however, nobody is trying to win. Everybody wins if anybody wins. There is a different sort of spirit to it. In a dialogue, there is no attempt to gain points, or to make your particular view prevail. Rather, whenever any mistake is discovered on the part of anybody, everybody gains. It's a situation called win-win, whereas the other game is win-lose – if I win, you lose. But a dialogue is something more of a common participation, in which we are not playing a game against each other, but with each other. In a dialogue, everybody wins.

As such, dialogue is a communicating tool where the intention is to hear the viewpoints of two or more people that come from different backgrounds, religions, and cultures, especially in this context of interreligious relations, together with their assumptions and opinions. The objective of dialogue, in contrast to debate, is to listen to all opinions, even if one does not agree them or, as Bohm (2004:30) suggests, 'It may turn out that the opinions are not really very important – they are all assumptions'. Of course, we should never be fooled into believing that all is hunky-dory in dialogue without any challenges. There would be the exceptions where some would want to assert themselves so as to dominate the dialogue, thus creating unwanted tension, especially with those who become overwhelmed with this domination that they would rather remain subdued, and therefore not contribute effectively in the discourse of the dialogue.

To sum up and formulate a definition of dialogue, I turn once again to Bohm (2004:30) who succinctly offers a working definition of dialogue as 'a frank exchange of viewpoints between two or more persons with the scope of enriching each other, leading to increase in the knowledge about each other's beliefs and convictions, and the removal of ignorance and or prejudice about the same'. And, in the words of Schein (2003:27),

> Dialogue… is a basic process for building common understanding, in that it allows one to see the hidden meanings of words, first by seeing such hidden meanings in our own communication. By letting disagreement go, meanings become clearer, and the group gradually builds a shared set of meanings that make much higher levels of mutual understanding and creative thinking possible.

With this understanding of dialogue, we now turn to how dialogue can be used advantageously in developing better relations with other faiths and religions in Africa.

Interreligious dialogue

When considering the African context, Christianity and Islam have always accepted the *bona fide* term 'religion' to denote its belief and faith traditions. Of note, one should not ignore the fact that before the arrival of Christianity and Islam on the African continent, and according to Brenner (2000:144), most African languages did not have a word for religion. Chidester (2018) maintains that 'religion' is a Protestant, and as such, a Western construct. What can be gathered from Chidester's critique of religion affirms the nature of material religion in juxtaposition with the abstract nature of religion purported by Western constructs. As is the case with all indigenous beliefs and practices,[3] the idea of 'material religion' justifiably, and most appropriately, defines 'indigenous religion'. In this regard, Hutchings and McKenzie (2017:6) suggest that 'belief itself can be studied from a materialist perspective' and that '[b]eliefs are learned, experienced and adapted through embodied engagement in rituals, relationships and practices'.

Much reference has been made to interreligious dialogue as a communicative tool with the intention of fostering relations with other religions. But what exactly does interreligious dialogue entail? In this regard, Hall (2010:1) suggests that:

> To speak of interreligious dialogue is to speak of an encounter between human subjects, not a comparison of doctrinal belief systems. In saying this, I am not suggesting that religious beliefs should be bracketed out of the equation – the phenomenological epochè I wish to emphasise that first and foremost dialogue is an event of intersubjective communication.

There is nevertheless space for engaging issues of philosophy and theology within interreligious dialogue, as espoused by Küng (1991), but with the intention of also self-reflection. He therefore calls for:

---

3 I purposefully excluded the term 'faith' as even this term does not resonate with indigenous religions.

> ... a more intensive philosophical and theological dialogue of theologians and specialists in religion which takes religious plurality seriously in theological terms, accepts the challenge of the other religions, and investigates their significance for each person's own religion (Küng 1991:138).

From the above two citations, we glean two fundamental characteristics that are espoused within an understanding of interreligious dialogue. The first is that interreligious dialogue is an encounter between human subjects that is focused on intersubjective communication. The term 'intersubjective' is a philosophical term that relates to 'intersubjectivity'. Intersubjectivity, according to the Oxford Reference (n.d.), suggests: 'The process and product of sharing experiences, knowledge, understandings, and expectations with others'. An expanded explanation of intersubjectivity is found in AlleyDog.com which explains that:

> Humans are by nature gregarious, or social beings, but although they are designed to operate in group situations each experiences the world and relationships uniquely as an individual. A basic human example of intersubjectivity is having a shared, common agreement in the definition of an object. So most people would experience intersubjectivity when asked to picture an apple - the definition of an apple would be the same.[4]

Therefore, when Hall (2010) refers to intersubjective communication, the intention is to understand this as a more social engagement, that those participating have a common goal and share common experiences and expectations. This cannot be said when one refers to the second characteristic espoused by Küng (1991) who calls for a philosophical and theological dialogue.

Thangaraj (1999:95-96) lists four levels of interreligious dialogue, which closely correlates with Hall (2010) and Küng (1991) above:

1. *The dialogue of life*, where people strive to live in an open and neighbourly spirit, sharing their joy and sorrows, their human problems and preoccupations.
2. *The dialogue of action*, in which persons of all religions collaborate for the integral development and liberation of people.

---

[4] AlleyDog.com, n.d., 'Intersubjectivity', viewed 27 July 2022, from https://www.alleydog.com/glossary/definition.php?term=Intersubjectivity#:~:text=What%20this%20means%20is%20that,the%20definition%20of%20an%20object.

3. *The dialogue of theological exchange*, where specialists seek to deepen their understanding of their respective religious heritages, and to appreciate each other's spiritual values.
4. *The dialogue of religious experience*, where persons rooted in their own religious traditions share their spiritual riches, for instance, with regard to prayer and contemplation, faith, and ways of searching for God or the Absolute.

Similarly, Çetinkaya (2020:n.p.) proposes that 'interreligious dialogue takes place at four levels: (1) knowledge, (2) action, (3) spirituality and (4) morality'.

Challenges to interreligious dialogue

Stemming from the above discussions, it is noticeable how interreligious dialogue evolved on basically two fronts, namely: the *social engagement* (which involves the dialogue of life and action), and the *academic engagement* (which involves the dialogue of theological exchange and religious experience). These are described in more detail below.

Interreligious dialogue as social engagement

Interreligious dialogue as social engagement incorporates the dialogue of life and action. In this type of dialogue, matters pertaining to daily community life and action are considered. It is the participation in community life, irrespective of religious affiliation, which sets the foundation for living in harmony and peace with others. This is where due recognition is given to all that everyone is created by God and shares in the same grace and mercy which God bestows on them. Therefore, there should not be any prejudice that is espoused as all human beings are created in the image of God and, as such, reflect the image of God. Nwosu (2020:180-181), reviewing social engagement, refers to the importance of participating in community activities which should also include collaboration with other religious affiliates for peace, development of communities, liberation of people, and humanitarian purposes. In some instances, a forum may be established to represent the views of different religious groups to institutions, with the upliftment of communities for a cohesive civil society as its mandate.

Interreligious dialogue as academic engagement

Interreligious dialogue as academic engagement incorporates the dialogue of theological exchange and religious experience. In this type of dialogue, matters pertaining to philosophy and theology are considered. Although this includes community life, the focus is on the understanding of theological and philosophical ideals, beliefs and practices, which may incorporate faith[5] traditions. In this engagement, the community meets to share 'methods of prayer, spiritual efforts, scripture... own religious traditions (and) spiritual riches' (Nwosu 2020:181). One example of interreligious dialogue as an academic engagement is the term 'scriptural reasoning'.

In scriptural reasoning, 'The intention is not to seek agreement or disagreement about other religions' scriptures but to learn to accommodate or show hospitality toward the views of other religions regarding scripture, even though one may disagree' (Sukdaven 2018:2). Hardy (2006:530) provides a succinct explanation of the purpose of scriptural reasoning as the:

> Primary discourse of God in the particularities ... as seen through ... particular interpretation of ... particular Scriptures, not in order to compare them and derive what is thought to be common to them, but in order to allow them to disagree or agree and by doing so illuminate the others.

One of the shortcomings of interreligious dialogue as academic engagement and, which inherently will appear, is that emotions may be displayed especially if one is not accustomed to it, or has freely accepted the rules and adopted the skills[6] in this engagement. If one construes this engagement as a threat to one's faith, belief and practices, it may lead to conflict.

With this understanding of dialogue as a communicative tool, and in respect of this chapter with the focus on dialogue with other faiths, I return to the compelling questions Ani (2005:140) raises with regards to dialogue in mission, namely:

> Should interreligious dialogue replace mission, or is it now a matter of mission or dialogue? Do we say that mission and dialogue should go together?

---

[5] I have deliberately mentioned belief and faith as two different philosophical and theological terms. Faith is the actionable part of belief or belief in action. Belief, on the other hand, is the acceptance of a statement that is true, but upon which one may or may not act on.

[6] There are generally seven accepted skills of dialogue that are crucial. These are: deep listening, respecting others, inquiry, voicing openly, balancing advocacy and inquiry, suspending assumptions and judgements, and reflecting. These skills can be found in E.H. Schein, 2003, 'On Dialogue, Culture, and Organizational Learning', *Reflections: The SoL Journal*, 4(4), 27-38.

Or when we talk of interreligious dialogue do we mean that the content of the Good News be disseminated by Dialogue? Which religion should now operate with a flair of superiority, or are all religions just equal and the same?

The questions raised by Ani challenges the participation of the Christian church in interreligious dialogue. We now, therefore, turn our attention to mission as dialogue or dialogue as mission, where interreligious dialogue forms the central communicative tool in this discussion.

Mission and dialogue in Africa

How important is interreligious dialogue in Christian mission? Is Christian mission and interreligious dialogue mutually exclusive or complementary? In returning to the introduction of this chapter and the statistics cited there, it was determined that Africa is a continent of three major religions: Christianity, Islam, and ATRs. Ani (2005:141) correctly asserts that, 'Christian missionary activities took place in Africa with a flair of superiority', and that, 'In most parts of Africa interreligious dialogue lays much emphasis on relationship with adherents of Islamic faith and African Traditional Religion'. Finally, he asks what the content of such a dialogue will entail.

To answer the last question, Ani (2005:146) puts forward the suggestion that within his context in Nigeria, interreligious dialogue assumed only the social engagement that was discussed earlier. It would seem that the context Ani found himself in was ripe for this form of interreligious engagement due to violence, oppression, exploitation, abuse of basic human rights, and political and economic considerations. As was alluded to previously in this chapter, these common social ills galvanised religious communities, and through their representatives, brought people together to work 'on practical steps to achieve social cohesion in the concrete situations of life'. In this sense, and it would be true for most, if not all, countries in Africa, that this form of interreligious dialogue is more visible and dominant. This form of dialogue also satisfies the characteristics identified in my assertion of interreligious dialogue as social engagement which embodies the idea of dialogue in life and action.

Across Africa there are many forums comprising of adherents of different religious beliefs and practices that have been established to address social engagement, as described by Ani above, via interreligious dialogue. This is commendable as one of the calls to the Christian church is to work towards life in its fullness, as intended by God. So, in this way, the Christian church is fulfilling one of the mandates of the *missio Dei*. What about interreligious dialogue as academic engagement which embodies the dialogue of theological exchange and religious experience? This form of interreligious dialogue is far from prominence when compared to interreligious dialogue as social engagement. Interreligious dialogue as an academic engagement assumes that those engaging in this form of dialogue have a decent understanding of their beliefs and practice, to the extent of being able to engage in this field and succinctly put forward their best leg to converse with affiliates of other religious persuasions so as to meaningfully engage with them at a more philosophical and theological level. These engagements are not for the faint-hearted, especially when the idea of scriptural reasoning is adopted as a mode for this engagement. As the name suggests, at the core of this approach, in interreligious dialogue, Scripture forms the basis upon which adherents of different faiths and religious beliefs gather. This coming together is intentional because, as religion is generally at the forefront of religious violence and extremism, the religious text that is engaged takes the form of reasoning about the texts in Scripture, not with the intention to learn to accommodate or show hospitality towards the view of other religions regarding Scripture, whether one agrees or not.

When one enters into the area of academic engagement, one is confronted with three truth claims, namely: (1) My religion has the only truth (that only in Jesus can true revelation and salvation be found). This is regarded as the *exclusivist* type; (2) Jesus is operative in other religions (that Jesus includes other religions by being present in them anonymously). This is regarded as the *inclusivist* type; and (3) in as much as Jesus is unique, there are other ways to God. This view totally rejects the exclusive view and is known as the *pluralist* type.

These three types of truth claims have a marked influence on how one engages in interreligious dialogue by adopting the scriptural reasoning approach. By adopting any of these approaches, one can be accused of shutting the door on interreligious dialogue. When this door in the academic engagement approach is shut, mission is inhibited, and one does not have the opportunity to share the gospel via the scriptural reasoning approach. Even though the intention in the academic engagement is not to convince the other or bring the other to conversion, the Bible does call on the church to plant the seed of the gospel in any which way, and God will honour His word and it will not return void. Therefore, one cannot underscore the importance on interreligious dialogue as a source for missions.

Conclusion

The whole purpose of interreligious dialogue is about a 'frank exchange of viewpoints between two or more persons with the scope of enriching each other, leading to increase in the knowledge about each other's beliefs and convictions, and the removal of ignorance and or prejudice about the same' (Bohm 2004:30).

In relation to this, one needs to also answer the question raised by Ani (2005:140): Should interreligious dialogue replace mission, or is it now a matter of mission or dialogue? Do we say that mission and dialogue should go together? Or when we talk of interreligious dialogue, do we mean that the content of the Good News should be disseminated by dialogue? Which religion should now operate with a flair of superiority, or are all religions just equal and the same?

The answer to the first question is that interreligious dialogue should not replace mission, nor should one have to choose between mission and dialogue. This chapter answered succinctly that interreligious dialogue has a place at the table for mission which has opened a door for Christianity to engage other religions at two levels, namely: (i) social engagement, and (ii) academic and religions experience engagements. Both these terms have been well defined in this chapter to give credence to their importance in mission.

The last question raised by Ani relates to the notion of superiority of one religion over the other. This was also addressed in the types of truth claims: exclusivist, inclusivist, and pluralist. The chapter explained that none of these approaches assists in missions, and it will only shut doors to the Christian who would otherwise have had a wonderful open door to express the gospel under the most trying and challenging circumstance of political and ideological upheaval that is opposed to the spread of the gospel. Not that interreligious dialogue should be used for this purpose, but God will remain true to his word wherever and however it is told. Finally, and in the words of Emmanuel Martey (2008:11):

> Africa today is a multi-cultural and multi-religious society. As such, our very survival depends on how we learn to live and walk together in harmony with our nonChristian neighbours or, drift apart and destroy ourselves and others. In inter-religious dialogue and praxis, we learn how to live and walk together with our neighbours—how to struggle together; face the crises of poverty, oppression, injustice, racism, and sexism together; face diseases, death, and mourn together; and how to celebrate life together. In all this togetherness, we also articulate and convey that which is deepest in our lives and our hearts—that which has been the source of our inspiration, empowerment and resilience in the face of death and decay—namely, our faith which has guided all our actions.

References

AlleyDog.com, n.d., 'Intersubjectivity', viewed 27 July 2022, from https://www.alleydog.com/glossary/definition.php?term=Intersubjectivity#:~:text=What%20this%20means%20is%20that,the%20definition%20of%20an%20object.

Ani, I., 2005, 'What We are Dialoguing About? Some Reflections on Interreligious Dialogue in Africa', in J. Meili, E. Heiniger & P. Stadler (eds.), *Interreligious Dialogue*, 140-147, Brunner Medien AG, Luzern.

Bohm, D., 2004, 'On Communication', in L. Nichol (ed.), *David Bohm: On Dialogue* (2nd ed.), 1-5, Routledge, London.

Brenner, L., 2020, 'Histories of Religion in Africa', *Journal of Religion in Africa* 30(2), 143-167.

Çetinkaya, K., 2020, *Interreligious Dialogue*, Key Concepts in Intercultural Dialogue, 96, Centre for Intercultural Dialogue, viewed 27 July 2022, from https://centerforinterculturaldialogue.files.wordpress.com/2020/02/kc96-interreligious-dialogue.pdf

Chidester, D., 2018, *Religion: Material Dynamics*, University of California Press, Berkeley, CA.

Garfinkel, R., 2005, 'What Works? Evaluating Interfaith Dialogue Programs', United States Institute of Peace, Special Report 123, 1-12, viewed 5 June 2022, from https://www.usip.org/publications/2004/07/what-works-evaluating-interfaith-dialogue-programs.

Hall, G.V., 2010, 'Inter-or-Intra-Religious Dialogue?', *Australian eJournal of Theology* 15(1), 1-13.

Hardy, D.W., 2006, 'The Promise of Scriptural Reasoning', *Modem Theology* 22(3), 530-551. https://doi.org/10.1111/j.1468-0025.2006.00333.x.

Hutchings, T., & McKenzie, J., 2017, 'Introduction: The Body of St Cuthbert', in T. Hutchings & J. McKenzie (eds.), *Materiality and the Study of Religion: The Stuff of the Sacred*, pp. 1-13, Routledge, Abingdon.

Küng, H., 1991, *Global Responsibility: In Search of a New World Ethic*, Crossroad Publications, New York.

Martey, E., 2008, *The Challenge of Inter-Religious Dialogue and Praxis to the African Theological Community*, viewed 15 May 2022, from https://www.oikoumene.org/sites/default/files/Document/WOCATI_2008_-Presentation_on_INTER-RELIGIOUS_DIALOGUE__CATI_-_Emanuel_Martey.pdf

Nwosu, P.U., 2020, 'The Concept and Practice of Inter-Religious Dialogue in Africa', *International Review of Humanity Studies* 5, 176-183. https://doi.org/10.7454/irhs.v0i0.227.

Orton, A., 2016, 'Interfaith Dialogue: Seven Key Questions for Theory, Policy and Practice', *Religion State and Society* 44(4), 349-365. http://dx.org/10.1080/09637494.2016.124886.

Oxford Reference, n.d., 'Intersubjectivity', viewed 20 July 2022, from https://www.oxfordreference.com/view/10.1093/oi/authority.20110803100008603.

Schein, E.H., 2003, 'On Dialogue, Culture, and Organizational Learning', *Reflections: The SoL Journal* 4(4), 27-38.

Sukdaven, M., 2018, 'Exploring the Possibility for African Traditional Religion to be Included in a Reimagined Scriptural Reasoning Model', *HTS Teologiese Studies/Theological Studies* 74(3), a5224. https://doi.org/ 10.4102/hts.v74i3.5224.

Sukdaven, M., 2019, 'Religion, religion! Wherefore Art Thou, Religion? Enactment in Interreligious Encounters as Walking the Talk', *HTS Teologiese Studies/Theological Studies* 75(4), a5640. https://doi.org/10. 4102/hts.v75i4.5640.

Thangaraj, M.T., 1999, *The Common Task: A Theology of Christian Mission*, Abingdon Press, Nashville.

Worldometer, n.d., *Africa Population Live*, viewed 27 October 2021, from https://www.worldometers.info/world-population/africa-population/.

Chapter 14

Evangelism and Mission

Johannes Knoetze

Introduction

To write about evangelism in a book on mission is not only proper but also necessary. To attend to the distinction between mission and evangelism, as well as the relation between mission and evangelism, is just as important. Already in the 1950s Stephen Neill remarked that if everything becomes mission, then nothing is truly mission. Bosch (1979:12–14) gives a brief summary of the debates and discussion about the relation between mission and evangelism. At Uppsala, in 1968, the World Council of Churches (WCC) used 'mission' as an umbrella term to include a diverse range of aspects, such as health- and social services, youth projects, politics, socio-economic development projects, the use of violence, fighting against racism, human rights, and many more. Donald McGavran criticised the Uppsala meeting since they defined mission as 'any good activity at home or abroad which anyone declares to be the will of God!' (1979:12). However, since the Nairobi 1975 meeting of the WCC, the concepts of 'mission' and 'evangelism' have almost functioned as synonyms, but still keeping the comprehensive meaning.

In history there were at least three, may I add colonial, distinctions between mission and evangelism. The first was geographical. Mission was something done when you cross the borders to the Third (or global) World, while evangelism was done at home (Europe). Thus, the church in Europe sent 'missionaries' to the heathen in the rest of the world. If the same missionary worked in Europe doing the identical work, he/she would be called an 'evangelist'. A second distinction was made regarding faith. Mission was to those people who were not yet Christians, while evangelism was to those who are no longer Christians. But in a sense, it was the same as the first since Europe was the 'no-longer-Christians', and the rest of the world was the 'not-yet-Christians'. The third was to use mission and evangelism as synonyms. When the WCC established the Commission on World Mission and Evangelism (CWME) in 1961, their mandate was described as: '[T]o further the proclamation to the whole world of the Gospel of Jesus Christ, to the end that all men may believe in him and be saved' (Bosch 1979:14).

Today we acknowledge that the gospel is from anywhere to everywhere, from all seven continents to all seven continents, and what an enriching experience! John Stott has helped us to understand that the 'Great Commandment' and the 'Great Commission' are tied together and interdependent. While mission and evangelism both have to do with the church crossing borders to enter the world, it is definitely not the only task of the church. The church is also a worshipping community that has the responsibility to build her members (*oikodome*) through *leitourgia, koinonia, diakonia, and didaskalia (Hendriks 2004:34)*. But 'Evangelization as the heart of ministry happens as Christ commissions the community *to be* his witnesses, *to do* his witness, and *to say* his witness. Continuing conversion is to Christ's salvation and thus to his mission' (Guder 2000:159).

If we then define mission as the common witness of the whole church, bringing the whole gospel to the whole world, what then is evangelism? Evangelism is more than just a part of mission. Hans Burki stated that evangelism is 'the center of the all-embracing mandate of God to the church' (quoted in Bosch 1979:19). When we want to understand what evangelism is, we must not look at the evangelism objects, or objectives, or methods, but rather at the content. The content of evangelism is the *kerugma* of the New Testament: 'the gospel events', 'the gospel witnesses', 'the gospel affirmations', 'the gospel promises', and the 'gospel demands' (Bosch 1979:19). It must be understood that *euangelion* is always good news, and it always includes an invitation; the God of mercy is inviting us. But *euangelion* is not good news in general, it is always actually within a specific context, over and against the bad news of the world. Evangelism has to do with addressing the specific needs of people in their specific context. Evangelism is thus not the bringing of an 'objective' truth of the Bible, but truth as an encounter (Kritzinger 2008). The person or the church doing evangelism is not just the messenger but is part of the message. Evangelism is the incarnation of the Word. If the person or the congregation that evangelises does not become part and parcel of the message, the good news, then no evangelism has taken place. Only as a participant in the *missio Dei* will the truth become truth as an encounter. In this regard, Bosch (1979:20) quotes Paul Loffler:

> When referring to its theological meaning, "evangelism" is practically identical to "mission". When referring to the evangelistic witness "evangelism" more specifically means "the communication of Christ to those who do not consider themselves Christians". … Thus, evangelism is sufficiently distinct and yet not separate from mission.

Understandings of evangelism

In his latest book, Osmer (2021:1–7) describes two opposite but basic understandings of evangelism. The first understanding has to do with concepts like 'bringing people to Christ' and 'sharing the Word so people will know the Lord from the heart'. This understanding of evangelism focuses mainly on conversion. As such, evangelism is viewed as successful when people convert, and it is associated with revivals, evangelistic preaching, and evangelism campaigns. For a long time, this understanding of evangelism (especially from America) shaped the general understanding of evangelism. It is logically deducted from different biblical passages, especially Jesus' call to his disciples (Lk 5:10, Mk 3:14, Matt 10:5-15, Lk 10:1-24, Jn 15:27, Matt 28:16-20). The second understanding relates to people who are sceptical of using the word evangelism since it is associated with negative experiences and images of people knocking on doors and confronting individuals on the street. In Osmer's description, this 'group' moves from evangelism to hospitality, where the focus is not only on the Bible but on the social context too. In this approach, it is about showing God's love and not only talking about God's love; this is done by inviting people from all walks of life and making them feel welcome in the community. It is not about the number of conversions, but about people and their needs. This understanding is clearly deducted from Jesus reaching out to people outside the religious establishment like the tax collectors, the Samaritans, and the sinners. Jesus and the Early Church were constantly crossing boundaries to bring healing, freedom, and forgiveness to outsiders. Osmer is describing this movement as 'Progressive Protestantism' which emerged in the 19th century and the first decades of the 20th century.

Within a post-Christendom context, Paas (2019:5) pleads for 'a theology that does justice to the deep secularization of many areas in the West without saying goodbye to the missional nature of Christianity'. With regards to evangelism, he refers to the document *Together Towards Life*: '[E]vangelism is defined as that "mission activity which makes explicit and unambiguous the centrality of the Incarnation, suffering, and resurrection of Jesus Christ". … it is characteristic of evangelism that it invites people to follow Jesus, to become disciples' (in Paas 2019:14). Paas is writing this within a frame of mind where we accept Christian mission as a gift having a reward in itself rather in what it produces (2019:xvii). When Christians receive mission as a gift, then 'Mission begins with an explosion of joy' (2019:7). Then mission and evangelism become normal to life as we work, eat, play and live as family and friends, and as we bond and share our lives with each other and also share the 'tidings of great joy' (2019:7). From a post-Christendom perspective, Paas is concluding that we must no longer assume faith, but rather consume faith, since 'faith becomes a matter of the *will*' (2019:24). Mission is part of a Christian's life. As Christian believers we cannot not 'missionise'. 'Mission is intrinsically connected with the Christian core experience of Jesus and his story' (2019:8) and, as such, evangelism forms the spearhead of mission (cf. Armstrong 1978:8). 'Mission may not always begin with evangelism. But mission that does not ultimately include declaring the Word and the name of Christ, the call to repentance, and faith and obedience has not completed its task. It is defective mission, not holistic mission' (Wright 2006: 319).

Bosch (2012) described 13 elements of an emerging ecumenical mission paradigm. Amongst these elements he also discussed *Mission as evangelism, Mission as common witness,* and *Mission as witness to people of other living faiths.* In this distinction between evangelism, common witness, and witness to other living faiths, we must pick something of the uniqueness of evangelism. Although witness is distinct from evangelism, evangelism includes witness, but witness does not always include evangelism. Under the heading: 'Toward a constructive understanding of evangelism', Bosch (2012:421-430) discusses the following 18 points which, to remain within the scope of this chapter, I will only mention here:

- Missions is perceived to be wider than evangelism
- Evangelism is therefore not to be equated with mission
- Evangelism is an essential "dimension" of the total activity of the Church
- Evangelism involves witnessing to what God has done, is doing and will do
- Evangelism does aim at a response
- Evangelism is always an invitation
- The one who evangelises is a witness not a judge
- Although we ought to be modest about the character and effectiveness of our witness, evangelism remains an indispensable ministry
- Evangelism is only possible when the community that evangelises – the church – is a radiant manifestation of the Christian faith and exhibits an attractive lifestyle
- Evangelism offers people salvation as a present gift, and with it, assurance of eternal bliss
- Evangelism is not proselytism
- Evangelism is not the same as church extension
- To distinguish between evangelism and membership recruitment is not to suggest, though, that they are disconnected
- In evangelism only people can be addressed and only people can respond
- Authentic evangelism is always contextual
- Evangelism cannot be divorced from the preaching and practicing of justice
- Evangelism is not a mechanism to hasten the return of Christ
- Evangelism is not only verbal proclamation

These points define evangelism. Let's take a look now at other related concepts like faith, church, and salvation and the kingdom of God.

Faith

When finding himself in a changing multicultural context, Armstrong (1979:16) realised the need to help people discovering their own faith, before teaching and expecting them to share it with other people. Armstrong opted for a 'faith-sharing' approach of evangelism. He then defined 'faith-sharing' as 'three-way communication in which two or more persons relate to each other their personal experiences of God' (1978:15). The evangelist is not to argue a case but to state his or her own beliefs in a way that others may perceive them as true. 'Faith-sharing' is not a one-way communication; the evangelist needs to be a good listener that responds appropriately, rather than a clever talker trying to convince the other person.

> ... being a witness is not a question of clever or heartfelt words; we are not in the business of selling the gospel. At the end of the day, we can only witness to what God has done in our lives and to what God is doing in history. Whether or not people respond is the work of the Holy Spirit alone. Our responsibility is simply to share our story and God's story with an invitation to all to join God's story (Myers 2017:188).

Faith sharing is incarnational, to be with people and care for people, rather than propositional, telling people, offloading on them (Armstrong 1978:9). Therefore, to make a case for God is to share one's experiences of satisfied needs (Armstrong 1979:35), since it is impossible to rationally prove the existence of God to non believers (1979:21). Paas (2019:7) mentioned some of these experiences[1]:

- The awareness of having received a great privilege (election, grace, blessing) ...
- Love for and compassion for people, who are, in whatever way 'lost' ...
- Concern about the direction in which the world or the nation is heading ...
- Joy ...
- The awareness of having a vision of truth ...
- The conviction of being part of an advanced (Christian) culture, that spreads blessings and wealth ...

---

[1] Paas calls it motives.

Paas continues to say that not all of these motives are specifically religious or Christian; they are natural and human but the content we add makes the difference (2019:8). It is about who gets the credit; this is the difference between believers and unbelievers (Armstrong 1979:37). When believers look at life through the eyes of their faith and interpret life from their understanding of God, human life is inescapably missionary, everybody evangelises and lives in a culture of conversion. There is nothing 'high and lofty' about evangelism; 'It is fully wedded with our social nature; we are witnessing, sharing, helping beings. "The word is near you, on your lips and in your heart …" (Rom 10:8)' (Paas 2019:6). Armstrong (1979:28) describes how I find myself with faith. I cannot own it; it is not a possession I can make myself have, but it is a gift from God. I can only joyfully share my experiences with others, without claiming it to be normative for them. 'One can describe one's own experience without threatening the other person. Sharing the evidence of God, in one's own life does not put the other person on the defensive but allows that person the freedom to assess the evidence and make his or her own application' (1979:36).

Such an understanding of evangelism, and the style of serving people through evangelism, is the opposite of confrontational evangelism that needs to lead to conversion. I believe it is from this understanding that evangelical leaders start to question evangelism as 'conversionism'. Osmer (2021:10-11) describes the characteristics of evangelism as conversionism as follows:

- *People are saved when they convert.* As soon as people convert, they are no longer amongst the 'lost', since they are now 'saved'. 'People apart from Christ are lost (Luke 15), dead in sins (Eph 2:1), under sin (Rom 3:9), and under condemnation (John 3:18)' (2021:10).
- *Individuals have the freedom to decide whether they will convert or not.* Every individual has a choice; when a person makes the decision, he or she is saved or lost.
- *Conversion is life-changing and accompanied by a dramatic experience at a particular moment (or short period) of time.* 'Thus evangelism has focused on a single issue: accepting Jesus as Lord and Saviour – now at this moment in time' (2021:11).

Over and against evangelism as conversionism, Osmer (2021:12) describes evangelism as an invitation:

Evangelism is the invitation to respond to the gospel, the good news of God's salvation in the world in Jesus Christ, which is offered to others as part of the witness of the church under the guidance and persuasive power of the Holy Spirit.

In my view, this description of Osmer lacks some important concepts like 'kingdom of God' and the 'communion of the saints' which is found in the description of Armstrong (1978:15) that also hints at evangelism as an invitation:

> Evangelism is proclaiming in word and deed the good news of the kingdom of God, and calling people to repentance, to personal faith in Jesus Christ as Lord and saviour, to active membership in the church, and to obedient service in the world.

From the above it is clear that evangelism is not only about conversion but rather a calling 'to come and follow him [Jesus] as part of a community of disciples' (Osmer 2021:13). This brings us to the next section, namely, the understanding and place of the faith community (church) in evangelism.

Church – a called community

'Someone has commented that too many Christians share their faith with one another and have fellowship with the world, when it ought to be the other way around!' (Armstrong 1979:61). Throughout the Bible it is clear that God is 'calling' people to participate in the *missio Dei*. Hastings (2012:14) states: "If the church is an image of the Trinity, it should not be merely *communio* (communion), but *communio* in *ekstasis* (outpouring) – the communion of the Trinity flowed out in the creating of a universe in love, by an act of his will, and the reconciliation of a fallen creation." In the New Testament, Paul also refers to the congregations as the *ekklesia*, the called-out people. Osmer (2021:14-16) uses the theme of calling as an entry to understanding evangelism.

First, *it is God who calls*; we must not confuse our human actions with divine action in evangelism. God calls people, not us; He is present in their lives long before we arrived.

Second, *God's call comes through the gospel*. The gospel, which is the good news of God's salvation, includes both God's 'yes' and God's 'no' to this world. In evangelism, we invite people to respond to the salvation in Jesus Christ; we are not shaming or threatening people but witnessing to the love of God.

Thirdly, *those people who respond to God's call through the gospel receive a new identity; they become God's called people and followers of Jesus*. Evangelism is an invitation to become part of the *ekklesia*; it is not about individuals first. Paas (2019:191) says, '[T]he Church precedes the individual, and that the individual receives his or her Christian identity through the participation in the Church'.

God has a relationship with the church first, and through the church he builds relationships with individuals.

Fourth, *the community of disciples and its individual members have a common mission: to bear witness to the gospel of God*. As a called-out and sent community, the church builds and invites her members, but also loves and serves the world. Nel (2021:11), comments that the faith community exists for the sake of the world, therefore the preaching in the faith community must turn them towards the world.

Fifth, *the mission of witness encompasses saying, doing, and being the gospel*. 'Evangelism is at the heart of the church's mission. It is not only something the church does; it represents something the church is' (Armstrong 1979:66).

Sixth, *evangelism is the ministry of inviting others to hear Christ's call to come and follow him*. 'Evangelism involves ... – witnessing, advocacy, evidence, and testimony – but is neither equated with or limited to any or all of them. I may 'witness' to a fellow Christian, but that is not evangelism. I may share my personal testimony with an adult Bible class, and neither is that evangelism' (Armstrong 1979:56). The invitation to follow Christ will look different for individuals in diverse contexts and cultures.

Paas (2019:187) remarks that modern Christians, and more specifically Protestants, tend to separate their Christian identity from participating in a local church within their specific context. He gives much attention to the church as the priesthood of believers but points out that in a 'Christian world' this priesthood could only develop 'upwards' in relation to God and 'inward' in relation to other Christians. It was Barth who helped to develop the priesthood to also develop 'outward' in relation to the world. Pass (2019:188), however, warns about over-emphasising the importance of the individual calling where 'a kind of hyper-Protestantism' interprets the priesthood of all believers to question the phenomenon of church and live as so-called 'post-church-Christians'. In most of the 'post-church' cases, the focus is on the individual who has been 'touched directly by God' or 'is individually empowered by the vision of the kingdom', which some might describe as a calling. Reading Osmer and Paas, as well as from my own ecclesiological and soteriological understanding, calling will always include the church in some way or another. And as the body of Christ,

> A Christian community needs a positive missional vision above all, and too many so-called "fresh" or "experimental" Christian communities are predominantly therapeutic groups, where damaged people manage to maintain some fragments of their former faith, but without much appeal and witness to those who don't share their background and sensitivities (Paas 2019:189).

Within the context of Africa, I am not sure how this relates to the different groups of independent churches where in most instances an individual 'leader' received a specific calling, starting his or her own church. Although faith and our callings are definitely personal, they are not individual or private. Being a Christian implies belonging to the *body of Christ*, the church. We receive our identity as a Christian through baptism and we are baptised *into* the body of Christ. Our identity is our incorporation in the body of Christ, and as the body of Christ we participate in the *missio Dei*. Therefore,

> Salvation is impossible apart from the church, not because the church has received salvation as a possession and is now in a position to dispense it or with-hold it from others. *It is instead because salvation is, in the first place, a distinct form of social existence.* To be saved is to be made part of a new people and a new politics, the body of Christ (italics in the original Paas 2019:192).

Christ is the head of the church, and unless the church – as the body of Christ – is united with Christ, it does not exist. For Christ through the Holy Spirit calls the church into being out of the world; he is building it, and he is sending it into the world. 'It is this invisible, spiritual relationship between Christ and the church that constitutes the being of the church, moment by moment and day by day' (Osmer 2021:148). It is in this regard that I want to make clear the distinction between proselytising and evangelism. *Proselytising* is about converting a person from one religious belief to another. Armstrong is pleading for *service evangelism* where the focus is on the needs of people, including spiritual needs. 'Service evangelism is concerned about persons; proselytizing is concerned about converts' (Armstrong 1979:63).

It must be emphasised that the church is the evangelist, and she must evangelise with integrity, knowing *that* she believes, *why* she believes, and *what* she believes.

Salvation

Where evangelism is viewed as conversionism, the question about the relation between salvation and evangelism is unavoidable. It is also clear from most of the authors, Bosch (2011), Armstrong (1979), Paas (2019) and Osmer (2021), that evangelism expects a response of some kind. Osmer (2021) discusses two understandings of salvation, namely: soteriological existentialism and *soteriological objectivism*.

> Soteriological existentialism is characterised by the view that salvation in itself and as such is not constituted or complete until something decisive takes place in one's human existence. To that extent, what took place in Christ does not acquire validity and efficacy until something decisive also comes to take place in us (Osmer 2021:168).

In this instance, conversion is a condition to be saved, and evangelism is then focused on saving people.

> Soteriological objectivism ... signifies that Jesus Christ is regarded as the sole Mediator not only of revealed truth, but also as saving truth. ... [It] means that there is finally no other truth about us than the truth of who we are before God in Jesus Christ (Osmer 2021:169).

In this understanding, we receive salvation as a free gift, and we can add nothing to it. Salvation is not dependent on us in any way. The reconciling work of Jesus is complete, perfect, and unsurpassable.

Soteriological objectivism is universal in its scope. Christ has died and risen for all! Does this mean that all people will be saved? No, although everybody is saved in Christ, not everybody will be saved at the consummation. God is a righteous God. He will not force us to convert, but will respect those who consistently and persistently resist the truth of their complete salvation in Christ. Therefore, 2 Peter 3:9 (NIV): 'The Lord is not slow in keeping his promise, as some understand slowness. Instead he is patient with you, not wanting anyone to perish, but everyone to come to repentance' is true; God does not owe us eternal patience.

However, understanding the *missio Dei*, salvation is the work of the trinitarian God. It is the work of the Spirit to convince us of our salvation, joining us to Christ and allowing us to participate in his work. Romans 8:16: 'The Spirit himself testifies with our spirit that we are God's children'. It is the Holy Spirit who mediates all forms of communion: us with God, us with fellow believers, and us in solidarity with the world.

> Salvation is the outcome of God's gracious action in Jesus Christ. It is a free gift, undeserved and unmerited. We receive it in faith, by trusting in God's grace through the Holy Spirit (Osmer 2021:171).

Mission the "labour room" of theology

Experiencing God and being saved is not the same. Salvation is in essence the restoration of community or communion. It is in this regard that Cyprian said there is no salvation outside the church. '[T]o receive salvation means that we enter a forgiving and healing *relationship* with God. ... it is about forgiveness, reconciliation, intimacy and adoption as God's child, together with your brothers and sisters' (Paas 2019:197). If salvation is about the restoration of community, and the Holy Spirit is creating that community, then there needs to be a community where salvation is real, and this community is called 'church'. As such, the church is not an extra, but an essential part of what God is doing with humans. The church participates in the *missio Dei* in restoring creation, and is sign and foretaste of the kingdom of God through the empowerment of the Holy Spirit. As such, the Eucharist is central to the missional identity of the church since it is not only the affirmation of the community but also always open and inviting.

> The life of worship and celebration is radiated outside the Sunday worship, into the other days of the week and outside the community. All activities of the Church are considered as expressions of the same reality that is celebrated during the Eucharist – the community with Christ and one another (Paas 2019:200).

It seems something more needs to be said, especially within the African socio-economic context and the needs of Africans. How do our prayers relate to salvation if we pray: 'your kingdom come, your will be done, on earth as it is in heaven' (Matt 6:10)? Salvation must be about more than

> [T]he individual and his or her personal relationship with God. Hatred, injustice, oppression, war, and other forms of violence are manifestations of *evil*; concern for humanness, for the conquering of famine, illness, and meaninglessness is part of the *salvation* for which we hope and labour (Bosch 2012:406, italics in the original).

However, there might be similarities between well-being and salvation, but they are not the same. In salvation the 'Christian faith is a critical factor, the reign of God is a critical category, and the Christian gospel is not identical with the emancipation and liberation movements' (Bosch 2012:408). However, salvation is never out of this world but always of this world.

Evangelism is then to witness to and participate in God's involvement in the world, proclaiming in word and deed the crucifixion and resurrection of Christ and relying on the Holy Spirit's empowerment. In this life we will always be caught up between the 'already' and the 'not yet' of God's reign, 'from the tension between the indicative (salvation is already a reality!) and the salvation subjunctive (comprehensive salvation is yet to come!) there emerges the salvation imperative – get involved in the ministry of salvation!' (Bosch 2012:410).

Conclusion

Tarantal (2020:1) states that in the year 2020, 80% of the world's Christians would come from the Global South (Africa, Asia, and Latin America). The growth of Christianity, especially in Africa, has tremendous implications for the global church, as well as the church in Africa, particularly regarding evangelism.

The question is, what is the criteria we use to call someone a Christian (our understanding of salvation)? Can an illiterate person who has heard the gospel of Jesus Christ only convert his/her life to Christ once? Can a person who reads his/her Bible every day, pray to the trinitarian God and love his/her neighbour, but also keep to African traditionalism, be called a Christian? Fortunately for us, Bosch (2012) has already helped us to understand that the evangelist is a witness and not a judge. But the point I want to make is that we need to relook at evangelism, especially in Africa. Meaning a person who no longer believes in Christ for whatever reason does not go back to a previous status of pre-Christian but is rather a non-Christian or a post-Christian. Therefore, the evangelical contact point with such a person will be different to that of a pre-Christian. For example, when a person who is married divorces his or her partner, they do not go back to being the same status as they were before marriage. We will not talk about them as pre-married, but rather as divorced/post-married/not married; the point is, their lives have changed. When we talk to them about marriage, we will have to understand where they are, and what happened to them. We have to address their need. The question is, how do we handle it if they do not have a need, or do not even realise it? The same with evangelism. We may not address people who have heard about Christ and believed in him the same as someone who never heard about Christ. We need to understand something of why this person does not want to be a Christian anymore; or wants to be a Christian, but no longer associates with the church.

Within the African context, mission churches have focused for so long on the three-selves of Venn and Anderson, namely self-governing, self-supporting, and self-propagating, not on *self-theologising*. In this sense, they did not really witness but were proselytising. Evangelism does not only involve a decision but also growth, and this is the importance of belonging to a local faith community. But within Africa, churches should do their own theologising based on the Scriptures, while sharing with each other the theological insights gained by the church down through history and around the world (Hiebert 1994:130).

Let's remember 2 Corinthians 4:7: 'But we have this treasure in jars of clay to show that this all-surpassing power is from God and not from us'; therefore, I conclude with the definition of evangelism proposed by N.T. Niles (as quoted in Armstrong 1978:15): 'Evangelism is one beggar telling another beggar where to get bread'.

References

Armstrong, R.S., 1978, *Faithful witnesses. Participant's book*, The Geneva Press, Philadelphia, Pennsylvania.

Armstrong, R.S., 1979, *Service evangelism*, The Westminster Press, Philadelphia, Pennsylvania.

Bosch, D.J., 1979, *Heil vir die wêreld*, N.G. Kerkboekhandel, Transvaal, Pretoria.

Bosch, D.J., 2012, *Transforming mission. Paradigm shifts in theology of mission*, Orbis books, Maryknoll, New York.

Guder, D.L., 2000, *The continuing conversion of the church*, Eerdmans, Grand Rapids.

Hastings, R., 2012, *Missional God, Missional Church. Hope for re-evangelizing the West*, InterVarsity Press; Downers Grove, Illinois.

Hendriks, H.J., 2004, *Studying congregations in Africa*, Lux Verbi BM, Wellington, South Africa.

Hiebert, P.G., 1994, *Anthropological reflections on missiological issues*, Baker Books, Grand Rapids, Michigan.

Nel, M., 2021, 'Framing our understanding of missional', in M. Nel (ed.), *Mission moves: Cultivating communities of the Gospel* (HTS Religion & Society Series Volume 11), pp. 1–18, AOSIS, Cape Town. https://doi.org/10.4102/aosis.2021.BK256.01

Myers, B.L., 2017, *Engaging globalization. The poor, Christian mission, and our hyperconnected world*, Baker Academic, Grand Rapids, USA.

Osmer, R.R., 2021, *The Invitation. A theology of evangelism*, William B. Eerdmans Publishing Company, Grand Rapids, Michigan.

Paas, S., 2019, *Pilgrims and priests. Christian mission in a post Christian society*, SCM Press, London, UK.

Tarantal, P., 2020, 'Global South Christian leaders: An African perspective', in A.N. Botha & E. Baron (eds.), *Majority world perspectives on Christian mission*, pp. 1–16, KREATIV SA, George.

Wright, C.J.H., 2006, *The mission of God. Unlocking the Bible's grand narrative*, InterVarsity Press, Downers Grove, Illinois.

Chapter 15

Missional Church and Mission in Africa

Nelus Niemandt

Introduction

Christianity in Africa is vibrant and visible, and making a significant impact on community life and the public sphere. Henry (2016:1) observes that Christianity has resulted in the fastest growing, most controversial, most dynamic, and most schismatic churches in the world. Christianity thrives on African soil, especially on the congregational level, but in many countries also impacting on the political, social, and economic spheres. The missional church developed into a very particular kind of expression of church in Africa, and serves as both a sample of and challenge to missional ecclesiology and missional theology.

This chapter will introduce concepts of the theology of the missional church, explain the missional renaissance, and describe contours of the missional church as an introduction to missional ecclesiology. It will attend to a case study of Fresh Africa as an example of a comprehensive missional church movement and suggest the investigation of African Initiated Churches (AICs) as a particular expression of missional churches as a research challenge.

The missional church

Any reflection on the missional church in Africa must be understood against the background of the global theological discourses and ecumenical insights on the idea of and theology behind the concept of 'missional church'. Reflection on ecclesiology provides that basis for answering every question facing mission (Bevans & Schroeder 2004:275). Recent attention to missional theology was accompanied by an ecclesiological renaissance and a resurgence of the doctrine of the church. Goheen (2014:loc 1148) remarks that the theological perspective on the mission of God, and the missional nature of the church, emerged in close association with each other throughout the previous century. The nature of the church can only be understood in terms of its relationship to mission, as reflection on salvation always leads to reflection on the communal nature of God, and salvation, and thus the gathered and reconciled community. 'Mission is an extension and amplification of God's very being' (Niemandt 2012:2).

Missional theology has been profoundly influenced by the great ecumenical mission conferences of the previous century, and especially by the theology of Barth, Hoekendijk, Newbigin and Bosch.

Barth (1955:431) described the dogma of the Trinity as a dogma of the church and saw a deep relation between the mission of God and the mission of the church. For Barth, the church exists in being sent and in building up itself for its mission. He reshaped the theology of mission, and his understanding of the church has been described as a 'magnificent and consistent missionary ecclesiology' (cf. Guder 2015:7). Mission was put in the context of the doctrine of the Trinity. Barth laid the groundwork from which the idea of the *missio Dei* was developed (Burger 2022:385). Hartenstein also raised similar ideas, and at the Willingen Missionary Conference in 1952, the *missio Dei* was developed into a theological model. The idea of the *missio Dei* was in a certain sense birthed at the Willingen Conference. Hartenstein played an important role at this particular conference, where he emphasised that mission is primarily God's work. The *missio Dei* refers to the sending nature and posture of the triune God. The trinitarian God is a God of boundless loving and endless life. The Father, in His endless love, sends the Son; the Father and Son send the Spirit; and then the Spirit gathers, equips, and sends the church into the world. It is God's movement towards all of creation, and all in creation joining in a loving and restored relationship with the triune God (*perichoresis*). Mission is participation in the boundless love and endless life of the triune God. Mashau (2012:3) summarises this important approach: 'The three persons in the Trinity are all actively involved in history as a missionary God, the only true God who is Lord of the entire creation and all of humanity'. The idea of the church participating in God's mission to the world became a *leitmotiv* that dominated the ecumenical movement and missionary conferences for decades and perhaps even a century (cf. Burger 2022:386).

Newbigin was one of the seminal mission thinkers of the 20th century[1], and he follows much of the same line of argument: '[T]he mission of the church is to be understood, and only be rightly understood, in terms of the Trinitarian model' (1989:118). He affirms that God has revealed himself as Father, Son, and Holy Spirit, and understands Christian mission in three ways: '[A]s proclaiming the kingdom of the Father, as sharing the life of the Son, and as bearing the witness of the Spirit' (1978:29). The church is a hermeneutic of the gospel (1989:222–233), it has a missionary dimension as well as a missionary intention, and brings to the gospel story but is also, in its life and witness, the gospel. Burger (2022:386)

---

[1] Geoffrey Wainwright (2000:v) described the influence, status and range of his work as comparable to the Church Fathers.

explains: '... the concept of our mission flowing from God's mission to the world is a premise of almost everything Newbigin wrote'. This strong emphasis on a trinitarian foundation by Newbigin influenced much of mission theology, as is even evident in an important document of the Catholic Church such as *Ad Gentes* (Bevans & Schroeder 2004:289).

Hoekendijk approached God's mission from a 'cosmocentric-Trinitarian' perspective (Arthur n.d.). He focussed on God being active in all of the cosmos, but not dependant on the church. The church is an appendix to God's work. God is at work in the world, and although it might impact on or even involve the church, the emphasis is on the wider world. God is working out his mission in the world and its historical processes, and the church can even be regarded as unnecessary for the *missio Dei* (Bosch 1991:392). Mission is fundamental and more important than the church. The gospel was intended, says Burger (2022:388), for Christians and the church, but also for all people and all of life.

Bosch, one of the most influential African theologians, played a very important role in the formulation of the theological and ecclesiological relationship between the *missio Dei* and the church (cf. Kärkkäinen 2002: loc.1680). He supplied an eloquent definition of the *missio Dei*: 'The *missio* Dei is God's activity, which embraces both the church and the world, and in which the church may be privileged to participate' (Bosch 1991:391). In one of his last publications, *Believing in the future: towards a missiology of Western culture* (Bosch 1995), he underscored the importance and need for a missionary theology (1995:32). God is a missionary God, and God's people are missionary people (1995:32). Missiology precedes ecclesiology (1995:32), and the church exists in being sent and in building up itself for its mission. This results in the understanding of the church as a missionary church (1995:31) –'... mission refers to a permanent and intrinsic dimension of the church's life' (1995:32). In his important *Transforming mission*, Bosch (1991:372) argues that missionary activity is not so much the work of the church as simply the church at work – 'The *missio Dei* institutes the *missiones ecclesia*' (1991:370). There is no church without mission, and no mission without church. For Bosch the priority was to ground his final paradigm in ecclesiology because of his understanding that God's mission has been entrusted to the gathered community.

It is clear that the church is now understood as a missional community. Mission is seen as an essential and centering description of the church's purpose and action (Guder 2015:65).

The influence of the Roman Catholic Church must also be noted. The last century saw a fundamentally new understanding of church and mission developing in a church that plays a major role in Africa. Bosch (1991:371) noted that the Second Vatican Council inaugurated a rediscovery of a 'missionary ecclesiology'. It was especially in *Lumen Gentium* that this new ecclesiology became evident. The church is a mystery of God's presence in the world (Bosch 1991:371). The church is the pilgrim people of God, pointing towards the kingdom but not equated with it (Bevans & Schroeder 2004:250). In *Ad Gentes*, the decree that was accepted during the final session of the Council, the trinitarian *locus* of the origin of mission was confirmed. Mission has a trinitarian foundation and is part of the nature of the church (Bevans & Schroeder 2004:249). Bevans and Schroeder (2011:15) explain that God's mission has a church. Mission precedes the church, and God shares the *missio Dei* with ordinary men and women. The focus is not on the church, but on the reign of God. We participate by being co-workers, 'sacraments of God's movement of healing, reconciliation, and life-giving in our world' (Bevans & Schroeder 2011:17).

These insights and developments in both the Catholic Church as well as Protestant theology and the ecumenical movement, eventually led the World Council of Churches (WCC) to formulate a mission policy where they affirmed: 'Mission begins in the heart of the Triune God and the unifying love which binds together the Holy Trinity that overflows to all humanity and creation' (WCC 2013:52).

These developments laid the groundwork for the development of a missional ecclesiology.

Missional ecclesiology and missional church – The missional renaissance

Kärkkäinen (2002:loc.34) is of the opinion that the main catalyst for this rapidly growing ecclesiological interest has been the ecumenical movement. Niemandt (2019:8) mentions at least five important ecumenical events that attended to matters ecclesiological:

- The Centennial World Missionary Conference in Edinburgh, celebrating Edinburgh 1910 from 02 to 06 June 2010 – (Niemandt 2012:3).
- The Uniting General Council of the World Communion of Reformed Churches (WCRC) in Grand Rapids from 18 to 26 June 2010 (Niemandt 2012:3).
- The Third Lausanne Congress (Lausanne III) on World Evangelisation from 16 to 25 October 2010 – Cape Town 2010 (Niemandt 2012:3).
- The 10th Assembly of the WCC from 30 October to 08 November 2013 in Busan, Republic of Korea (Keum 2013).
- The World Council of Churches' Conference on World Mission and Evangelism (CWME) in Arusha, Tanzania, from 08 to 13 March 2018 (WCC 2018).

These developments eventually led to a more mature and fully fledged ecclesiology, initially labelled a *missionary* ecclesiology by Kärkkäinen (2002:loc.1680), and now more recently a *missional* ecclesiology.[2] Mashau (2012:5) reminds us that we '... should bear in mind that the church and the *missio ecclesiae* were born out of the *missio Dei* and, therefore, this understanding is critical in defining the being of a local and universal church of God ...'

The characteristics of the missional church can be summarised in terms of the following contours of a missional church.

The *missio Dei* is the foundation of a missional ecclesiology

Mission, argues Niemandt (2019:16), is an extension and amplification of God's very being. Mission begins with the triune God, and '... the unifying love which binds together the Holy Trinity that overflows to all humanity and creation' (WCC 2013:52). The God of the *missio Dei* is the triune God of Christian Scriptures – Father, Son, and Holy Spirit (Burger 2022:392). The Trinity is a community, and God in God's deepest triune nature is a communion-in-mission (Bevans & Schroeder 2011:26). The mission of the triune God is to bless creation with life in fullness, and the mission of the church is to participate in this mission of God. This is the gospel story – God revealing Godself as a creating, redeeming, and transforming God. Ecclesiology starts with God and God's mission to the world. The church and the church's mission are understood as being from the very being of God Himself. Bevans and Schroeder (2011:10-11) summarise it, stating that God is mission: 'That is what God is in God's deepest self: self-diffusive love, freely creating, redeeming, healing, challenging that creation'.

The church is God's people gathered around Jesus Christ and empowered by the Spirit

Through the Word and Spirit God calls, gathers, equips, and sends the church. God's mission has a church! God establishes the community of saints from all nations. The people of God are called to demonstrate the gospel as a community and gather in congregations. The church participates in God's life as communion-in-mission and is therefore missionary by its very nature (Bevans & Schroeder 2011:26). The gospel is entrusted to the church, and the church proclaims the gospel, but is also a vital sign, instrument, and foretaste of the gospel, reflecting the gospel. Through the gathered and sent congregations, the Word of God is proclaimed in word and

---

2 Earlier ecclesiologies, such as Bosch (1991) and *Mission shaped church* (Church of England 2004) refer to 'missionary' churches, although the concept is now generally described by the term 'missional' (cf. Saayman 2010: 'Missionary or missional? A study in terminology', *Missionalia* 38(1) for an interesting discussion of the two terms.) Guder also explains the origin of the term 'missional' (cf. Guder 2015:63).

deed. God is served by serving those in need. Bosch (1991:516) says the church does not inaugurate God's kingdom but helps to make it more visible and tangible. God's kingdom is present, and whenever and wherever His righteousness and reconciliation are proclaimed, the kingdom breaks through. Congregations plays a vital role in the *missio Dei* – congregations are the cradle of the Christian faith, the communities in which children of all ages are supported, encouraged, and formed for lives of service (Nel 2021:3).

The church is a community equipped and sent by the Spirit

The Holy Spirit plays an important part in the gathering, equipping, and sending of the church. Burger (2022:395) explains that the Spirit is a Helper and Enabler: 'He is the One who empowers the church and Christians to perform and execute the gospel'. A number of theologians argue for the temporal and experiential priority of the Spirit. Bevans states: 'If the Spirit is the first way that Gods sends and is sent, the Spirit's activity becomes the foundation of the church's own missionary nature' (Bevans & Schroeder 2004:293). The WCC (2013:8), in their recent mission affirmation, also emphasise the important role of the Spirit in gathering and sending the church: 'The Holy Spirit is seen as the continuing presence of Christ, his agent to fulfil the task of mission. This understanding leads to a missiology focusing on sending out and going forth'. This is so important that the WCC (2013:4) underscores the following: 'Life in the Holy Spirit is the essence of mission, the core of why we do what we do and how we live our lives'. It is clear that the church finds its identity in the activity of the Holy Spirit, so much so that mission has been described as finding out where the Spirit is working and joining in with the Spirit (Kim 2009:1). The church exists in being sent, and every congregation as well as each and every member, participates in God's mission as God's missionary people (Bosch 1991:372). The core of the *missio Dei* is the idea of sending, and a life in the trinity leads to being equipped and sent by the Spirit.

Congregations as vibrant communities where the practices of Christian life flourish

Nel (2021:3) states that congregations are the habitat in which the practices of the Christian life flourish. The church is called to build vibrant communities (congregations) where real sharing, mutuality, justice, service, and solidarity can take place (Bevans & Schroeder 2004:298). The church is a sacrament, sign and instrument, but, as Bosch explained, the church is not the focus holding itself up as a model, but rather a community not proclaiming 'Come to us!' but 'Let us follow him!' (Bosch 1991:376). When this happens, the church can become a sign and foretaste of its own destiny, a hermeneutic of the gospel where the church proclaims the gospel but also becomes the gospel (Newbigin 1989:222-233).

These congregations are relational communities that reflect the relationality of the triune communion. God invites his children into the community of the Trinity, and participation in the Trinitarian dance (*perichoresis*) is to do in the world what God in community is doing in the world (Aldous 2019:35). Mission is expressed in relationships (Niemandt 2019:28). The WCC (2013:63) calls the Spirit the 'Spirit of Community' in its affirmation that the Spirit is creating community and a communion that opens the hearts and lives of the people of God to live in the movement of love overflowing from the Trinity.

Proclaiming the gospel to people who do not know the gospel or are alienated from it

The sent church serves the gospel in all its dimensions to people who do not know the gospel or are alienated from it. The sent church witnesses to the person and work of Jesus Christ and salvation that embraces all of humanity and creation. Evangelism is regarded as an essential part of the church's participation in God's mission. Bevans and Schroeder (2011:102) remind us that, from the early days of the church, followers of Christ shared their faith outside their homes, mostly by 'gossiping the gospel'. The Early Church experienced phenomenal growth due to the witness and informal proclamation of the gospel by ordinary Christians. Witness and proclamation are an essential part of the calling of the church and an indispensable ministry. Witnesses are followers of Jesus living their lives in the light of their faith, as well as local congregations being a hermeneutic of the gospel – a community where people are faithfully present, exhibiting a lived Christian authenticity. Proclamation is communicating the gospel about Jesus and the gospel of Jesus. It is about introducing others into a relation with God through and in Jesus (Bevans & Schroeder 2004:358), extending an invitation that is aimed at a response (Bosch 1991:413). The conclusion of the WCC (ed. Keum 2013:29) in the mission affirmation serves as an excellent summary of the importance of evangelisation: 'Evangelism is mission activity which makes explicit and unambiguous the centrality of the incarnation, suffering, and resurrection of Jesus Christ without setting limits to the saving grace of God'.

Incarnational, contextual and inculturated

The missional church is incarnational and represents a movement from an attractional to an incarnational model. This entails a shift in focus from church to community; a shift from church life to real life; a shift from the Christian life in the church to the everyday. Aldous (2019:35) underscores the important relationship between incarnation and contextualisation, stating that 'the reality of the incarnate one amongst us can only be experienced contextually'. This implies that the missional church is an incarnational movement sent to engage its context (Niemandt 2012:4). Incarnation underscores the importance of contextualisation and inculturation. Bosch (1991:421) explains that the Christian church incarnated itself in the life and world of those who had embraced it. Followers of Jesus are learning habits and routines to embody, demonstrate, and announce God's life and reign for the sake of the world (Niemandt 2010:15). Inculturation implies a three-way conversation between the gospel (and the tradition interpreting the gospel), the church, and the culture in which the gospel is being shared. The church acts as bridge connecting the gospel and tradition to the relevant culture, and contextualisation can be described as a bridge-building process. The WCC (2010:35) explains:

> The gospel takes root in different contexts through engagement with specific cultural, political, and religious realities. Respect for people and their cultural and symbolic life-worlds are necessary if the gospel is to take root in those different realities.

Pillay (2015:3) clarifies this contextual approach with four practical missional questions one needs to ask: (1) What is the mission context? (2) What is God already doing in this context (3) What is God calling us to do? and (4) How can we do what God is calling us to do in such a context?

This contextual approach is especially relevant when one considers the African missional church.

An African missional church

Henry, an African missionary and missiologist now working at a global missionary society in the United States, attended to the issue of developing a clear understanding of an African missional church.

Henry (2016:2) proposes that reflection on the mission of the church in Africa must consider the culture and worldview of people among whom mission is done. This is of course the same approach as that followed by Newbigin, who understood the importance of a genuine missionary encounter with culture. Goheen and Bartholomew (2008:10) are of the conviction that the gospel must be released from its bondage to modern Western culture, and this necessitates attending to the challenge of recovering the gospel on its own terms. This is also explained in the brief description of incarnation, contextualisation and inculturation above.

Henry argues that to find the source of an African missional church, one must develop a framework within which people may understand and actively respond to political, social and religious issues, and one that is not in isolation from global trends and Christianity. He (2016:5) argues: 'What is needed is the utilisation of an African epistemology as the governing factor defining the meaning of "text" within the world view of the people it is presented to'. There are a plethora of sources which can contribute to the epistemological core of the broader spectrum of African theology, and by implication, missiology.

He then proposes the following framework:

1. The Bible as a primary source for the Christian worldview. The Bible must be contextualised.

2. The African experience, referring to the history of Africa, which includes issues such as colonisation, violence and suffering.

3. The African heritage of struggle, inter-continental pollination, suppression, exclusion and African nationalism.

4. African religious thought and experience.

   I suggest that further exploration of the missional church in Africa tends to especially two important ecclesial phenomena – the Fresh Expressions movement and AICs.

Fresh expressions

The Fresh Expressions movement is closely associated with work done in the Anglican community. The groundwork was laid by a report by the Church of England published as *Mission shaped church* (2004). Using the concept of a 'mixed economy', the report encouraged existing 'expressions of church' to a complementary process to plant new or 'fresh expressions' of church. The latter is an expression of church for our changing culture, established for the benefit of people who are not yet members of any church (Crowther 2022:347-348).

The theology of the movement can by summarised in the following values of missional churches formulated in *Mission shaped church* (Church of England 2004:81-82):

- A missionary[3] church is focused on God the Trinity. This approach emphasises the doxological nature of the church, the fact that worship lies at the heart of the missional church and to 'love and know God as Father, Son and Spirit is its chief inspiration and primary purpose'.

- A missionary church is incarnational. This implies a discerning sensitivity towards the community in which the church is found. 'A missionary church seeks to shape itself in relation to the culture in which it is located or to which it is called'.

---

3   *Mission shaped church* (Church of England 2004) still refers to 'missionary' churches.

- A missionary church is transformational. The church exists for the sake of the community and to transform that community through the power of the gospel and the Holy Spirit.
- A missionary church makes disciples. The church calls people to faith but also to develop a Christian lifestyle appropriate for the culture in which it operates.
- A missionary church is relational. Communities of faith are formed – and these communities are characterised by welcome and hospitality.

This brief overview clearly shows the fact that the Fresh Expressions movement was deeply influenced and formed by the missional church movement and theology. The theological and ecclesiological similarities are obvious.

Pillay observes that the Fresh Expressions movement has found its way into Africa. He explains:

> I may add that this is different from the church growth model which primarily focuses on building the local church. This is not about making the church attractable, but missional. It is not about bringing people into the church, it is about taking the church into the world – to transform the world to reflect the glory of God and God's kingdom or sovereign rule (Pillay 2015:1).

This movement is mostly found in mainline African churches, or mission-initiated churches (MICs).

Exposure to the ideas of the Fresh Expressions movement in Southern Africa started when Prof Nelus Niemandt and Dr Willem Pretorius of the North Synod of the Dutch Reformed Church (DRC) invited Bishop Graham Cray to visit South Africa after both of them visited Bishop Cray in London in 2010. Bishop Cray spoke at a seminar on 10 June and 11 June 2011 at the DRC Weltevreden in Johannesburg and Kameeldrift in Pretoria, South Africa, and 13 June in Stellenbosch (Fresh Africa 2022). This was the first of several visits and his insights ignited considerable interest, so much so that a South African chapter of Fresh Expressions was established as Fresh Expressions Southern Africa (FESA). In 2013 a formal agreement between Ekklesia, related to the University of Stellenbosch, and the board of Fresh Expressions United Kingdom was ratified. A South African board was established, and the board now consists of senior denominational leaders and a national executive from various mainline churches or MICs (Mission Initiated Churches) (Crowther 2022:352). This includes the Anglican (Anglican Church of Southern Africa [ACSA]), Dutch Reformed (DRC), Netherdutch Reformed (NDR), Baptist (Baptist Union [BU]), Methodist (Methodist Church of Southern Africa [MCSA]),

Presbyterian (Uniting Presbyterian Church in Southern Africa [UPCSA]), Uniting Reformed (Uniting Reformed Church in Southern Africa [URCSA]), United Congregational Church (UCC), and Vineyard (Association of Vineyard Churches South Africa [AVCSA]) churches. FESA describes their reason for existence as the 'purposeful accompaniment of missional communities' and serving churches and denominations as they 'rediscover and seek to join God's mission in the world and in so doing become co-workers with God in the transformation of their communities in order to start new missional communities' (Crowther 2022:352). FESA developed a Mission Shaped Introduction Africa (MSIA) course in Afrikaans, English, Xhosa, and Zulu. The course aims to assist congregations to:

- Understand God's passion for mission better;
- Rediscover the main purpose of the congregation;
- Become more involved both inside and outside of the church;
- Become part of disciple making processes;
- Grow spiritually and to be renewed.

This is also evident when one notes the themes of the course, namely: 'Rediscovering the mission of God'; 'Rediscovering a missional calling in a changing world'; 'Rediscovering missional church'; 'Rediscovering disciple making'; 'Rediscovering missional spirituality'; and 'Rediscovering missional listening'. Fresh Africa (cf. Fresh Africa 2022) mentions a number of key concepts in its self-understanding: Relationships; listening to God, congregations and communities; formation of partnerships; empowerment of the church and congregational leaders; and contextualising. Fresh Expressions Southern Africa changed its name to Fresh Africa (cf. Fresh Africa 2022)[4].

The ACSA also established a movement called Anglicans Ablaze, initially under the leadership of Bishop Martin Breytenbach. This movement introduced the theology and practices of Fresh Expressions to an African audience and regularly uses the material of Fresh Africa (Anglican Communion News Service [ACNS] 2014).

In conclusion, one can regard Fresh Africa as an expression of the missional church that exhibits the core ecclesiology and values of the latter.

AICs as African missional churches?

Henry (2016:6) mentions the need for a missional ecclesia that is uniquely Afrocentric and seriously addresses the specific needs of the African landscape. He proposes that AICs might provide a unique lens to study and understand African

---

4 Cf. The PhD of Aldous (2019) on Fresh Expressions in Southern Africa. .

missional churches. In Africa, social life has been fundamentally impacted by the growing urbanisation of Africans. Urbanisation exploded together with another phenomenon, and the two phenomena are interrelated – AICs. Henry (2016:6) says:

> AICs have taken bold steps in ensuring that urban centres are permeated with the gospel and many communities have been established with the sole purpose of replicating family life in urban centres bringing harmony through relationships in order to cope with the challenges of modern urban dwelling.

The AICs are a very significant source of African theology and must be included in any attempt to develop a unique and contextually relevant African ecclesiology. Henry (2016:7) underscores that the AICs can contribute significantly to the idea of missional identity (ecclesiology) as well as the churches' missional praxis. Although an in-depth investigation into the plethora of AICs and the diversity in theologies are outside the scope of this chapter, the phenomena of AICs do receive attention in section A of this book.

The challenge for ongoing research and a better understanding of AICs as a contextually relevant expression of the missional church in Africa, might ask the following questions:

- What is the trinitarian basis of an AIC, and to what extent does its theology and praxis reflect the *missio Dei*? This question does not imply a fully developed Trinitarian theology, but most certainly gives attention to the idea of God sending his people. There must be continuity with the Christian faith in its current and historical forms.

- To what extent does an AIC understand itself as a community gathered around Christ, but also a community called to proclaim the gospel? This question might also attend to the particular community as a sign, instrument, and foretaste of the gospel, reflecting the gospel. Is the Word of God proclaimed in word and deed, and more particularly, is God being served by serving those in need?

- Does the AIC understand itself as a community gathered, equipped, and sent by the Spirt? Does this sense of calling and being sent function in the offices (leadership) of the AIC as well as in the ordinary membership?

- Does the AIC function as a vibrant relational community where the practices of Christian life flourish? What are these practices? Does one find practices of hospitality and welcoming the stranger?

- To what extent does the AIC proclaim the gospel to people who do not know the gospel or are alienated from it?

- How do the concepts of incarnation and contextualisation function in these communities? Can one identify practices in inculturation that show the intention of the community to bridge the gap between the context of the Bible and tradition, and the context of the community where the church finds itself in? Henry (2016:4) explains:

> If we are to believe that theology is always contextual and the Christian faith and message "liquid" and inherently adaptable and translatable, then it naturally follows that what we need to do in Africa is to establish continuity with the African world view and bridge the gap between the Christian faith and traditional religion.

- To what extent does the AIC attempt to transform the context and community it finds itself in? Does it exhibit a public theology? Henry (2016:6) pleads for a framework that assists faith communities to understand and respond to political, social and religious issues. This includes '… an uncovering of the African world view and life that will lead to critical reflection, movement, continuity and discontinuity'.

Engaging AICs as missional communities might open up exciting insights for them, but it might also enrich traditional (MIC) churches in the endeavour to become more missional, and it might just serve ecumenical bridge-building between these communities.

Conclusion

There is a clear and important connection between the general operative theology of churches and the expression of beliefs about the church (ecclesiology), and how churches understand their calling and witness in terms of the *missio Dei*. What the church *is*, determines what the church *does*. This research explained the idea of missional church and the vital relationship between ecclesiology and missionality, and how this development was influenced by the ecumenical movement, mission conferences and important theologians. It placed these developments as being part and parcel of the burgeoning growth of churches in the African context. Fresh Africa was investigated as an example of a comprehensive missional church movement in Africa. The research concluded with research suggestions in terms of investigating African Initiated Churches (AICs) as a possible unique expression of missional churches.

References

Aldous, B.J., 2019, 'Towards an assessment of Fresh Expressions of Church in ACSA (The Anglican Church of Southern Africa) through an ethnographic study of the community supper at St Peter's church in Mowbray, Cape Town', PhD-thesis, University of Stellenbosch.

Anglican Communion News Service (ACNS), 2014, *Fresh ways of being Church excite, inspire Anglicans*, viewed 29 April 2022, from https://www.anglicannews.org/news/2014/07/fresh-ways-of-being-church-excite,-inspire-anglicans.aspx.

Arthur E., n.d., *Missio Dei and the mission of the church*, viewed 15 March 2022, from https://www.wycliffe.net/more-about-what-we-do/papers-and-articles/missio-dei-and-the-mission-of-the-church/.

Barth, K., 1955, *Die Kirchliche DogmatikI/1. Die Lehrevom Wort Gottes, Prolegomenazurkirchlichen Dogmatik*, Evangelischer Verlag, Zollikon-Zürich.

Bevans, S.B., & Schroeder, R.P, 2004, *Constants in context. A theology of mission for today*, Orbis, Maryknoll, N.Y.

Bevans, S.B., & Schroeder, R.P, 2011, *Prophetic dialogue. Reflections on Christian mission today*, Orbis, Maryknoll, N.Y.

Bosch, D.J., 1991, *Transforming mission. Paradigm shifts in theology of mission*, Orbis, Maryknoll, NY.

Bosch, D.J., 1995, *Believing in the future: towards a missiology of Western culture*, Trinity Press International, Valley Forge.

Burger, C., 2022, 'A missional ecclesiology and our theological tradition', in C. Burger, F. Marais & P. Van der Walt (eds.), *Missional ecclesiology*, 384–401, BM Biblecor, Wellington.

Church of England, 2004, *Mission shaped church: Church planting and fresh expressions of church in a changing context*, CHP, London.

Crowther, G., 2022, 'Fresh Expressions in the missional movement in Southern Africa', in C. Burger, F. Marais & P. Van der Walt (eds.), *Missional ecclesiology*, 346–364, BM Biblecor, Wellington.

Fresh Africa, 2022, *Serving the church in developing mission shaped communities*, Fresh Africa, viewed 29 April 2022, from https://www.freshafrica.org.za/our-beginnings.

Goheen, M.W., 2014, *Introducing Christian mission today. Scripture, history and issues*, InterVarsity, Downers Grove.

Goheen, M.W., & Bartholomew, C.G., 2008, *Living at the crossroads: An introduction to Christian worldview*, Baker Academic, Grand Rapids.

Guder, D.L., 2015, *Called to witness: Doing missional theology*, The Gospel and Our Culture Series (GOCS), [Kindle Edition], Eerdmans, Grand Rapids.

Henry, D., 2016, 'Reflections on a missional ecclesiology for Africa's expressions of Christianity through the Tswana lens', *Verbum et Ecclesia* 37(1), a1612. htp://dx.doi.org/10.4102/ve. v37i1.1612.

Kärkkäinen, V.-M., 2002, *An introduction to ecclesiology: Ecumenical, historical & global perspectives*, [Kindle Edition], InterVarsity, Downers Grove.

Kim, K., 2009, *Joining in with the Spirit. Connecting world church and local mission*, Epworth, London.

Keum, J. (ed.), 2013, *Together towards life. Mission and evangelism in changing landscapes*, World Council of Churches Publications, Geneva.

Mashau, T.D., 2012, 'A reformed perspective on taking mission and missiology to the heart of theological training', *In die Skriflig/In Luce Verbi* 46(2), 8 pages. http://dx.doi.org/10.4102/ ids.v46i2.64.

Nel, M., 2021, 'Framing our understanding of missional', in M. Nel (ed.), *Mission moves: Cultivating communities of the Gospel* (HTS Religion & Society Series Volume 11), 1–18, AOSIS, Cape Town. https://doi.org/10.4102/aosis.2021.BK256.01.

Newbigin, L., 1978, *The open secret. An introduction to the theology of mission*, Eerdmans, Grand Rapids.

Newbigin, L., 1989, *The Gospel in a pluralist society*, Eerdmans, Grand Rapids.

Niemandt, C.J.P., 2010, 'Five Years of Missional Church – Reflections on Missional Ecclesiology', *Missionalia* 38(3), 397-413.

Niemandt, C.J.P., 2012, 'Trends in missional ecclesiology', *HTS Teologiese Studies/Theological Studies* 68(1), a1198. https://doi.org/10.4102/hts.v68i1.1198.

Niemandt, N., 2019, *Missional leadership*, AOSIS Academic, Cape Town.

Pillay, J., 2015, 'The missional renaissance: Its impact on churches in South Africa, ecumenical organisations, and the development of local congregations', *HTS Teologiese Studies/Theological Studies* 71(3), Art. #3065, 6 pages. http:// dx.doi.org/10.4102/hts. v71i3.3065.

Saayman, W., 2010: 'Missionary or missional? A study in terminology', *Missionalia* 38(1), 5–16.

Wainwright, G., 2000, *Lesslie Newbigin: A theological life*, Oxford University Press, New York.

World Council of Churches (WCC), 2013, *Resource book WCC 10th Assembly, Busan 2013*, World Council of Churches Publications, Geneva.

World Council of Churches (WCC), 2018, 'The Arusha call to discipleship', in *World Council of Churches' Conference on World Mission and Evangelism, Moving in the Spirit: Called to Transforming Discipleship*, viewed 16 May 2022 25, from https://www.oikoumene.org/en/resources/documents/commissions/mission-and-evangelism/the-arusha-call-to-discipleship.

Chapter 16

Missional Ethical Issues in Africa Through the Lens of 2 Corinthians 2:12-17

Annette Potgieter

Introduction

In 2001, in a footnote to the life and ethos of the church, M. Douglas Meeks (2001) coined the term 'missional ethics'. Since then, it has been used by numerous scholars, particularly missiologists. *Missional ethics* describes the ways in which the believing community's behaviour is in and of itself missional (Salter 2017:1). However, missional ethics remains embroiled in a framework undergirding a renewed focus on what 'missional' entails. Missions and Western culture have been entangled as the growth of European civilisation spurred the spread of Christianity (Neill 1964:243). Maluleke (2007:503) marvels at the fact that Africans continue to be Christian as missions have been deeply complicit in colonial oppression.[1] Neill (1964:510) puts it as follows,

> [P]resumably all missionaries from the beginning have had at the back of their minds that as a result of their labours churches would sooner or later acquire all the characteristics and qualities that are subsumed under the term church.

This being said, Christianity in the West has undergone significant changes. Secularisation has caused a gulf between culture and what happens in the church,

---

1   In this regard, Patric Tariq Mellet (2020:312) mentions the dangers of adopting the language and practices of the so-called 'development' accompanied by the developer and developed paradigm, and refers to this practice as a 'colonial trap'.

one which seems irreconcilable. Lesslie Newbigin and David Bosch have been instrumental in addressing the divide through a critical engagement with the philosophical and epistemological roots of modernity, of Western and Reformed theology and culture (Hendriks 2007:1001). For Newbigin, a church is not a church if it is not a church in mission (Newbigin (1978/1995:2). In turn, Bosch (1991:470) understands the church as being sent as the *missio Dei* which grounds and institutes the *missio ecclesiae*. A flurry of interest has followed, reinterpreting the church as missional.

This chapter will work within a missional framework, understanding the church as sent. Paul establishes within early Christian communities a missional ethos of living as a follower of Jesus. Paul's interpretation of Christ permeates a bodily perspective. The ancient understanding of body entails a permeable system that is open to influences from the environment (Punt 2005:367). An embodied understanding of missional ethics guides our understanding of the missional church having an impact on its environment, but also the environment having an impact on the missional church. Moreover, concerning the question of behaviour and how one should act is encompassed in a bodily view. Missional behaviour is lived, and what is right and wrong is relational to the situation. It should be kept in mind that missional theology considers a link between anthropology and ecology as important (Hendriks 2007:1003). Missional ethics is a field with a comma after it, especially in the light of an African context. There are a vast array of topics and themes that need to be studied. This chapter will delimit the discussion using 2 Corinthians 2:12-17 as a lens for contouring pitfalls and areas of thought concerning missional ethics in a South African context particularly. Themes such as justice, the abuse of power, digital church, and ecology, will be under its scope. However, these themes are just scratching at the surface and would require more research. Due to the, limited scope, important topics for missional ethics such as migration, xenophobia, decolonisation, gender-based violence (GBV), land, ecumenism, networking and artificial intelligence in Africa are not even covered in this chapter. Missional ethics is an open field that requires in-depth research, which could aid our framing of *missio Dei* and being a missional church. The pendulum swing of the Global South becoming the new hub of Christianity, underscores the importance of discussing the behaviour of Christian communities especially in Africa, and for the purposes of this chapter, South Africa.

Through the lens of 2 Corinthians 2:12-17

The body is central in Paul's theology (Punt 2005:368). Paul fundamentally understands himself as being sent by God. He continually refers to himself as a slave of God, understanding his own body as being in the service of God. Second Corinthians 2:12-17 is not a typical passage to employ in order to speak about Paul's bodily perspectives. It is clear that Paul often uses the body metaphor for the church and the manner in which believers should conduct themselves. However, 2 Corinthians 2:12-17 contains more implicit bodily imagery.

The passage reads staccato. Paul goes to Troas to preach the gospel of Christ (εἰς τὸ εὐαγγέλιον τοῦ Χριστοῦ).[2] In typical Pauline fashion, the city of Troas was a strategic location as the cosmopolitan population was often joined by travellers experiencing delays on their way to other parts of the Roman world (Harris 2005:237). An opportunity presents itself as the door is open (καὶ θύρας μοι ἀνεῳγμένης ἐν κυρίῳ), since the metaphor of an open door illustrates the promising prospects of evangelism (Harris 2005:237). The phrase ἐν κυρίῳ is important, as the preposition ἐν signals location, painting a picture of a believer being engulfed in the Lord denoting being 'in the Lord's service'. However, it seems that not much happens in Troas as Paul is filled with unrest on account of not meeting with Titus in Troas and moves on to Macedonia. The passage then abruptly shifts to 2 Corinthians 12:14, containing imagery of a triumphal procession. This is the only instance along with Colossians 2:15 where the image is found in Pauline literature. But what is significant about this passage for the purposes of this chapter, is the use of δι' ἡμῶν ἐν παντὶ τόπῳ ('through us in all places') in 2 Corinthians 12:14 in conjunction with the imagery of the triumphal procession. A triumphal procession implies a victorious general leading his troops through the city (Furnish 2008:174).[3] Whether Paul is truly drawing on the triumphal procession is disputed. The verb θριαμβεύω ('to lead in triumphal procession') fits the best according to the rhetorical pattern in 2 Corinthians 2:14 (Bauer, Danker, Arndt & Gingrich [1957] 2000:459). Accordingly, Paul envisions himself as a captive of the victor, namely God through Christ as the *Praesens* participle θριαμβεύοντι refers to τῷ θεῷ. It seems suitable to regard the triumph as God's with the more ἐν τῷ Χριστῷ illustrating 'in the cause of Christ or through our union with Christ' (Harris 2005:246).

What is significant is the whole body is subjected to Christ. All actions are permeated with Christ. Moreover, we know that the victor is different to that of a conquering Roman general. The bodiliness of believers is implied with the personal pronoun ἡμᾶς ('us'). However, the personal pronoun ἡμᾶς must be understood with reference to ἐν τῷ Χριστῷ ('litt. in the Christ'). The preposition ἐν denotes location. 'In Christ' is a space of freedom – a space which is free to do something, and to be 'in Christ' is to be working in God's service (Plummer 1915:69). What is more, a shift occurs from ἡμᾶς (2 Cor 2:14a) to δι' ἡμῶν (2 Cor 2:14b), moving from the passive captive to an active evangelist (Harris 2005:247). These contradicting positions are of course typical to Paul.

---

2   The preposition εἰς indicates purpose.
3   This custom is documented in, e.g. Josephus, *War* VII.v.4-6 (the triumph of Vespasian and Titus after the fall of Jerusalem), and Dio Cassius, *Roman History* VI.

Mission the "labour room" of theology

The imagery is continued, as Paul proceeds to illustrate that it is through believers that the fragrance of the knowledge of him manifests in every place. The participle φανεροῦντι ('is making known') should also be understood against the backdrop of disciples who claim to manifest God in their life and ministry seen in connection with 2 Corinthians 4:2 (Martin 2014:186). The smell is manifested by believers, and although it cannot be seen, it is active in places where believers work and live. The effect of the body on its environment is prevalent in the smell the body produces. The association of scent stems from the triumphal imagery, as incense was burnt to the gods with the fragrance being smelt by the spectators (Kruse 2015:119). What is significant is that the question of whether the smell is positive or negative is subject to a person's location within this triumphal procession. For the victor, the smell is pleasant and stirs positive associations, but for the conquered, the smell recalls imminent slavery or death (Kruse 2015:119). However, it is difficult to argue that this is the manner in which the victor and conquered would have perceived smell. Martin (2014:187) sees a link with the application of Old Testament wisdom literature (Sir 24:15; 39:14; 50:15) between 'the knowledge of God' with wisdom and sweet odour. What is clear is that Paul uses 'fragrance' to delineate two groups. Thus, the orientation of the believer with reference to God boils down to life and death. The triumphal imagery may be shocking for modern hearers as slavery is not acceptable. However, Paul uses this image which would have been well known to any first hearer of the text and reapplies the image to communicate to believers to locate themselves in Christ. Plummer (1915:70) puts it that believers 'are not independent agents, but instruments'.

The fragrance image continues in 2 Corinthians 2:15, as the reason clause marked by ὅτι illustrates that believers are the aroma of Christ to God. However, the association with smells are diverse as some smells are enjoyable and others can be poisonous. Accordingly, Paul draws on the contrast with an antithetical parallelism, repeating the preposition ἐν, emphasising the two different locations one could find oneself at, namely saved (ἐν τοῖς σῳζομένοις) or not saved (ἐν τοῖς ἀπολλυμένοις). The antithetical parallelism also communicates a dual effect, as being saved entails that eternal life is an outcome, whereas, in contrast, not being saved entails death as an outcome (Harris 2005:252). What is more, the smell that brings life is unequivocally associated with Christ with God as the source. To some, the smell of the aroma is pleasant, and to others, it is a stench.

Paul continues this line of reasoning in the relative clause 2 Corinthians 2:16a, illustrating a specific group for whom the stench of death leads to death (οἷς μὲν ὀσμὴ ἐκ θανάτου εἰς θάνατον). This could refer to false prophets as Paul has continually had a struggle in the Corinthian community with false preachers. In contrast, another relative clause – 2 Corinthians 2:16b – illustrates the opposite, which is that the fragrance of life leads to life (οἷς δὲ ὀσμὴ ἐκ ζωῆς εἰς ζωήν).

Paul continues by asking the question of who is equal to the task of dispensing the fragrance of Christ. Paul does not answer the question in this instance, but he makes it clear in 2 Corinthians 3:6 that he is competent on account of God who has affirmed him (Matera 2013:74).

The passage concludes with Paul contrasting himself with the many. Paul's message is ἐκ θεοῦ ('from God'), κατέναντι θεοῦ ('in the presence of God') and ἐν Χριστῷ ('in Christ') (Martin 2014:190). The many peddle the gospel of God for profit which Paul sharply rejects. Paul rather points to the responsibility of preaching the gospel as he refuses to manipulate or tamper with God's word for personal gain (Kruse 2015:120-121).

Summary

Paul draws on two images, that of the triumphal procession and that of fragrance. Both metaphors aid in shaping our understanding that as believers we orientate ourselves to God through Christ. The fragrance metaphor is especially lingering as one cannot see it but for some, it is a pleasant smell resulting in life, and for others, a stench that results in death. Being in Christ entails having a pleasant scent that gives life. Believers are instruments of Christ, spreading the gospel and the fragrance of life in all places. This manifests when believers are functioning as sent people, or as Paul would put it, people who are in Christ.

Missional ethics in Southern Africa

Looking through the lens of 2 Corinthians 2:12-17, being a believer entails having a pleasant fragrance. Being in Christ entails bringing a positive effect wherever you are situated. For Paul, the preaching of the gospel is crucial. He does not miss an opportunity to spread the good news, but also, the good news is lived. In a South African context, there are a multitude of issues that require believers to make a difference. The church has a vital role to play in Africa in particular. Hendriks (2007:1000) quotes Radoli (1998:257) on the important role the church has to play in Southern Africa, but adds that this is not applicable if the theological methodology adheres to old clerical paradigms. Accordingly, the challenge is constructing how the missional church will cultivate intentional missional behaviours to these questions bearing the aroma of Christ. Some implications of a bodily understanding for *missio Dei* and the missional church are also under the scope, especially in a South African context concerning issues that impact missional ethics.

Justice

One of the biggest challenges facing the missional church is that of the theme of justice. Whether justice refers to the legacy of apartheid, poverty, inclusivity (e.g. Lesbian, gay, bisexual, transgender, queer, intersex, and questioning [LGBTQI+] and racism), and systems of oppression undergirding social problems, such as GBV or the continued influence of colonisation, it is essential for the missional church to address these issues. It could seem like a daunting task, as justice needs to be defined within the community where the missional church is functioning.

However, the interpretation of the church as missional is not straightforward. At the core, the movement focussing on the missional church intends to bridge the gap between popular culture and church. Inadvertently, this also condones secularisation and the transmission of identity found in churches. The danger is that the church becomes a place that is entertaining. South Africa has one of the highest rates of unemployment as well as inequality, making the society particularly susceptible to experiencing the church as a place of entertainment (Baron & Maponya 2020:7). People come to church to be encouraged and motivated (Baron & Maponya 2020:7). A church that participates in this type of culture only manages to attract people by being a form of entertainment. In this case, Kruger's (2013:7) argument against a missional church rings true, as this type of church does not form identity. Kruger (2013:7) mentions the necessity of the church in order to be successfully transferred to the next generation to cultivate a lifestyle which is embodied by the institution.

Accordingly, how does the missional movement address injustices and act as bringers of justice that is also identity forming for the younger generation, instilling a love for Christ, and continuing the community of believers? Perhaps imaginative leadership may play a role by empowering congregants. Baron and Maponya (2020:1) comment on how the church has lost its prophetic voice and attributes this to a lack of imagination. More importantly, they proffer discipleship as a means of identity formation. Part of identity formation, however, lies in communicating to the poor that they have a role to play in the kingdom of God. Instead of 'mission to the margins', the focus should be 'mission from the margins' (ed. Keum 2013:5). For Baron and Maponya (2020:9), churches should develop and inspire an 'ecclesial imagination' amongst their members that would reflect God's intention for the church, and by so doing would enhance the 'prophetic' nature of the churches in South Africa. Prosperity gospel preachers are aware of the power of imagination as they provide an imaginary space where people address their longing for a prosperous way of life (Cezula 2015:146-147). What is more, there is a concern for the African culture as most Africans share a worldview of spirits and witchcraft. Eyo, Essien and Ekong (2020:440) mention that prosperity preachers promise followers the tools to overcome witchcraft, demonic forces, as well as malignant spirits through the Holy Spirit. The effect of living in poverty, the experience of being victimised and vulnerable to powers beyond your control, opens the door for the interpretation of hope that prosperity preachers bring (Eyo et al. 2020:450). There is a need for leaders who understand what is truly intended by the missional church, but these leaders need to come from within their communities.

Niemandt (2017:216) indicates how missionary imagination has been abducted by the prosperity gospel, resulting in a materialistic and consumerist orientation. Churches involved in the prosperity gospel, however, have managed to make a difference in their communities and also install rituals, ritual enactments of offerings, and elaborate rituals of gift exchanges (Niemandt 2017:207). Ritual is a vital part of community formation. Missional church does not mean meetings at coffee cafés to suit the busy lifestyle of congregants. Rather, from a missional ethical perspective, a focus on justice should become part of the lifestyle of a missional church. Marches and awareness events contribute in facilitating these matters. But leaders that start to incorporate practices within church services, even if these services are digital, start to ignite the missional imagination of their community. We live in a country where the majority of people identify as being Christian, but yet violence, corruption and injustice remain rampant. Thus, the missional church needs to actively empower the marginalised. This can only be done when the church hears and admits the suffering the marginalised have experienced. Missional ethics should consider talking about injustices as correcting wrong with an immense focus on trauma and healing. A similar space to the Truth and Reconciliation Commission (TRC) where parties are allowed to tell these stories is important. A person's imagination is limited to their context. The missional church needs to cultivate a story that inspires and invites people to see Christ and themselves in a different role. The aroma of Christ can only be smelt when a person is engulfed by the love of Christ.

The abuse of power

One of the greatest challenges facing churches concerning missional ethics is the abuse of power. As important as leaders are, simultaneously unethical leaders are troublemakers. It has become necessary for the South African Commission for the Protection of Rights of Cultural, Religious and Linguistic Communities to investigate the suspicious practices of some pastors. Dangerous religious practices such as pastors forcing congregants to eat grass, snakes, drink gasoline, and to discontinue the use of medicine, as faith healers spread misinformation that holy water, which they are selling, will cure them from HIV/AIDS (Dreyer 2016:1; Kgatle 2018:1). Apart from the physical harm of these practices, the theology and persons conducting these types of churches are guilty of exploiting the poor. A ministry needs money, but soliciting for money is problematic (Mpofu 2020:3). Although the prosperity gospel is a global phenomenon, Africa is home to some of the richest religious leaders (Mashau & Kgatle 2019:3). Mashau and Kgatle (2019:1) propose an alternative to the abuse of the poor and manipulation of power, drawing on the African philosophy of 'ubuntu'. They want to move away from the negative elements of the prosperity gospel to the correct biblical understanding of prosperity (Mashau & Kgatle 2019:1). *Ubuntu* encompasses values in life different to that of capitalist and self-interests based on reciprocity; it creates a space where a person can flourish (Mashau & Kgatle 2019:4).

The concept of *ubuntu* also becomes important in light of fighting corruption. Coetzer and Snell (2013:30) mention that in South Africa, the growing black elite has been separated from the values of *ubuntu*, which has increased the levels of corruption in the public and private sector, costing rising numbers in expenditure. However, South Africa is not the only country to be affected by corruption. This is in fact a worldwide problem with the World Bank estimating the cost of bribery to the global economy of $1 trillion (Khotseng & Tucker 2013:2). On the Africa continent, however, corruption is such a big problem as it prevents the alleviation of poverty (Allaby 2020:83). But ultimately, corruption impoverishes all (Khotseng & Tucker 2013:3). Mbaku (1998:53) describes the African context as a target and breeding ground for corruption as there exists a low sense of national interest and commitment to public service with an inherent cultural ethic favouring obligations to family and friends rather than civic virtues.

Khotseng and Tucker (2013:10) consider the church in South Africa to be in a unique position to make a difference in combatting corruption and intervening as large numbers of people, including government workers, profess to worship in local congregations. This presents an opportunity to reflect on the Scripture and God's expectation that his people should be incorruptible in both government and business (Khotseng & Tucker 2013:10). Allaby (2020:90) suggests that theologies that reflect God's concern for justice in the present time need to be taught in ways that lead Christians to apply biblical teachings to the challenges of corruption in their own contexts. What is more, a theology of *ubuntu* may aid in correcting the need of the rich to become richer, but to take responsibility with their positioning as people who can effect change.

Digital church

The impact of the Fourth Industrial Revolution has been in the periphery of research. Scholars have been exploring the link between religion and social media (Kgatle 2018:1). However, COVID-19 has increased the necessity to rethink what is church in an online community, and moreover, how accessible it is to South Africans. Buhle Mpofu (2020:3) sheds light on the challenge the church faces, as the poor are excluded from the church on account of not being able to afford Internet and electronic devices. Edward-John Bottomley (2020) reports in the *Business Insider* that South Africa fosters some of the highest data costs in Africa.

Although it is cheaper than the United States and Canada, it is much higher than some African countries such as Nigeria, Kenya, Rwanda and Tanzania, for example. Part of the problem the data reports are that it obscures how expensive it is for the poor. If a person buys data in bulk, then the cost is not as exorbitant, however, the majority of South Africans cannot buy in bulk with the result of the cost of megabytes becoming absurdly expensive. Mpofu (2020:3) mentions the financial strain the church has undergone during COVID-19 as congregants were no longer able to make electronic payments to the church. Here the church has increasingly entered a virtual sphere with services online.

However, as important as church gatherings are, Jacques Beukes (2021:2) points out that church attendance started dwindling before COVID-19 and calls for a renewed understanding of church as an opportunity. Mpofu (2020:4) adds that church membership, not church attendance, should be the focus. Although Beukes is positive about the possibility of a digital church, he is not unaware of the challenges – that, for example, the role of the pastor becomes renewed under the spotlight. Following Niemandt (2019:1), Beukes (2021:6) argues that the digital era is a favourable time to focus on spiritual disciplines, emphasising missional spirituality. Luc Kabongo (2021:5) similarly argues for the necessity of spiritual disciplines from the perspective of doing work as a part of InnerChange in the township of Soshanguve near Pretoria. Although Kabongo is not directly addressing a digital era, the call for spiritual discipline ties in with the concept of community that Beukes envisions. Kabongo (2021:5) writes about the noises in a township and how important silence becomes to avoid being just another addition to the cacophony of noises, being present in order to be agents of change (Kabongo 2021:5).

The challenge of the digital church in Southern Africa remains its capacity to proffer possibilities as well as pitfalls. Kgatle (2018:6) mentions how, for example, Facebook can cause online gospel preaching harm with the spread of viral videos of fake prophecies and staged miracles. In an era of misinformation and fake news, the missional church should be particularly mindful of its online presence. Also, with the risk of account hacking, the missional church should keep a close eye on how it wants to be portrayed and what message it wants to convey.

This being said, Mpofu's (2020:3) call for rethinking new ways of ministering to the poor remains a burning question. If the missional church is serious about reaching the marginalised in a digital manner, a way will have to be sought to make it possible with devices and data. This presents another ethical quandary, as a household with hungry people would rather sell a given electronic device than watch a service online. What is more, cultivating missional identity-forming practices online should be a priority to move onlookers to a position of being participants.

Theological education and reading the Bible

The growth of Christianity in the South renders a new spotlight on what good theology is. This is a question that could easily be misrepresented. Within an African context, it is salient to respect African culture and not use the Bible as a means to enforce Western identity. Cezula (2015:133) remarks that biblical interpretation still tends to be predominantly dominated by Europeans. The Bible is an African book according to Maluleke (2007:515). This renders the need to create more spaces of biblical interpretation for communities from communities. Niemandt (2019:4) suggests the need for a missional hermeneutic that correlates and compares various perspectives that provide a springboard for a transformative theological education. He also proposes that this must be part of theological education and the curriculum as this will trickle into congregational life. What is more, Derrick Mashau (2009:112) mentions that a focus on 'winning souls' has led to dichotomies by narrowing the gospel to its vertical dimensions with little, if any, social involvement. This is pertinent within the reality of a country like South Africa, a land that perpetuated the apartheid fallacy, as well as in a post-apartheid period that includes a majority of Christians but is a society crippled by high crime rates and corruption, to mention but a few social problems.

Theological education in Africa, and particularly South Africa, constantly needs to be under review as a 'good' theology is a theology that constantly reassesses what it means to follow Jesus, using the Bible as the point of departure. There is a need to teach different ways of thinking that will enable pastors to preach with imagination, but also keeping to a missional hermeneutic. Pastors need to mobilise people to make a difference in their communities.

Ecology

As devasting as the COVID-19 lockdowns have been to the economy and livelihoods of people, not even to mention the loss of life, the environment thrived. The disruption of normal life has caused an 8% drop in global carbon emissions according to the International Energy Agency (Mpofu 2020:4). It is alarming that a pandemic provides alleviation to the current and pending ecological crises. Awojobi and Tetteh (2017:39) predict that Africa will be one of the places profoundly stricken by climate change. Africa's impoverished population is particularly vulnerable as poverty limits the ability to adapt to adverse conditions (Conradie 2008:7). Jacques Beukes's work has focussed on youth involvement in the climate change context. Beukes (2021:5) defines the youth as both victims and problem-solvers. He mentions the vital role the youth have played in South Africa to bring about change, for example, the role of youth during apartheid, and campaigns such as #FeesMustFall and #RhodesMustFall (Beukes 2021:6). The mobilisation and support of the youth of Africa is vital to aid in climate change. Beukes (2021:5-6) lists the various skills youth have, such as the ability to understand the complexity of the ecological problem, as well as their technological prowess which is often underestimated. Africa is a young continent, as youth constitute the majority of the populace (Beukes 2021:6). The missional church should be more vocal and involved in identifying young climate advocates.

But what is more, the reason why the missional church is involved with climate change should also be communicated from a biblical foundation. Christianity has been a culprit in abetting a poor theological understanding of stewardship, allowing theological arguments that buttress a misuse of the environment. The plundering of nature goes against the heartbeat of Africa. Kaunda (2016:178) argues that colonialism has separated the Africans from the traditional African environmental philosophy and knowledge based on kindness, familial relationships amongst humans, and the environment. A missional church must not repeat the mistake of early missionaries and so should respect African culture (Mashau 2009:122). A focus on ecology could open new avenues of supporting African theological voices to be heard, and moreover, bring healing for communities in terms of human dignity.

Kaunda (2016:196) brings attention to a renewed interest in research on ecogender theology that proffers a 'life-centred' concept of creation that generates a community of wholeness, justice, equality, respect and unconditional love. The restoration within climate change in Africa is fundamentally also a restoration of human relationships and the relationship with God. African theology has much to contribute to the ecological crisis discourse, especially with regards to an 'ecological pneumatology', as Sakupapa (2012:429) puts it. Mbiti (1975:1) stated that Africans are renowned for their religiosity. Each people have their own religious system pervasive to their interaction with their environment (Mbiti 1975:1). Mamati and Maseno (2021:9) call for a resuscitation of African awareness and engagement to conserve the environment. They purpose that the approach of governments, religious organisations, world agencies and civil movements should adopt a holistic approach that is cultural and context-based. In this sense, the missional church has much to offer in providing missional ethics on ownership and responsibility. Moreover, the missional church should have discussions on how to involve youths to participate in the advocacy in governments to change policies concerning $Co2$ gas emissions and environmental conservation. In South Africa, the military has even been employed in order to help with rhino poaching. This type of action will become even more necessary as the environment suffers the greed of people. Moreover, a successful ecological missional ethics will also need to address the minority of rich people who exercise a monopoly in the exploitation of land and resources for their own financial gain. The monetary gain of selling water, for example, needs to be addressed, as water is a basic human right. The focus should be on protecting rivers and water supplies so that it is available to all.

Summary

Missional ethics is a vast field that requires more research with this chapter only highlighting a few issues. As the pendulum of Christianity moves to the South, the way in which theological students are taught will have to be under scope. These students will minister in places faced with poverty, corruption, and difficulties; and apart from a formal skillset of analysing the Bible, they will also need to be able to think practically, to nourish the spirit as well as nourish the body with food in sustainable ways. The role of leaders living a life by example, and particularly inspiring youth leaders that are contributing to saving the ecology, is necessary. Africans live close to nature and the relationship needs to be cherished. Leaders who are servants and not preaching for their own bank account is also something that should be taught at seminary already. In this sense, subjects like Spiritual Formation need to be implemented early in the first year of study, with congregants also being invited to discover spiritual disciplines and understand their identity in Christ as sent persons.

Conclusion

This chapter used 2 Corinthians 2:12-17 as a lens to illustrate embodiment as something that should also render a scent, or differently put, make a difference. The field of missional ethics has not been explored nearly enough. Missional ethics should be different instead of merely explicating difficult matters, it should aid in cultivating lived faith behaviours. It is imperative that missional ethics keep a deep respect for the African culture as a parameter. Cultivating an African missional ethic of *ubuntu* may serve as a springboard to launch discussions concerning ecology, corruption, and identity. It is only by discovering African culture that it will be able to reason why theologies, such as the prosperity gospel, are so successful. The growth of the church in the South presents a unique opportunity for the missional church to be a transforming influence, bringing people closer to their identities as being sent people. God's sent people include the youth of Africa, who have been neglected for far too long. A missional church ethic should focus on restoring the bond between Africa and its environment, but also allow the biblical narrative to restore this identity. However, it is only from within an African culture that solutions can be found. Moreover, it is pertinent that biblical hermeneutics from an African perspective needs to be voiced, honed, and supported in order to bring the vital contact with God that reshapes the human behaviours of creeds and the need to dominate. The missional church is necessary to reinstall and rediscover the sent identity, with missional ethics spurring Christians to continue living from their sent identity.

References

Allaby, M., 2020, 'Protestant Christianity and control of corruption, past and present', *Christian Relief, Development, and Advocacy* 1(2), 83–92.

Awojobi, O.N. & Tetteh, J., 2017, 'The impacts of climate change in Africa: A review of the scientific literature', *Journal of International Academic Research for Multidisciplinary* 5(11), 39–52.

Bauer, Walter, Danker, F.W., Arndt, W.F. and F.W. Gingrich. 2000. *A Greek-English Lexicon of the New Testament and Other Early Christian Literature*, 3d ed. Chicago: The University of Chicago Press.

Baron, E. & Maponya, M.S., 2020, 'The recovery of the prophetic voice of the church: The adoption of a "missional church" imagination', *Verbum et Ecclesia* 41(1), a2077. https://doi.org/10.4102/ ve.v41i1.2077.

Beukes, J.W., 2021, 'Seen and heard: The youth as game-changing role-players in climate change and environmental consciousness – A South African perspective', *HTS Teologiese Studies/Theological Studies* 77(2), a6893. https://doi.org/10.4102/hts.v77i2.6893.

Bosch, D.J., 1991, *Transforming mission: paradigm shifts in theology of mission*, Maryknoll, Orbis.

Bottomley, E-J., 2020, 'SA has some of Africa's most expensive data, a new report says – but it is better for the richer', viewed 7 March 2022, from https://www.businessinsider.co.za/how-sas-data-prices-compare-with-the-rest-of-the-world-2020-5.

Cezula, N. 2015, 'Reading the Bible in the African context: Assessing Africa's love affair with prosperity Gospel', *Stellenbosch Theological Journal*, Vol 1, No 2, 131–153 DOI: http://dx.doi.org/10.17570/stj.2015.v1n2.a06.

Coetzer, W. & Snell, L.E. 2013, 'A Practical-theological perspective on corruption: towards a solution-based approach in practice', *Acta Theologica* 33(1): 29-53 DOI: http://dx.doi.org/10.4314/actat.v33i1.2 ISSN 1015-8758.

Conradie, E.M., 2008, *The church and climate change*, Signs of the Times Series – Volume 1, Cluster Publication, Pietermaritzburg.

Cassius Dio, C., 1914, *Dio's Roman history* (transl. E. Cary & H.B. Foster) W. Heinemann, London.

Dreyer, W., 2016, 'Church, mission and ethics. Being church with integrity', *HTS Teologiese Studies/Theological Studies* 72(1), a3163. http://dx.doi. org/10.4102/hts.v72i1.3163.

Eyo, U., Essien, E. & Ekong, G., 2020, 'Beyond Prosperity Gospel and Socio-Economic Insecurity in Africa: Ethical Implications of Spiritualizing Poverty', in E. Essien (ed.), *Handbook of research on the impact of culture in conflict prevention and peacebuilding*, pp. 440–463, ICI Global. doi:10.4018/978-1-7998-2574-6.ch026.

Furnish, V.P., 2008, *II Corinthians: translated with introduction, notes, and commentary* (Vol. 32A), Yale University Press, New Haven and London.

Harris, M.J., 2005, *The Second Epistle to the Corinthians: a commentary on the Greek text*, Eerdmans, Grand Rapids, MI.

Hendriks, H.J., 2007, 'Missional theology and social development', *HTS Teologiese Studies/Theological Studies* 63(3), 999–1016.

Josephus, F. (translated Haverkamp, S. 1900. *Complete works of Josephus*. Bigelow, Brown, New York.

Kabongo, K.T.L., 2021, 'Contextualisation: A case study of a team within an international missional order', *Verbum et Ecclesia* 42(1), a2171. https://doi.org/10.4102/ve.v42i1.2171.

Kaunda, C.J., 2016, 'Towards an African ecogender theology: A decolonial theological perspective', *Stellenbosch Theological Journal* 2(1), 177–202. http://dx.doi.org/10.17570/stj.2016.v2n1.a09.

Keum, J. (ed.), 2013, *Together towards life: Mission and evangelism in changing landscapes, with a practical guide*, World Council of Churches Publications, Geneva.

Kgatle, M.S., 2018, 'Social media and religion: Missiological perspective on the link between Facebook and the emergence of prophetic churches in southern Africa', *Verbum et Ecclesia* 39(1), a1848. https://doi.org/10.4102/ve. v39i1.1848.

Khotseng, B. & Tucker, A.R., 2013, 'They worship in our churches' – An opportunity for the church to intervene in order to diminish the corruption that is hindering service delivery in South Africa?', *HTS Teologiese Studies/Theological Studies* 69(2), Art. #1933, 11 pages. http://dx.doi.org/10.4102/ hts.v69i2.1933.

Kruger, J., 2013, 'Filosofies- teologiese uitgangspunte van "missionale" kerkwees: 'n Kritiese evaluering', *In die Skriflig/In Luce Verbi* 47(1), Art. #711, 8 pages. http://dx.doi.org/10.4102/ids. v47i1.711.

Kruse, C.G., 2015, *2 Corinthians: An introduction and commentary* (Second edition, Vol. 8, p. 119), InterVarsity Press, Nottingham, England.

Maluleke, T.S., 2007, 'Postcolonial mission: Oxymoron or new paradigm?', *Swedish Missiological Themes/Svensk Missionstidskrift*, 503–528.

Mamati, K. & Maseno, L., 2021, 'Environmental consciousness amongst indigenous youth in Kenya: The role of the Sengwer religious tradition', *HTS Teologiese Studies/Theological Studies* 77(2), a6690. https://doi. org/10.4102/hts.v77i2.6690.

Martin, R.P., 2014, *2 Corinthians* (2nd ed., Vol. 40), Zondervan, Grand Rapids, MI.

Mashau, T.D., 2009, 'A Reformed missional perspective on secularism and pluralism in Africa: Their impact on African Christianity and the revival of traditional religion', *Calvin Theological Journal* 44, 108–126.

Mashau T.D. & Kgatle, M.S., 2019, 'Prosperity gospel and the culture of greed in post-colonial Africa: Constructing an alternative African Christian theology of ubuntu', *Verbum et Ecclesia* 40(1), a1901. https://doi.org/ 10.4102/ve.v40i1.1901.

Matera, F.J., 2013, *II Corinthians: A commentary*, Westminster John Knox Press, Louisville, KY.

Mbaku, J.M., 1998, 'Bureaucratic and political corruption in Africa', in J.M. Mbaku (ed.), *Corruption and the crisis of institutional reforms in Africa*, pp. 33–83, Edwin Mellen Press, New York.

Mbiti, J.S., 1975, *Introduction to African religion*, Heinemann Educational, London.

Meeks, D.M., 2001, 'Being human in the market society', *Quarterly Review* 21(3), 254–265.

Mellet, P.T., 2020, *The lie of 1652 – a decolonised history of land*, Tafelberg, Cape Town.

Mpofu, B., 2020, 'Mission on the margins: A proposal for an alternative missional paradigm in the wake of COVID-19', HTS Teologiese Studies/Theological Studies 76(1), a6149. https://doi. org/10.4102/hts.v76i1.6149.

Neill, S., 1964, *A history of Christian missions*, Penguin Books, Middlesex.

Newbigin, L., 1978/1995, *The open secret: An introduction to the theology of mission*, Eerdmans, Grand Rapids.

Niemandt, C.J.P., 2017, 'The Prosperity Gospel, the decolonisation of Theology, and the abduction of missionary imagination', *Missionalia* 45(3), 203–219, http://dx.doi.org/10.7832/45-3-199.

Niemandt, N., 2019, 'A missional hermeneutic for the transformation of theological education in Africa', *HTS Teologiese Studies/Theological Studies* 75(4), a5406. https://doi.org/ 10.4102/hts.v75i4.5406.

Plummer, A., 1915, *A critical and exegetical commentary on the Second epistle of St. Paul to the Corinthians*, T&T Clark, New York.

Punt, J., 2005, 'Paul, body theology, and morality: Parameters for a discussion', *Neotestamentica* 39(2), 359–388.

Radoli, A., 1998, 'Editorial', *African Ecclesial Review* 40(5&6), 257.

Sakupapa, T.C., 2012, 'Spirit and ecology in the context of African theology', *Scriptura* 111, 422–430.

Salter, M.C., 2017, 'An exegetical definition of missional ethics', PhD Thesis, University of Aberdeen.

Chapter 17

Missional Diaconate:
A Focused Holistic Ministry

Johannes Knoetze

Introduction

Why must we deal with missional diaconate? Is this not a tautology? Indeed, some would say that it is, yet there is, for many reasons,[1] a great need in the church to closely define mission. Therefore, we find many different descriptions of mission to describe it as more than just witnessing through our words, because, in mission, we want to proclaim the whole gospel, in service to the whole person and the whole world. To establish this understanding of mission, concepts like 'missional diaconate', 'wholistic mission', 'incarnational mission', and 'integral mission' are used. All these concepts attempt to emphasise that mission is more than just spiritual. Mission is more than only witnessing through words, and it is more than mere evangelism – if evangelism is understood as just bringing people to make a choice for Christ. Maybe the important question is not what is mission, but rather, why do we do mission? The main purpose of mission and of diaconia is to honour the presence of God in the world and to worship him (doxology).

In the brief space of this chapter, I will provide a short biblical perspective and then describe three current influences on our understanding of missional diaconia. The first of these influences is the movement of the centrality of Christianity from the West and the North to the Global South with a focus on Southern Africa; the second is the implication of the new understanding of diaconia; and the third is the implication of understanding mission as *missio trinitatis Dei*.

Biblical perspectives

In the New Testament (Matt 3:1; Lk 4:18-19; Rom 10:14) the word *kerygma* is translated as 'preaching', and it is related to the verb *kerusso*, meaning 'to cry or

---

[1] Collins, in his 1990 work Diakonia: *Re-interpreting the Ancient Sources*, gives proof that the *diak-* word group implies not only servant but also proclaimer.

proclaim as a herald'. With the launching of Jesus' public ministry in Luke 4:17-21, he reads from Isaiah 61 and proclaims and identifies himself as the Good News to the poor, the blind, and the captive. From this, Christopher Wright (2010:118ff) argues that the 'gospel' and 'evangelism' have their roots in the Old Testament, and more specifically, in the Book of Isaiah. In the Septuagint, the Hebrew word *basar* is translated with *euangelizomai*, the word used for the preaching of Jesus in the New Testament. *Basar* means announcing good news, and the messenger is called *malak*. In Isaiah 52:7, the *malak* brings the good news of a victory: 'It is peace'. God reigns, this implies *shalom*, the end of brokenness.

When the understanding of Jesus – as Good News – is directly linked to the suffering servant songs in Isaiah: First, Jesus is *God reigning* – the reign becomes more visible through Jesus (Mk 1:14-15). Second, Jesus was *God returning* – with Jesus, the day of the Lord has arrived. Jesus will return in the same way that he went to heaven (Acts 1:11). Third, Jesus was *God redeeming* – Jesus is the one who was going to redeem Israel (Lk 24:21). On the cross, in his 'powerlessness and vulnerability', he redeems the world (Col 2:14-15). Thus, the core message of *kerygma* is 1 Corinthians 15:3-5: 'that Christ died for our sins according to the Scriptures, that he was buried, that he was raised on the third day according to the Scriptures ...' (Jorgensen 2016:9). Thus, mission is the proclamation of the Lordship of Jesus Christ.

If we accept that mission belongs to the essence of being church, then *diaconia* is part of the very nature of the church (Angell 2014:155). In this regard, God's covenant is important for our understanding of *diaconia* since it links the life of the church to God's mission and calls the church to be obedient and faithful to God in every context. Therefore, *diaconia* can be understood as the invitation to participate in God's caring and liberating actions towards all people, especially the marginalised. In this regard, *diaconia* has a prophetic task to unmask injustice and to promote justice. As with mission, the best example and understanding of *diaconia* today is the starting point of Jesus' earthly ministry (Jesus as the great *Diakonos*) and his statement in Luke 4:18-19. Since *diaconia* grows out of the incarnation and sacrificial life of Christ, *diaconia* is never neutral. It is this Christ-centredness of *diaconia* that distinguishes it from development actions or a good life; it is the gospel in action. In this regard Noordegraaf (1991:9) mentioned for the necessity to reinterpret the diaconate as "dienend getuigen" or missionary diaconate.

Christianity in the Global South

Our world is changing every minute. One of the most influential changes today is the explosion of Christianity in the Global South as well as in South(ern) Africa. While the centre of Christianity was in the West and the North, and mission was done from the centre (Europe & North America) to the margins, the message of the gospel was in many instances reduced to 'the forgiveness of sins', and a personal choice for Christ. The main purpose was the winning of souls for Christ. This closely relates to the first two aspects of the threefold mission purposes of Voetius, namely: the conversion of the Gentiles, and the planting of churches; however, the third purpose, the glory and manifestation of God's divine grace (Kritzinger, Meiring & Saayman 1994:1), was neglected. The focus and the motivation were (and in many instances still are) the needs of people – whether it is expanding their own territories and prosperity or attending to the poor and broken in the world – and not the glorification of God. Recently, as many societal ills have been viewed as the consequence of wider injustices from the colonial and Christian era, it is realised that less attention has been given to doxology (the glory and manifestation of God's grace in society) as the purpose of mission and diaconia, than the winning of souls. With the movement of Christianity to the Global South, the church is faced with extreme social-political issues of poverty, racism, greed, health, education, and human sins in every manifestation, since in a sense the church (again) becomes the church of the marginalised. The changing world asks for a mission conversion from a reduced Christian message of 'the forgiveness of sins' to a more wholistic message of the 'Good News of the Kingdom of God' (Sider 2010:19).

The phrase 'the kingdom of God' is central to Jesus' ministry. Of the 122 times the phrase appears in the first three Gospels, he used the phrase 92 times himself. Jesus defines his own mission in Luke 4:43 as: 'I must proclaim the good news of the kingdom of God to the other towns also, because that is why I was sent'. Mark's understanding of the ministry of Jesus is captured in Chapter 1 verses 14 and 15 of his Gospel: 'After John was put in prison, Jesus went into Galilee, proclaiming the good news of God. "The time has come", he said. "The kingdom of God has come near. Repent and believe the good news!" When Jesus sent out the 12 disciples, he commanded them: 'As you go, proclaim this message: "The kingdom of heaven has come near. Heal the sick, raise the dead, cleanse those who have leprosy, drive out demons. Freely you have received; freely give"' (Mt 10:7-8), and in Luke 10:9, he sent out the 72 with the same command: 'Heal the sick who are there and tell them, "The kingdom of God has come near to you"'. Reading the Gospels, it is clear, the demonstration and the announcement of the kingdom of God is the core of Jesus' ministry. Jesus announces both the kingdom and the King. The kingdom is experienced in submission to the King in obedient discipleship. This obedience and witness to the reign of God takes place in the tension between the 'already' and the 'not yet' of the kingdom (Guder 2000:66). Many missionaries and evangelists who claim to be biblical do not define the gospel in the same way Jesus did. This contributes to the reduction of salvation to a spiritual and individualistic relationship between a person and God, which boils down to cheap grace and the neglect of the social implications of the gospel (Sider 2010:18). This contributes to the fact that the gospel becomes 'too small' (Guder 2000:102). Within the majority world, this contributes to what is called the 'missing middle' where no attention is given to folk religion. When salvation is reduced to the forgiveness of sins, it becomes, '... in effect, a property or status that gradually was [is] determined, at least in part, by human actions – the assertion again of the human desire to exercise control' (Guder 2000:112).

It is important to realise that salvation and a relationship with God is always personal, but it is never private. Paas (2019:204) clearly argues that the nature of salvation is the restoration into community with God and with each other and, as such, it cannot take place outside the body of Christ. Christianity is most visible in doxology, in the celebration of a liturgical community, which becomes evident in the missional and diaconal acts of the faith community, not necessarily as acts of ministry, but as doxology.

New understandings of diaconia

Diakonia/diaconia is mostly translated in English as 'ministry' or 'service' which immediately brings some challenges to how we understand mission. It further prompts the question of what the relation between mission and diaconia is? While the secular cultural context contests the nature of diaconia, ministry further challenges the traditional understanding of diaconia. It needs to be stated that one's ecclesiology will be influenced and will influence our understanding of the relation between mission and diaconia. Hartley (2015:n.p.) refers to the debate between Hoekendijk and McGarvan in the 1960s regarding the 'God-world-church' and 'God-church-world'. However, it will become clear later in this chapter that our understanding of the Trinitarian God will have the greatest influence on our understanding of the relation between mission and diaconia. Rather than going into a detailed discussion on diaconia, this chapter attends to the concern of how diaconia and mission interrelates. We will focus on the implications of the new understandings of diaconia for mission today.

The language we use to describe diaconia influences the way the church engages with institutions and non-governmental organisations (NGOs) involved with diaconia. It also influences the ministry of the deacons in our churches which is described as both the most challenging and the most promising ministry in the church (Hartley 2015:n.p.).

Hartley (2015:n.p.) indicates three important paradigm shifts for missiology in relation to Collins' study on the *diakon*-word group. The first has to do with the field of meaning which is 'focused on intermediary or emissarial relationships of persons and less on the caring, ethical, nature of the acts performed, such as in taking care of or helping someone'. In this instance, the importance is to recover the relations between the diaconia in the world and the church, not the officious status. The point to note here is that the diaconal work is in some way accountable to the church, in the same way that mission is accountable to the church. This implies that the church is the agent. The second point is already alluded to, that *diakon* is more focused on the missionary meaning like *diakonos* (minister), or *Apostolos* (messenger), than the previous understandings with a focus on lowly, humble, service. 'At a personal level, a more apostolic understanding of a minister's vocation may further guard against an unhealthy victim complex whereby one perceives oneself as a burned-out servant of the people more than a sent emissary of God' (Hartley 2015:n.p.). This new understanding of the *diakon*-word group must help to free the church from a humility of 'let the world set the agenda' like the World Council of Churches (WCC) claimed in 1968. Embracing the revised definition, the *diakon*-words, while holding on to true Christian humility, deacons, deaconesses and missionaries may embrace the radical missionary values of God's reign when crossing borders and when the whole church, brings the whole gospel, to the whole world. Holding on to God's reign, we can focus on the doxology and not let the world set the agenda. This might seem like a contradiction as if we no longer care about the world. However, nothing is further from the truth since we can never truly honour God where his love has not conquered our lives.

The third implication for mission from this new understanding of the *diakon*-word group is 'Ministry is not synonymous with activities of Christian discipleship' (Hartley 2015:n.p.). Loving your neighbour, taking care of the poor, and witnessing are activities all Christians ought to do and are not necessarily ministries, although they could be. The intention here is not to 'take back' the diaconia of the lay person and make diaconia exclusive to the ordained. The important dimension here is the 'accountability' of the deacons, deaconesses and missionaries who received a specific call.

Some Trinitarian perspectives on *diaconia*

One of the most important questions are: What are the theological grounds for missional diaconia? Is missional diaconia just a way to follow Jesus? And therefore, an expression of discipleship? Or is missional diaconia grounded in the theology of creation? And therefore, we have the calling to be God's co-workers? We need a more comprehensive understanding of missional diaconia than just the Christian nature or the emphasis on the public domain. A more comprehensive understanding is rooted in the being of the Triune God: The Father as Creator and Sustainer; Jesus Christ as Saviour and Liberator; and the Holy Spirit as the Giver of Life, the one who equips with gifts and empowers with faith. As such, the theological grounds for missional *diaconia* is doxology, to worship God for being God. One of the most essential perspectives of the Trinity is *koinonia*, the love, the relations between the three persons of the Trinity, and the relation of the Trinity with all of creation. In light of this, the departure of a missional diaconate ministry is the Great Commandment: loving the Lord with all of who you are and have, and loving your neighbour as yourself (Matt 22:34-40).

The Father

In a sense it is easy to talk about God as the Father. Within the Trinity it is the one Person that helps us to think and talk in universal terms of our belief in a god. Many Christians also think of God as the Father, the One who created/s, and the One who sustains. This is also true of at least the Abrahamic religions: Judaism, Islam, and Christianity. But it is also true for African Traditional Religions which refer to him as the Supreme Being (Turaki 2006:17).

Focusing now from a Christian perspective, God the Father is the One who loves and wanted to be loved. God is a relational being who created out of love; he is the encountering God who wants to be known by his creation. To ensure humans of his love and encounters with us, he made several covenants with certain individuals as representatives of those who believe in him. Here we think of the covenants with Noah, Abraham, Moses, David, and the new covenant in Jesus Christ. All these covenants refer to God's love and commitment to his creation, through the calling of his people. With the enormous privilege and security of God's covenant, love comes with the great responsibility of making his love known. A noteworthy point is that when God calls people, he always calls them *out* of a people or a known context and sends them to witness in a strange uncertain context for them. He does not call them *out of this* world, he calls them out of their (comfortable) world into a new (unknown) world, where they will be strangers and pilgrims. It is in these unknown circumstances that they need to make God known through their words and deeds.

The Father's one desire is to be known and to be loved, not only by his people but by his whole creation. We show our love, and we make him known when we glorify his name, when we talk about the great deeds he had done (Acts 2:11; 1 Pet 2:9). In the covenant with Abraham (Gen 12:1-3), believers (children of Abraham) are called to be a blessing to the nations. We will only be a blessing to the nations if our words and deeds witness to and imitate the love and the commitment of the Father to his whole creation. Believers are called to act as priests of God amongst the nations. Reading through the Old Testament, we notice how Israel (God's people) struggled to be a blessing to the nations since they again want to create their own comfortable circumstances and not live as a blessing (priests) and strangers (pilgrims) amongst the people. Therefore, God did not break his covenant to love them, but he always created new circumstances that made his people a blessing and strangers in a foreign land. Think for example about the slavery in Egypt, the exile in Babylon. But Israel, like us, always falls back into their comfort zones. Therefore, the Father had to send his Son – Jesus Christ –so that the whole creation may know about his love (Jn 3:16) and that we are able to love him.

In a post-Christendom era, we are still thinking about Christianity as this powerful religion. Paas (2019) elucidated that the church in the post-Christendom era in Europe is in the same pilgrimage situation as the people of God in the Bible.

This is why it is so important that we not only confess the Father as the Creator, but also as the Sustainer of Life. The question is, What is the role of God as Creator and Sustainer in the current post-Christian context?

Jesus Christ

Out of love for the creation, the Father honours his covenant by sending his Son, Jesus Christ, to save those who believed in him from his judgement and wrath. Through Jesus Christ, God forgave us and wants us to live from his forgiveness. It is in the footsteps of Jesus, whom the Bible describes as the great *Diakonos*, that we must do missional diaconate to the glory of God from an attitude of forgiveness

Thinking from a missional diaconate point of view, we must take the whole story of Jesus Christ serious and as an example of the calling of the church. The incarnation of Jesus confirms what we have already said about God's calling to pilgrims and priests (Paas 2019). According to Philippians 2:6-8, Jesus 'did not consider equality with God something to grasped, but he made himself nothing'. He stepped out of his 'comfort zone' into a world where people were hostile towards him and treated him as a stranger. Although he came into this world as a Priest, they always treated him as a stranger. 'His own people did not recognise him' (Jn 1:11). He was always a pilgrim with no home, no place to lay his head (Lk 9:58). His incarnation is the ultimate calling of the church to a life of mission and diaconate as a self-giving and other community. Jesus' earthly ministry was characterised by love, justice and humility through grace and forgiveness with a focus on the kingdom of God. Jesus did not only forgive people; his focus was on the kingdom of God and honouring the Father; he also attended to the hungry, the sick, the marginalised, the prisoners, and the broken. He gave them food. He healed them. He taught them.

Despite all this grace and these wonders, he was still treated as an outcast through suffering and crucifixion. Through his death, he showed us the price of forgiveness, but through his resurrection and ascension, he showed us the fruit of forgiveness. If we are prepared to die to ourselves, our self-interests, and our own delusions, it is possible to accept his forgiveness and, in turn, to forgive others. Forgiveness creates new life and life possibilities and makes living in the (ever) present possible. He forgave us, and he sent his disciples to do the same. He sent us to create new life possibilities in the present at the cost of our own lives. But God knows we are not able to live accordingly from our own abilities, so he gave us his Spirit.

The Holy Spirit

Jesus did not leave us as orphans (Jn 14 & 16); together with the Father, he sent us his Spirit. The Spirit continues with the ministry of Jesus – the great *Diakonos* – to serve creation in all its brokenness and to empower believers to participate in his service. Jesus' main purpose was to worship the Father which he did when reconciling creation and God when he died on the cross. It is in light of this that Calvin could say that the primary work of the Spirit is to unite us with Christ, because it is the Spirit who gives us faith and witnesses together with our spirit as we are children of God (Rom 8:16). The Spirit does not only serve us – work *for* us – but he also empowers us, giving us *charismata* – working *in* us and *through* us in the reconciling work. As such, reconciliation is not only a spiritual occurrence; it must also be embodied in real life. That is what Pentecost is about. When believers confess that the Spirit of God lives within and through them, they confess that they are able and willing to serve others, and to be served by others, because they are also broken people. This serves to happen when we use the charismata that we received as a gift to serve others and to work towards the reconciliation of the creation with God through a ministry like the missional diaconate. Living in obedience to the Spirit who is not only the One who empowers us but also the One who gives life (*Spiritus Creator*). As such, the Spirit gives life to faith communities. Central to the life in the Spirit is inclusive communities. Therefore, the church may/can never lose hope and must continue to participate in creating new life possibilities, regardless of the context, whether it is problematic, complicated, or destructive.

The church as a window of the kingdom

The kingdom of God – *basileia tou Theo* – is central in the Gospels and in Jesus' understanding of his ministry. When the Father and the Son send the Spirit, he creates the church, through giving people faith in the reconciliation work of the Lord Jesus, which he did through his words (teachings) and his actions (life, death, and resurrection). The church may be viewed as a window through which the world can see how the kingdom of God is coming on earth. Therefore, the Spirit not only creates a faith community, but he also equips the church with charismata to benefit those within and outside the faith community (1 Cor 12:7). God loves, forgives (grace), and serves (empower) the believers so that they may know themselves and know him through the reconciliation work of Jesus, so that those who believe may participate in the *koinonia* with the Father and the Son (1 Jn 1:3) (Knoetze 2013:40). We know God and ourselves better if we find ourselves in the *koinonia* of the faith community, because it is in the faith community that we experience the love, forgiveness, and empowerment – the *koinonia* of God. As a community, we are called to do missional diaconate and be a window of the kingdom of God. If we preach the gospel that the kingdom of God is here, our preaching will only have meaning within the context of *diaconia*, because our preaching presupposes that something is happening that needs to be explained. Actually, our *kerygma* is the explanation of the why of our *diaconia*. 'Word without deed can be abstract and powerless, and deed without word can be mute and open for any interpretation' (Jorgensen 2016:17)

References

Angell, O.H., 2014, Diakonia, Hospitality and Welfare, in Stephanie Dietrich, Knud Jorgensen, Kari Karsrud Korslien & Kjell Nordstokke (eds), *Diakonia as Christian Social Practice. An Introduction*, WIPF & STOCK; Eugene, Oregon

Collins, J.N., 1990, *Diakonia: Re-interpreting the Ancient Sources*, New York: Oxford University Press.

Guder, D.l., 2000, *The continuing conversion of the church*, William B. Eerdmans Publishing Company, Grand Rapids, Michigan.

Hartley, B., 2015, 'Diakonia and Mission: Charting the Ambiguity', *Faculty Publications - College of Christian Studies*, 217. http://digitalcommons.georgefox.edu/ccs/217

Knoetze, H., 2013, Missionary diaconate: Hope for migrated people, in *Missionalia*, 41:1, p 40-52

Jorgensen, K., 2016, 'Biblical perspectives on kerygma and diakonia', in R. Dowsett, I. Phiri, D. Birdsall, D.O. Terfassa, H. Yung & K. Jorgesen (eds.), *Evangelism and diakonia in context*, 7-18, Regnum Books, Oxford, UK.

Kritzinger, J.J., Meiring, P.G.J., & Saayman, W.A., 1994, *On being witnesses*, Orion Publishers, Johannesburg.

Noordegraaf, A., 1991, *Orientatie in het diakonaat*. Zoetemeer: Uitgeverij Boekencentrum

Noordstokke, K., 2016, 'Trinitarian perspectives on diakonia', in R.R. Dowsett, I. Phiri, D. Birdsall, D.O. Terfassa, H. Yung & K. Jorgesen (eds.), *Evangelism and diakonia in context*, 141-152, Regnum Books, Oxford, UK.

Paas, S., 2019, *Pilgrims and priests: Christian mission in a post-Christian society*, SCM Press, London, UK.

Sider, R.J., 2010, 'What if we defined the Gospel the way Jesus did?' in B. Woolnough & W. Ma (eds.), *Holistic mission: God's plan for God's people*, Regnum Books, Oxford, UK.

Turaki, Y., 2006, *Foundations of African Traditional Religion and Worldview*, WorldAlive Publishers Limited; Nairobi, Kenya

Wright, C.H.J., 2010, *The mission of God's people: A Biblical theology of the church's mission*, Zondervan, Grand Rapids, Michigan.

Chapter 18

Church and Development in Africa: Looking Back, Moving Forward

Nadine Bowers Du Toit

Introduction

Our continent is a lively and flourishing one with an abundance of mineral wealth, but it is also plagued by persistent poverty and caught in the unequal power relations between the Global North and Global South. On the continent, churches and other faith-based organisations (FBOs) have long been at the forefront of seeking to address issues of poverty and injustice, believing it to be part of the mission of God; nevertheless, there remains the opportunity to reflect on the ways in which churches are actively engaging these issues in the current context. Furthermore, the emergence of the Sustainable Development Goals (SDGs), and also recent development thinking which foregrounds issues such as gender and the need to decolonise development have emerged, providing challenges and opportunities for churches on the continent to engage. This chapter therefore seeks to explore both the ways in which African churches have responded and are responding to issues of poverty and injustice, as well as highlight possible emerging tensions and opportunities from the field of development itself to the African context using local examples that draw on the recent works of African scholars in the field of church and development.

The legacy of colonialism in Africa with regards to charity and welfare provision

The double legacy that the colonial missionary enterprise has played in both contributing to what we now understand as development via the establishment of soft infrastructure and social justice with regards to issues such as slavery, as well as its complicity in the colonial enterprise, have been well documented with reference to the African context.

Gifford (2009:20, 46), for example, affirms that the long history of mainline church involvement in Africa with regards to their contributions to health, education and infrastructure provision is well documented. Deacon and Tomalin (2015:71), for example, note that 'From the early construction of isolated mission stations came forth the building of roads, schools and hospitals, as well as, of course, churches', which, in effect, 'laid the groundwork for the colonists'. They further articulate that between the mid-19th century and mid-20th century, the New Imperialism, as evidenced via the Berlin Conference and 'scramble for Africa', were particularly intertwined with the missionary enterprise. Post-colonial critiques therefore identify missionaries as tacitly supporting colonial interests via their faith-based projects (Deacon & Tomalin 2015:71). In this respect, Manji and O'Coil (2002:3) are particularly critical, identifying the ways in which missionary Christianity not only provided 'material support in education, health or other social services', but that 'in providing such services, they were also concerned with evangelizing among the African population, discouraging what they perceived as ignorance, idleness and moral degeneracy and promoting their own vision of civilization'. In so doing, they observe these 'works of benevolence as a solution to social unrest', although, '[i]n short, [such] charity was not only designed to help the poor, it also served to protect the rich' (Manji & O'Coil 2002:7). Eale (2021:187) maintains that diaconia is a recent development within the African church as it was not the primary agenda of mission work, but rather arose out of a felt need.

Nevertheless, it should be noted that the missionaries also played a role in addressing the abuses of colonial powers. South African theologian John De Gruchy, for example, indicates that while some missionaries indeed played a role in the racial segregation propounded by the colonial powers, still others not only evangelised the indigenous peoples, but also 'took their side in the struggle for rights, justice and land' (De Gruchy 1979:13). Deacon and Tomalin, citing Comaroff and Comaroff (1986:2), state that:

> Many mission-educated subjects seem to have questioned their altered universe: mission education often meant that Biblical texts were interrogated and those who had attended mission schools were the first to express open rejection of the colonial order by pointing to the inconsistency with biblical injunction and by freeing from the holy text itself a charter for liberation.

This, according to Mtata (2013:29), meant that not only did mission education assist Africans in their fight against colonialism, but it also provided them with tools to challenge the missionaries in their complicity with the colonisers.

The process of decolonisation, during which we saw many states in Africa become independent of their former colonial masters during the 1950s and 60s, was one which resulted in 'most of the schools, hospitals and other properties in the hands of the missionaries being taken over by the new local governments' (Mtata 2013:29). Mtata comments that sadly during this era it became evident that, nevertheless, 'at some level, the missionary churches' ambivalent (and sometimes even supportive) relationship with the colonial regime disempowered it from playing any public role in the aftermath of the colonial period'. He also reflects on the way in which missionary Christianity promoted a dualistic spirituality that weakened the church's role in society (Mtata 2013:29).

The current African context with regards to poverty

As commonly stated: 'Africa is not a country', which complicates the task of discussing the features of poverty and inequality for an entire continent. Nevertheless, I will attempt to briefly highlight some key issues and their complexities on the context with regards to these issues.

The causes of poverty on our continent are numerous and not least shaped by the colonial project which continues in the destruction of the many natural resources on our continent and the perpetuation of unequal trade – issues which continue today. This domination has also led to environmental degradation, which sees a depletion of our national capital and the 'overexploitation of natural resources', which frequently increases poverty by 'destroying the means to production' via practices such as water pollution, deforestation, and illegal mining – often by multinational companies which then export the wealth elsewhere (Boaheng 2020:32; Anim 2020:206). Boaheng avers that 'in Africa, poverty is often politically driven'. This results in politicians' exploitation and gaining unjust wealth via state power, which is of course only possible due to weak governance in many African countries who continue to display political instability and at times lack of 'proper governmental machinery and oversight'. Such factors create a context within which Africa's socio-economic development is hindered.

This problem goes hand in hand with the issue of corruption, a concern that has been recognised as a contributor to poverty in Africa. In fact, corruption is cited by scholars as not only hampering investment and economic growth, but increasing the inequality gap between the rich and poor, 'creating obstacles to economic and political reform and in the long run can cause considerable human welfare losses' (Justesen & Bjornskov 2014:106). The Corruption Perception Index, for example, names several African countries amongst the most corrupt in the world (Boaheng 2020:35). Corruption has been shown to not only eat into the economy, but also affects service delivery and the ensuring of justice, as officials themselves who are expected to safeguard justice, the rule of law and promote the welfare of citizens, are implicated. As a result, 'corruption undermines national development, weakens the economy, leads to economic inequality amount citizens and makes a country poorer' (Boaheng 2020:35). Nevertheless, it is further noted that poverty is also a causal factor with regards to corruption as studies show that 'poverty significantly increases the probability of paying bribees' (Justesen & Bjornskov 2014:113).

Moreover, political instability is an outcome of the ongoing conflict and civil wars in many African countries. Didier (2017:1) argues that one of the root causes of Africa's poverty lies in the rise of conflicts on the continent, which he contends stems from the colonial period which deepened ethnic divisions and 'rivalry for resources' (Calderisi 2006:222). Didier (2017:1) further argues that conflict and development are both interconnected and interdependent in the following way:

> That is to say, here there is conflict there is no sustainable development, and where there is no development there is conflicts. At the same time, where there is development that is not equitably shared there will be conflicts.

Other developmental issues which plague our continent include natural disasters, high rates of illiteracy, poor health, and unemployment. The crisis of HIV and AIDS, for example, has had a significant impact on the continent and much of the continent is still reeling from its effects. Boaheng (2020:41) affirms the devasting effects of this epidemic on our continent as it resulted in many sick people no longer being able to work and left many children and youth orphaned. Youth unemployment and poverty on the continent also remains a worrying trend as Africa is a continent where the vast majority of its people are under the age of 30.

In Sub-Saharan Africa, which comprises a total of 21 countries, there is nevertheless some positive movement as the region is experiencing what scholars term 'pro poor growth' – despite high levels of chronic poverty. It is also interesting to note that the more resource rich and middle-income countries have more upward mobility with post-secondary education which is 'especially strongly associated' with this factor and which even holds true for some female headed households (Dang & Dabalen 2017:2). Chronic poverty nevertheless continues to persist. The following is noted with regards to long term goals for addressing this chronic poverty:

> Although the long-term goal is to increase upward mobility, or exit from poverty, the immediate and medium term goals may be to protect the incomes of the poor and to minimize downward mobility, especially for the vulnerable. Some of the policies that have been shown to achieve these goals include safety net programs and building the assets (especially human capital

– education and health) of the poor and the vulnerable, such as investments in early years of the children of the poor, and providing a basic package of health services (Dang & Dabalen 2017:22).

It is interesting to note here that the building of social capital and provision of basic needs in the areas of education and health – both areas in which the church has been prominent since the missionary era – are recognised as contributing to stemming the tide of poverty on the continent.

Emerging tensions and opportunities

Deacon and Tomlin (2015:73) mention that it was only in the 1980s that African Christian churches began to speak out with regards to critical engagement with oppressive national regimes and that at that time we also witnessed what they term 'paradigmatic changes' in the African church with the rise of Pentecostalism. Towards the 1990s and early 2000s, it became clear that within the global development discourse the role of spirituality in development was gaining traction and bodies such as the World Bank were paying attention to faith actors on the continent (Deacon & Tomlin 2015:75). This section now turns to more recent developments and some of the emerging tensions and opportunities with regards to current trends pertaining to the church and development on the continent. In each of the aspects raised here, both the tensions and opportunities are discussed.

The rise of Neo-Pentecostalism and its role

Heuser (2013:54) remarks that since the 1980s (despite missionary/classical Pentecostalism having taken root much earlier in Africa), neo-Pentecostalism – often aligned to the 'Word of Faith' movement in the United States of America (USA) and its prosperity gospel 'which connects an elevated religious stature with social status represented by material wellbeing' – as growing in astounding numbers on the continent. This is unsurprising considering that Africa has high levels of poverty and illiteracy, 'leaving many lives in despondency and powerlessness', and thus more vulnerable to messages of prosperity (Pondani 2019:ii). Much has been written with regards to the harm that this movement has caused in terms of preying on poor communities who believe that their only way out of poverty is the 'sowing' of money towards the church so that they may partake in financial blessing. In this way prosperity preaching has done much harm and has often seen the poor left further impoverished while the 'man of God' – a kind of spiritual entrepreneur – is living in material wealth. In recent years, we have also seen the rise of a new, yet more harmful, form of neo-Pentecostalism in Southern Africa where neo-Pentecostal prophetic figures perpetuate dangerous healing practices such as snake eating, petrol drinking, and even the spraying of congregants with insecticide, thus 'endangering the lives of congregants who are desperate for a special miraculous touch' (Pondani 2019:ii).

Nevertheless, neo-Pentecostalism has shown that it has another side to it. This movement which 'offers God's blessings to transform an individual's life are also viewed as having the power to transform society' – so much so that Birgit Myer names it the 'pentecostalisation of the public sphere' (Heuser 2013:53). Heuser (2013:56) cites, for example, the way in which the former chair of the Church of Pentecost in Ghana 'encourages financial responsibility in the discourse on poverty' and encourages congregants to also invest in social services in the areas of health and education. Heuser also notes the way in which these forms of Pentecostalism have encouraged impoverished African believers with a sense of discipline and hard work via a renewed protestant work ethic founded on a 'theology of success' (Heuser 2013:58). There is also the rise of middle-class Pentecostalism – 'a specific category of churches that emphasizes active social/development ministries' (Heuser 2013:59). These churches invest in the social needs of their community and are involved in what they would term outreach ministries to the poor. Examples of such congregations in South Africa would be Grace Bible Church and Rhema, both of whom have sophisticated social development outreach arms. Such churches have also been seen to engender greater self-esteem in their members so that they 'feel less powerless, less afraid of the future and more willing to accept change' – thus providing fertile ground for the development of social capital and in mobilising for social change (Heuser 2013:65).

The push to decolonise development

As already alluded to, colonialism's double legacy has meant that the church in Africa has been both a proponent of liberation and social welfare and development on the continent, and a force for colonial exploitation. This double legacy appears to carry on in various ways currently in the way in which Northern donors and Southern receipts interact within a neo-colonial framework. While my own study of FBOs in the context of Cape Town, South Africa, reveals that there is far less Global North donor dependency in a middle-income African country such as ours, which larger donors do not support, this may well not be the case for lower income African countries (Bowers Du Toit 2019). A case study from Angola between a Reformed denomination and its international faith-based donor reveals, for example, extreme imbalances of power in the partnership, which resulted in undue interference by the donor in internal denominational issues as well as ultimately a lack of sustainability of projects and the complete collapse of the projects upon donor exit (Fabiao 2021). Sadly, such engagement is often tinged with a distinct lack of understanding of the cultural context, charity and welfarist discourse rather than participatory development and white supremacy which often lingers in unexpected power dynamics (Bowers Du Toit 2018).

What Öhlmann, Grab and Frost's (2020) book reveals, however, is that the African Initiated Churches (AICs) (and here they include both neo-Pentecostal churches together with AICs) are doing development on their own terms and thus changing the development landscape in the process. Their book focuses mainly on the contexts of Nigeria, Ghana and South Africa, and argues that while AICs are 'not yet recognized as development actors', they have great potential for shifting the faith and development discourse on our continent (Öhlmann et al. 2020:12-15). By de-centring development discourse and praxis away from the Global North and firmly centring it on indigenous religious culture and praxis, the decolonisation of development is taking place in surprising ways. In this discourse, the relevance of overarching global frameworks, such as the SDGs, are brought into question on a continent like ours, as often these indicators 'are imposed on national and then by design on local contexts – priorities set outside of context and often used by donors in determining funding priorities' (Bowers Du Toit 2020:315). The challenge for faith actors – whether it be FBOs, congregations, or denominational ministries – on our continent is certainly to resist global imperialism and donor influence of the kind that dictates agendas from the outside in, rather than working with local peoples and drawing upon their spiritual resources to engage in diaconal and development work that will ultimately be more sustainable in the long run.

Holism in development

While as briefly noted, bodies such as the World Bank and other faith and secular actors began to take renewed interest in the role of spirituality from the late 1980s – as Mbiti once stated, Africa is an inherently religious continent and so for Africans there is no separation between religion and life. This is certainly a feature of much social development work on the continent. Bansah and Dzunu (2021:198) therefore reiterate that in a West African context, 'most churches are involved in community engagement efforts because of the belief that the church cannot divorce itself from its community, and because of the understanding that it is unbiblical for sections of communities to have comfort while many others go without this comfort'. These writers further contend that within the West African region, churches are, therefore, not only interested in the spiritual well-being of their members, but also in their physical and mental well-being, with many churches making a concerted effort to address poverty and inequality via church hospitals, schools, micro credit, and even via church farms and other agricultural initiatives.

This holistic approach is not limited to humans but also stretches to the need for creation care; moreover, it not only focuses on charitable actions, but also on advocacy initiatives which additionally address the socio-political issues of the day. Kalengyo's (2021) chapter on East African engagement with issues of diaconia and development reveal both sophisticated ministries offered mostly by mainline (former mission) churches such as the Evangelical Lutheran Church in Tanzania, The Anglican Church of Uganda, and the Catholic Church in Uganda, as well as the issue that some churches in East Africa – more especially those affected by prolonged civil conflict – are still 'underdeveloped and largely serviced by foreign relief agencies and local NGO's' (Kalengyo 2021:213). In the South African context, Bowers Du Toit opines that there remains within a country such as South Africa a dualistic spiritualisation of the gospel which sees local congregations either remaining apathic or focusing on relief and charity, rather than advocacy and participatory development – a feature which can be traced to missionary spirituality. Yoms' (2015) thesis on the 'People Centred Development Programmes' of his own denomination in Nigeria reveals a more subtle picture with regards to the challenge of holistic mission, namely that while his denomination regards both the spiritual (evangelism) and the physical (development) as important – these are still functioning as separate ministries and are viewed as separate aspects of mission rather than both as part of God's integral mission. This practice is possibly more an outcome of dichotomous enlightenment missionary praxis than indigenous thought, however.

Foregrounding gender in church and development

Despite the fact that poverty is femininised on our continent, Chilongozi (2016:49) asserts that 'without gender equality where women are empowered and allowed to participate equally in development projects – sustainable development is unachievable', the issue of gender in mission and development discourse and practice is still one that requires much attention. The latter is identified as being rooted in ways in which conservative and fundamentalist religious attitudes have had a negative influence and impact on the social status of women in society. In an African context, this is, furthermore, often bound up with culture. These cultural practices are both overt (child marriage, wife inheritance, widow cleansing, female genital mutilation/cutting, etc.) and more subtle (stereotypical gender roles, ritual impurity when menstruating, exclusion from community rituals, etc) (Oduyoye 1993:09). Myambo's (2017) thesis which deals with the way in which the Shona culture, when combined with fundamentalist Christian beliefs, often reinforces the oppression of girl children in Zimbabwe. In this regard, Myambo (2017:18) notes the following:

> What is clearly revealed by the findings is the patriarchal nature of Shona society defines the role of women in marriage, community and has infiltrated the church. Cultural and societal norms shape the people's theological understandings and beliefs as evidenced by their response to social transformation, social justice and their view of salvation.

Of course culture shapes the way Scripture is often interpreted, and toxic interpretations of Scripture also perpetuate patriarchy and oppressive practices with regards to women. Le Roux and Bowers Du Toit (2016:32), for example, cite numerous studies which show the way in which the Bible has been used to facilitate and justify wife beating, marital rape and other forms of gender-based violence. It is further argued that religious leaders in Africa have been key in using the Scriptures in life giving ways and have thus played a significant role in turning the tide against such heinous practices – cultural or otherwise.

Over the past 30 years, the Circle of Concerned African Women Theologians (the Circle) have not only begun to challenge the church on the kind of scriptural hermeneutics which facilitates the oppression of women but have also 'sought to uncover liberating and empowering resources in African culture and religion' (Le Roux & Bowers Du Toit 2016:555). It is noteworthy to mention that grassroots African Christian women also have their own agency. A study done on the Zambian Anglican Women's Union, for example, showed that women were exercising their agency, while a more recent study that focused on the way that rural women in Malawi are empowering themselves by means of the microfinance Village Savings and Loans model is truly inspiring (Le Roux 2019; cf. Chilongozi 2022). In an African context, it is also important to note that issues of gender and mission cannot be approached from a Western feminist framework and that any engagement with issues of gender, church and development must be recognised within the framework of gender partnership. As the mother of the Circle, Mercy Amba Oduyeye, notes: '[T]he partnership of women and men is… necessary if the church is to be whole and to be the light of Christ for the world' (in Onwunta & August 2011:11). African Church leaders themselves have been shown to be able to address issues of gender-based violence (GBV) when working in partnership with women and addressing texts in a responsible hermeneutic manner (Le Roux & Bowers Du Toit 2016).

The need to develop a theological perspective of church and development

One of the key challenges identified by Kalengyo (2021:2019) is the need for churches to develop a sound theological understanding of the church's role in development

– more especially as diaconia is a biblical mandate (cf. Bansah & Dzunu 2020:202). Kalengyo (2021:2019) mentions the following in this regard:

> The churches have not yet taken time to reflect and understand diaconia as a dimension integral to the nature and mission of the church and rather than as an optional extra. Secondly, nearly across the board, churches are lacking explicit framework documents that spell out theological and biblical perspectives on the understanding of diaconia. Following from these two challenges, thirdly, there is a lack of theological resources and trained personnel which would help move the diaconal ministry in churches forward and in other agencies who would promote the diaconal ministry.

This challenge, while prominent in the context of East Africa, is echoed by scholars on other parts of the continent such as in South Africa (Bowers Du Toit 2014; De Gruchy 2015) and Zimbabwe (Webster 2019) who argue for theological training in the field of church and development to be taught more, especially within seminaries and universities that offer theological education across the continent as part of clergy training. Although the field of theology and development is well established in South Africa, having been recognised at universities since the late 1990s, and despite its rapid expansion through the teaching and works of continental scholars and it being taught at universities (such as Daystar University and St Paul's University in Kenya, amongst others), there is a need for the field to broaden across the continent (De Gruchy 2015). In addition, international FBOs, such as Tearfund[1], have expressed a keen interest in developing this field within the seminary context, and in late 2022 the All Africa Conference of Churches (AACC) held an international symposium to 'encourage theological education initiatives throughout the African region'; this conference had a distinct focus on the need for theological education to address the socio-economic and political challenges facing the continent.[2] Also worth mentioning here is that prominent African theologians, such as Prof Isabel Phiri and Bosale Eale, to name but two, continue to drive these conversations both locally and worldwide.

---

[1] Cf. NetACT, 2019, *Tearfund 'Collaboration in Theological education and Training in Africa' Group* [Online forum], viewed 3 May 2022, from https://landtportal.netact.org.za/?q=forum/2

[2] Cf. World Council of Churches (WCC), 2022, *AACC supports theological education projects in Africa*, viewed 3 May 2022, from https://www.oikoumene.org/news/aacc-supports-theological-education-projects-in-africa

Conclusion

It is clear that in looking back, the missionary enterprise has a double legacy in terms of the African church and its engagement with the welfare and flourishing of peoples on our continent, and that our continent still faces many development challenges with regards to issues of poverty and its related ills. It, nevertheless, becomes clear, too, that God is doing something new. Churches are rising up to dictate their own terms for development by working from the grassroots and, in effect, decolonising development; Pentecostals – long critiqued for their problematic role in the spread of the prosperity gospel on the continent – are also arising as key players in addressing social issues; African men and women are recognising the harmful role of patriarchy and are being called upon to address the feminisation of poverty together on our continent; and there are revived discussions and praxis with regards to holistic development and the church's role therein. There is much that still awaits the African church in its push to address the integral nature of mission; nevertheless, from my perspective, we are well on our way.

References

Anim, E.K., 2020, An Evaluation of Pentecostal Churches as Agents of Sustainable Development in Africa: the case of the Church of Pentecost, in P. Öhlmann, W. Grab & Frost, M. (eds)., *African Initiated Christianity and the decolonization of development: Sustainable development in Pentecostal and Independent churches*, 195-211, Routledge, London.

Bansah, C.W. & Dzunu, E., 2021, 'Diaconia in West African Christianity', in G. Ampony, M.

Büscher, B. Hofmann, F. Ngnintedem, D. Solon & D. Werner (eds.), *International handbook on ecumenical diakonia*, 197-202, Regnum, Oxford.

Boaheng, I., 2020, *Poverty, the Bible and Africa: Contextual foundations for helping the poor*, ACTS Publishing, Bukuru.

Bowers Du Toit, N., 2018, 'Decolonising development? Re-claiming Biko and a Black Theology of Liberation within the context of faith based organisations in South Africa', *Missionalia* 46(1), 26-35.

Bowers Du Toit, N., 2020, 'Contested Development(s)? The possible contribution of the African Independent Churches in decolonizing development. A South African perspective', in P. Öhlmann, W. Grab & M. Frost (eds.), *African Initiated Christianity and the decolonization of development: Sustainable development in Pentecostal and Independent churches*, Routledge, London.

Bowers Du Toit, N.F., 2014, '"Rise up and walk": Tracing the trajectory of the Carnegie discourse and plotting a way forward', *NGTT*, http://ngtt.journals.ac.za/pub/article/view/651.

Bowers du Toit, N.F., 2019, 'Unapologetically faith based: The nature of donor engagement in the context of South African faith-based organisations', *HTS Teologiese Studies/Theological Studies* 75(4). https://doi.org/10.4102/hts.v75i4.5529.

Calderisi, R., 2006, *The trouble with Africa: why foreign aid isn't working*, Palgrave, New York.

Chilongozi, M., 2016, 'The role of the church with regards to maternal health: A case study of the Church of Central Africa Presbyterian, Livingstonia Synod', Master's thesis, University of Stellenbosch.

Chilongozi, M., 2022, 'Microfinance as tool for socio-economic empowerment of rural women in Northern Malawi: A practical theological reflection', Doctoral dissertation, University of Stellenbosch.

Comaroff, J. & Comaroff, J., 1986, 'Christianity and colonialism in South Africa', *American Ethnologist* 13(1), 1-22.

Dang, H.H. & Dabalen, A.L., 2017, *Is poverty in Africa mostly chronic or transient? Policy Research Working Paper*, World Bank Group.

Deacon, G. & Tomalin, E., 2015, 'A history of faith-based aid and development', in E. Tomalin (eds.), *The Routledge handbook of religions and global development*, pp. 68-79, Routledge, London.

De Gruchy, J., 1979, *The church struggle in South Africa*, Eerdmans, Grand Rapids.

De Gruchy, S., 2015, 'Theological education and social development; politics, preferences and praxis in curriculum design', In B. Haddad (ed.), *Keeping body and soul together: reflections by Steve De Gruchy on Theology and Development*, 106-121, Cluster, Pietermaritzburg.

Didier, K.W.W., 2017, 'Conflict resolution for sustainable development in the Democratic Republic of Congo: a practical theological perspective', Doctoral dissertation, University of Stellenbosch.

Eale, B., 2021, 'Diaconia in Southern and Central African Christianity', in G. Ampony, M. Büscher, B. Hofmann, F. Ngnintedem, D. Solon & D. Werner (eds.), *International handbook on ecumenical diakonia*, pp. 186-190, Regnum, Oxford.

Fabiao, T., 2021, 'Exploring the relationship between the church and FBO's: A practical theological study of Igreja Reformada em Mozambique – Maphatso Synod', Master's thesis, University of Stellenbosch.

Gifford, P., 2009, *Christianity, politics and public life in Kenya*, Hurst, London.

Heuser, A., 2013, 'Trajectories into the World: Concepts of "Development" in Contemporary African Pentecostal Christianity', in K. Mtata (ed.), *Religion: help or hindrance to development? LWF Documentation 58*, pp. 51-68, Lutheran World Federation, Geneva.

Justesen, M.K. & Bjornskov, C., 2014, 'Exploiting the poor: bureaucratic corruption and poverty in Africa', *World Development* 58(2014), 106–115.

Kalengyo, E.M., 2021, 'Examples and concepts of Diaconia in East African Christianity', in G. Ampony, M. Büscher, B. Hofmann, F. Ngnintedem, D. Solon & D. Werner (eds.), *International handbook on ecumenical diakonia*, pp. 213-2019, Regnum, Oxford.

Le Roux, E., 2019, *Religion, Development and GBV: Suggestions for a Strategic Research Agenda*. Research report, Washington, DC, Joint Learning Initiative on Faith and Local Communities, viewed 15 July 2019, from https://jliflc.com/resources/pard-gee/?utm_source=JLI+Network&utm_campaign=20365d87f9-6-4-gbv-hub-justice-webinar&utm_medium=email&utm_term=0_17f3b763b6-20365d87f9-297210313

Le Roux, E. & Bowers Du Toit, N., 2016, 'Men and women in partnership: mobilizing faith communities to address gender based violence', *Diaconia* 2016, 23–37.

Manji, F. & O' Coil, C., 2002, 'The missionary position: NGO's and development in Africa', *International Affairs*, 178(3), 567-583.

Mtata, K., 2013, 'Religion and development: friends or foes?' in K. Mtata (ed.), *Religion: help or hindrance to development? LWF Documentation 58*, pp. 23–36, Lutheran World Federation, Geneva.

Myambo, V., 2017, 'Churches as community development locus: addressing the challenges of the girl child in the Eastern Highlands of Zimbabwe', Master's thesis, University of Stellenbosch.

NetACT, 2019, *Tearfund 'Collaboration in Theological education and Training in Africa' Group* [Online forum], viewed 3 May 2022, from https://landtportal.netact.org.za/?q=forum/2

Oduyoye, M.A., 1993, 'A critique of Mbiti s view on love and marriage in Africa', in J.K. Olupona, S. Sulayman & S. Nyang (eds.), *Religious plurality in Africa: Essays in honour of John S. Mbiti*, pp. 341-365, Mouton de Gruyter, Berlin.

Öhlmann, P., Grab, W. & Frost, M. (eds.)., 2020, *African Initiated Christianity and the decolonization of development: Sustainable development in Pentecostal and Independent churches*, Routledge, London.

Onwunta, E. & August, K., 2011, '(Gender) Partnership as Transforming Paradigm for Development in Church and Society', *HTS Teologiese Studies/Theological Studies*, 68(2), 1-9.

Pondani, S., 2019, '"Prophets of Doom": the phenomenon of healing and power dynamics in Neo-Pentecostal African churches', Master's thesis, University of Stellenbosch.

Webster, V., 2019, 'Towards the introduction of community development within a theological curriculum: Murry Theological College of the Reformed Church in Zimbabwe', Master's thesis, University of Stellenbosch.

World Council of Churches (WCC), 2022, *AACC supports theological education projects in Africa*, viewed 3 May 2022, from https://www.oikoumene.org/news/aacc-supports-theological-education-projects-in-africa

Yoms, E., 2015, 'Transformational Development as theological challenge: an evaluation of the ECWA People Orientated Development Programmes', Doctoral dissertation, University of Stellenbosch.

Chapter 19

Mission as Theological Education (Curriculum) in Africa

Johannes Knoetze
Jones Hamburu Mawerenga

Introduction

This chapter discusses the topic of mission as theological education (in Africa) with the aim of creating an all-embracing missional framework for curriculum development of theological education in Africa. Bosch (2011) draws our attention to the fact that most of the New Testament was written within a missionary context. He then says, '[I]n the first century, theology was not a luxury of the world conquering church but was generated by the emergency situation in which the missionizing church found itself. In this situation mission became the "mother of theology"' (2011:501). Later, when Christianity became an established religion in Europe, theology lost its missionary dimension. With the Enlightenment, this one discipline was subdivided into two areas, namely: *theology as practice* and *theology as theory*. From there it developed into the 'fourfold pattern' known as: the disciplines of the Bible (text), church history (history), systematic theology (truth), and practical theology (application). Schleiermacher established this pattern, and it was universally accepted for Protestant theological schools and seminaries, as well as theological education in general, on the different continents. While practical theology keeps the church going, the other disciplines were seen as 'pure science'. Theology as practice and theology as theory were kept together by the 'clergy paradigm'. 'The horizon of theology, in both cases, was the church or, at most, Christendom. And theology was, by and large, thoroughly un-missionary' (Bosch 2011:501).

Within Protestantism, the situation was even worse. Bosch (2011:501–502) describes how a Lutheran theological faculty in 1652 stated 'that the church has no missionary duty or calling at all'. While Voetius was the first theologian to develop a 'theology of mission', it did have a lasting effect on generations to come when mission was treated as something on the margins of the church. While the theory aspects of theology focused mainly on the reality of the divine revelation, the practical aspect of theology focused mainly on service to the institutional church.

> This was true even in the case of the new seminaries established in the Third World for the training of native clergy. Since the "daughter church" had to imitate the "mother church" in the minutest details and had to have the same structure of congregations, dioceses, clergy, and the like, it went without saying that the theology taught there would be a carbon copy of European theology. The focus was, once again, on conceptualizing and systematizing the faith along the line that had been laid down once and for all (Bosch 2011:502).

Because of the continuous engagement with the 'mission territories' of the younger churches, new attention was given to mission. A first strategy was implemented by Schleiermacher when he appended missiology to practical theology. This understanding is still followed in some institutions. According to Bosch (2011:502), Rahner defines practical theology as the self-realisation of the church in all its dimensions, of which missiology, then, is one dimension. As such, missiology

> becomes the study of self-realization of the church in missionary situations (that is the self-expanding church) and practical theology proper the study of the self-realization of the existing church (that is the church building itself up). ... practical theology has to do with the *pastorate* of the church, missiology with the *apostolate* – but in such a way that the apostolate is clearly tending toward the pastorate (italics in the original).

A second strategy is evident in the example of Gustav Warneck who advocated for missiology as a separate theological discipline in its own right 'not only as a guest but as having the right of domicile in theology' (Bosch 2011:503). Over time, some chairs of missiology were converted into chairs for world Christianity, comparative theology, ecumenical theology, intercultural studies and, more recently, development studies. All these new names for 'chairs of missiology' are of great concern to the authors of this chapter as they only represent certain focusses in missiology, while mission is a more holistic concept.

A third strategy, which was mainly followed in Britain, was to incorporate missiology in all the other disciplines and abandon it as a separate discipline. Although this sounds good, it has some serious defects since teachers of other disciplines 'usually are not sufficiently aware of the innate missionary dimension of all theology; neither do they have the knowledge to pay due attention to this dimension' (2011:504).

However, none of the three strategies really succeeded. The chapter argues that the contemporary theological and missiological discourses of the *missio Dei* have implications on the theological curricula in Africa. The *missio Dei* defines the essence, substance, and purpose of the church because it expounds God's salvific plan for humanity and the entire universe (Niemandt 2019:3). Therefore, the main research question is not what *missiology* is, but what *mission* is?

Herein lies the knowledge gap to be filled by this chapter. The existing knowledge gap can be amply represented by the following research questions: (1) How should we consider mission as theological education? (2) How do we form missional congregations in Africa that actively participate in the *missio Dei*? (3) How do we assess the barriers and opportunities for contemporary missions in Africa? (4) How do we develop missional leadership for the transformation of theological education institutions in Africa?

Mission as theological education in Africa

Saayman (2013:133) argues that mission should also be understood as theological education. Bosch (1982) states that mission as theological education in Africa demands the proper positioning of the missiological discourses in the theological curricula.

The basic problem is thus not with missiology, but how we define mission. When mission is defined exclusively in terms of soteriology or ecclesiology, then mission can only be a science for the missionary and viewed as a practical (even pragmatic) subject responding to the how question. How do we execute our task? If mission is defined in this way, then missiology as a subject remains an expendable extra. But when mission is defined as *missio Dei*, and the church is understood as 'missionary by its very nature', then we are back where mission is: 'the mother of all theology'. Wright (2006:45) argues that the trinitarian founding of mission should make it clear that God is the primary subject and source of mission, and not the church. In this understanding, the church does not have a mission, but God's mission has a church. He then defines mission:

Fundamentally, our mission (if it is biblically informed and validated) means our committed participation as God's people, at God's invitation and command, in God's own mission within the history of God's world for the redemption of God's creation (Wright 2006:23).

When mission is understood in this way, it must be the core of the theological education curriculum in Africa. Niemandt (2019:3) illustrates that a missional centre reframes all the other disciplines and that the place, role and content of the various disciplines derives from this centre. Mashau (2012:2) explains that the entire theological curriculum should be missional, reflecting God's mission and the missionary nature of the church as an instrument participating in the *missio Dei*.

In the rest of the chapter, we will reflect on mission as theological education in Africa in seven ways, namely: having a clear mission focus; missional hermeneutic; missional spirituality; contextualisation; inclusive of marginalised groups like women, youth, and children; community engagement; and dialoguing with public theology.

Theological education must form missional congregations in Africa

Theological education as mission must contribute to form congregations which realise that they are participants in God's mission. As participants in God's mission, congregations are working towards the kingdom of God, and are indeed signs of the kingdom of God; in principle, this implies ecumenical theological education. In this regard, theological education must equip congregations and leaders with the following:

A clear mission focus

Mission as theological education (in Africa) demands an articulation of a clear mission focus within the specific context of Africa. Theological education institutions and the church need to understand that it is not our ecclesiology and soteriology that determines the curriculum but our understanding and participation in the *missio Dei*. Baron (2019:1) contends that the focus of theological curricula in Africa must be clearly missional because the church's reason for being is missional.

Penner (1997:85–87) insists that theological education has a binding missionary vocation for the Christian community:

> The concept mathetes (disciple) is very important for the understanding of theological education as mission. Here the Judaic tradition and the Christian tradition overlaps ... It is prescribed in the Great Commission in Matt 28:18-20 in such a way that didasko (servant) is included in our understanding of the concept ... An outstanding example of comprehensive theological education [in this sense] we find in the student of Gamaliel, the first theologian, apostle to the pagans, and missionary, Paul ... he not only educated the congregations, but left us a practical example for future

generations of educators. His great value can be found in his formulation of a [missionary] theology for the young churches, also a theology of education and formation.

Therefore, for theological education to be transformational, mission studies need to be at the very heart of the curriculum. In other words, 'we need to bring a passion for serving God's transforming mission, and for seeing it given its rightful place at the heart of our endeavours in theological education' (McCoy 2005:7).

Mission-oriented theological education must entail two things: (1) it must be faithful and focussed on God who is a missionary God; and (2) it must be focussed on serving the church which, by definition, is a church in mission (Ott 2001:91).

A missional hermeneutic

Mission as theological education in Africa implies the employment of a missional hermeneutic. Wright (2006:39) argues that a missional hermeneutic at least includes the recognition of 'the multiplicity of perspectives and contexts from which and within which people read the biblical text'. Hendricks (2012:5) asserts that the realisation of mission as theological education in Africa can be made possible by doing theology with a missional hermeneutic lens. Using a missional hermeneutic lens in theological education will influence all theological disciplines as Wright (2006:48) proposes that the whole of Scripture is a 'missional phenomenon'. Niemandt and Niemandt (2021:3) argue that a missional hermeneutic provides the framework for the transformation of theological education in Africa, and the authors believe also a mission praxis that will transform the Africa context.

Though Peters (1984) articulates a biblical theology of missions, Bekele (2011:153) maintains that authentic hermeneutics is always missional. Thus, we need to move from a (biblical) theology of mission to a missionary (biblical) theology. Du Preez, Hendriks and Carl (2014:3) affirm that a missional hermeneutic for theological curricula should be trinitarian based. First, it should acknowledge that God the Father is the source, initiator, and telos of the *missio Dei*. Second, it should acknowledge that God the Son is the incarnation of the *missio Dei*. Third, it should acknowledge that God the Holy Spirit is the empowering presence of the *missio Dei*.

Barriers and opportunities for contemporary theological education in Africa

In a certain sense Africa is in a catch-22 situation. On the one side, it is struggling to create its own theological understanding applicable to the context of Africa. In this sense, it is dealing with issues of decolonisation and Africanisation. On the other side, Africa is part of world Christianity and a globalised world, and it is not possible to escape or distance Africa from the world. The interdependence of Africa and the world is also captured in the African Union (AU) document, Agenda 2063. From this understanding, the following are opportunities and barriers for theological education in Africa.

Contextualisation

It is worth noting that the word 'contextualisation' was first coined in the circles of the Theological Education Fund in the early 1970s, with a specific understanding of education and the formation of people for church ministry (Bosch 2011:430-431). According to Bosch (2011), there are two main types of contextualisation: the indigenisation model and the socio-economic model. These two models then also have two further subtypes. He then concludes with his own understanding of contextual theology in the following two types: as inculturation and as revolutionary. Mission as theological education in Africa generates contextualisation. Terms like 'contextualisation', 'decolonisation', or 'Africanisation' have been used by some as synonyms to capture the need for theological education to respond effectively to the needs arising in the African context (Pillay 2018; Kaunda 2016; Sakupapa 2018; Musopole 1998; Bujo 2006; Magesa 2014; Methula 2017).

Africanisation can be defined as liberation, i.e., the comprehensive liberation of all of Africa and all Africans. Unless Africans do theology in Africa to address issues that are arising in the African context, theological relevance will remain questionable (Maluleke 1998:3-4). Ramose (2004:140) argues that Africanisation holds that the African experience in its totality is simultaneously the foundation and the source for construction of all forms of knowledge (cf. Naidoo 2016; Mugambi 2013; Makgoba, 2005). As such, there is a need to construct indigenous Christian theologies for an independent Africa since Africa needs a theology that is, to use a metaphor, cooked in an African pot (Musopole 1998:7).

Knoetze (2021:3-5) discusses the implications of Africanisation or decolonisation of theological education in Africa as doing theology from 'below'. Theology develops when we are participating in the *missio Dei*. De Vries (2016:3) points out that one major implication of the Africanisation or decolonisation process is missional theologising with specific reference to Africa's socio-cultural context. This can be demonstrated from Acts 15 where a discussion about contextualisation is inextricably linked to missionary concerns.

Theologians from the North and West must be aware of their own contexts influenced by the Greek spirit containing 'ideas and principles which were considered to be prior to and more important than their application' (Bosch 2011:431).

The Christian church is always in the process of becoming; the church of the present is both the product of the past and the seed of the future. For this reason, theology must not be pursued as an attempt at reconstructing the pristine past and its truths; rather theology reflects the church's own life and experience (:432).

Contextualised theological education will, according to Bosch (2011:435-442):
- Affirm that God has turned towards the world
- Involve the construction of a variety of 'local theologies'
- Be aware of the danger of relativism, but also the danger of absolutism of contextualism
- Read the 'signs of the times'
- Not take the context as the sole and basic authority for theological reflection
- Not only interpret context as a problem of the relationship between praxis and theory
- Hold together the creative tension between theory, praxis and poiesis.

Inclusive of marginalised groups like women, youths and children

Mission as theological education in Africa stresses a deliberate inclusion of marginalised groups such as women, youths, and children. Phiri (2012:255) avers that the church in Africa marginalises women in its missional initiatives because of the lack of a theological framework that recognises and celebrates women's inherent giftedness, dignity, and equality. Makgaka (2017) demonstrates that God's mission is inclusive and not exclusive of women.

Wyngaard (2015:410) observes that African youths are marginalised from participating in the *missio Dei*. In agreement, Knoetze (2015a:4-5) argues for the creation of an African youth ministry as a paradigm of the trinitarian *missio Dei*. Consequently, making God known to the youth and empowering them to participate in the *missio Dei*.

It is impossible to omit children from the scope and coverage of the Great Commission. It is God's will for the children to be saved, to be baptized and to be disciples in God's Word to praise God and to become witnesses so that the *missio Dei* will continue from generation to generation (ed. Bunge, Fretheim & Gaventa 2008:370).

Knoetze (2015b:5-6) highlights three missional implications concerning the church's efforts in reaching and equipping children in Africa. First, making the trinitarian God known to children. Second, helping them to realise that they are part of the God story. Third, giving the children of Africa a voice in theology as participants in the *missio Dei*. Jesus' words in Matthew 18:14: 'it is not the will of your Father in heaven that one of these little ones should be lost', incudes children in the *missio Dei* (Jones 2011).

Community engagement

Theological education in Africa from a missional ecclesiology will have a strong focus on both a mission praxis (evangelism) and a diaconal praxis (practical service). Diaconal studies within the theological education curricula in Africa demands community engagement. Magezi (2017:1) confirms that churches and other faith-based organisations (FBOs) play a critical role in community development as a way of fulfilling the *missio Dei*. Amanze (2009:130) observes that

> [I]n view of the bad performance of African countries to realise a sustainable socio-economic growth and development it has become incumbent upon the churches to advocate and insist that development is authentic where it uplifts and equips communities with skills to deal with their own situation.

Klaasen (2019:2) demonstrates the shift in the development discourse from giver-receiver to a more inclusive participatory community development paradigm. Amanze (2009:130) claims that the successful implementation of community engagement initiatives requires that mission as theological education in Africa should be development oriented.

Church planting

Mission praxis of a missional church involves planting other missional churches across Africa. McGavran (1999) suggests that the goal of Christian mission should be to preach the gospel and to plant a church, or a cluster of churches, in every unchurched segment of mankind. Murray (1998:57) asserts that,

> [T]he practice of church planting indicates that reproduction is as fundamental a feature of the church as it is of biological organisms. A healthy church does not just develop internally and expand in size and social impact, but naturally expresses its life in new forms and structures.

Mutavhatsindi (2009:v) demonstrates how the missional church can participate in church-planting mission in Africa. He states that:

> Christ called the church to be His witness (martyria) to the world (Ac 1:8) by proclaiming the Word of God (kerygma) to the people, by serving people (diakonia), and by entering into fellowship of love with people (koinonia). The main goal of witnessing Christ in Africa should be the *glorificatio Dei*, "to glorify God", this is the liturgical dimension.

Alawode (2020:2-3) mentions four church planting strategies used by the Apostle Paul that can inform contemporary church planting missions in Africa. First, Paul focused on preaching to responsive people. Second, Paul and his team established churches in strategic cities and towns of the Roman Empire. Third, Paul employed the strategy of house churches, which was useful in reaching out to families. Fourth, Paul contextualised the message of the gospel to various audiences.

Develop missional leadership for transformation at theological education institutions in Africa

Theological institutions in Africa need missional leaders to train leaders and congregations for the transformation of the church in Africa. Different studies have shown a direct link between spirituality and leadership. Therefore, leaders and teachers at theological institutions must operate from a missional spirituality, equipping students with the abilities of public dialogue, evangelism, and making disciples.

Missional spirituality

Mission as theological education in Africa entails the formation of a missional spirituality. Niemandt and Niemandt (2021:1-2) state that theological education should cultivate a missional spirituality aimed at forming missional leaders for the church. Niemandt (2019:4-6) avers that missional spirituality influences Christian leaders to engage in the church's missionary praxis. Therefore, missional spirituality has two implications. First, it is foundational to the process of equipping the church to participate in the *missio Dei*. Second, it equips the church to make missional disciples who actively participate in the *missio Dei*.

Niemandt (2012:87) reiterates the call to the church to cultivate missional spirituality with a threefold consequence. First, the church will become missional in orientation. Second, the church will rediscover the missiological thrust that lies at the heart of the Christian faith. Third, it will allow Christianity to remain vibrant and faithful in the contemporary era. Nonetheless, he points out the missing gap in bringing the discourse of missional spirituality, orientation, and leadership into the realm of theological education in Africa. In this regard, Murithi (2014:6) argues for the interdependence of theological education and missional spirituality. Missional spirituality is part and parcel of the missional formation of students, teachers, ministers, the laity, and their communities.

Dialoguing with African public theology

Mission as theological education in Africa involves dialoguing with African public theology by being competent in providing political direction (Forster 2020:21; Smit 2013:11).

Mission as theological education in Africa should be able to capture the desire of Africans to move 'towards the Africa that God wants' (Hendricks 2012:391). Agang (2020:3) correlates the missional role of African public theology with 'the African Union's Agenda 2063 which advocates for the implementation of public policies in combatting Africa's darkest demons: bad governance, corruption, socio-economic injustice, religious competition, tribal and ethnic conflicts and political domination'. Therefore, this underscores the need for a public theology in Africa as a way of fulfilling the *missio Dei*.

Evangelism

The missional church participates in the *missio Dei* through evangelism. Stott (2012) intimates that the Lausanne Covenant defined evangelism in terms of the evangel. Paragraph four states that:

> [T]o evangelize is to spread the good news that Jesus Christ died for our sins and was raised from the dead according to the Scriptures, and that as the reigning Lord he now offers the forgiveness of sins and the liberating gift of the Spirit to all who repent and believe (cited by Stott 2012:39).

Stott (2009:3) articulates a fourfold biblical basis for world evangelisation: mandate for world evangelisation (Gen 12:1–4; Matt 24:14, 28:18-20; Acts 1:8); message for world evangelisation (1 Cor 15:11; 1 Tim 6:20; 2 Tim 1:12-14; 2 Cor 4:1–2); model for world evangelisation (Jn 1:14; 2 Pet 1:21; Heb 1:1); and the power for world evangelisation (Rom 1:16; 1 Cor 2:1–5; 2 Cor 12:9–10).

Niemandt (2016:3) underscores the significance of evangelism for the missional church. He states that:

> Evangelism is a vital part of God's mission and the church's calling. The call to share this message and tell the story of God's mission - in brief, the call to evangelise – is part and parcel of this mission. It belongs to the very being of the church.

Discipleship

Niemandt (2016:3) insinuates that the missional 'church is called to invite the whole of humanity in the whole world to a costly and radical discipleship in mission'. Therefore, discipleship accords the missional church's participation in the triune God's life-giving mission (ed. Keum 2013).

Van Aarde (2017:3) hints that the discipleship initiatives of the missional church entail the equipping of the saints to function in the missional church. He mentions five different equipping functions of the missional church, namely: the apostolic equipping, the prophetic equipping, the evangelistic equipping, the pastoral equipping, and the equipping for teaching (Eph 4:11-12).

Gibson (2016:157) infers that discipleship stimulates and sustains transformation in society by influencing the believers to be good citizens/disciples as they engage in the socio-political and economic life of the society. Hence, the notion of missional discipleship serves as a stimulus for inclusive transformation in African societies.

Conclusion

Some denominations in Africa perceive theological education as not always being applicable to Africa and the context of Africa. In this chapter the authors postulate that theology and the church are constantly developing and transforming as they engage with different contexts outside of the church both locally and globally. It is only in these engagements, when the church participates in the *missio Dei,* that it can be relevant to Africa in glorifying God. It is for this reason that the authors confirm mission as the mother of all theology and theological education.

References

Africa Union Commission, 2017, 'Agenda2063-The Africa We Want.'

Agang, S.B., Forster, D.A. & Hendriks, H.J. (eds.), 2020, 'The Need for Public Theology in Africa', *African public theology*, Langham Publishing, Cumbria.

Alawode, A.O., 2020, 'Paul's biblical patterns of church planting: An effective method to achieve the Great Commission', *HTS Teologiese Studies/Theological Studies* 76(1), 1-5.

Amanze, J.N., 2009, 'Paradigm shift in theological education in southern and central Africa and its relevance to ministerial formation', *International Review of Mission* 98(1), 120-131.

Baron, E., 2019, 'The call for African missional consciousness through renewed mission praxis in URCSA', *Studia Historiae Ecclesiasticae* 45(3), 1-19.

Bekele, G., 2011, 'The biblical narrative of the missio Dei: analysis of the interpretive framework of David Bosch's missional hermeneutic', *International Bulletin of Missionary Research* 35(3), 153-158.

Bosch, D.J., 1982, 'Theological education in missionary perspective', *Missiology* 10(1), 13-34.

Bosch, D.J., 2011, *Transforming mission: Paradigm shifts in theology of mission*, American Society of Missiology Series, No. 16, Orbis Books, Maryknoll, NY.

Bujo, B., 2006, *African theology in its social context*, Wipf and Stock Publishers, Eugene, Oregon.

Bunge, M.J., Fretheim, T.E. & Gaventa, B.R. (eds.), 2008, *The child in the Bible*, Wm. B. Eerdmans Publishing, Grand Rapids.

De Vries, B.A., 2016, 'Towards a global theology: Theological method and contextualisation', *Verbum et Ecclesia* 37(1), 1-12.

Du Preez, K.P., Hendriks, H.J. & Carl, A.E., 2014, 'Missional theological curricula and institutions', *Verbum et Ecclesia* 35(1), 1-8.

Forster, D.A., 2020, *The Nature of Public Theology*, in S.B. Agang, D.A. Forster & H.J. Hendriks (eds.), *African public theology*, pp. 15-25, Langham Publishing, Cumbria.

Gibson, E.L., 2016, 'Missional discipleship: A transforming paradigm for the churches in Africa', *International Review of Mission* 105(2), 157-168.

Hendriks, J.H., 2012, 'Contextualising theological education in Africa by doing theology in a missional hermeneutic', *Koers* 77(2), 1-8.

Jones, D.J.C., 2011, 'An evaluation of the Accelerate Christian Schools for reaching children for the Kingdom of God as part of Missio Dei in South Africa', Doctoral dissertation, North-West University.

Kaunda, C.J., 2016, 'Towards an African ecogender theology: A decolonial theological perspective', *Stellenbosch Theological Journal* 2(1), 177-202.

Keum, J. (ed.), 2013, *Together towards life. Mission and evangelism in changing landscapes*, World Council of Churches Publications, Geneva.

Klaasen, J.S., 2019, 'Theology and development: Taking personal responsibility for community development', *HTS Teologiese Studies/Theological Studies* 75(2), 1-7.

Knoetze, J., 2015a, 'Perspectives on family and youth ministry embedded in the missio Dei – An African perspective', *In die Skriflig/In Luce Verbi* 49(1), Art. #1874. https://doi.org/10.4012/ids.v49i1.1874

Knoetze, J.J., 2015b, 'Spiritual transformation: Reaching and equipping sub-Saharan African children', *In die Skriflig/In Luce Verbi* 49(1), Art. #1919. https://hdl.handle.net/10520/EJC173057.

Knoetze, J., 2021, 'Decolonising or Africanization of the theological curriculum: a critical reflection', *Scriptura* 120(1), 1–15.

Magesa, L., 2014, *Anatomy of inculturation: Transforming the church in Africa*, Orbis Books, Ossining, NY.

Magezi, V., 2017, 'Making community development at grassroots reality: Church-driven development approach in Zimbabwe's context of severe poverty', *In die Skriflig/In Luce Verbi* 51(1), 1–12.

Makgaka, B.T., 2017, 'Women in the missio Dei: problems, achievements and challenges in post-colonial Africa', Doctoral dissertation, North-West University.

Makgoba, M.W., 2005, The African University: Meaning, penalties & responsibilities towards African scholarship. *Public Affairs and Corporate Communication. University of KwaZulu-Natal, South Africa.*

Maluleke, T.S., 1998, 'The Africanization of theological education: Does theological education equip you to help your sister?' *Journal of Constructive Theology* 4(2), 3–20.

Mashau, T.D., 2012, 'A reformed perspective on taking mission and missiology to the heart of theological training', *In die Skriflig/In Luce Verbi* 46(2), 1–8.

McCoy, M., 2005, *Restoring mission to the heart of theological education A South African perspective.* Anglican Standing Commission on Mission and Evangelism (South Africa).

McGavran, D.A., 1999, *The bridges of God. A study in the strategy of missions*, Friendship, New York.

Methula, D.W., 2017, 'Decolonising the commercialisation and commodification of the university and theological education in South Africa', *HTS Theological Studies* 73(3), 1-7.

Mugambi, J.N., 2013, 'The future of theological education in Africa and the challenges it faces', in I.A. Phiri & D, Werner (eds.), *Handbook of theological education in Africa*, pp. 117-125, Regnum Books, Oxford.

Murithi, S., 2014, 'Contextual theological education in Africa as a model for missional formation', *The Asbury Journal*, 69(2), 6.

Murray, S., 1998, *Church planting, laying foundations*, Pinnacle Publishers, New York, NY.

Musopole, A.C., 1998, 'Needed: A theology cooked in an African Pot', in K. Fiedler, P. Gundani & H. Mijoga (eds.), *Theology cooked in an African Pot*, pp. 7–47, Kachere, Zomba.

Mutavhatsindi, M.A., 2009, 'Church planting in the South African urban context– with special reference to the role of the Reformed Church Tshiawelo', Doctoral dissertation, University of Pretoria.

Naidoo, M., 2016, 'Overcoming alienation in Africanising theological education', *HTS Teologiese Studies/Theological Studies* 72(1), 1–8.

Niemandt, C.J.P., 2016, 'Rediscovering joy in costly and radical discipleship in mission', *HTS Teologiese Studies/Theological Studies* 72(4), 1–7.

Niemandt, C.J.P.N., 2012, 'Missional leadership – Entering the trialogue' [Inaugural address], University of Pretoria.

Niemandt, D. & Niemandt, N.C., 2021, 'Missional metanoia: Missional spirituality in holistic theological education', *HTS Teologiese Studies/Theological Studies* 77(4), 1–10.

Niemandt, N., 2019, 'A missional hermeneutic for the transformation of theological education in Africa', *HTS Teologiese Studies/Theological Studies* 75(4), 1–10.

Ott, B., 2001, 'Mission and theological education', *Transformation* 18(2), 87–98.

Penner, P., 1997, 'Theologische Ausbildung-eine Verpflichtende Mission: Faktoren zur Bestimmung von Leitlinien für theologische Ausbildung in der GUS', Doctoral dissertation, UNISA.

Peters, G.W., 1984, *A biblical theology of missions*, Moody Publishers, Chicago.

Phiri, I.A., 2012, 'The church and women in Africa', in E.K. Bongmba (ed.), *The Wiley-Blackwell Companion to African Religions*, pp. 255-268, Blackwell Publishing, UK.

Pillay, J., 2018, 'Theological education and missional formation in the South African context', *Transformation* 35(3), 179–191.

Ramose, M.B., 2004, 'In search of an African philosophy of education: perspectives on higher education', *South African Journal of Higher Education* 18(3), 138–160.

Saayman, W., 2013, 'Mission as theological education: Is Christian mission history coming full circle?', *Missionalia* 41(2), 133–145.

Sakupapa, T.C., 2018, 'The decolonising content of African theology and the decolonisation of African theology reflections on a decolonial future for African theology', *Missionalia* 46(3), 406–424.

Smit, D.J., 2013, 'The paradigm of public theology? Origins and development', in H. Bedford-Strohm, F. Höhne & T. Reitmeier (eds.), *Contextuality and intercontextuality in public theology,* pp. 11-24, Lit Verlag, Münster.

Stott, J., 2012, *The Lausanne Covenant: Complete text with study guide*, Hendrickson Publishers, Peabody, Massachusetts.

Stott, J.R., 2009, 'The Bible in World Evangelization', in R.W. Winter & S.C. Hawthorne (eds.), *Perspectives on the world Christian movement: a reader*, pp. 3-9, William Carrey Library, Pasadena, CA.

Van Aarde, T.A., 2017, 'The missional church structure and the priesthood of all believers (Ephesians 4: 7-16) in the light of the inward and outward function of the church', *Verbum et Ecclesia* 38(1), 1-9.

Wright, C.J., 2006, *The mission of God: Unlocking the Bible's grand narrative*, IVP Academic, Downers Grove, Illinois.

Wyngaard, J., 2015, 'Missio Dei and youth ministry-mobilizing young people's assets and developing relationships', *Missionalia* 43(3), 410-424.

Chapter 20

Normal(ised) Christianity/Religiosity in the Public Arena – A Mission of the Mind

Christo Lombaard

The pathway below: A mission of the mind

Below, the argument unfolds as follows:

- Change is always present:
  - At present (for the past centuries and decades, ever increasingly so), change has been so rapid, that humanity seemed to lose its heritage, including the foundationally orienting Christian faith in Western/ised contexts;
  - This meant that Christianity fell victim to the presuppositions of what is popularly termed secularism;
  - However, faith did not become extinct, as was broadly supposed, but it changed – for the greatest part, doing so unnoticed;
  - At present the realisation is dawning that faith has been as present in and amongst us as always.
- Appreciating this reality now requires a *mission of the mind*: that we see anew who we really are and have always been (i.e. believers), and not who we think people think we think we are[1].

Panta rei

Πάντα ῥεῖ – *Pánta rheī* ('Everything changes') – with this 6th to 5th century BCE formulation, the early Greek philosopher Heraclitus (cf. Hussey 1999:88–112) captured an insight which has always been sound. An implication from this Heraclitus

---

[1] The latter formulation is a play on identity formation as foundationally argued by Richard Cooley (1902).

wisdom, is that the dynamism of our contexts and of humanity itself is such, that non-change is almost synonymous with non-existence. This has continuously been both our social and our physical reality. The modern period of human civilisation has however superlatively been subject to dramatic increases in the pace of change. This to such an extent that 'social acceleration' has been identified by Hartmut Rosa (2013; cf. Lombaard 2018:1–7) as the central distinguishing aspect of our times, sociologically speaking. That is to say, in the current era, the rate of change outpaces by far that in any other era, both in the degree of modification, even revolution, and in the speed of adjustment that we as humans live through. The *now* and the *new* are ever greater intensifiers of our existence. This is certainly valid for the African context too – and always has been, as acknowledged by sayings already in Greek and Latin antiquity that Africa both brings and absorbs what is new (cf. Ronca 2014:146–158).

One of the corollaries of what has therefore become a reflexive human focus in such societies on the now and on the im/pending future, is that the *past* is not given due attention. In our modern view of time as a flow that unfolds along the line of Past – Present – Future, as new possibilities now unfurl abundantly and quickly and all too temporarily (impermanently), it is easy to forget the past. Alternatively, the past is viewed as no longer being of any consequence. The stabilising, identity-giving and therefore enlightening presence of history is not acknowledged. In the same way as when philosophy or religion or culture are perhaps not explicitly recognised in broader society, these influences certainly remain present, palpably and discernibly; yet, they are not given attention, thus leading to a superficial life, and even to a false sense of ourselves.

In such a situation, tradition is often neglected, along with anything that is rooted also in the past (cf. Scruton 2012). The argument here is not (as could easily be misunderstood) that active awareness of the past should act as a conservative impulse, in the sense that it diverts attention from the now and the new and, in doing so, tries to hold back advances. Rather, the opposite is the case, in two ways:

- The past often has a transforming effect on the present (with the Renaissance being a classic example), because the imagined past that is habitually drawn on by those in power in order to provide legitimacy for current practices, is characteristically contrived and sectarian. Drawing more completely on the past undercuts falsely-conceived power structures (– ironically, in much the same way as new technologies can do);
- A focus on the now and the new that excludes the past, narrows the reality of our existence in a manner that cuts us off from a great deal of who we really are. The same kinds of criticisms that are valid, if we were to ignore the *present* (the criticism would be: contextual irrelevance; a common metaphor for this: arguing how many angels could stand on a pin-point), or if we were to shirk from

the immediately-unfolding *future* (the criticism would be: naivety; a common metaphor for this: an ostrich burying its head in the sand), apply to when we are ignorant of the past. Why would we close off the years, decades, centuries and millennia that have, in many and varied ways, made us who we are? In the flow that unfolds as Past – Present – Future, all three are important.

Religion has, amongst many other values, also these two roles: that it transforms the present in the light of both the past and the future. In theological terms: revelation (the past) and eschatology (the future) surround the now, making the present a fuller, more mature reality than it would be without Scripture, nature and culture (the past) or goals, ideals and hopes (the future). Faith thus brings together all three of these dimensions of Past – Present – Future; not uniquely so, but certainly foundationally so, for most people in the world[2]; not as a special event, but in their everyday lives.

Again not uniquely so, but certainly more pronounced than any other dimension of the human experience (which includes thoughts and awarenesses, actions, emotions, language, technology, art, sustenance and care; cf. Van Huyssteen 2006), faith integrates horizontal and vertical dimensions of life. The earthly and the heavenly; more philosophically formulated: the physical and the metaphysical; more theologically formulated: creation and Creator are in lives of faith not regarded as disconnected. Rather, a fuller reality unfolds in religion – a lifeworld that is not contracted to only limited dimensions. (Such dimensions could include rationality, or the empirically observable, or the ideologically palatable). It remains constantly possible to reduce humanity in some ways: politics or war may for instance at times regard us as mere fodder; economics and entertainment may perhaps see humans as simply consumers, and so forth. In matters of faith, however, the full horizontal and vertical breadth of our existence may never be reduced (cf. e.g. Tillich 1955).

Seen from yet another angle: as humans we are both victims and perpetrators; creators and consumers; sinners and saints, and so forth. It remains an error hence to think that religion, anchored as it also is to the past, cannot bring something truly new; that it cannot act as a cultural accelerant. At best, the importance of history and the practice of faith lie therein that they can r*enew* – in that line of thinking. In themselves, however, tradition and religion are then, erroneously, not thought of as being the agents of primary change. Rather, history and faith are considered to require one-sidedly *return*, which implies recouping something old; not a turn *to* but a turn (away) *from*… new technology/different sexualities/alternate politics/avant-garde aesthetics/experimental economics/revolutionary research, etc.

---

[2] It is well worth keeping an eye on the demographic trends related to matters of faith, internationally, published on www.pewresearch.org/topic/religion/.

Given this dominant conception, outside of religious circles but not infrequently amongst pious believers too, it is not surprising, therefore, that in the modern period religion is all too easily publicly discounted. When 'everything changes' as it has in our past (with such stimuli as the early Renaissance and the invention of the printing press in the 15th century; the Industrial Revolution from ± 1760 and the subsequent iterations thereof; Capitalism, with a key publication, Adam Smith's 1776 *The wealth of nations*; the French Revolution from 1789 onwards), religion is seen to fall by the wayside. Matters of faith – God, church, Bible – no longer seems to hold everything together, no longer giving cohesive, coherent meaning to all that is. This religious Bigger Picture is in the public mind replaced by ever more Smaller Pictures, each of which initially has hardly any tradition – in the sense that faith traditions each have a past and a conducting social circle that render stability, hence conveying a sense of social and individual security and of belonging (cf. Goosen 2007; 2015). All these new things – industrial technology, the market economy, democratic freedoms – by their very natures initially have no active past. Their meanings lay elsewhere. That is to say, their significances are found in the dynamisms, which are the instabilities and strangenesses that innately go along with novel ways of working, buying, living, and more.

God, church, Bible, faith, and related matters, were therefore in modern times either eliminated from public life or marginalised within societies. This happened as quite a natural, almost logical consequence of these many rising Smaller Pictures. These demanding complexities seemed to suppress the comfortable simplicities of a Bigger Picture. It became ever more the small things that count, which then occupy increasing portions of time and mind and energies.

This *physical* busy-ness diminishes, for many, *metaphysical* wakefulness. A primary orientation towards the context (i.e. a more strongly horizontal disposition) inhibits a primary orientation towards the Divine (i.e. a more strongly vertical disposition). This framework of understanding in time would enable and enhance the public success of declarations such as that 'Die Religion ... ist das Opium des Volkes' ('Religion ... is the opium of the people' by Karl Marx in 1844: meant to critique the non-socially-critical Christianity of the time[3]), or that '*Gott ist todt*' ('God is dead', by Friedrich Nietzsche in e.g. 1887:125, meant as a criticism of superficial Christianity of the time[4]), and of turning around by 180° the meaning

---

[3] The quote (from Marx 1844:71–72) gives a description of how religion is related to by those suffering; '...of the people'. It was however quite soon mistranslated as 'for the people', thus instrumentalising religion more sharply, rather than describing a social situation.

[4] The fuller quote (from Nietzsche 1887:125) is, 'Gott ist todt! Gott bleibt todt! Und wir haben ihn getödtet!' ('God is dead! God stays dead! And we have killed him!')

of the term *secular* (by George Holyoake in 1896): from approximately *living as a religious person in society* (rather than in e.g. a monastery) to something like its opposite, *living within a religionless society*.

The thrust was already then, when pronounced, or else soon afterwards, and certainly by our time, that public society and individual meaning-making would be emptied of God. This would – in that line of thinking – be a logical unfolding of the maturing of humanity. In Western/ised, modern democracies, life would then be characterised most conspicuously in this respect not by freedom *of* religion (though that certain still, in principle), but by freedom *from* religion.

All of these voices, stated by influential figures or (as it were) whispered in the corridors of our board culture, on Christianity, have been influential: we picked up on them and internalised their gist. For all the great value that critical theologies (theologies of liberation, of feminism, of the ecology, and so forth) have brought to us, they also drew on the conceptual systems and central insights of these significant voices – at times doing so explicitly, at times doing so without being aware of this heritage. When accepting the valuable insights and subsequent conversions to greater practical love ethics brought about by these theologies, and also when rejecting them[5], to a great extent Christianity was drawn into the underlying conceptual spheres. For the greater part, hence, the communities of the faithful (the churches, their leaderships, and individual Christians) fell victim in an unpleasantly surprising way, unacknowledged, to the underlying problems identified by these critical diagnoses. A particularly good example of this, is the concept of secularism.

πάντα πλήρη θεῶν εἶναι

Πάντα πλήρη θεῶν εἶναι – Panta plērē theôn inae ('Everything is full of gods') – with this 7th – 6th century BCE formulation, the very early Greek philosopher Thales (quoted in Aristotle's *De Anima* 411a7–8; cf. Hett 1957:60–61) captured an insight which has over the past centuries only, and then in select circles only, been thought of as unsound. This, *viz.*, is the period known as modernism, with as its corollary on the religious side, what has been termed – albeit inaccurately – 'secularism'. It is during this cultural phase that the world was thought of as 'secular', which was taken as meaning, free from religion – an understanding which, as already hinted to above, was mistaken. This error in thought, which consequently requires a conversion of mind, will now (in some respects, at least, and all too briefly) be traced.

---

5   When rejecting such more inclusive extensions of practical love ethics, rather than viewing these critical theological voices as therapeutically beneficial, if uncomfortable, diagnoses of the state of religious affairs, Christians reject such analyses, or react against them, or ignore them. As with any diagnosis, though, not accepting the doctor's advice does not make the illness disappear.

In a series of publications, members of the 'small circle' interdisciplinary group of scholars have traced these developments. Iain T. Benson, Kristof K.P. Vanhoutte and Christo Lombaard, in conversation with researchers who follow similar and opposite trains of thought, have developed their insights in, among others, these three publications (each of which are easily accessible publications, in South Africa, which may be read as a next step to expand one's understanding of the matters touched on below):

- Vanhoutte, K.K.P., 2020, 'The revenge of the words: On language's historical and autonomous being and its effects on "secularisation"', *HTS Teologiese Studies/ Theological Studies* (Special Issue: Christianity as a Change Agent in the 4th Industrial Revolution World) 76(2), 1–9;
- Lombaard, C., 2018, '*Spiritualityd...* Spirituality in our time – In conversation with Hartmut Rosa's theory on social acceleration', *HTS Teologiese Studies/ Theological Studies* 74(3), 1–7;
- Benson, I.T., 2013, 'Seeing through the secular illusion', *Nederduitse Gereformeerde Teologiese Tydskrif* 54(4), 12–29.

Summarising here the arguments in and implications from these publications, it becomes clear that the way the term 'secular' is commonly used in our time, reflects the expectation amongst its users – outside *and* inside church circles – that religion has for long been on the wane, and remains so. This by now reflexive expectation is simply incorrect, on most counts, and ought not to be entertained.

Countering this use of the term 'secular' and its false reference are equally simple:

1. The term 'secular' was in the earlier church never used to refer to a world that was somehow without faith; rather, the term then referred to faith practiced outside of the closest precincts of the church as institution. A 'secular priest' was hence a priest who worked outside of the monastery; still, avowedly, as a priest. The priest had not become irreligious; nor had the sense been that the world outside of the precincts of the religious orders of the church, was free from faith. 'Secular' meant simply practicing one's faith in the world, in the manner that might be formulated in our time as 'contextually' – as would a minister/pastor/priest serve in a parish, in our time. Faithlessness is not implied. The same holds true for every believer who, like by far the most believers, hold no ordained position. Faith is lived, quite simply, 'secularly' – which means, *within* day-to-day life (rather than in a convent or monastery); it does not mean that the faith has been lost. Quite the contrary, it means that faith is active precisely *in* the world, and as a fully normal practice.

    (The idea that 'secular spirituality' – a formulation which some books have also included in their titles – refers to people who have more or less lost their belief in God and/or sense of the divine, and/or do not live religiously-coloured lives, yet gently seek fuller meaning in life beyond the merely mundane, is therefore an unsatisfactory use of the terminology. To describe this important and growing group of seekers, or their journeys/quests/experiences, a better formulation ought to be sought, since 'secular spirituality' means, unfancifully, experiencing one's already established religious convictions not only in church, but in many other aspects of life besides, 'Secular spirituality' means, properly, 'normal, active, daily faith'.)

2. The idea that a faith-free public or political world is, a.) possible, and is b.) a worthy, and c.) a neutral ideal, came from developments not *in* the first (and still most influential) two declarations of modern democratic statehood, those of the United States of America (USA) (1789) and of France (1791). These were ideas that developed in time *from* them, through reinterpretation, and are now often misunderstood as being expressions of those founding declarations themselves. (This, parallel to the way some central Christian ideas – the Trinity being a good example – are thought by many to be found in the Bible, but are, more accurately, later theological refinements.) Rather, these declarations of modern statehood, in order to prevent violence between Roman Catholics and Protestants and among the latter groupings, intended to reorder societies in such a way that the state may give no preference to any of these. The idea was not to exclude religion from public society. The intention was, rather, that the state should not understand itself as Roman Catholic or as any of the Protestant options of the time, and then go on to prosecute its citizens who are of an alternate persuasion. It was therefore not religion (specifically Christianity, in both those contexts) that was renounced in these important political manifests; it was prejudicial government choices (with violent consequences) on matters religious that were being averted.

Although subsequent modern democracies have, in the wake of a series of further interpretations of these two models of governance from the late 1700s, come to understand themselves as secular, meaning religion-free (i.e. formally atheist), three problems present themselves in this regard. These problems are, that a religion-free/atheist political organisation of society presented as a.) possible, b.) worthy, and c.) neutral ideals, could never and has never been logically, ethically or demographically valid. Though recited as such by its adherents, as a kind of mantra on democracy, these three possibilities falter (following here the same matters twice numbered a., b. and c. above):

   a. The idea that a formally atheist public life (politics, the economy, education etc.) is religion-free because it is atheist, is logically false. To enforce through social and legal (supported by state policing) means public atheism, is simply to enforce a clearly *religious* idea – that of atheism. Atheism is, indeed, as much a religious orientation as any other: it takes a position on God (the vertical or metaphysical orientation), and enforces the consequences of that taken position on society (the horizontal or physical dimensions), doing so by requiring certain acts and attitudes and by disallowing others. To promote public/societal atheism, is therefore not to promote *no* religious orientation; it is to promote the religious orientation that God does not exist, or alternatively, that if God does exist, faith in this God should not feature in the public arenas of society. Political atheism is, reasonably speaking, hence no more and no less an active religious orientation to arranging the public sphere, than a political stance from any other religious orientation have always been (for instance, political Calvinism or political Islam).

On the open marketplace of religious possibilities available to humanity, political atheism can of course be judged to be as valid a religious orientation as any other would be (e.g. Christianity, Judaism, Islam, Buddhism, African Traditional Religions, etc.), where these options are weighed rationally and politically. Political atheism is indeed one option among many. However, political atheism is *no less a religious approach* as is any of these others. All of these constitute, actively, a position of faith on faith, from which consequences for public life are then deduced. Atheism is not a non-faith; promoting public atheism is not a non-orientation to religion. These are, indeed, active religious stances. The idea that political atheism is *non-religious politics*, therefore cannot be accepted. That political atheism may be acceptable within a society as a religious orientation, remains a valid and fair possibility. However, the pretence that political atheism is in truth non-religious, should not be accepted; greater honesty is required.

b. The reason why a public a-religiousness or atheism (*had* it been possible; which we have just seen in a., immediately above, is not the case) is promoted as benefitting the social good, is ethical in nature. The argument is twofold: that i.) religious adherence is held inherently to cause violence, which sense then commonly leads to the conclusion, or just the unstated implication, that ii.) official public atheism would not be violent.

However, both parts of such an understanding are misleading:

   i. Even though religions usually are involved in acts of conflict and war, religions are seldom the cause of such conflict, but are drawn into the fray by powerful figures involved, who thus exploit religious sentiments for other purposes. What is more, religion more often than not provides the impetus for peace-making –

either preventatively or during a conflict. A simplistic 'religions cause violence' equation falters on these dynamics.

ii. Additionally, the most murderous socio-political system the world has ever known, namely 20th century Soviet (and Soviet-style) Communism-Socialism, had been formally atheist. Religion was not required; in fact, non-religion was actively obligated, by the ideology and system that caused the death of some 20 million Soviet subjects and of another at least 60 million people across the world.

Relating religious adherence in any one-sided manner to violence, as is often done in arguing for democracies to be formally atheist, is contrived, ignoring stark realities to the contrary.

c. Related to a.) and b.) directly above, the position favouring a formally atheist public life almost always assumes to itself that this position is neutral. Whereas an explicitly religiously committed government (an Islamic state is the usual current example; the 'Christian national' self-identification within the 1948-1994 South African government is a local instance) takes on a well-defined confessional role, a 'secular' government that divorces or separates state and church (which is the usual metaphor), promotes no confessional stance – so this position holds. Government is therefore thought of as impartial, and also has the task of promoting a religiously unbiased society in its important constituent spheres.

By extension, if the thinking is pursued in this direction, any official support to any religiously affiliated (or inclined) expression or institution, would render the government illegitimate, as a result of an implicating faith commitment. If this thinking is pursued in another direction, the so-called sword power of the state – its policing and armed services – ought to be deployed in cases the affirmed public a-religiosity is contravened; doing so for the sake of the political legitimacy of the government and hence for the upkeep of the stability of society.

Sketched in this manner, it becomes clear that in all such cases, the instruments of state are steered in order to promote an active stance of public atheism. Rather than religious tolerance or diversity, one position of faith on faith, which is that of atheism, is strongly promoted. Drawing on the paragraphs above, it is clear that such an orientation of the state is not related to a vacuum on religion that is thus politically maintained; no such vacuum (or void) exists. Rather, such state actions constitute an activated promotion and defence of the public atheism stance – with an explicitly religious orientation; one which demands loyalty and bears no alternatives.

(However, pointing this out could in certain contexts unleash responses, the vehemence of which is matched by other religious fundamentalists' reactions. Tolerance, along with freedom of and diversity of religious expression, are adhered to only as long as one subscribes to, and remains subordinate to, the mandated views on public atheism, in some democracies. The point being made here, is however not one of revolution; the argument here is from Christian pacifist grounds, in the search for expanded honesty on the manner in which public life is arranged: that such unpalatable parallels, sensitivities and blind spots ought to be shown. This, for the virtuous sake of greater intellectual clarity and for the social sake of living together most justly with diversities, as they occur in various societies.)

3. Lastly, here, an argument that may be understood as related either to demography or to fate (alternatively formulated as 'chance' or, with reserved piety, as 'providence'). This is the understanding, meant as a criticism against commitment to any given faith, that one's religion is largely determined by the place of one's birth. Therefore – the point is then developed – atheism is a preferred state of being; which is to say, atheism seems more logical, more socially tolerant and offers a more broadminded alternative to any specified religion.

This is a common contention in debates on faith commitment versus atheism (with the latter then understood as *not* a faith commitment, which position has above been discredited). The claim – which is valid, as a statement on demography and on fate/chance/providence – is that one's religious adherence is, to a great extent, related to the geography in which one happens first to see life. For instance, if one is born in Thailand, one will almost certainly be Buddhist; if one is born in Turkey, Muslim; if in Portugal, Roman Catholic; in each case, with relatively rare occurrences of conversion from one faith to another. So far, that assessment is sound.

The conclusion drawn from this given, though, is without merit; on two counts. The conclusion is usually that, because religion is so determined by chance of birth, atheism is a more logical choice, by reason of it being more universally applicable. The errors of reasoning here are easy to see:

a. Like all religious orientations, atheism too is by no means free from such *geographic influence* (or more strongly stated: geographic determinism). The nearer one is born to Western Europe, the more so if born to (aspiring) middle-class families, the greater the chance that one would be atheist. Precisely equal to the examples above from Thailand, Turkey and Portugal, if one is born in the Netherlands or Germany (or as more extreme examples, though outside of the Western part of Europe: in the

Czech Republic or in Estonia), the likelihood is exponentially increased that one would be atheist, than it would be if one were born in Poland, Nigeria, Japan or Argentina.

The 'faith by region' argument does not render atheism a special case or an elite position from which to evaluate others' commitments; atheism is as subject to it as is any other faith.

b. Atheism seems reflexively to claim for itself a *sense of universal applicability* in this regard. This is shown both in the initial argument, meant to detract from the validity or authenticity of religion by indicating its geographic grounding, and by the secondary argument. The latter is the retort to the point made in the immediately preceding paragraph (a., directly above). This retort holds that one however finds atheists more or less everywhere, as people convert from other religions to atheism. Therefore, atheism is more universal – in this line of (often unstated) thinking.

Here too, this sense of a unique universalism on the part of atheism is unreasonable to maintain, in two ways. First, one finds most religions, equally to atheism, more or less everywhere; present in those localities not only through birth, but in much the same way, also through conversion. Atheism is consequently in no manner unique in this respect. Second, this same sense of unique universalism (present by implication in atheism's claims on geographic determinism and in the mentioned retort), is present in most religions: inherent to almost every faith, as a kind of phenomenological necessity to religion, is the implicit understanding that all people everywhere can benefit most profoundly from *this* faith, if only they would accept *this* worldview…

In none of these respects is atheism substantially different from most other religions. This includes, not infrequently, an intrinsic awareness that taking this position now promulgated, offers a much more valid approach than any other to matters religious in particular, and to life in general. Hubris had replaced humility in all such cases, substantively equally; navel-gazing has replaced the (always beneficial) awareness of the contingency of the own position. In such regards too, atheism displays the same characteristics as most religions.

To summarise the above: The word 'secular' does not inherently mean religion-free, but refers to (e.g. Christian) faith that is active in the world. Neither were modern democracies meant to be religion-free. The arguments that a-religiosity as a political ideal (the technical French term is *laïcité*) implies a publicly non-religious society, is self-deception by us adherents to democracy, perpetrated on ourselves. Atheism is as much a religion as any other; it portrays all the characteristics of religion: a vertical orientation with horizontal effects, with all the traits – good and bad – common to faiths. Pretending that a modern democracy that promotes the good liberal ideals of all the freedoms involved maximally pursued, functions without the dimension of the religious, is simply deceitful. As was done above, socio-political introspection leaves one with the uncomfortable realisation that our self-concept of public life, had been inaccurate. The idea of a religion-free public sphere does not exist.

Acknowledging as much requires a kind of conversion; an acknowledgement that we live inescapably religious lives. Returning to the headings above: religion is in fact everywhere. Now, the change that is required – the mission of the mind – is to work out the specifics of this more honest self-acknowledgement. Such a conceptual rearrangement of understanding the public sphere, will require no less dramatic adaptations from us who live in modern, liberal democracies, than do adapting to new technologies, mores, ecological problems, and other innovations.

However, Christianity, as is the case with any other religion, is better suited to such advances, given that the present is overtly acknowledged to be built on the past, at least in some important ways; and that is the case with the future too – avowedly and confessionally. Many of the conceptual (legal, philosophical, theological) tools for building such a better, more self-honest present and future, are already existent and well thought through – for instance in the three Vanhoutte, Lombaard and Benson publications on which much of the aforegoing here is built, and more. In a palpable sense, a new religio-political future is upon us; one in which greater scrupulousness and circumspection about also our religious situatednesses will play a constitutive part. In this regard too – with reference to the opening paragraph of this contribution – the various parts of Africa have as much to bring to as to absorb from the rest of our integrated world (cf. e.g. Hacket 2011:853–897), in interaction, internally and externally; co-textually and contextually. A mission of the public mind still lies ahead, in order to correct widespread misconceptions about these matters; doing so always in humility, in the spirit of openness to be corrected.

In this, though, religions/religiosity/Christianity will not constitute the reactionary forces, trying to avert or divert immanent changes. Here, these commitments will be the steering forces towards greater clarity and, hence, freedom. As an early Reformation-era adaptation by Caspar Huberinus (cf. Huberinus 1999; ed. Franz 1973) of a 1st century BCE – 1st century CE Ovid (cf. Walter 2022:257–271) saying formulated this: *Tempora mutantur, nos et mutamur in illis* ('Times change; we, yes, change with them') (Huberinus 1554:354).

References

Benson, I.T., 2013, 'Seeing through the secular illusion', *Nederduitse Gereformeerde Teologiese Tydskrif* 54(4), 12–29.

Cooley, R., 1902, *Human nature and the social order*, Charles Scribner's Sons, New York.

Franz, G. (ed.), 1973, *Huberinus – Rhegius – Holbein. Bibliographische und druckgeschichtliche Untersuchung der verbreitetsten Trost- und Erbauungsschriften des 16. Jahrhunderts*, de Graaf, Nieuwkoop.

Goosen, D., 2007, *Die nihilisme, Notas oor ons tyd*, Praag, Pretoria.

Goosen, D., 2015, *Oor gemeenskap en plek. Anderkant die onbehae*, FAK, Pretoria.

Hackett, R., 2011, 'Regulating religious freedom', *Emory International Law Review* 25, 853–897.

Hett, W., 1957., *Aristotle, Volume VIII: On the Soul. Parva Naturalia. On Breath* (Loeb Classical Library 288), Harvard University Press, Cambridge, Massachusetts.

Holyoake, G.J., 1896, *English secularism: a confession of belief*, Library of Alexandria, Chicago.

Huberinus, C., 1554, *Postilla Deudsch*, Johan Eichorn, Frankfurt an der Oder.

Huberinus, C., 1999, *Works by Caspar Huberinus (1500-1553)*, Brill, Leiden.

Hussey, E., 1999, 'Heraclitus', in A.A. Long (ed.), *The Cambridge companion to early Greek philosophy*, pp. 88–112, Cambridge University Press, Cambridge.

Lombaard, C., 2018, 'Spiritualityd… Spirituality in our time – In conversation with Hartmut Rosa's theory on social acceleration', *HTS Teologiese Studies/Theological Studies* 74(3), 1–7.

Marx, K., 1844, *Deutsch-Französische Jahrbücher*, Bureau der Jahrbücher, Paris.

Nietzsche, F., 1887, *Die fröhliche Wissenschaft*, Neue Ausgabe, E. W. Fritzsch, Leipzig.

Ronca, I., 2014, '*Semper aliqvid novi africam adferre*: philological afterthoughts on the Plinian reception of a pre-Aristotelian saying', *Akroterion* 37(3-4), 146–158.

Rosa, H., 2013, *Social acceleration: A new theory of modernity*, Columbia University Press, New York.

Scruton, R., 2012, *The face of God. The Gifford lectures 2010*, Bloomsbury Academic, London.

Smith, A., 1776, *An inquiry into the nature and causes of the wealth of nations*, W. Strahan; and T. Cadell, London.

Tillich, P., 1955, *Biblical religion and the search for ultimate reality*, University of Chicago Press, Chicago.

Vanhoutte, K.K.P., 2020, 'The revenge of the words: On language's historical and autonomous being and its effects on "secularisation"', *HTS Teologiese Studies/Theological Studies* (Special Issue: Christianity as a Change Agent in the 4th Industrial Revolution World), 76(2), 1–9.

Van Huyssteen, J.W., 2006, *Alone in the world? Human uniqueness in science and theology*, William B. Eerdmans Publishing Company, Grand Rapids.

Walter, A., 2022, 'Tempora Mutantur: Metamorphic Imagery in Ovid's *Fasti*', in J.S. Clay & A Vergados (eds.), *Teaching through images. Imagery in Greco-Roman didactic poetry*, pp. 257–271, Brill, Leiden.

Chapter 21

Mission 'and' Ecology in Africa

Ernst Conradie

Introduction

This contribution explores the ecological dimension of mission in the African context. It notes that such an ecological dimension of mission is widely recognised in ecumenical discourse, also in (South) Africa. Nevertheless, by juxtaposing the terms 'mission' and 'ecology', it unpacks various layers of the troubling 'and' that connects these two terms. Does earthkeeping form part of God's mission or is mission itself part of something else, for example, of God's household or God's economy? How is the alignment of mission with colonialism and the ecological impact of colonialism to be addressed in the African context? Could a focus on missional theology help to overcome the underlying problem?

Earthkeeping as a dimension of mission!

In an editorial for *Missionalia* published in 1991, David Bosch (1991a:1) observed that a Christian responsibility towards the environment 'has only very rarely been linked with the church's missionary enterprise' (an odd phrase!). In *Transforming Mission* (Bosch 1991b) published in the same year, the role of 'ecology' in mission received no attention. Thirty years later there is sufficient ecumenical consensus in Christian discourse on mission that 'ecology' forms an integral part of mission. Such consensus is found across geographic, confessional, and other divides.

At the World Convocation on 'Justice, Peace and the Integrity of Creation' (JPIC) in Seoul in 1990, churches entered into a covenant solidarity on JPIC. However, the word mission does not appear in the final document from that conference (cf. ed. Niles 1992). The 1991 annual meeting of the South African Missiological Society focused on the theme of 'Justice, Peace and the Integrity of Creation', as did the 1992 annual meeting of the Theological Society of South Africa. By that time Sean McDonagh made connections between mission (in the Philippines) and ecology in books such as *To care for the earth* (1986) and *The greening of the church* (1991). Calvin Dewitt and Ghillean Prance (ed. 1992) edited a volume on *Missionary earthkeeping* following a lecture at the Au Sable Institute which included several essays on the African context. In Zimbabwe, Marthinus Daneel and associates were exploring the significance of tree-planting Eucharists amongst African Initiated Churches (AICs) (cf. Daneel 1991, especially 1998 and 1999).

Since that time, various confessional bodies and ecumenical documents have recognised earthkeeping as a crucial dimension of mission. A few examples may suffice:

a) The United Ministry for Service and Witness of the Dutch Reformed family of churches in South Africa developed a thoroughly Trinitarian understanding of mission that includes this:

> In the power of the Holy Spirit the Church is sent … to: 3.1.1 live in the presence of God (*coram Deo*), obedient to the word of God, 3.1.2 a ministry of worshipping God and praying for the world (*leitourgia*), 3.1.3 minister the Gospel of God's salvation to all people through word (*kerugma*), deed (*diaconia*) and in a relationship of love and unity (*koinonia*), 3.1.4 seek justice, reconciliation and healing, testifying to the hope that we live by and 3.1.5 conserve and cultivate creation in the name of God and for the sake of all who live in it (see Botha et al., n.d., also quoted in Dreyer 2020:265, italics in the original).

b) In 1990 the Anglican Consultative Council (ACC) decided to add a fifth mark of mission, stating that: 'We now feel that our understanding of the ecological crisis, and indeed of the threats to the unity of all creation, mean that we have to add a fifth affirmation':[1]

- To proclaim the Good News of the Kingdom;
- To teach, baptise and nurture new believers;
- To respond to human need by loving service;
- To seek to transform unjust structures of society; to challenge violence of every kind and to pursue peace and reconciliation;
- To strive to safeguard the integrity of creation and sustain and renew the life of the earth.

---

1   Anglican Communion Office, 2022, *History of the five marks of mission*, viewed 9 January 2022, from http://www.anglicancommunion.org/mission/marks-of-mission/history.aspx.

c. In a public lecture entitled 'The Third Mission of the Church', the Australian Lutheran biblical scholar Norman Habel (1998) suggested that there have been three phases in the history of Christian mission, where each subsequent phase includes but expands the previous phase. In the first phase, mission was understood as 'saving souls'. The second phase of mission widened the scope to include the whole human being. The scope of the third mission is wider and deeper still to include the whole earth, to announce the reign of God, and to aim for wholeness, inclusion, and service (diakonia) rather than domination. For Habel (1998:33), 'The task of this mission may be variously understood as saving, redeeming, restoring, liberating, or healing the earth'.

d. The Methodist Church of Southern Africa states its vision for 'A Christ healed Africa for the healing of nations'. Its mission statement follows from that, namely: 'God calls the Methodist people to proclaim the Gospel of Jesus Christ for healing and transformation'. It believes that the church is called to –

- A deepening spirituality.
- A resolve to be guided by God's mission.
- A rediscovery of every member of ministry, or the priesthood of all believers.
- A commitment 'to be one, so that the world may believe'.
- A re-emphasis of servant-leadership and discernment as our model for ministry.
- A redefinition and authentication of the vocation of the clergy in our church.
- A commitment to environmental justice.[2]

e. The World Council of Churches' (WCC) Commission on World Mission and Evangelism (CWME) presented a new mission statement entitled 'Together towards Life: Mission and Evangelism in Changing Landscapes' to the WCC 10th Assembly at Busan, Korea, in 2013 (cf. ed. Keum 2013). This document adopts an explicitly Trinitarian understanding of God's mission, affirms the Spirit of Mission as the 'Breath of Life' (para. 12-18), and recognises the cosmic scope of such mission, for example, in paragraphs 4 and 19:

4. God did not send the Son for the salvation of humanity alone or give us a partial salvation. Rather the gospel is the good news for every part of creation and every aspect of our life and society. It is therefore vital to recognize God's

---

[2] The Methodist Church of Southern Africa, 2021, *Who we are*, viewed 9 January 2022, from https://methodist.org.za/who-we-are/vision-mission/.

mission in a cosmic sense and to affirm all life, the whole oikoumene, as being interconnected in God's web of life.

19. Mission is the overflow of the infinite love of the Triune God. God's mission begins with the act of creation. Creation's life and God's life are entwined. The mission of God's Spirit encompasses us all in an ever-giving act of grace. We are therefore called to move beyond a narrowly human-centred approach and to embrace forms of mission which express our reconciled relationship with all created life. We hear the cry of the earth as we listen to the cries of the poor and we know that from its beginning the earth has cried out to God over humanity's injustice (Gen 4:10).

f. In the Roman Catholic context, the two themes of 'mission' and 'integral ecology' are both addressed in papal documents, albeit not together. In the apostolic exhortation *Evangelii Gaudium* ('The Joy of the Gospel'), Pope Francis explored the proclamation of the gospel in today's world. He maintains that the church must understand itself as 'a community of missionary disciples' (para. 24), who are 'permanently in a state of mission' (para. 25). There is little if any attention to integral ecology. In the papal encyclical *Laudato Si'* (2015), Pope Francis addressed the 'care for our common home' at some length. He developed a notion of integral ecology but did not address the role of mission or evangelism, except for several cross-references.

Some caveats

Despite such emerging consensus, at last four caveats need to be noted:

First, religious discourse on 'ecology' is of course not restricted to Christianity – which raises complex issues over what mission entails. Is engagement in earthkeeping merely an opportunity for evangelism, or does Christian mission form part of something larger, captured by umbrella categories such as 'the faith-based organisation (FBO)-sector', 'civil society', or 'language, religion and culture'? Again, does ecology form part of mission, or does Christian mission form one (perhaps crucial) dimension of Christianity which itself is one religion amongst others and, as part of human engagements with nature, have to adhere to ecological ground rules?

Second, not all Christians are engaged in discourse on 'mission', at least not explicitly. Ever since mission became inextricably entangled in colonial history, some Christians refrain from using the term mission and opt, instead, for evangelism, prophetic witness, service, ministry, and so forth. If 'ecology' is a dimension of mission, does 'ecology' not also operate outside of such a notion of mission?

Third, even where an ecological dimension to Christian mission is recognised, the vocabulary to describe that is divergent. Earthkeeping is used in the heading above, but others prefer care for creation, ecological responsibility, struggling for ecojustice (e.g. climate justice), or environmental stewardship. These words mean very different things to different people, with diverging theological assumptions on an adequate rationale for such earthkeeping (Conradie 2011b). The crucial question is how the place and vocation of humanity within the community of life on earth (understood by Christians as part of God's creation) is framed. To introduce any 'and' to speak of 'humanity *and* nature' is to suggest that humans are somehow separate from nature. This can only yield an anthropocentric way of thinking. Put differently, are human beings nothing but 'dust of the earth', or are they 'little less than angels'? To emphasise human responsibility is of course crucial, but to what extent does such a notion of responsibility assume human dignity, human rights, and behind that, human exceptionalism?

Fourth, even where a word such as 'environment' is used, this can serve as a key to very different agendas, namely: regarding nature conservation (the so-called 'green' agenda focusing on endangered species, land degradation, deforestation, loss of biodiversity), or regarding environmental justice (the so-called 'brown' agenda focusing on the impact of environmental destruction upon the poor, marginalised, people of colour, women, the elderly, and indigenous people (in the southern African context) (cf. For example, Conradie & Field 2016). Is the main problem overpopulation (amongst the poor) or overconsumption (amongst the consumer classes)? How should prosperity be assessed theologically?

Despite these caveats, the emerging consensus is still remarkable.

Creation at the heart of mission?

The mission statement *Together towards Life* not only regards earthkeeping (a term that it admittedly does not use) as a dimension of mission. It adopts a phrase that has been widely used in ecumenical circles to describe creation as 'the heart of mission':

> 20. Mission with creation at its heart is already a positive movement in our churches through campaigns for eco-justice and more sustainable lifestyles and the development of spiritualities that are respectful of the earth. However, we have sometimes forgotten that the whole of creation is included in the reconciled unity towards which we are all called (2 Cor. 5:18-19). We do not believe that the earth is to be discarded and only souls saved; both the earth and our bodies have to be transformed through the Spirit's grace. As the vision of Isaiah and John's revelation testify, heaven and earth will be made new (Is. 11:1-9; 25:6-10; 66:22; Rev. 21:1-4).

But what does this phrase actually mean?³ If 'creation' in the phrase 'Creation at the heart of mission' is understood as shorthand for 'care for creation', this would suggest that earthkeeping forms an integral part of the mission of the church. It is no longer to be understood as a marginal item on an over-crowded mission- or social agenda. Indeed, care for creation lies at the heart of mission. Wherever it is indeed marginalised, *Together towards Life* would suggest a form of mission 'from the margins'. Likewise, one may argue that earthkeeping is not a marginal concern in terms of the biblical roots of Christianity, its subsequent history, the deepest convictions of the Christian faith or of Christian praxis.

However, the phrase becomes awkward if 'creation' is understood as the product of God's work (*creatura*). The underlying problem becomes evident when the core ecological insight is taken into account, that we as human beings form part of the evolutionary history of the earth as a planet in an evolving universe. If Earth is re-described by Christians as 'God's creation', how could creation then be 'at the heart of mission'? If mission is understood as the mission of the church (which is admittedly disputed) and the church as a fellowship of believers emerging rather late in the history of the human species, how could the planet form part of such mission? If the focus would be on the vocation of humanity or our responsibilities towards the planet within which we live, that would still make sense, but not if the word 'mission' is used to describe this. Who is sending whom and where to with what message? Instead, the umbrella term should be God's creation, while mission could perhaps be regarded as lying 'at the heart of God's creation', not the other way around!

The 'and' in 'mission and ecology'

The discussion above clearly raises profound questions regarding the relationship between mission and ecology. To regard earthkeeping as a dimension of mission is to assume that this is one dimension along others, perhaps a crucial one, but mission is then the larger concept so that earthkeeping forms part of that. This would not make sense if the focus is on the church's missions. It would make sense if earthkeeping is understood as part of God's mission to the world. If so, the phrase could mean that God's work of creation forms a core aspect of God's work as a whole (God's mission) – in relation to other aspects of God's work such as providence, salvation, election, and consummation. This raises thorny theological questions: is the aim of salvation to allow God's creation to flourish again or is salvation (and consummation) an aim in itself?⁴ Applied to mission: if mission is tied primarily to God's work of salvation

---

3   For a more detailed discussion, see Conradie (2010).
4   Cf. Conradie 2011a and 2012 for an exploration of this question.

(understood, e.g. as liberation, reconciliation or 'reconstruction and development'), is mission an aim in itself or the aim of salvation (and thus mission) something else, perhaps the reign of God 'on earth as it is in heaven'?[5]

One may also suggest that mission forms part of the whole household of God (*oikos*). Accordingly, the household has an ecological dimension that addresses the underlying logic (*logos*) of the planetary household. Following the same Greek root *oikos* one may then also identify an economic dimension of the household to speak of the rules (*nomoi*) for the management of the household. An ecumenical dimension of the household then addresses the inhabitation of the household – by plants, animals, and humans alike. If so, the church cannot be equated with God's household but forms part of that larger household. Accordingly, God's mission is to allow the whole household to flourish again given the destruction wreaked by human sin (cf. eds. Ayre & Conradie 2016).

Another option is to regard God's mission and God's household as part of something even larger, namely the Triune God's economy. This term then refers to the whole work of the Triune God – which is also expressed by the classic notion of the 'economic Trinity' (the Triune God as this God may be known through God's work), as distinct from the 'immanent Trinity' (God's Triune Being in itself). The whole work of God then includes God's work of creation (of heaven and earth, of what is seen and unseen), ongoing creation, the emergence of humanity, human sin, providence, the history of salvation, the election of Israel, the formation and up-building of the church, its missions, and the expected consummation of God's work (cf. Conradie 2015). One may then say that God's economy is a more differentiated and more encompassing way of speaking about God's mission.

One may therefore conclude that the 'and' in the phrase 'mission and ecology' is awkward as it does not clarify the theological relationships between God's mission, God's household, and God's economy.

Mission and ecology in the African context

In the African context the conceptual connections between God's mission and ecology have indeed been made, but then almost exclusively by South African male scholars classified as 'white' under apartheid. This could be illustrated in the oeuvres of especially David Bosch, Ernst Conradie, Marthinus Daneel, Steve de Gruchy, Jannie Du Preez, David Field, Dons Kritzinger, Nelus Niemandt, Klaus Nürnberger, Phil Robinson, and Willem Saayman. Except for Nürnberger, all of these scholars come from the Reformed tradition. One may add a few others such as Rachel Mash (British Anglican), Susan Rakoczy (Polish/American Catholic), and Annalet van

---

[5] For a discussion, see Conradie 2014.

Schalkwyk (South African Reformed). There will be some exceptions from other evangelical theologians, but this observation cannot but elicit a hermeneutics of suspicion.

This observation by no means suggests a lack of theological interest in ecological concerns elsewhere in the African context. However, such interest is hardly expressed with reference to mission. Put bluntly and in overgeneralised terms, besides such white South African scholars, those who are interested in mission are not that interested in 'ecology', while those who are interested in 'ecology' are not that interested in mission. At least they do not frame earthkeeping responsibilities in terms of mission. What should one make of this?

Given the focus on *mission* 'and' ecology, this is not the place to offer an overview of theological reflection on earthkeeping in the African context (cf. Conradie 2016). Such reflection covers the full range of theological sub-disciplines. While a missional dimension may or may not be present throughout, the focus here has to be on an explicit missionary/missional intention (as proposed by Bosch 1980).

Five general impressions may suffice:
First, there is extensive literature, from within African Christian theology, seeking to retrieve an indigenous African ecological wisdom in response to deforestation and land degradation due to mining, commercial agriculture, and urban sprawl.[6]

Second, in African women's theology there is a widespread recognition of the intricate connections between (black) women's bodies and the 'rape of the Earth'. A female sense of being embodied is then employed to develop an ecofeminist spirituality.[7] In such contexts, the metaphor of the household of God does play a significant role, especially in terms of the distinction between, a house, a home, and a warm hearth (cf. ed. Kanyoro & Njoroge 1996).

Third, in prophetic and liberation theologies, the dangers imposed by global threats associated with climate change, droughts and storms, and the spread of diseases are clearly recognised through efforts to address international debt, reproductive health and climate justice.[8] Such contributions could be, but are hardly ever, framed in terms of Christian mission.

---

6   For monographs, see, for example: Gitau 2000; Kaoma 2013; Mante 2004.

7   See the PhD theses by Chirongoma 2013; Moyo 2011; Nalwamba 2017 from Zimbabwe, Malawi, and Zambia, respectively.

8   See, for example: the addenda in the SACC statement on climate change, 2009; ed. Chitando and Conradie (2017); eds. Chitando, Conradie and Kilonzo (forthcoming).

Fourth, in some evangelical and Pentecostal circles, also in AIC theologies, the need for environmental stewardship is recognised and framed as such. However, this is not yet fully developed at any length (cf. Golo 2012). In fact, the debate on Pentecostal forms of ecotheology in Africa is dominated by a critique of the prosperity gospel.

Fifth, there are numerous local projects that focus on sustainable agriculture, sustainable livelihoods, deforestation, endangered species, appropriate technologies, climate resilience, environmental education, and so forth. There is ample practical experience and wisdom that emerge from such projects and some theological reflection on what this entails. It would be impossible to provide an adequate overview of such projects here.

Again, in none of these trends is theological reflection on mission prominent. The simple reason may be that the association between mission and colonialism remains deeply entrenched so that those with ecological concerns refrain from over-complicating their agendas by using the term mission to describe what they are doing. More specifically, the ecologically destructive impact of colonialism is widely recognised. If so, and through guilt by association, the ecologically destructive impact of (some forms of) mission is recognised, if not presupposed. As a result, 'mission' hardly seems to be an appropriate concept to express earthkeeping responsibilities, at least not in the African context outside of South Africa or where the legacy of foreign mission by churches in South Africa is still tangible.

Ecology and missional theology

This negative assessment, namely that 'mission' hardly seems to be an appropriate concept to express earthkeeping responsibilities, at least not in Africa outside of South Africa, is hard to accept for South African scholars like myself with longstanding commitments to both mission and ecology.[9]

In my view it would *not* do to reinterpret the term 'missionary' by replacing it with a 'missional' theology. Following the insights of Leslie Newbigin, Darryl Guder, and David Bosch, a missional theology has become widely discussed and appreciated amongst South African scholars in the fields of missiology and congregational studies. Such theological developments are discussed in other contributions to this volume. Missional theology helps to recognise that mission is not merely one activity of the church but that the church itself forms part of God's mission and is a therefore 'missional' by its very nature. Moreover, the ecological dimension of missional theology has been recognised by several scholars, including Nelus Niemandt (cf. 2015), one of the most significant exponents of South African missional theology (cf. Niemandt 2019).

---

9   For an overview, see Conradie (2014).

Nevertheless, there is a danger that missional theology would be missing the point that Leslie Newbigin, the father of missional theology, so clearly recognised. The point is that the church (e.g. in England, but also in the USA and in South Africa) has become the recipient (not only the agent or instrument) of its own missionary message so that the church's accommodation of the dominant cultural patterns under conditions of Christendom in such countries (shaped by power, privilege, and nowadays, consumerism) is challenged by the gospel. The self-critique of consumerism and of the prosperity gospel is certainly highly appropriate in order to resist ecclesial self-legitimising. The same would apply to a tacit legitimation of modernity, British imperial rule, the 'American dream', a Eurocentric outlook, or Christian nationalism. The messengers are challenged by their own message.

However, to 'export' such a missional theology to other African countries, for example to emphasise the church's earthkeeping responsibilities, would be missing that very point. The proverbial elephant in the room needs to be confronted, namely the problem of whiteness, with its associated concepts of white supremacy, white privilege, white fragility, white-speak, implicit or unconscious bias, institutional racism, and the so-called ignorance contract.[10] To address this will be crucial in order to overcome the association between mission and colonialism. Only on that basis would it become possible to associate a missional theology with the church's earthkeeping responsibilities in the wider African context.

A very brief conclusion

A very brief conclusion may suffice. From the perspective of discourse on 'mission', there can be no doubt that 'ecology' forms an integral part of God's mission, God's household, and the missions of the church. From the perspective of discourse on 'ecology', this connection is far less obvious, although many environmental activists are on a proverbial 'mission', but then understood in purely secular or quasi-religious terms. In the context of African Christianity, the intricate relation between mission and ecology can only become fruitful if the ecologically destructive legacy of Christian mission under conditions of coloniality is addressed.

References

Anglican Communion Office, 2022, *History of the five marks of mission*, viewed 9 January 2022, from http://www.anglicancommunion.org/mission/marks-of-missio-n/history.aspx.

---

[10] Such concepts are being explored in an ongoing Ph.D. project by Johannes Mouton entitled 'Facing the image in the mirror: "Whiteness" in South African missional discourse', registered at the University of the Western Cape.

Ayre, C.W. & Conradie, E.M. (eds), 2016, *The church in God's household: Protestant perspectives on ecclesiology and ecology*, Cluster Publications, Pietermaritzburg.

Bosch, D.J., 1980, *Witness to the world: The Christian mission in theological perspective*, John Knox, Atlanta.

Bosch, D.J., 1991a, 'Editorial: Mission and ecology', *Missionalia* 19(1), 1-2.

Bosch, D.J., 1991b, *Transforming mission: Paradigm shifts in theology of mission*, Orbis Books, Maryknoll.

Botha, J., Knoetze, H., Orsmond, E., van der Merwe, W., & van Deventer, H., n.d., *Our calling to service and witness in unity. A theological basis for the DRC family's missional ministries*, viewed 9 January 2022, from http://witnessministry.christians.co.za/wp-content/uploads/sites/16/2017/12/Our-calling-to-service-and-witness-in-unity-final-book.pdf.

Chirongoma, S., 2013, 'Navigating indigenous resources that can be utilized in constructing a Karanga theology of health and well-being (Utano): an exploration of health agency in contemporary Zimbabwe', Ph.D. thesis, University of KwaZulu-Natal.

Chitando, E. & Conradie E.M. (eds.), 2017, 'Praying for Rain? African Perspectives on Religion and Climate Change', *The Ecumenical Review* 69(3), 311-435.

Chitando, E. & Conradie E.M., & Kilonzo, S. (eds.), 2022, *African perspectives on religion and climate change*, Routledge, London (forthcoming).

Conradie, E.M., 2010, 'Creation at the heart of mission', *Missionalia* 38(3), 380-396.

Conradie, E.M. (ed.), 2011a, *Creation and salvation, Volume 1: A mosaic of essays on selected classic Christian theologians*, LIT Verlag, Berlin.

Conradie, E.M., 2011b, *Christianity and Earthkeeping: In search of an inspiring vision*, SUN Media, Stellenbosch.

Conradie, E.M. (ed.), 2012, *Creation and salvation, Volume 2: A companion on recent theological movements*, LIT Verlag, Berlin.

Conradie, E.M., 2014, 'Missiology and ecology: An assessment of the current state of debate', *Australian Journal of Mission Studies* 8(1), 10-16.

Conradie, E.M., 2015, *The earth in God's economy: Creation, salvation and consummation in ecological perspective*, Studies in Religion and the Environment, Vol. 10, LIT Verlag, Berlin.

Conradie, E.M., 2016, 'Approaches to religion and the environment in Africa', In E.K. Bongmba (ed.), *Routledge companion to Christianity in Africa*, pp. 438-453. Routledge, New York.

Conradie, E.M. & Field, D.N. et al., 2016, *A Rainbow over the land: Equipping Christians to be earthkeepers* (edited by Rachel Mash), Bible Media, Wellington.

Daneel, M.L., 1991, 'The liberation of creation: African traditional religious and independent church perspectives', *Missionalia* 19(2), 99-121.

Daneel, M.L., 1998, *African Earthkeepers. Volume 1. Interfaith mission in earth-care*, African Initiatives in Christian mission 2, Unisa, Pretoria.

Daneel, M.L., 1999. *African Earthkeepers. Volume 2. Environmental mission and liberation in Christian perspective*, African Initiatives in Christian mission 3, Unisa, Pretoria.

DeWitt, C.B. & Prance, G.T., (eds) 1992. *Missionary earthkeeping*. Mercer University Press, Macon.

Dreyer, W.A., 2020, 'Missionale ekklesiologie in die Afrikaanse gereformeerde kerke sedert 1990', *Stellenbosch Theological Journal* 6(3), 249-175.

Francis (Pope), (n.d.), *Evangelii Gaudium: The Joy of the Gospel*, Apostolic exhortation of the Holy Father Francis to the bishops, clergy, consecrated persons and the lay faithful on the proclamation of the gospel in today's world, 9 January 2022, from https://www.vatican.va/content/francesco/en/apost_exhortations/documents/papa-francesco_esortazione-ap_20131124_evangelii-gaudium.html.

Francis (Pope), 2015, *Laudato Si: On Care for Our Common Home* (Encyclical Letter), Vatican City, Liberia Editrice Vaticana.

Gitau, S.K., 2000, *The environmental crisis: A challenge for African Christians*, Acton Publishers, Nairobi.

Golo, B-W.K., 2012. 'Creation and salvation in African neo-Pentecostalist theology', In: E.M. Conradie (ed.), *Creation and salvation, Volume 2: A companion on recent theological movements*, pp. 334-339, LIT Verlag, Berlin.

Habel, N.C., 1998. 'The third mission of the church', In *Trinity Occasional Papers*, XVII, I, pp. 31-43, Trinity Theological College, Brisbane.

Kanyoro, M.R. & Njoroge, N.J. (eds), 1996, *Groaning in faith: African women in the household of God*, Acton, Nairobi.

Kaoma, K.J., 2013, *God's family, God's Earth: Christian ecological ethics of ubuntu*, Kachere Series, Zomba, Malawi.

Keum, J. (ed.), 2013, *Together towards life: Mission and evangelism in changing landscapes with a practical guide*, World Council of Churches, Geneva.

Mante, J.O.Y., 2004, *Africa: The theological and philosophical roots of our ecological crisis*, Sonlife Press, Accra.

McDonagh, S., 1986, *To care for the earth*. Geoffrey Chapman, London.

McDonagh, S., 1991, *The greening of the church*, Orbis Books, Maryknoll.

Moyo, F.L., 2011, 'Religion, spirituality and being a woman in Africa: gender construction within the African religio-cultural experiences', Ph.D. thesis, University of KwaZulu-Natal.

Nalwamba, K., 2017, 'Vital force as a triangulated concept of nature and s(S)pirit', Ph.D. thesis, University of Pretoria.

Niemandt, C.J.P., 2015, 'Ecodomy in mission: The ecological crisis in the light of recent ecumenical statements', *Verbum et Ecclesia* 36(3), 1-8.

Niemandt, C. J.P., 2019, *Missional leadership,* Aosis, Durbanville.

Niles, D.P. (ed.), 1992, *Between the flood and the rainbow,* World Council of Churches, Geneva.

South African Council of Churches (SACC), Climate Change Committee, 2009, *Climate change – A challenge to the churches in South Africa,* SACC, Marshalltown.

The Methodist Church of Southern Africa, 2021, *Who we are,* viewed 9 January 2022, from https://methodist.org.za/who-we-are/vision-mission/.

Conclusion

Collective works such as this usually develop according to a once-off dynamic that generates outcomes that could not be predicted beforehand. Whilst protagonists of a central and unified leitmotif may feel this to be a shortcoming, differing voices and viewpoints in collective undertakings are beneficial as they provide some indication of the multidimensional challenges that confront mission studies within the reality of fragmented and diverse communities and contexts (in Africa). It thus tends to make the volume authentic in its reflection of reality.

As suggested by the title of this book, theology is conceived where mission is done in the name of the Father, the Son, and the Holy Spirit. Let us remember that every birth – the creation of new life is the work of God alone – is a miracle, and we as humans have the privilege to participate in it. If we then keep in mind that when Christian mission came to Africa at the beginning of the 15th century, 'there was no developed theology of mission' (Oborji 2020:6), and as we read through the pages of this book, we cannot but be amazed at what God is doing in and through Africa. It is indeed a miracle. For the church, mission is and will be a continuous process of listening, seeing, sifting, testing, reformulating, discerning, and discarding because everything the church does is not mission. In this regard, quoting Neil, Bosch (2012:523) contends: 'if everything is mission, nothing is mission'. It must always be remembered that the crux of mission – the cross of Jesus Christ – is both God's 'yes' and God's 'no' to the world.

It was argued in several chapters of this book, by different authors, that mission can only be understood as *missio Trinitatis Dei*. Mission comes from the being of the trinitarian God; therefore, mission is to participate in whatever God is doing in different contexts and amongst different people. The church then participates in God's six major 'salvific acts' as portrayed in the Bible: 'the incarnation of Christ, his death on the cross, his resurrection on the third day, his ascension, the outpouring of the Holy Spirit at Pentecost, and the Parousia' (Bosch 2012:524). Then it becomes clear that, every ministry of the church, if it is focussed on God and his kingdom, must have a mission intention and dimension. As was stated, mission is the mother of all theology. Missiology is a major dimension of all theology. Thus, any mission that does not conceive, or build new or on current theology, would be incomplete.

We might be overwhelmed by the challenges of our faith in the trinitarian God. We might be overwhelmed by Christ's calling on our lives to participate in his salvation acts. But Christ is also our hope, because he is the Good News, and he has both the power to save and to transform our world. May he grace us with obedience because the Lord has shown what is good and what he requires of us according to Micah 6:8 (emphasis added):

> To act justly and to love mercy and to walk humbly with your God.

References

Bosch, D.J, 2012, *Transforming mission: Paradigm shifts in theology of mission*, Orbis Books, Maryknoll, New York, NY.

Oborji, F.A., 2020, *Towards African Missiology. Issues of new language for African Christianity,* Collection of Essays, Volume 1, Xlibris, Bloomington, Indiana.

Index

Ad Gentes: 53, 263-4
Advocacy: 190, 242, 255, 287
Accra Declaration: 43
Africae Munus: 58
African:
- agency: 101, 168, 169
- Christianity: 26, 28, 39, 41, 42, 77, 85, 88, 101, 171
- continent: 35, 38, 86, 97, 154, 212, 220, 221, 228, 230, 231, 235, 237, 239
- culture: 28, 30, 37, 83, 100, 101, 168, 282, 286, 287, 288, 309
- experience: 59, 269, 320
- Theology: 42, 97, 101, 102, 216, 269, 272, 287
- Traditional Religions (ATRs): 55, 68, 79, 297, 337

African Independent/Indigenous/Initiated/Instituted Churches (AICs): 40, 75ff
Africanisation: 320
Afrocentrism: 91, 98, 101
Afro-pessimism: 42
Afro-xenophobia: 101
Agency: 39, 101, 103, 150, 168, 169, 200, 203
Alexandria: 28, 29, 47, 79, 342
All Africa Conference of Churches: 43, 310
Anglican (Church): 33, 35, 201, 269-271, 309
Anthropology: 56, 57, 61, 66, 163, 218, 278
Apartheid: 38, 98, 99, 103, 162, 163, 182, 190, 196, 216, 286, 350
Apostolic Church: 64
Arusha Call to Discipleship: 43
atheism: 337-339

Barth, Karl: 57, 111, 225, 262
Biblicism: 31
Blackness: 98
Bosch, David: 89, 90, 91, 121, 124, 170, 178, 344

Calling: 31-34, 37, 39, 69, 84-86, 112-114, 121-126, 128, 143, 151, 165, 166, 172, 178, 189, 209, 254- 268, 271-273, 296-298, 315, 325, 354, 357)
Calvin, John: 32, 33ff, 56, 119, 299, 344
Carthage: 29, 127
Charismata: 299
Charismatic: 41, 44, 64, 65, 111, 147, 211, 218
Charity: 190, 301-307
Children: 63, 91, 98ff, 123, 134-136, 180, 182-183, 189, 194, 196-203
Christology: 66
church/es:
- body of Christ: 47, 110, 112, 114, 116-119, 133, 147, 255
- community: 202,
- denomination: 23, 26, 28, 36, 40, 62, 64, 78, 103, 110-115, 120, 132, 146-147, 170-171, 198, 208-211, 215-216, 228, 270, 306-308, 325
- local: 48, 53-54, 58, 62, 112, 114-118, 186-190, 210, 223, 230, 255, 270
- mainline: 64-65, 76-78, 81, 97, 133, 146, 210-212, 270, 301, 308,
- mega: 41,
- planting: 33, 70-72, 108, 124-125, 150, 157, 167, 210-211, 293, 322-323

climate change: 200, 286-287, 351,
collaboration: 27, 40, 110, 209ff, 241

colonial/colonialism: 27, 32, 34, 36, 38, 48, 52, 88-102, 116, 151-155, 158-159, 166, 197-204, 216, 248, 277, 287, 294, 301-306, 344, 347, 352-353
community: 248, 250, 254-255, 258, 260, 261-267, 269-273, 277, 280, 282-285, 287, 295, 299, 305, 307-309, 318, 321, 347
communication: 48, 65, 134, 143, 185, 188-189, 199-201, 205, 215, 236-240, 249, 252,
Commission on World Mission: 248
congregation(s): 54, 64, 81, 82-83, 90, 110, 113-118, 125, 160-161, 164, 187-189, 204, 249, 254, 261, 265-267, 270, 284, 286, 306-307, 308, 316, 318, 352,
context/contextual/contextualisation/ contextual analysis: 21, 23, 26-27, 32, 35, 37, 39, 40-43, 46, 48-49, 51, 53, 59, 63, 66-72, 81, 88-95, 97-98, 101-104, 113, 129ff
Coptic Church: 28-29, 47, 226,
Corpus Christianum: 109
corrupt/corruption: 140, 181, 212, 220-224, 231, 283-286, 288, 303-304
cosmology: 41,
COVID-19 pandemic: 13, 90, 98, 136, 182, 212-213, 284-285
creation/Creator: 12, 47-49, 57-58, 63, 79-80, 88, 101, 111, 113, 122, 128, 130, 141, 166, 185, 189, 195, 203, 223-226, 230, 232-233, 258, 262, 265, 287, 296-299, 307, 317, 321, 332, 344ff
crime: 103, 136, 138, 140, 181-182, 193, 286
Crowther Samuel: 35
curriculum/curricula: 42, 149-159, 162-170, 200, 286, 315ff

decoloniality/decolonisation: 39, 52, 87, 92ff, 306
deliverance: 41, 66, 69, 80
democracy/democratic: 139, 336, 340-341
demography/demographic: 134
Desert Fathers: 28

development (community): 36-37, 42, 54, 71, 86, 91, 136, 144, 182, 185, 190-191, 194, 212, 229, 241, 301ff, 350
dialogue: 92, 103, 122, 152, 156, 204, 235ff, 324
diakonia/diaconia/diaconal/diaconate: 123, 292ff
digital: 278, 283-285
discipleship: 43, 204, 282, 294, 296, 325
discipline/s: 27, 99, 102, 149ff, 222, 226, 234, 285, 288, 315-319, 351
discrimination: 84, 136, 138-140, 147
displaced people: 140-145
diversity: 56, 62, 66, 72, 89, 103, 165, 188, 272, 338-339, 348,
dogma: 32, 64, 66, 162, 195, 211, 262,
Dutch Reformed Church (DRC): 63, 161, 189, 270

Early Church/Christianity: 28 ff, 49, 67, 91, 108, 120, 126, 250, 267,
Earth keeping: 344
Ecclesia in Africa: 55
Ecclesiology: 13, 63, 66, 67, 69-72, 198, 232, 261-265, 271-273, 317-318, 322
ecology/ecological: 189, 286, 334, 344ff
economy/economic: 137-140, 144, 195, 269, 284, 286, 303-304, 333, 336, 350
ecumenical: 42, 58, 63, 66, 70, 91, 110-113, 120-121, 156, 159, 185, 211, 217, 251, 261-264, 273, 318, 344-350
education (theological): 34, 37, 47, 51, 71-72, 77, 86, 99-101, 136, 144, 149ff, 181, 193, 195, 216-217, 225, 228-233, 286, 302-305, 310, 315ff
Egypt: 28-29, 200, 297,
empire/imperialism: 28-29, 52, 108, 151-152, 302, 307, 323,
Enlightenment: 36, 40, 53, 91, 308, 315
environment: 41, 114, 131, 141-143, 189, 200, 227, 232-234, 278, 286-288, 303, 344, 348, 352,

ethics/ethical issues: 97, 147, 157, 182, 223, 230, 277ff
Ethiopia: 28-29, 40, 64, 77, 144, 226,

Index

ethnic/ethnicity: 100-101, 134, 140, 147, 185, 226, 304, 324
Eurocentric(tism): 88, 101
Europe/European: 109, 115, 145-146, 151-152, 159, 232, 248, 277, 286, 297, 315-316, 339
eschatology: 66, 332
evangelism: 72, 131, 150, 162-163, 167, 216, 248ff, 267, 279, 292, 322-325, 346-347,

faith/s: 27, 29, 30, 32, 35, 37, 39, 41-42, 49-50, 52-58, 68-69, 82-83, 93, 95-97, 109, 119, 122, 127, 148, 156, 170, 188, 196-197, 222, 226-228, 232, 235-254, 267, 270-273, 283, 288, 296, 299, 307, 324, 330-340, 349
faith-based organisations (FBOs): 158, 301-302, 306, 347
Faith and Hope Gospel: 63, 67-69, 72, 77-79,
Family: 39, 47, 50, 56, 66, 119, 124, 133, 135, 182-183, 188, 204, 210-211, 250, 272, 284
food scarcity/security: 181-183
forgiveness: 225, 227, 230-231, 250, 258, 293-294, 298, 324,
Fresh Expressions: 269-270
fundamentalism: 31,

gender: 15, 42, 91, 99-103, 124, 135, 140, 147, 154, 163, 170, 190, 278, 282, 287, 301, 308-309
global/globalisation 43, 90-91, 99, 102, 143-146, 151, 156, 158, 160-161, 169, 177, 181, 199, 201, 205, 209-212, 220, 227, 231, 237, 248, 259, 261, 268, 283-286, 305, 307, 320, 325, 351
Global North: 144, 159, 165-166, 301, 306-307
Global South: 26, 40, 76, 144, 152, 166, 278, 292, 293-294, 301
God the Father: 195, 225, 296-297, 319,

gospel: 26ff, 49, 51-55, 58, 66-69, 71, 77, 98-103, 108-117, 120-127, 132- 134, 147, 150, 179, 202, 209, 217, 221, 227-229, 267
grace: 26, 30, 33, 55, 57, 69, 114, 122, 127, 203, 241, 252, 257, 267, 294, 298, 347, 348, 357
Great Commission: 31, 46, 178, 209, 249, 318, 321

healing: 41, 47, 53, 64, 66-69, 77, 81-86, 114, 122, 157, 189, 204, 228, 250, 258, 264-265, 183, 287, 306, 345-246
health: 68, 79, 81, 135-136, 141-144, 182-188, 248, 294, 296, 302-306, 351
hermeneutic: 67, 197-203, 262, 266-267, 286-288, 309, 318-319, 351
history:
 – African: 40, 48, 59, 77, 101
 – Christianity: 47, 58, 67, 77, 349
 – Church: 28, 29, 52, 101, 301, 315
 – colonial: 89, 90, 94, 347
 – general/secular/human: 27, 58, 84 91-92, 109, 252, 260, 262, 269, 317, 331-332, 349
 – mission: 23, 26-29, 110, 346
 – salvation: 350
 – theological: 97, 102-103
holism: 307
Holy Spirit/Pneumatology 33, 41, 53, 63-67, 70, 72, 83, 89, 103, 109-113, 199, 225, 298, 234, 256-259, 262, 265-266, 287, 296, 270, 298, 319 345, 357
human/humanity: 21-22, 30, 31, 33, 36, 42, 47, 49-57, 65-68, 79, 88, 91-92, 97-99, 101, 111, 122, 126, 128, 131, 138, 141, 150, 161, 165-166, 172, 178, 179-184, 190, 201, 221-232, 234, 236, 240-241, 248, 253-254-258, 262-267, 287-288, 294-297, 303, 317, 357
identity/identities: 29, 42, 52, 64, 71, 80, 84, 88, 90-92, 96-99, 101, 112, 158, 169, 197-203, 210-214, 254-258, 266, 272, 282-288, 331

immigrants/migrants: 85, 90, 101, 136- 145, 183
incarnation/incarnational: 26-28, 40, 55, 60, 71, 221, 230, 232, 249-252, 267-269, 273, 292-293, 298, 319, 357
independence/independent: 28, 35, 38-41, 52, 64, 76ff, 88, 102, 139, 152-153, 158, 197, 210-217, 231, 256, 280, 303, 320,
inculturation: 55-56, 88, 98, 102, 267-268, 273, 320,
intercultural: 154, 159-161, 316
internet: 185, 284
interreligious: 235-244
Islam: 29-30, 42, 47, 79, 139, 154-161, 168-169, 213, 216, 297, 235ff, 337-338

Jesus Christ: 22, 30, 31, 57-60, 67-69, 78-80, 100, 108, 117, 122, 220-223, 248, 250, 254, 257, 259, 265-267, 293-298, 346, 357
Justice: 29, 42-43, 92-93, 97-99, 117, 124, 145, 153, 166, 179-186, 190, 202, 224-226, 278, 282ff, 294, 301-303, 344ff
Justification: 30, 38, 69, 162, 229

kerygma/kerygmatic/proclamation: 121-122, 292-293, 299, 323
kingdom: 121, 152, 171, 176-180, 186-189, 202, 205, 210-217, 299
koinonia/koinonial: 124, 249, 296, 299, 232, 345

language: 34-36, 49, 71, 80, 90, 101, 134, 140, 152, 158, 166, 189, 198, 213-214, 217, 239, 332, 347
leadership: 29, 38, 40-42, 53, 59, 64-65, 72, 94, 98, 125, 147, 161, 179, 182, 187, 272, 282, 317, 323-324, 334, 346
liberty/liberalism/liberation/Liberator: 46, 65, 68-69, 79-80, 92, 98, 102, 122, 147, 150, 152-153, 157-160, 169, 203, 228, 240-241, 259, 296, 302, 306, 320, 334, 346, 350-351

liturgy/liturgical/*leitourgia*/worship: 53, 65, 70-71, 81-85, 90, 113-114, 121-122, 126, 198, 230, 258, 269, 284, 296, 299, 345
Livingstone, David: 36,
Luther, Martin/Lutheran Church: 30-33, 120, 126, 221, 233, 308, 315,

marginalise/marginalised 63, 90-92, 99, 103, 120, 124-125, 149, 158-159, 163-166, 186, 193-203, 249, 283, 293, 298, 318, 321, 249
martyrs/*martyria*: 29, 126-127, 323,
Methodist: 33, 85, 120, 178, 270, 346,
migrants/migrancy/migration: 136, 138, 140-145, 183
mind: 53, 83, 222-227, 330ff
ministry: 23, 37, 41, 46, 59, 69, 71, 80, 83-86, 116, 122-123, 133, 162, 193ff, 345-347, 357
missio Dei: 22, 26, 32-33, 42, 62ff, 111-113, 118-119, 169, 178, 193ff, 201, 243, 249, 254-266, 272, 278, 281, 317-322, 323-325
mission(nes) ecclesiae 112, 263
missio trinitatis Dei 26, 111, 292, 357
Missiology: 147, 150, 178, 194, 197-198, 202, 295, 315ff
missional: 116, 261ff, 315-323-325, 344, 351-353
mission:
 – agent of: 108, 110, 170, 197
 – as common witness: 249, 251
 – incarnational: 292
 – praxis: 31, 63, 66, 72, 156, 319, 322
 – dimensions 114, 120-128, 150, 157-159, 167
 – societies: 27, 33-34, 110, 147
missionary: 27-43, 47-60, 70-71, 76-80, 85, 88, 90-96, 100, 108-110, 117-127, 129, 132-134, 138-143, 151-152, 160, 165, 178, 201-202, 211, 216, 225, 248, 262-265, 268-270, 283, 294-296, 301-303, 315-319, 323, 352-353
modernism: 146-147, 334

Index

Moffat, Robert: 34
Monasticism: 29, 31-32

neo-Pentecostal(ism): 40-41, 64-65, 68, 305-307
new-Prophetic: 63, 65ff, 168
networking/networks: 39, 113, 133, 185, 187, 209ff
North Africa: 28-29, 47, 127, 144,

oppression: 84, 89-92, 99, 103, 124, 202, 243-245, 258, 277, 282, 308-309

Panta rei: 330
paradigm: 59-60, 69, 91, 98, 102, 121, 161, 196-200, 228, 234, 251, 263, 281, 295, 305, 315, 321-322
partnerships: 40, 42, 167, 187, 211-212, 271, 306, 309
peace: 29, 49, 68, 92, 97, 150, 157-159, 194, 203, 228, 241, 293, 345
Pentecostal: 62ff, 120, 133, 147, 161, 168, 210-211, 305-306, 352
Pietist: 32ff
Pollution: 141-143, 181, 189, 303
poor/poverty: 29, 42, 49, 69, 79, 90-94, 102-103, 114-117, 120-124, 138-139, 145, 152, 170-171, 178-179, 181-186, 190, 193-196, 212, 223, 282-286, 293-294, 300ff, 348
Pope:
 – Benedict XVI: 58
 – Francis: 347,
 – John XXIII: 52-53
 – John Paul II: 55
 – Paul VI: 54,

Population: 42, 46-54, 60, 64, 137-144, 176-177, 183, 196-198, 235, 279, 302, 348
post-Christendom: 146, 250, 297
post-colonial: 101, 152-153, 200, 302
post-conciliar: 54
post-modernism: 146

power: 101, 103, 109-113, 139-140, 169-170, 179-180, 188, 198, 221-229, 237, 258-260, 265, 270, 278, 282-284, 299, 301-309, 319, 331, 337-338, 353, 357
priesthood of all believers: 31, 255, 346
Presbyterian: 90, 156, 271
Propaganda Fide: 48
prophecy/prophesy/prophets: 41-42, 46, 64-66, 81-83, 116, 184, 201, 280-282, 293, 325, 347, 351
Protestant: 26ff, 97, 109-110, 116, 124, 146, 164, 239, 250, 255, 264, 306, 315, 336,
Padroado: 30
public theology: 42, 220ff
public space: 220-223

racism: 136, 139-140, 200, 216, 245, 248, 282, 292, 353
reconciliation: 97, 114, 120, 125, 150, 157-159, 194-195, 204, 226, 258, 264, 266, 299, 345, 350
reconstruction: 88, 97
Reformation: 30ff, 48, 56, 91, 119, 166, 341,
religion: 131, 134, 235ff, 284, 294, 297, 307, 309, 331-341, 347
revival: 33, 64, 250
Roman Catholic Church: 30, 46ff
rural: 134, 135, 138, 144, 176, 181, 183-186, 198, 209, 309

Sacra Congregatio de Propaganda Fide: 48
salvation: 31, 32, 47, 50, 53, 64, 66, 79-80, 84, 88, 92, 103, 108, 124, 126, 199, 202, 221-227, 230, 244, 249-252, 254-259, 261, 267, 294-295, 309, 345-350
secular/secularisation: 37, 38, 41, 48, 134, 146, 152-156, 171, 201, 224-228, 250, 277, 282, 295, 307, 330-338, 340, 301-306,
slavery: 27, 35, 42, 49, 221, 280, 297, 301,

363

social: 134, 231-232, 240-245, 248, 250, 261, 268, 272-273, 282, 284, 286, 294, 306-309, 331, 333-339
sources: 53, 59, 142, 151
spiritual/spirituality: 37-43, 54, 64-69, 77, 79, 82-85, 90-91, 98, 100, 113, 130, 134, 150-151, 164, 168, 170, 171, 211, 220, 228, 230-232, 241-242, 256, 271, 285, 288, 292, 294, 299, 303-308, 323-324, 335-336, 346, 348, 351
Sub-Sahara Africa (SSA): 26, 79, 85,
Supreme Being: 35, 297,

technology: 21, 54, 65, 91, 138, 185, 209, 215, 217, 230, 232, 333,
Together Towards Life (TTL): 61, 250
tradition/traditionalism/Traditional African Faith: 28, 33ff, 47, 54, 55, 59, 63-72, 77-79, 83-84, 95-101, 111, 115, 122, 130-135, 142-147, 150, 154-157, 163, 189, 201, 212, 231, 236, 239, 242, 259, 268, 273, 287, 297, 318, 331-333, 337, 350
translating/translation: 26, 37,
Trinity/Trinitarian: 26, 47, 70, 83, 111, 119, 150, 195, 212, 257, 262-267, 269, 272, 295-297, 317, 319, 321-322, 336, 345-346, 350, 357,
triumphalism: 170

ubuntu: 284, 288
unemployment: 135, 181, 193, 195-196, 282, 304
unity: 118, 194, 348
University:
 - Cape Town (UCT): 154
 - Ghana: 157
 - Malawi: 156
 - Stellenbosch: 161
urban/urbanisation: 65, 134-138, 143-144, 169, 176ff, 198, 209, 272, 351,

Van der Kemp, Johannes: 34
Vatican: 49, 53-57
Voetius: 33, 293, 315

war:
 - Civil: 231, 304
 - First World 52
 - Second World 52
West/Western: 26, 27, 29, 36, 37-42, 52, 71, 76-79, 83-85, 88-99, 101, 109-110, 117, 132, 139, 146, 151-152, 159, 163-166, 210, 217, 231, 239, 250, 268, 277, 278, 286, 293, 309, 320, 334
witness/witnesses: 26, 29, 39, 42, 46-47, 68, 69, 83-84, 108, 112, 117-120, 122, 127-128, 131, 133, 140, 143, 145, 147, 150, 157, 163, 170, 171, 222, 229, 249-255, 259-260, 262, 267, 292, 296-299, 305, 321, 323, 347
women: 21-22, 39, 48, 91, 98, 103, 108, 110, 115-118, 120, 123-124, 127, 138, 143, 147, 169-170, 181-182, 197, 200-201, 227, 230, 232, 234, 309, 318, 321, 351
World Communion of Reformed Churches 43, 264, 308-309
World Council of Churches: 42, 63, 103, 120, 127-128, 198, 211, 248, 264, 296, 346
Worldview: 68, 71, 79, 83, 131-134, 145-146, 201, 223, 268-269, 282, 340

xenophobia: 101, 124, 136, 141, 278,

youth: 103, 164, 193ff, 248, 286-288, 304, 318, 321

Zion/Zionist: 41, 77-81, 133

www.ingramcontent.com/pod-product-compliance
Lightning Source LLC
Chambersburg PA
CBHW072038160426
43197CB00014B/2548